The People Want

The publisher gratefully acknowledges the generous support of the Joan Palevsky Literature in Translation Endowment Fund of the University of California Press Foundation.

The People Want

A Radical Exploration of the Arab Uprising

Gilbert Achcar

Translated from the French by G. M. Goshgarian

UNIVERSITY OF CALIFORNIA PRESS

Berkeley · Los Angeles · London

University of California Press, one of the most distinguished university presses in the United States, enriches lives around the world by advancing scholarship in the humanities, social sciences, and natural sciences. Its activities are supported by the UC Press Foundation and by philanthropic contributions from individuals and institutions. For more information, visit www.ucpress.edu.

University of California Press
Berkeley and Los Angeles, California

University of California Press, Ltd.
London, England

Library of Congress Cataloging-in-Publication Data
Achcar, Gilbert.
    The people want : a radical exploration of the Arab uprising / Gilbert Achcar.
        pages   cm
    ISBN 978-0-520-27497-6 (hardback)
    ISBN 978-0-520-28051-9 (pbk)
    1. Arab Spring, 2010– 2. Protest movements—Arab countries—History—21st century. 3. Revolutions—Arab countries—History—21st century. 4. Arab countries—Politics and government—21st century. 5. Arab countries—Economic conditions—21st century. 6. Youth—Political activity—Arab countries. 7. Unemployment—Arab countries. 8. Information technology—Political aspects—Arab countries. I. Title.
    JQ1850.A91A336 2013
    909'.097492708312—dc23   2013014452

Manufactured in the United States of America

22 21 20 19 18 17 16 15 14
10 9 8 7 6 5 4 3 2

In keeping with a commitment to support environmentally responsible and sustainable printing practices, UC Press has printed this book on Rolland Enviro100, a 100% post-consumer fiber paper that is FSC certified, deinked, processed chlorine-free, and manufactured with renewable biogas energy. It is acid-free and EcoLogo certified.

Contents

Figures and Tables   *vii*

Acknowledgments   *ix*

Preliminary Notes   *xi*
> *On the Arab Countries and "the Middle East and North*
>   *Africa" (MENA)*   *xi*
> *On Transliteration of Arabic*   *xi*

Introduction: Uprisings and Revolutions   *1*

1. Fettered Development   7
    The Facts   *10*
    Poverty, Inequality, Precarity   *15*
    Informal Sector and Unemployment: The Bouazizi Syndrome   *22*
    Youth Underemployment   *26*
    Female Underemployment   *29*
    Graduate Unemployment   *32*
    Fetters on Development   *35*

2. The Peculiar Modalities of Capitalism in the Arab Region   *38*
    The Problem of Investment   *39*
    Public and Private Investment   *41*
    A Specific Variant of the Capitalist Mode of Production   *50*
        1. Rentier and Patrimonial States   *54*
        2. A Politically Determined Capitalism: Nepotism and Risk   *60*
    The Genesis of the Specific Regional Variant of Capitalism:
       An Overview   *67*

3. Regional Political Factors   76
   The Oil Curse   77
   From "Arab Despotic Exception" to "Democracy Promotion"   85
   The Muslim Brothers, Washington, and the Saudis   93
   The Muslim Brothers, Washington, and Qatar   100
   Al Jazeera and the Upheaval in the Arab Mediascape   108

4. Actors and Parameters of the Revolution   114
   Overdetermination and Subjective Conditions   114
   The Workers' Movement and Social Struggles   123
   New Actors and New Information and
      Communications Technologies   129
   States and Revolutions   136

5. A Provisional Balance Sheet of the Arab Uprising   144
   Coups d'État and Revolutions   144
   Provisional Balance Sheet No. 1: Tunisia   145
   Provisional Balance Sheet No. 2: Egypt   148
   Provisional Balance Sheet No. 3: Yemen   155
   Provisional Balance Sheet No. 4: Bahrain   160
   Provisional Balance Sheet No. 5: Libya   163
   Provisional Balance Sheet No. 6: Syria   172

6. Co-opting the Uprising   188
   Washington and the Muslim Brothers, Take Two   189
   Nato, Libya, and Syria   197
   The "Islamic Tsunami" and the Difference between Khomeini
      and Morsi   208

Conclusion: The Future of the Arab Uprising   218
   The Difference between Erdogan and Ghannouchi . . .   218
   . . . And the Difference between Erdogan and Morsi   225
   Conditions for a Genuine Solution   235

Notes   243
References and Sources   281
Index   303

Figures and Tables

FIGURES

1.1   GDP per capita average annual growth rate / *11*

1.2   Egypt—GDP per capita annual growth rate / *12*

1.3   Average annual population growth rate *13*

1.4   GDP average annual growth rate / *14*

1.5   Human Development Index (HDI), 1980–2010 / *15*

1.6   Informality in labor force and employment / *23*

1.7   Unemployment rate / *24*

1.8   Unemployment rate youth and adults / *26*

1.9   Youth in total population, 2010 / *27*

1.10 Unemployment rate by sex, 2010 / *29*

1.11 Employment-to-population rate by sex, 2010 / *30*

1.12 Population with advanced education / *33*

2.1   GDP per capita annual growth; MENA—1969–2010 / *39*

2.2   Gross fixed capital formation / *40*

2.3   Gross capital formation annual growth; MENA without GCC—1969–2007 / *41*

2.4   Gross capital formation annual growth; MENA without GCC—1969–2007 / *42*

2.5   Gross fixed capital formation, public sector, 1995–2007 / *43*

2.6 Net official financial flows / 43

2.7 Gross fixed capital formation, private sector; 1995–2007 / 44

2.8 Gross fixed capital formation, total and public; Egypt—1982–2010 / 47

2.9 Public sector revenue, 2006 / 57

TABLES

1.1 Distribution of Consumption / 19

1.2 GDP per Capita 2008 / 22

1.3 Gross Enrollment Ratio in Tertiary Education (2009) / 32

1.4 Graduate Unemployment Rates 1984–2010 / 34

4.1 Percentage of Individuals Using the Internet (2010) / 132

Acknowledgments

This book is the outcome of intensive work that started shortly after the beginning of the revolutionary wave engulfing the Arabic-speaking region. It is based, however, on the course on Problems of Development of the Middle East and North Africa that I have taught at the School of Oriental and African Studies (SOAS, University of London) since the academic year 2007–8. This means that I owe much to my institution, which offers an ideal environment and one of the richest libraries for the research on the region that is the object of this study. The students who attended my lectures and who will remember them when they read the following pages have contributed with their questions to forming the answers this book provides.

Yet scholarly teaching and research are but one of the sources of this work. My major debt is toward the great number of those whom I met and with whom I had a chance to discuss during my travels in different countries of the region over decades, and most particularly since the beginning of the uprising. I clearly cannot name them all. Four key stages in this experience occurred in 2011, when I was honored to be invited to take part in the "Spring University" of ATTAC Morocco in Casablanca, in April; the "Socialist Days" organized in Cairo after the uprising by the Egyptian Center for Socialist Studies, in May; the meeting of prominent members of the Syrian Opposition, many of whom came directly from Syria to the place near Stockholm where it was held, in October; and the festivities celebrating the first anniversary of the beginning of the uprising in Sidi Bouzid, the Tunisian town where it all started, in December. I thank here one more time the organizers of these meetings, as well as the team of the Haus der Kulturen der Welt in Berlin, which gave me the opportunity to take part in a gathering of persons involved in cultural activities in the Arab region in January 2012.

I am also grateful to all those who invited me to submit some of this book's theses to the critical attention of audiences including people knowledgeable about the region in various academic institutions—in particular Henry Laurens at the Collège de France; Robert Wade at the London School of Economics; Rashid Khalidi and Bashir Abu-Manneh at Columbia University in New York; Joel Beinin at Stanford University; Ronit Lentin at Trinity College in Dublin; Haideh Moghissi and Saeed Rahnema at York University in Toronto; Farid al-Alibi at the University of Kairouan, Tunisia; Tullo Vigevani at the Universidade Estadual Paulista (UNESP) in São Paulo; and the Brazilian National Social Science Postgraduate and Research Association (ANPOCS) at its annual convention in Caxambu.

The friends whose names follow have read the manuscript of this book in part or in whole and given me the benefit of their comments in finalizing it: Henry Bernstein, Ray Bush, Franck Mermier, Saleh Mosbah, Alfredo Saad-Filho, Fawwaz Traboulsi, and Lisa Wedeen. Very acute remarks by Omar El Shafei, who translated this book into Arabic, were most useful. My collaboration for the second time with Geoff Michael Goshgarian, who translated this book into English most elegantly after my previous one, *The Arabs and the Holocaust*, was equally an opportunity for useful exchanges between us. I beg those whom I failed to mention in these acknowledgments to excuse me. None of the above-mentioned persons can in any way be held responsible for the theses of this book and the errors that it may include.

Preliminary Notes

ON THE ARAB COUNTRIES AND "THE MIDDLE EAST AND NORTH AFRICA" (MENA)

In the following pages, "Arab" refers to the member states of the Arab League (with the exception of the Union of the Comoros, Djibouti, and Somalia). These countries are called "Arab" because Arabic is their main language of administration, communication, and instruction. Thus "Arab" and "Arabic" are, here, geopolitical and linguistic terms (whence also the occasional reference to the "Arabic-speaking region"); neither is in any sense an "ethnic" description. Non-Arab groups comprise a significant segment of the populations of these countries, notably the Amazigh in North Africa (Maghreb) and the Kurds in the Middle East (Mashriq). They have taken an active part in the uprisings in the region.

Several international institutions whose studies and statistics are copiously cited in the present book focus on a group of countries they call "Middle East and North Africa" (MENA or the MENA region). In addition to the countries identified above, MENA includes Iran. When data limited to the Arab states are lacking, data for the MENA region have been used.

All the figures published in this book are original; the sources of the data used in making them are indicated.

ON TRANSLITERATION OF ARABIC

The method adopted for the transcription of Arabic words and names in the Latin alphabet is a simplified version of the transliteration system in use in specialized literature; the aim is to make it easier for nonspe-cialists to read the text, while allowing the knowledgeable to recognize the original Arabic. Special characters and diacritical marks have been avoided, except for the inverted apostrophe representing the Arabic let-ter *'ayn*. The common spellings of the names of the best-known indi-viduals have been retained. Finally, when Arabs have published in European languages, their own transliteration of their names in Latin letters has been respected, as has, in the citations, the transliteration of Arabic names in the form in which it occurs in the original.

Introduction:
Uprisings and Revolutions

"The people want!" This proclamation has been and still is omnipresent in the protracted uprising that has been rocking the Arabic-speaking region since the Tunisian episode began in Sidi Bouzid on 17 December 2010. In every imaginable variant and every imaginable tone, it has served as the prelude to all sorts of demands, from the now famous revolutionary slogan "The people want to overthrow the regime!" to highly diverse calls of a comic nature—exemplified by the demonstrator in Cairo's Tahrir Square who held high a sign reading: "The people want a president who doesn't dye his hair!"

"The people want . . ." first emerged as a slogan in Tunisia. It echoes two famous lines by Tunisian poet Abul-Qacem al-Shebbi (1909–34) inserted in the country's national anthem:

> If the people want life some day, fate will surely grant their wish
> Their shackles will surely be shattered and their night surely vanish.[1]

The coming of the day of reckoning expressed in this collective affirmation that the people *want*, in the present tense—that they want here and now—illustrates in the clearest possible way the irruption of the popular will onto the Arab political stage. Such an irruption is the primary characteristic of every democratic uprising. In contrast to the proclamations adopted by representative assemblies, such as the "We the People" in the Preamble to the Constitution of the United States, here, the will of the people is expressed without intermediary, chanted at lung-splitting volumes by immense throngs such as those that the world has seen packing the streets of Tunisia, Egypt, Yemen, Bahrain, Libya, Syria, and many other countries besides.

The use of the term "revolution" to qualify the upheavals under way in the Arab region has nevertheless been, and continues to be, hotly debated and stoutly contested, even in those victorious cases in which the people have succeeded in ridding themselves of an oppressive tyrant. The more neutral term "uprising" has been used in this book's subtitle not only to avoid settling the debate on the cover, but also because the word "revolution" has more than one sense.

The Arab region has unquestionably witnessed *uprisings*. Indeed, it has witnessed the whole gamut of what that word designates, from outpourings of demonstrators to armed insurrections. The Arabic term *intifada*, which the Palestinian population of the territories occupied by Israel in 1967 has added to the international lexicon, covers the same semantic range. The Arabic term *thawra* also has a broad range of meanings: derived from the verb *thara* (to revolt), it originally corresponded more closely to the idea of revolt than to that of revolution. Thus *thawra* is accurately translated in the familiar English names of other events that have shaken the Arab region: the Great Arab Revolt of 1916–18, the 1920 Revolt in Iraq, the Great Syrian Revolt of 1925, and the Great Palestinian Revolt of 1936. For the same reason, insurgents, rebels, and revolutionaries alike are called *thuwwar* in Arabic.

Farsi, together with the languages it has most deeply influenced, has for good reason settled on the Arabic term *inqilab* (overturning) to translate the Western concept of revolution. In Arabic itself, however, *inqilab* has come to mean "coup d'état," whereas *thawra* means not just revolt, but also revolution—in the sense of a radical upheaval including, at the very least, a change in the political regime accomplished in ways that violate existing legality. These diverse semantic developments can help us bring out the imprecision of the terms in our own ordinary lexicon.[2]

The concept of revolution generally evokes, in Western languages, a movement in which the people seek to overthrow the government from below, although a "revolution" need not lead to the use of arms. A coup d'état, in contrast, is the work of a faction, usually originating in the army, which seizes power at the pinnacle of society, always by force of arms. It so happens that the history of the Arab region is dotted with coups d'état that were unquestionably revolutionary, in that they culminated in profound transformations of political institutions and social structures. To cite just one example, the 23 July 1952 coup of the Free Officers led by Gamal Abdel-Nasser unquestionably led to a transformation of Egypt much more radical than anything that has so far resulted from the Revolution of 25 January 2011.

The 1952 coup led to the overthrow of a dynasty, the abolition of the monarchy and parliamentary regime, the creation of a republican military dictatorship, the nationalization of foreign assets, the subversion of the old regime's property-holding classes (big landed property, commercial and financial capital), a major drive to industrialize, and far-reaching progressive social reforms. These changes certainly better deserve to be called a "revolution" than do the results of the uprising set in motion in January 2011, which so far (at the time of writing) has led only to the overthrow of the small clan that dominated the state, and the democratization of the semipresidential regime, pending a change in the constitution by means that seek to maintain juridical continuity with the old institutions.

Indeed, we might go so far as to say that the passive counterrevolution led by Anwar al-Sadat after Nasser's death on 28 September 1970 also brought about deeper socioeconomic changes than those seen in Egypt since the downfall of Hosni Mubarak on 11 February 2011. Yet the immense uprising that began on 25 January 2011 constitutes a bursting of the masses onto the political stage that had no precedent in the very long history of the land of the pyramids. Hence it has, beyond the shadow of a doubt, set a revolutionary *dynamic* in motion. It is too soon to pronounce on the consequences. The most radical results of the 1952 coup appeared only many years later. We would do well to bear that in mind.

In this sense, it takes no extraordinary acumen to identify, from the outset—from the very first hours of its existence—a revolutionary *dynamic*, like the Duke of La Rochefoucauld-Liancourt, who, "during the night of July 14–15, 1789"—according to a story that became famous after Hyppolite Taine retold it—"caused Louis XVI to be aroused to inform him of the taking of the Bastille. 'It is a revolt, then?' exclaimed the King. 'Sire!' replied the Duke; 'it is a revolution!' "[3] If the duke really did make this remark, he could only have been referring to the rioters' *intentions*; they had indeed set out, not to vent their disgruntlement in an ephemeral revolt, but to have done with Absolutism once and for all. They plainly had revolutionary aims, identifiable as such from the moment they took the Bastille.[4]

Yet, the *intentions* of those who rioted on 14 July aside, no one could then have predicted the ultimate consequences of the event: whether it would culminate in radical change or, instead, join the long list of abortive revolutions demoted to the rank of revolts. We should, moreover, read the rest of Taine's narrative and his description of the uprising, a description typical of the conservative historian he was:

> The event was even more serious. Not only had power slipped from the hands of the King, but also it had not fallen into those of the Assembly. It now lay on the ground, ready to the hands of the unchained populace, the violent and overexcited crowd, the mobs, which picked it up like some weapon that had been thrown away in the street. In fact, there was no longer any government; the artificial structure of human society was giving way entirely; things were returning to a state of nature. This was not a revolution, but a *dissolution*.[5]

This is how conservatives of all stripes (some of those in the region discussed in this book even proclaim themselves "progressives" and "anti-imperialists") defame uprisings against the despotic regimes with which they identify, dismissing them as "pure mayhem" when they do not see them as the fruit of a conspiracy. This does not in the least alter the fact that the emergence of the people freed from the shackles of servitude (voluntary or involuntary), the assertion of collective will in public squares, and success in overthrowing tyrannical oppressors are the unmistakable marks of a political revolution.

Beyond the shadow of a doubt, this description applies to the uprisings in Tunisia, Egypt, and Libya, whereas the one in Yemen has, so far, yielded only a sorry compromise. The Tunisian and Egyptian political revolutions have, nevertheless, left the state apparatuses of the fallen regimes essentially intact; only in Libya was the old state machine largely dismantled by a civil war. However, none of these countries has yet experienced a *social* revolution, in the sense of a thorough transformation of its social structure. Only factions at the pinnacle of the social hierarchy—big or small, depending on the case—have been affected. Nowhere has that hierarchy itself been modified.

I myself have, from the first months of 2011, described the ongoing uprisings as a *protracted* or *long-term revolutionary process*. Such a formulation reconciles the revolutionary nature of the event with its incompleteness. It is motivated by two major considerations:

- First is the fact that the revolutionary shock wave has shaken virtually all the countries in the Arab region; although it has so far (at the time of writing) led to a general uprising in only six, it is highly likely others will follow their example in the months and years ahead.

- Second is the fact that the political revolutions in the three aforementioned countries cannot by themselves eliminate the profound causes of the explosion that has set the region ablaze; only profound socioeconomic transformations can do that.

The very fact that the revolutionary wave that arose in Tunisia has swept through the entire Arabic-speaking region shows that its causes are not confined to the political dimension. They run deeper. This sweep cannot be due to the linguistic factor alone: where revolution is concerned, contagion by example occurs only when there is favorable ground. For a spark to start a conflagration that spreads from one end of a geopolitical and cultural zone to the other, there must be a *predisposition* to revolution. Given the diversity of the region's political regimes, logic suggests we search for underlying socioeconomic factors which may have laid the common ground for the regional shock wave. Despotism by itself, moreover, can hardly be sufficient cause for the outbreak and subsequent success of a democratic revolution. Otherwise, there would be no explaining why it triumphed when it did: why 2011, after decades of despotism in the Arab region? Why 1789 in France, after a long history of Absolutism and peasant revolts? Why 1989 in Eastern Europe, rather than, say, 1953–6?

If socioeconomic factors are at the very heart of the Arab uprising, it follows that there are still radical changes to come. At the very least, they will bring in their wake new episodes of revolution and counter-revolution in the countries that have already experienced upheavals, and in others as well; and they will do so over a protracted period. After all, while there is a consensus that 14 July 1789 is the day the French Revolution began, the debate as to when it ended is still raging (1799, 1830, 1851, or even 1870–5). The French Revolution lasted, by the most conservative estimate, more than ten years. The revolutionary process in the Arab region will soon pass the two-year mark. It is highly likely that it will go on for many years to come.

These are the things that this book tries to explain. It does not seek to recount the histories of particular uprisings; there are several accounts about each of them already. In the years ahead, these accounts will surely be joined by innumerable other works written with the benefit of hindsight, after the dust of events has settled and the archives have been sifted through. Because the revolutionary process in the Arab region is still under way, and long will be, any chronicle that strives to be up-to-date risks being outstripped by events even before it comes off the press. This book proposes, rather, to analyze the dynamics informing events, to scan their horizon and draw their significant lessons. It is a *radical* exploration of the Arab uprising in both senses of the word. It aims to identify the deep roots of the uprising; but it is also written with the conviction that there can be no lasting solution to the crisis unless those roots are transformed.

Gilbert Achcar
London, 30 October 2012

CHAPTER I

Fettered Development

At a certain stage of development, the material productive
forces of society come into conflict with the existing
relations of production. . . . From forms of development
of the productive forces these relations turn into their
fetters. Then begins an era of social revolution.

—Karl Marx, 1859, Preface to *A Contribution to the Critique of
Political Economy*

When a revolutionary upheaval is not an isolated phenomenon attrib-
utable to specific political conditions in a particular country, but constitutes a shock wave that goes beyond the merely episodic to initiate a veritable sociopolitical transformation in a whole group of countries with
similar socioeconomic structures, Marx's thesis cited above takes on its
full significance. From this perspective, the "bourgeois" revolutions at
the heart of the Age of Revolution—from the sixteenth-century Dutch
War of Independence and the seventeenth-century English Revolution
through the long process comprising the French Revolution to the 1848
European Revolutions sometimes called the Spring of Nations—appear
as a series of earthquakes triggered by the collision of the two tectonic
plates Marx identified as developing productive forces and existing relations of production. The latter are represented by what the author of
Das Kapital calls the "legal and political superstructure," with the state
at its core. These revolutions accelerated the transformation of the predominantly agrarian societies of the late feudal period into societies
dominated by the urban bourgeoisie. They thus paved the way for capitalist industrialization.

A comparable instance of the existing relations of production
blocking the development of the forces of production was at the origin of the shock wave that, beginning with Poland in 1980, overturned

all the Central and Eastern European "communist" regimes and culminated in the 1991 collapse of the Soviet Union (USSR). This shock
wave put an end to the bureaucratic mode of production of the USSR
and Eastern Europe, undermined by stagnation at its very center, and
put a "market economy" in its place. With that, the process of capitalist globalization was essentially completed. It has not been sufficiently stressed just how striking an illustration of Marx's thesis this
historic turn provides—a new irony of history, since the overturned
regimes claimed to take their inspiration from his "doctrine." Yet it
was a Marxist critic of the Soviet regime, Leon Trotsky, who was the
first to predict—in 1936, at a time when the "socialist fatherland" was
posting record growth rates—that the bureaucratic command economy would ultimately founder on the "problem of quality."[1] Trotsky
thus anticipated the period beginning in the early 1970s, later named
the Era of Stagnation, which culminated in the collapse of the regimes
descended from Stalinism.

Is what we have been witnessing in the Arab region since 2011 an
"era of social revolution" brought on by a blockage impeding the development of productive forces? If so, is this blockage due to factors common to the countries of the region and specific to them, as in the two
historical cases just mentioned? The question is worth asking, if only
because the tremor running through the region has affected the whole
of it, from Mauritania and Morocco to the Arab-Iranian Gulf. That,
moreover, is why observers have compared the upheaval under way in
the Arab countries with the shock wave that traversed Eastern Europe
in the 1980s. Yet this upheaval has not—at any rate, not yet—brought
about a radical change in the mode of production. There seems to be no
change on the horizon of the revolutionary process unfolding today in
the Arabic-speaking region profound enough to invite comparison with
the great upheaval that ultimately integrated the "communist" countries
into globalized capitalism.

Whereas the European upheaval of the 1980s resulted from a crisis at the very heart of the bureaucratic mode of production, the crisis
in the Arab region affects only one of the peripheral zones of today's
globalized capitalist mode of production. Hence it cannot, by itself, be
regarded as a manifestation of a general blockage of this mode of production, nor even—since capitalism continues to generate development
in other peripheral zones—a blockage confined to the capitalist periphery. Indeed, even if the crisis currently besetting the highly developed
economies central to the world system (the European economies, above
all) eventually proves to be the expression of an insurmountable block-

age leading to sociopolitical upheaval, the coincidence of this crisis with that rocking the Arabic-speaking region can hardly be interpreted in terms of cause and effect.

The fact that the crisis in Arab countries is clearly limited to them as far as its peculiar modalities are concerned plainly shows that specific factors are at work. It is neither a symptom of the general crisis of globalized capitalism, nor even a symptom of the crisis of "neoliberalism," the dominant management mode in the current phase of capitalist globalization. To identify the specific factors at work, we must compare the Arabic-speaking region with others on the periphery of the world economic system—particularly the countries of the Afro-Asian group of which the Arab region is a part.

Nevertheless, Marx's paradigmatic thesis on revolution should not be ignored when explaining the ongoing upheaval in the Arab world. Simply, we have to derive variants that are less sweeping in historical scope: the development of productive forces can be stalled, not by the relations of production constitutive of a generic mode of production (such as the relation between capital and wage labor in the capitalist mode of production), but, rather, by *a specific modality of that generic mode of production*. In such cases, it is not always necessary to replace the basic mode of production in order to overcome the blockage. A change in modality or "mode of regulation" does, however, have to occur.

Such changes do not necessarily presuppose social or even political revolutions. They can result from economic crises that induce the economically dominant class to change tack. Capital has negotiated more than one such turn in the course of its history. Both the 1930s Great Depression, followed by World War II, and the generalized recession of the 1970s precipitated sharp changes of tack, leading in two diametrically opposed directions. Certainly, the social balance of forces entered into the equation in both cases: the workers' movement was strengthened by the first crisis, weakened by the second. But these were not periods of social revolution or counterrevolution in the proper sense.

These changes in the management mode occurring within a basic continuity of capitalist relations of production illustrate, in some sense, another of Marx's theses. He presents it shortly after the passage in the 1859 Preface to *A Contribution to the Critique of Political Economy* that serves as the epigraph to this chapter:

> No social formation is ever destroyed before all the productive forces for which it is sufficient have been developed, and new superior relations of production never replace older ones before the material conditions for their existence have matured within the framework of the old society.[2]

Yet there also exist situations in which the development of productive forces is held back, not by a "simple" crisis in regulation or management mode, but by a particular type of social domination, one sustaining a specific variant of the generic mode of production. In such cases, the blockage can be overcome only if the dominant social group is overthrown, that is, only by a social revolution. Yet that revolution will not necessarily precipitate a radical change in the mode of production. We may here make use of Albert Soboul's definition of "revolution" as a "radical transformation of social relations and political structures on the basis of a renewed mode of production,"[3] as long as we admit that such renewal may be limited to a profound change in the modalities of a mode of production, with no accompanying change in the generic mode itself.

For capitalist development can be blocked by a distinct configuration of dominant social groups sustaining one particular *modality of capitalism*, rather than by the general relations of production between wage laborers and capitalists and the attendant property relations (private ownership of the social means of production). Later we will discuss the conditions under which such a blockage can be overcome, as well as the social dynamics that may accompany that process. What matters for present purposes is the blockage itself. We must therefore first determine whether, in the case at hand, such a blockage exists.

THE FACTS

The most frequently cited indicator of economic development—in the sense of growth, considered without regard to other aspects of human development—is an increase in gross domestic product (GDP), both in absolute terms and also relative to the size of the population. This indicator is, of course, very much open to discussion (a point to which we will return), but it does provide some idea of the relative development of the production of goods and services: its growth over time as well as variations in the pace of development in the various countries and regions of the world.

It so happens that, of all the regions still referred to as the Third World, the Middle East and North Africa (MENA) region is the one facing the most severe developmental crisis. After the 1960s, when most of this region's economies were dominated by the public sector in line with a state-led developmentalist perspective, the 1970s saw the inauguration and gradual extension of policies of *infitah* (opening), the name

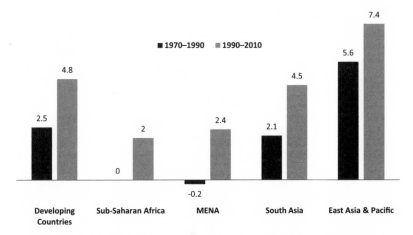

FIGURE 1.1 GDP per capita average annual growth rate (%). (Source: UNICEF)

then given to economic liberalization in the Arabic-speaking region. *Infitah* went hand in hand with public-sector privatization and an erosion of social gains. Certain MENA countries, notably Egypt, thus prefigured the "structural adjustment programs" that would be imposed on the whole planet from the 1980s onward in the framework of neoliberal deregulation.[4]

The available data plainly show that the two decades between 1970 and 1990 saw stagnation in per capita GDP in MENA: the GDP's per capita average annual growth rate (at constant prices in local currencies) was even slightly less than nil. Although that growth rate became positive again in the two following decades, it remained at levels well below—fifty percent below—the average rate of increase in developing countries (Fig. 1.1).

It goes without saying that the regional average masks disparities between individual cases. But the fact remains that most of the positive performances in the 1970–90 period were inferior, or at best equal, to the average performance in developing countries. Egypt was set apart from the other countries in the region with an average annual rate of 4.1% in 1970–90; this growth rate, substantially higher than that posted by the other MENA countries, was fueled by Egypt's rising oil revenues, remittances from migrant Egyptians working abroad, aid grants from oil monarchies and Western powers, and the expansion of tourism. (All these factors, combined with compensation for the nadir due to the October 1973 war, explain the 1976 apogee.) In 1990–2010,

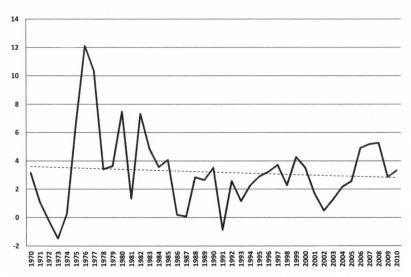

FIGURE 1.2 Egypt—GDP per capita annual growth rate (%) 1970–2010.
(Source: World Bank)

however, Egypt's growth rate fell to 2.7%, despite exceptional performance from 2006 to 2008 (to which we will return).[5] For the forty years
under consideration, Egypt's per capita GDP exhibited a declining trend
line (Fig. 1.2).

It is not unreasonable to suppose, of course, that MENA's poor results
in per capita GDP find their explanation less in exceptionally slow economic growth than in exceptionally rapid demographic growth. It is
indeed true that the region's average population growth rate was the
world's highest in the 1970–90 period, thanks to the growth spurt in the
population owing to 1960s social reforms and health care sector investment. Population growth was, however, stabilized in 1990–2010 at a
level lower than sub-Saharan Africa's (Fig. 1.3).[6] It was still 17% higher
than in Southern Asia in the same period. However, GDP per capita
growth was 47% lower in MENA than in Southern Asia (see Fig. 1.1).

Let us also point out that the average annual population growth rate
in Arab countries—2.2% in 2010, according to the World Bank's World
Databank—has been driven upward by the unusually high figures of
certain oil monarchies whose population growth is to a great extent
due to the importation of migrant labor. In 2010, all the countries represented in the Gulf Cooperation Council (GCC) showed average population growth rates above the Arab average; they ran from 2.4% for
the Saudi kingdom to 9.6% for Qatar, with 2.6% for Oman, 3.4%

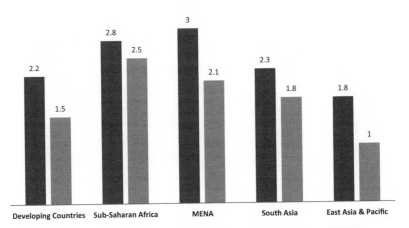

■ 1970–1990 ■ 1990–2010

FIGURE 1.3 Average annual population growth rate (%). (Source: UNICEF)

for Kuwait, 7.6% for Bahrain, and 7.9% for the United Arab Emirates (UAE). For the other MENA countries, again in 2010, the rates were, according to the same source, Lebanon, 0.7%; Morocco and Tunisia, 1%; Algeria and Libya, 1.5%; Egypt, 1.7%; Syria, 2%; Jordan, 2.2%; Mauritania, 2.4%; Sudan, 2.5%; Iraq, 3%; and Yemen, 3.1%.[7]

It should also be noted that MENA GDP growth figures over the four decades in question have in large measure been determined by the sharp fluctuations in oil prices during this time, since oil is the region's main export. Nevertheless, the variation in the real prices of crude oil—which soared between 1973 and 1981, then fell until 1986, only to increase again from 1988 onward—cannot explain the negative balance of the years 1970–90. Similarly, the steady but slight decrease in the prices of crude until 1998 and a new dip in 2008 did not suffice to counterbalance the hefty increase from 1998 to 2008.[8]

We can verify that the MENA region's especially poor performance does not just reflect the vicissitudes of oil markets by looking at the years 2000–8, during which oil prices rose spectacularly. The real price of crude (in 1973 US$) went from $7.99 in 2000 to $16.04 in 2008; that is, it more than doubled (more precisely, it soared from 2005 on).[9] Let us compare the total GDP average annual growth rates of the various developing regions of Africa and Asia in 2000–8 (Fig. 1.4).

The result is surprising. MENA's growth rate is not merely far lower

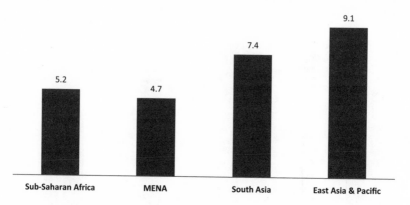

FIGURE 1.4 GDP average annual growth rate (%). (Source: World Bank)

than South Asia's and East Asia's, it is below even that of sub-Saharan Africa. This comparison of total GDPs also neutralizes the impact of the demographic factor on per capita GDP growth, although it is perfectly legitimate to argue that the latter is the sole valid indicator of growth. Indeed, underscoring the oil wealth of this region of the world—richly endowed in both raw materials and capital, and with no shortage of labor supply, so that it has the three basic prerequisites for industrialization—throws the acuteness of the problem plaguing it into even sharper relief.

However, as is well known, GDP has only limited validity as an index of development as opposed to growth, both because it fails to take the so-called informal economy into consideration and because it is hard to measure public services such as education or health in terms of money. Moreover, GDP ignores both environmental costs and the qualitative aspects of the public services just mentioned.[10] To take these aspects into consideration, the United Nations Development Program (UNDP) has devised a "Human Development Index" (HDI) of its own. The HDI is, according to the official definition, "a composite index measuring average achievement in three basic dimensions of human development—a long and healthy life, knowledge and a decent standard of living."[11]

As measured by HDI, the Arab states were outperformed by East Asia in the period 1980–2010 (Fig. 1.5), despite the fact that the Arab region is much richer. The PPP-adjusted per capita GDP was on average $8,256 in the Arab states in 2009, according to UNDP data, as opposed to $6,227 in East Asia.[12] ("PPP" stands for "purchasing power parity":

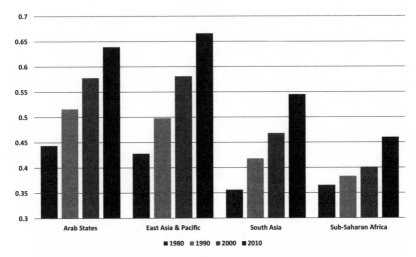

FIGURE 1.5 Human Development Index (HDI), 1980–2010. (Source: UNDP)

simply put, a PPP-adjusted dollar has the same purchasing power in any given country that a dollar has in the United States.) Similarly, the disparity between the Arab countries' and South Asia's performance is, again as measured by HDI, far smaller than the disparity in wealth between the two regions (with a per capita GDP at PPP of $3,368 for South Asia).

POVERTY, INEQUALITY, PRECARITY

The social situation confronting the Arab region's population can be summed up in three words—poverty, inequality, precarity—ironically reminiscent of the motto of the French Revolution: Liberty, Equality, Fraternity.

Poverty is, of course, a relative notion, even, or perhaps especially, when it is a question of expressing it in numbers. We need only consider how the World Bank revised its 1993 assessment of poverty in the world in 2005, using a new method to determine purchasing power parities. Rather like sudden currency devaluations and revaluations, the new estimates considerably modified the World Bank's assessment of many countries' relative wealth. Per capita GDP figures plunged dramatically in some cases and soared in others.[13]

One of the most striking results of this readjustment was a radical change in estimates of poverty in some countries. A good example is the claim that over forty percent of Egyptians live on less than $2 a day, a figure that has been endlessly bandied about, even in economic publications, since the protest movement in Egypt began in January 2011.[14] This figure in fact stems from estimates based on 1993 purchasing power parities, which continued to appear in World Bank publications up to and including its *World Development Report 2008*, released in autumn 2007. This *Report* still estimated that 43.9% of Egypt's inhabitants were living on less than $2 a day, on the basis of a survey conducted in 1999–2000. In *World Development Report 2010*, however, the assessment of the number of Egyptians living on that amount, based on the 2005 parities and a 2004–5 survey, fell to 18.4%. Conversely, the proportion of the populace living on less than $2 a day in Tunisia went from 6.6% when 1993 purchasing power parities were used, to 12.8% when they were replaced by their 2005 counterparts; both figures were based on the same 2000 survey. For a few other countries, such as Morocco and Yemen, poverty rate estimates were hardly affected.

The radical drop in the figures for Egypt, the MENA country with the biggest population, merely accentuates the difference between MENA and other parts of the developing world as reflected in statistics published by international institutions. Thus, according to World Bank data, the percentage of people living in extreme poverty—that is, under the international poverty line of $1.25 (PPP) per day—is lower in MENA than in all other developing regions. In 2008, it was 2.8% in MENA as opposed to 6.5% in Latin America, 14.3% in East Asia, and a shocking 36% in South Asia and 47.5% in sub-Saharan Africa. The percentage of inhabitants living on less than $2 a day was the lowest in MENA (and Latin America): again according to the 2008 figures, the rate was 13.9% in MENA and 12.4% in Latin America, compared with 33.2% in East Asia and the even more appalling rates of 69.2% in sub-Saharan Africa and 70.9% in South Asia.[15]

The fact remains that, according to the same data, the proportion of people living on less than $2 a day is high in several Arab countries, even if poverty is very extensive only in Mauritania, Sudan, and Yemen, as well as among Palestinians (particularly in Gaza). To restrict ourselves to countries for which estimates have been made in the last few years, those living on less than $2 a day make up 14% of the population in Morocco (2007), 15.4% in Egypt (2008), 16.9% in Syria (2004), 21.4% in Iraq (2007), 46.6% in Yemen (2005), and 47.7% in Mauritania (2008).[16] The fact, for example, that in Morocco, which has the lowest rate of all the countries just mentioned, one inhabitant out of seven has to get by on less than $2 (PPP) a day means that a substantial segment of society lives in poverty. Morocco's rate may, to be sure, seem relatively benign when compared with South Asia's and sub-Saharan Africa's. For the individuals involved, however, dire poverty is quite as onerous whether they represent one-tenth of the population or two-thirds of it. Indeed, poverty is even harder for the poor to accept when it affects a minority, which must daily be confronted with the sight of overconsumption and ostentatious luxury.

Yet these figures are highly dubious indicators of poverty. They are questioned in *Arab Human Development Report 2003*, the second in a series published by the UNDP. It affirms that "the data base on the extent and features of poverty and income distribution in Arab countries is extremely weak," referring to estimates showing that "poverty in Arab countries is more widespread than is usually reported in international data bases, particularly those compiled by the World Bank and the International Monetary Fund" (IMF).[17] *Arab Human Development Report 2009*, the fifth report in the same series, points out that "applying the two-dollar-a-day international line and the lower national poverty line respectively yields a virtually identical picture of extreme poverty in the region," inferring that "it would be reasonable to expect a significantly higher percentage of the population at or below the upper poverty line."[18]

The upper national poverty line defines the revenue needed to obtain both basic nutrition and essential nonfood items in a given country, whereas people living at the lower poverty line have to make hard choices between these two kinds of minimum expenditure. The image that emerges when we focus on the number of people in the Arab region living below the "upper" line, which varies between $2.43 and $2.70 (PPP) a day, differs sharply from the one that appears when we apply the international poverty line of $2 (PPP) a day. According to the UNDP report, poverty rate statistics for the MENA countries for which such data (collected between 2000 and 2006) are available are as follows: 11.33% in Jordan, 23.8% in Tunisia, 28.6% in Lebanon, 30.1% in Syria, 39.6% in Morocco, 40.9% in Egypt, 53.9% in Mauritania, and 59.9% in Yemen. The average rate of poverty for all the countries in question is 39.9%. This is a much higher figure than the 16.9% of MENA inhabitants supposedly living below the $2 a day international poverty line.[19]

In an enlightening critique of the (under)estimates of Egyptian poverty in general and poverty in greater metropolitan Cairo in particular,

Sarah Sabry provides one key to explaining the substantial disparity between the 18.4% of Egyptians living below the international poverty line according to World Bank statistics and the 40.9% of those living beneath the line of $2.70 a day according to national estimates. Sabry calls attention to "the large percentage of the population, almost 35 per cent, that is considered to live fairly close to the poverty line" and adds, "This means that small differences in methodology could have very large effects on the numbers of poor people in Egypt."[20] It should also be noted that it helps explain the recent jump in the proportion of Egypt's population living under the lower national poverty level: from 19.6% in 2004–5 to 25.2% in 2010–11, according to national statistics.[21]

It is no wonder that what we have just noted about assessments of poverty also holds for assessments of socioeconomic inequalities. In World Bank data on the latter, figures based on surveys carried out after 2000 are available for only nine Arab states. In inequality statistics, Gini coefficients are used to measure inequality in income or expenditure on a scale running from 0, indicating absolute equality, to 100, indicating absolute inequality (one person receives or spends the total amount). The Gini coefficient for Japan and Sweden, the most egalitarian countries (in income), are 24.9 and 25 respectively; that for the Seychelles, the least egalitarian (in expenditure), is 65.8. The nine Arab states are located in a zone of medium to high consumption inequality, ranging between 30.8 for Egypt and 41.4 for Tunisia (Table 1.1). These are relatively average levels in comparison with India's 33.4 and Indonesia's 34, Iran's 38.3, Turkey's 39, Nigeria's 48.8, the Philippines' 43, or South Africa's 63.1, to mention only countries for which the Gini coefficients bear on consumption inequality.

Like poverty level data, these data were also challenged in *Arab Human Development Report 2003*. Here again, Egypt is the touchstone for the international financial institutions' statistics on Arab states:

Even when field surveys of income and expenditure (which constitute the basic source for estimates of income distribution) exist, such surveys suffer from defects that diminish their credibility, particularly with regard to the parameters of income distribution, as a result of bias in the collected data. In Egypt, for instance, relying on the results of income and expenditure surveys in the first part of the 1990s leads to an improvement of the Gini coefficient—i.e., income distribution becomes more equal. But this does not correspond to the overall economic situation, particularly unemployment and poverty criteria and the observations made of wealth distribution during the same period. . . . Labour's share of the value added declined from nearly

TABLE 1.1   DISTRIBUTION OF CONSUMPTION

	Survey year	Gini index	Lowest 10%	Lowest 20%	Second 20%	Third 20%	Fourth 20%	Highest 20%	Highest 10%
					Share of expenditure (%)				
Egypt	2008	30.8	4	9.2	13	16.4	21	40.3	26.6
Iraq	2007	30.9	3.8	8.7	12.8	16.7	22	39.9	25.2
Jordan	2010	35.4	3.4	7.7	11.6	15.7	21.5	43.6	28.7
Mauritania	2008	40.5	2.4	6	10.4	15.1	21.5	47	31.6
Morocco	2007	40.9	2.7	6.5	10.5	14.5	20.6	47.9	33.2
Qatar	2007	41.1	1.3	3.9	...	...	...	52	35.9
Syria	2004	35.8	3.4	7.7	11.4	15.5	21.4	43.9	28.9
Tunisia	2005	41.4	2.4	5.9	10.1	14.7	21.3	47.9	32.5
Yemen	2005	37.7	2.9	7.2	11.3	15.3	21	45.3	30.8

SOURCE: World Bank, 2012

40% in 1975 to nearly 25% in 1994, which indicates a deterioration of GNP distribution in favour of wealth returns.[22]

The inequality estimates available for Arab countries are all based on the shares of overall consumption accruing to deciles or quintiles of the population classified according to per capita expenditure.[23] These calculations provide a very rough idea of social inequalities. Income inequalities are necessarily much greater than inequalities in consumption, but it is impossible to determine them in countries lacking all transparency in this domain. It is even harder to shed light on inequalities in wealth distribution. Although *Arab Human Development Report 2009* confuses consumption inequality with income inequality when it calls the latter "moderate" in the Arab countries, it nevertheless points out the divergence between this (mistaken) observation and social reality as experienced and perceived there. It also underscores the difference between inequalities in income and wealth:

> Despite moderate levels of income inequality, in most Arab countries social exclusion has increased over the past two decades. In addition, there is evidence to suggest that the inequality in wealth has worsened significantly. In many Arab countries, for example, land and asset concentration is conspicuous and provokes a sense of exclusion among other groups, even if absolute poverty does not increase. Furthermore, the crowding of the poor in slums without sanitation, safe water, recreational facilities, reliable electricity and other services aggravates such exclusion. These trends, combined with high unemployment rates, result in the ominous dynamics of marginalization, visible in the high rates of urban slum dwellers in Arab cities and towns: 42 per cent in 2001.[24]

World Bank data indicate that the expenditure of the 10% of the population that consumes the most in all the Arab countries for which figures are available is 10.4 times higher, on average, than the expenditure of the 10% that consumes the least (see Table 1.1). These figures are hardly credible, even as far as the countries surveyed are concerned. Let us again take Egypt as our example: according to the same set of statistics, the bottom decile of the population has a 4% share of national consumption, while the top decile has a 26.6% share, that is to say, consumes (only!) less than 7 times as much. Anyone familiar with Egypt and Egyptian standards of living, however, knows perfectly well that the disparity between the expenditure of the poorest 10%— which lives mainly in rural areas—and richest 10% is much greater, to say nothing of income and wealth inequalities. If the World Bank's figures were accurate, this would mean that, in a country in which more than 40% of the population lives on less than $2.70 (PPP) a day (the upper national poverty line), while 18.4% lives on less than $2 (PPP) a day (the upper international poverty line), the richest 10% spends less than $14 (PPP) a day, on average—that is, $420 (PPP) a month, or $155 at the market rate that prevailed in 2008.[25] That seems highly unlikely.

The reported disparity in consumption levels in Qatar may seem more credible. According to World Bank data, the top decile there spends 27.6 times more than the bottom decile. This disparity will nevertheless seem to fall far short of the mark to anyone aware both of the wretched living conditions of the emirate's most poorly paid Asian migrant workers, who comprise well over ten percent of the population and spend less than $75 per month, and, on the other hand, the frenetically conspicuous consumption typical of Qatar's privileged social strata. Moreover, here as everywhere else, lumping all those in the top decile together masks the inequality that becomes immediately evident when we focus on the small percentage of super-rich at the tip of the social pyramid, whose extravagant consumption makes them all the more conspicuous.

Qatar is the richest state in the region in per capita terms. It vies with Liechtenstein and Monaco for the world title of the state with the highest per capita national income. Income inequalities between individuals in each of the Arab countries taken separately are exacerbated by inequalities in average per capita income *between* these countries. Country-to-country disparities are higher in the Arab region than in any other geopolitical region. They provide a good reflection of the inequalities that occur on a world scale, since this region includes countries whose per capita GDP is considerably above average for the group of the world's richest countries, and others whose per capita GDP is considerably below world middle income (Table 1.2). Per capita GDP in Qatar was 66.6 times higher than in its neighbor Yemen in 2008. If they were available, the figures for gross national income per capita, which takes into account the income that states and their citizens derive from foreign sources, would display even greater disparities.

Thus the Arab region, as we have seen, exhibits poverty and inequality rates that are quite high, although they are on average lower than those found in other developing regions in Africa and Asia. But MENA indisputably breaks a number of world records when it comes to the third element of our triad, precarity—understood as a combination of informal labor relations, unemployment, and underemployment.

TABLE 1.2 GDP PER CAPITA 2008 (CURRENT US$)

Qatar	79,303	Tunisia	3,954
Kuwait	58,383	Jordan	3,922
UAE	42,108	*World middle income*	*3,491*
World high income	*39,631*	Iraq	2,867
Oman	22,968	Morocco	2,793
Bahrain	20,813	Syria	2,678
Saudi Kingdom	18,203	Egypt	2,079
Libya	15,150	Sudan	1,401
Lebanon	7,219	Yemen	1,190
Algeria	4,967	Mauritania	1,089

SOURCE: World Bank

INFORMAL SECTOR AND UNEMPLOYMENT: THE BOUAZIZI SYNDROME

Mohamed Bouazizi was the young man who, by setting himself on fire in Sidi Bouzid, a city in central Tunisia, on 17 December 2010, triggered the revolutionary process that would spread to the whole Arabic-speaking region in the space of a few months. He has come to symbolize the millions of young people too poor to pursue their education beyond a few years at secondary level. The memorial statue representing a cart with two handles that was erected on the main square of his native city as a tribute to his martyrdom poignantly underscores the fact that his tragedy originated in his precarious condition as a poverty-stricken fruit-and-vegetable street vendor.

It takes all the neoliberal complacency of Peruvian economist Hernando de Soto to be able to claim that Bouazizi sacrificed himself for the cause of the "free market." According to de Soto, "the forces of the market have come to the Arab world—even if governments didn't invite them in. Political leaders must realize that, since Bouazizi went up in flames and his peers rose in protest, poor Arabs are no longer outside but inside, in the market, right next to them."[26] The outrageousness of neoliberal dogmatism defies the imagination; the suggestion is that to satisfy the "poor Arabs," one need only simplify administrative procedures and make it easier to get microcredits. One is reminded of the "Great Princess" in Jean-Jacques Rousseau's *Confessions*, who,

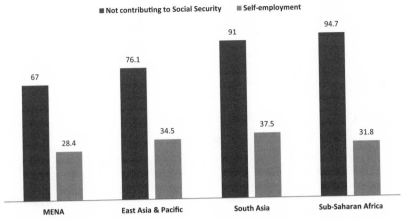

FIGURE 1.6 Informality in labor force and employment (%) (latest available figures in 2011). (Source: Gatti et al.)

informed "that the peasants did not have bread, replied: Let them eat cake."

Yet the fact remains that the so-called informal sector—"informal" because it is not subject to state regulation—is, overall, smaller in Arab countries than in other developing regions in Asia and Africa, even if it accounts for a sizable proportion of those countries' labor force and total employment (Fig. 1.6).

It should, however, be noted that the proportion of the labor force not covered by any form of social insurance varies considerably from one Arab country to another, depending on the nature of the state and its socioeconomic regime. The overall proportion of those not covered in the region is driven downward by the remarkably low average of 6.4% of the economically active in the six very tightly controlled oil monarchies of the GCC; here undeclared work is a negligible phenomenon (compare the 8.9% average in developed countries). For the remaining Arab countries, the proportions range from 34.5% in Libya, 44.5% in Egypt, and 49.9% in Tunisia, through 63.3% in Algeria, 66.9% in Lebanon, and 67.2% in Jordan, to 80.1% in Morocco and 82.6% in Syria and peaking at 90% in Yemen.[27] As for the proportion of the self-employed (above all, peasants and craftspeople) in the active labor force outside the GCC states, where that, too, is very low (6.2%), the disparities between Arab states are smaller, varying between Tunisia's 24.7% and Syria's 35.8% (33.2% in Yemen).[28]

A recently published World Bank study of the informal sector in

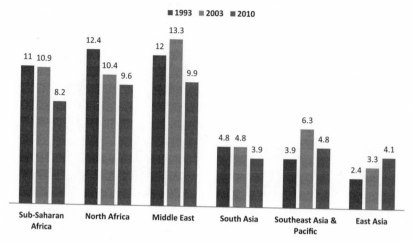

FIGURE 1.7 Unemployment rate (%). (Source: ILO)

MENA emphasizes the positive correlation between informal labor and poverty, even hazarding the paradoxical formulation: "those who can afford to be unemployed, i.e. those who are relatively better off."[29] The study likewise points out the correlation between informal labor and low levels of education, noting that the better educated generally find work in the public sector or the most productive private enterprises[30] when they do not swell the ranks of those seeking employment. Paradoxically, the fact that income and educational levels are higher in the Middle East and North Africa than in the other developing regions of Asia and Africa is responsible for MENA's significantly higher unemployment rates (Fig. 1.7).

These figures, however, offer a very pale reflection of the realities of unemployment and underemployment in MENA. In line with prevailing definitions, the statistics of the International Labour Organization (ILO) treat as "employed" all people old enough to work (15 or above) who, during a brief reference period, such as a week or a day, "performed some work," if only for an hour, in exchange for a wage or salary in cash or in kind or for profit or family gain in cash or in kind.[31] In other words, both individuals underemployed to various degrees and the hidden unemployed who, for lack of salaried employment, join the ranks of the informal sector's "self-employed" in order to survive, fall into the category of the "employed" in this organization's tables and charts.

As for the unemployed, they are, by ILO definition, people "seeking work."[32] This criterion is, however, a very fuzzy one in countries where it is impossible to keep count of those hunting for a job, since the unemployed are not systematically registered. In reality, the official MENA unemployment figures basically reflect the proportion of those looking for work who fall into this category on a rigid interpretation of ILO criteria. As is the case everywhere else as well, these unemployment figures exclude the mass of people who have renounced looking for a job because they have no hope of finding one and who are accordingly relegated to the ranks of the "inactive." In sum, the official MENA unemployment figures by no means accurately reflect the real situation, as observers on the ground agree.

The negative socioeconomic impact of these unemployment figures is heightened by the fact that Arab countries are vying with sub-Saharan Africa for the unenviable distinction of occupying last place in the international ranking of countries' social unemployment coverage: in the Arab states, 97.8% of the unemployed receive no allocations at all (the corresponding figure for sub-Saharan Africa is 99.3%). In fact, in most Arab states, 100% of the unemployed receive no unemployment benefit at all; the sole exceptions before 2011 were Algeria (where the proportion was 96.1%), Tunisia (97%), Bahrain (65.8%), and Egypt (the figure is not available, but probably close to 100%).[33]

Emigration long functioned as a safety valve that made it possible to absorb a large proportion of regional unemployment. Since the 1960s, however, its effectiveness in this regard has appreciably diminished since the population explosion of recent decades coincided with restrictions on immigration to Europe imposed as a result of the crisis of the 1970s, the saturation of the effects of the two oil shocks of the 1970s and 1980s on immigration to the GCC countries, and the competition offered by South Asian immigration to the GCC. Thus the percentage of total MENA emigrants to total MENA population decreased from 9.5% in 1960 to 3.4% at the beginning of the first decade of this century: from 14.5% to 5.5% for North Africa (13% to 5.7% for Tunisia) and from 9.3% to 3.3% for the Arab countries of the Middle East (8.1% to 3.3% for Egypt and 8.7% to 2.4% for Syria).[34]

With the economic crisis in the West and the political upheavals in Arab countries, this safety valve has largely been closed. As for the contribution to GDP that emigrants' remittances represent, it varies considerably from one Arab country to the next. In 2004, it was the highest in Lebanon (25.7%, where, however, it was offset by remittances, totaling 19.5% of GDP, made by workers who had immigrated to Lebanon), followed by Jordan (20.4%), the Palestinian territories of the West Bank

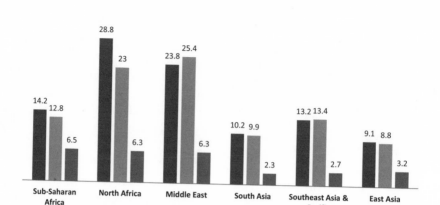

■ Youth 2000   ■ Youth 2010   ■ Adults 2010

FIGURE 1.8 Unemployment rate youth and adults (%). (Source: ILO)

and Gaza (15.5%), Yemen (9.3%), and Morocco (8.4%). It was under 5% in Tunisia (4.9%), Egypt (4.3%), and Syria (3.5%).[35]

YOUTH UNDEREMPLOYMENT

A major distinguishing feature of MENA unemployment is that the percentage of those seeking work is substantially higher among the "youth" (in ILO statistics, "youths" are people between 15 and 24 years of age) than among "adults" (people over 24), as is attested by the figures for 2010 (Fig. 1.8). Youth unemployment thus contributes massively to driving the overall rate upward.

Unemployment rates, it should be noted, exclusively concern the "labor force," defined as all those who have jobs or are looking for them. Thus these rates ignore not only young people who are not seeking employment because their social situation allows them to pursue their education, but also the large number of those who in reality need to find work but have become discouraged or resigned. World Bank researchers seem to have recently discovered this banal and all but self-evident truth, judging from a January 2011 report by the organization's Arab World Initiative: the report ingenuously declares that the actual number of unemployed youths in the region "could be much higher [than reported]. Many young people who are out of school and out of work are not reflected in the statistics because they are not looking for work."[36]

This explains why the labor force participation rate, which mea-

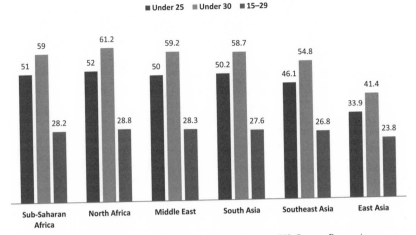

FIGURE 1.9 Youth in total population, 2010 (%). (Source: US Census Bureau)

sures the "labor force" as a percentage of the total population, was in the Middle East in 2010 only 30.3% for young people between 15 and 24, and in North Africa only 33.6%. The corresponding figures in South Asia, sub-Saharan Africa, and East Asia were 41.3%, 53.6%, and 60.3% respectively. This confirms that the rate of unemployed youth in MENA is exceptionally high.[37]

Yet contrary to a pervasive notion very often held out as a key to explaining the "Arab Spring," MENA societies are not particularly young compared with the world's other developing regions. More precisely, they are *no longer* especially young. They are, today, still younger than East Asian societies but scarcely younger than societies in sub-Saharan Africa or South Asia and only just younger than those in Southeast Asia, as is shown by the percentage of young people under 25 or under 30 in these regions today (Fig. 1.9). As for the proportion of adolescents (10 to 19 years of age) in the general population, it was 20% in MENA in 2010, that is to say, equal to the corresponding figure for South Asia and lower than the one for sub-Saharan Africa (23%).[38]

Thus the MENA youth unemployment rate is plainly exceptional, and a broad-based age pyramid is not the sole explanation for this, as proponents of the Youth Bulge theory would like to believe.[39] Formulated in Central Intelligence Agency (CIA) circles, this rather unoriginal theory purports to explain how conflicts originate. Graham Fuller appealed to it in a paper presented at a 1993 conference organized by the CIA's Geographic Resources Division.[40] His thesis was subsequently taken up and popularized by Samuel Huntington in his all too well-known *The Clash of Civilizations,* which cites Fuller.[41] Since then, it has been cast in outrageously systematic form by the controversial German sociologist Gunnar Heinsohn, notably in a 2003 work that has become a best seller in his country and a handful of others.[42]

In an essay published in 2003, Fuller develops his thesis with respect to the Middle East, his area of expertise.[43] However, like a number of other writings disseminated by the CIA since the 1990s that fall back on the same thesis to explain zones of sociopolitical turbulence, his essay attributes unrest and violence not to the high percentage of young people in and of itself, but to the absence of mechanisms for the political and economic absorption of this "bulging" youth population. According to Fuller and his cothinkers' analysis, it is for reasons of this kind that demographic explosions are transformed into political explosions. The palliatives and remedies prescribed by Fuller himself, as well as by other researchers working for the CIA, turn on political liberalization, democratization of the societies involved, educational reform, and birth control. These measures do not challenge, at least not directly, the economic and social order or dependency on Western powers. They aim, rather, to preserve them in the long term.

Heinsohn's provocative thesis, in contrast, is unabashedly reactionary. In his estimation, young people tend to become rebellious as their socioeconomic level rises, so the West would be well advised to stop subsidizing the populations in question and fostering, by the same stroke, their demographic growth. Thus Heinsohn cold-bloodedly advocated, in a *Wall Street Journal* piece published during the Israeli forces' intensive bombardment of Gaza in January 2009, that the Western states stop contributing to the United Nations Relief and Works Agency (UNRWA), created in 1949 to provide relief for Palestinian refugees.[44]

Heinsohn's thesis is as simplistic as it is wrongheaded. By his reckoning, propensity to violence in a given society is directly proportional to the percentage of the population between 15 and 29. However, as we have seen (Fig. 1.9), people in this age group represent approximately the same percentage of society from one developing region to the next, with the exception of East Asia, for which the disparity with other regions is somewhat greater. Comparison of these figures shows that, with respect to unemployment, what distinguishes the condition of young people in MENA from that of their peers in other developing regions is not demographics, but, plainly, the social and political conditions responsible for an economic situation thanks to which nearly one-

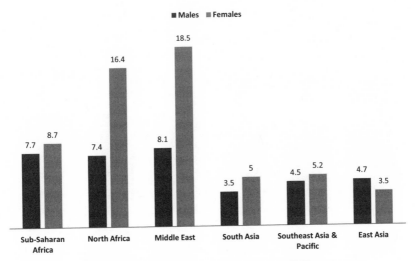

FIGURE 1.10 Unemployment rate by sex, 2010 (%). (Source: ILO)

quarter of youth between the ages of 15 and 24 are, according to official statistics, looking for work.[45]

FEMALE UNDEREMPLOYMENT

The other major distinguishing feature of MENA unemployment is the disparity, greater than anywhere else in the world, between the proportions of men and women in the "labor force" seeking employment. The percentage of unemployed women is more than twice that of men in MENA. It is also twice that of women in sub-Saharan Africa, the region with the next highest rate of female unemployment. It is three times that of women in South Asia and Southeast Asia, to say nothing of East Asia, where proportionately fewer women than men are looking for work (Fig. 1.10).

As with young people, the number of unemployed women represents only a small proportion of all women without employment. In this respect, too, MENA holds an unenviable, even more memorable record. Whereas in 2010, 18.5% of Middle Eastern and 16.4% of North African women in the "active population" were seeking work, only 14.8% and 20%, respectively, of women in those regions who were old enough to work (15 or older) had a job (Fig. 1.11). When we combine the numbers of employed women and those seeking employment, it appears that only 18.1% (in the Middle East) and 24% (in North

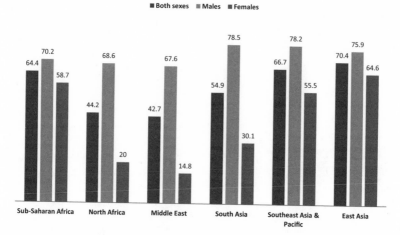

FIGURE 1.11 Employment-to-population rate by sex, 2010 (%). (Source: ILO)

Africa) of the women old enough to work were counted as part of the "labor force," a particularly low rate, as becomes clear when we compare it with the rate for men in the two regions (73.6% and 74.1% respectively) or with the rate for women in the other developing regions of Africa and Asia (in 2010, 31.7% in South Asia, 58.6% in Southeast Asia, 64.4% in sub-Saharan Africa, and 66.9% in East Asia).[46]

These rates of women without jobs comprise, along with youth unemployment rates, the other feature distinguishing MENA from the rest of the world. The demographic explanation commonly given for youth unemployment cannot, of course, hold for the high proportion of women without jobs, since there are not more women than men in the region (in fact, there are slightly fewer women). Here, a cultural explanation is most often held out. Unlike the demographic argument about youth unemployment—we have seen what that is worth—there is little doubt that a cultural factor does indeed play a role, albeit to different degrees in different countries, in generating the extraordinary female nonemployment rates just noted. In order to legitimately take it into account in our analysis, we have to begin by acknowledging that culture is not nature and that mores and customs are themselves social realities that vary considerably over time. Suffice it to compare contemporary with medieval European cultures.

The variety of patriarchal male chauvinist culture predominant in MENA is not the efficient cause but overridingly the product of a par-

ticularly oppressive system of male domination that succeeds in repro-
ducing itself the same way that despotic regimes do, that is, thanks to
a combination of force and consent internalized by way of what Pierre
Bourdieu calls "symbolic violence." To grasp this is to understand that
culture is not eternal, but that "the eternal" itself "cannot be anything
other than the product of a historical labor of eternalization." That is the
term Bourdieu employs in *Masculine Domination*,[47] a work that offers
a useful account of the ideological sources of domination, although it
has been criticized by Western feminists, notably for underestimating
women's self-emancipation. Bourdieu adds, in his idiosyncratic style,
that a history of women "which brings to light, albeit despite itself, a
large degree of constancy, permanence, must, if it wants to be consistent
with itself, give a place, and no doubt the central place, to *the history of
the agents and institutions which permanently contribute to the maintenance of these permanences*—the church, the state, the educational system etc., and which may vary, at different times, in their relative weight
and their functions."[48]

A good overview of MENA women's economic situation was provided by a 2004 report for the World Bank put together by a predominantly female team, advised by Iranian dissident and Nobel Peace Prize
laureate Shirin Ebadi. Released under the title *Gender and Development
in the Middle East and North Africa*,[49] the report laudably considers
cultural factors to be social factors. Thus it considers what it calls "the
traditional gender paradigm" in MENA: the fact that the family rather
than the individual is the basic social unit; that the man of the house has
the breadwinner's role; that a "code of modesty" is imposed on women;
and that a form of inequality perpetuated by the law gives men advantages in the private sphere.[50] This traditional paradigm, however, should
have been demolished by the same factors that have proven decisive in
other climes. This is what the report calls "the gender paradox" specific
to the region:

> MENA's achievements in many areas of women's well-being compare favor-
> ably with those of other regions. Indicators such as female education, fertil-
> ity, and life expectancy show that MENA's progress in those areas in recent
> decades has been substantial. Where MENA falls considerably short is on
> indicators of women's economic participation and political empowerment.
>
> MENA's rate of female labor force participation is significantly lower
> than rates in the rest of the world, and it is lower than would be expected
> when considering the region's fertility rates, its educational levels, and the
> age structure of the female population.[51]

TABLE 1.3 GROSS ENROLLMENT RATIO IN TERTIARY EDUCATION (2009)

Algeria	31	Oman	26
Bahrain	51	Qatar	10
Egypt	28	Saudi kingdom	33
Jordan	41	Tunisia	34
Lebanon	53	UAE	30
Mauritania	4	West Bank & Gaza	46
Morocco	13	Yemen	10

SOURCE: UNESCO

This paradox comes at a price, and it is a high one. A study carried out by two University of Munich economists for the report just cited calculates the growth differential associated with gender inequalities, comparing a group of MENA countries (excluding most of the rich oil monarchies) with East Asia. It comes to the conclusion that if MENA had since 1960 enjoyed a rate of female employment equal to East Asia's, its per capita GDP in 2000 would have been $2,173 dollars higher (in constant 1996 dollars) than it was that year.[52] This finding, which, of course, provides only a rough order of magnitude estimate, should be compared with per capita GDP in the region as a whole, which was, *in 2009*, only $2,361 (in 1996 dollars, the equivalent of $3,281 in 2011 dollars).[53] According to the same study, if MENA had had a female employment rate equal to East Asia's only from 1990 on, its per capita GDP in 2000 would still have been $518 higher, a very substantial difference.

As the 2004 report quoted above points out, the main obstacle to female employment in MENA is not situated at the level of objective factors involving health and education, the evolution of which has led to a marked improvement in women's condition in other parts of the world. If there is a paradox here, it is precisely because MENA has seen significant progress in these areas over the past few decades but has failed to experience the changes in women's political and economic roles that have gone hand in hand with such progress elsewhere.

GRADUATE UNEMPLOYMENT

The third major characteristic of unemployment in the Arab region is the high percentage of unemployed people who have completed their tertiary education. The average gross enrollment ratio in tertiary educa-

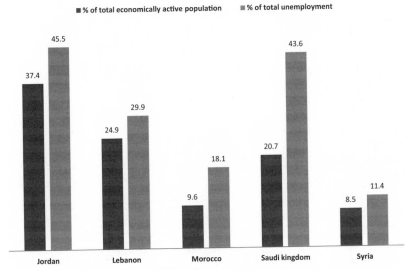

■ % of total economically active population   ■ % of total unemployment

FIGURE 1.12 Population with advanced education (latest available ILO figures in 2011). (Source: ILO)

tion in Arab countries—in other words, the number of those enrolled as a proportion of the total number of individuals of college age—reached 22% in 2009, considerably higher than South Asia's and West Asia's 13% or sub-Saharan Africa's 6%, yet lower than East Asia's and Pacific Asia's 28%.[54] This rate does, it is true, vary considerably from one Arab country to the next, among those Arab countries for which data are available (Table 1.3).

Similarly, while the share of graduates in the total number of the unemployed varies considerably from one Arab country to the next, depending on the proportion of graduates in the labor force, the proportion of people with a tertiary education among the unemployed is everywhere higher than their proportion in the labor force (Fig. 1.12).

Moreover, the unemployment rates of people with a tertiary education are rising fast. The data below, compiled from various national statistics by a Tunisian economist,[55] show how the unemployment rate has ballooned in the three central Maghreb countries over the past twenty to twenty-five years (Table 1.4). The acute nature of the problem in Tunisia, exacerbated by regional disparities, was a major contributing factor to the explosion in that country.[56]

The most common explanation for this rise in the unemployment

TABLE I.4   GRADUATE UNEMPLOYMENT RATES
1984–2010

	1984–1990	2008–2010
Algeria	8.4 (1990)	20.3 (2010)
Morocco	6.0 (1984)	17.7 (2010)
Tunisia	5.3 (1989)	21.6 (2008)

SOURCE: Jaballah

rate among graduates is inspired by the logic of the economic ortho-doxy prevailing in international financial institutions. It is patent that the number of graduates has been increasing in step with the growth of the population as a whole, thanks to the democratization of tertiary education in most of the region in the 1960s. The increase in graduate unemployment results, the argument runs, from the mismatch between supply and demand regarding qualifications.

By this very rudimentary logic, college students need only study the right subjects to resolve the problem—as if the existing economies already had the capacity to absorb all those with a tertiary education, if only they had different qualifications. This logic also postulates that demand creates supply. But MENA students are apparently not studying the right subjects, since they are not finding jobs. Hence they are criti-cized for majoring in useless subjects at college, while their governments are criticized for not channeling them in authoritarian fashion toward the right majors.

By the same logic, the demand that remains unsatisfied by locally available supply should lead to the importation of the qualifications required, or, in other words, to immigration of graduates from the rest of the world to MENA. Nothing of the sort is happening. Quite the contrary: outside the GCC countries, which have indeed attracted such immigrants because of the absolute insufficiency of their native human resources (and not merely because of their human resources' inappro-priate qualifications), Arab countries are in fact disadvantaged by the emigration of their graduates; they are victims rather than beneficiaries of the "brain drain."

According to the most recent available figures in the World Bank's *Migration and Remittances Factbook 2011*, figures dating from the year 2000, the emigration rates of people with tertiary education from MENA to countries outside the region (essentially, OECD countries) were, for the countries with the highest emigration levels in relative terms, 38.6% for Lebanon, 17% for Morocco, 12.5% for Tunisia, 11.1% for Iraq, 9.4% for Algeria, 7.2% for Jordan, 7.2% for the West Bank and Gaza, and 6.1% for Syria.[57] According to a study carried out by the Population Policies and Migration Department of the League of Arab States, the overall rate of emigration from all Arab countries of people who had completed tertiary education had reached 9% in 2000, after increasing an average 8.9% annually from 1990 on.[58] This rate has most probably continued to rise since 2000. Very many of the emigrants had qualifications that are sorely lacking in the region. For example, 2,300 physicians left Syria and 3,000 left Egypt in the year 2000.[59]

To account for the high graduate unemployment rate in MENA, a 2004 study carried out by a World Bank research team provides an explanation more convincing than the "mismatch" thesis. "The conclusion that emerges" from this study, its authors affirm,

> is that unemployment in MENA is a phenomenon that primarily affects young new entrants and women at the middle and upper ends of the educational distribution. Thus, the unemployed are essentially those who would have had a chance at a formal job in the public sector in the past and continue to have expectations of acquiring such a job.... To survive, those with no education must either accept whatever employment is available to them, no matter how casual, or create their own job. Although they might be underemployed, they are less likely to be openly unemployed.[60]

This is insightful. The authors point out that there exists an incompressible number of people whom the local economy is incapable of absorbing, and that this number is incessantly growing due to the arrival of new people on the job market. But the more social requirements and aspirations that unemployed people have, the less they are inclined to content themselves with slapdash expedients in the world of the "informal sector"—in other words, to pull the wool over the eyes of international institutions or people conducting local surveys, if not to deceive themselves and those around them by disguising what is in fact unemployment as undeclared "employment," "self-employment," or even a "microenterprise."

FETTERS ON DEVELOPMENT

In sum, what is incontestably revealed, both by economic growth rates, especially when we take demographics into account, and also by the data on employment and participation in the labor force, is that a number of factors are seriously inhibiting development in MENA. The weaker economic growth is, the less the economy is capable of absorbing a potential labor force that is expanding in step with population growth. The underemployment of the region's population as a whole indicates, in the clearest possible way, the extent to which its potential for development is being thwarted, with an employment/population ratio well under 50% in 2010: 42.7% (Middle East) and 44.2% (North Africa), as opposed to rates of 54.9% for South Asia, 66.7% for Southeast Asia, 64.4% for sub-Saharan Africa, and 70.4% for East Asia.[61]

When Marx talks about relations of production and property becoming fetters for the productive forces after serving as forms for their development, he does not mean just material forces in the sense of the application of technology. In his view, productive forces also include the force of human labor, which sets the factors that determine the mode of production and level of wealth—namely, science and technology—in motion. The question of the population held a central place in Marx's thinking as he worked on his magnum opus, *Das Kapital*, especially as it bore on the basic contradictions of the capitalist mode of production. In the preparatory manuscripts for *Das Kapital* known as the *Grundrisse* (the first word of their German title), he develops the idea encapsulated in the 1859 Preface that serves as the epigraph to this chapter:

> Beyond a certain point, the development of the powers of production becomes a barrier for capital; hence *the capital relation [becomes] a barrier for the development of the productive powers of labour.* . . . The growing incompatibility between the productive development of society and its hitherto existing relations of production expresses itself in bitter contradictions, crises, spasms. . . . It is not only the growth of scientific power. . . . It is, likewise, *the development of the population* etc., in short of all moments of production; in that the productive power of labour, like the application of machinery, is related to the population.[62]

Capitalism is a global mode of production and accumulation. Accordingly, its major periodic crises and convulsions manifest themselves on a global scale: the ones that mark its advance toward a level of development at which it will find it harder and harder to overcome the gridlocks inevitably provoked by the logic of profit informing it. It has so far managed to overcome these blockages, thanks either to the systematic destruction caused by wars or to changes in the mode of capitalist regulation.

As was stressed at the beginning of this chapter, however, on the regional scale that concerns us here, we have to deal, not with a manifestation of the contradiction between the capitalist system and the development of the productive forces in absolute terms, but, rather, with a blockage specifically linked to particular capitalist modalities. We must go on to identify these modalities that, in a context of unequal development on a world scale, are inflicting economic growth rates on the Arab region that are lower than those in other parts of the developing world—despite that region's wealth in factors of production (capital, labor, and natural resources)—and, most importantly, saddling it with unemployment rates considerably higher than those found elsewhere.

CHAPTER 2

The Peculiar Modalities
of Capitalism in the Arab Region

Examining the way the average annual growth rate of GDP per capita has evolved in the MENA region (Fig. 2.1) draws attention to several facts. This rate is subject to frequent sharp variation. It depends closely on political events: nationalization, regional wars (1967 and 1973 Arab-Israeli wars, 1980–8 Iran-Iraq war, wars that US-led coalitions waged on Iraq in 1991 and 2003), and so on, as well as oil price fluctuations. The latter, in turn, correlated with the recurrent political tensions in the MENA region, the main exporter of this highly strategic commodity. Yet, since its 1972 peak due to the 1971 nationalizations of oil, and its 1974 and 1976 peaks due to the price surge that followed the 1973 Arab-Israeli war, the region's per capita GDP growth rate has exhibited a clear downward trend, in a context marked by the dismantling of the state-led developmentalist model.

In the 1980s, this downward trend was exacerbated by the "oil glut" that followed the second, 1979–80 oil shock, which had far more limited consequences than the first. The increased influence of the oil-exporting monarchies of the Arab-Iranian Gulf, which, from 1974, suddenly found themselves with substantially higher petrodollar revenues, went hand in hand with the introduction of *infitah* policies (see Chapter 1) at the regional level by republican regimes that had previously claimed to be "socialist": Egypt, Iraq, and Syria, joined by Algeria late in the decade. (Tunisia likewise went through a "socialist" phase in the 1960s. As for South Yemen, it was annexed by North Yemen in 1990–4.)

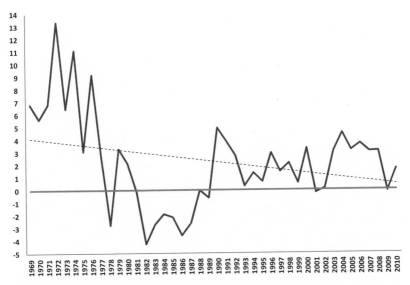

FIGURE 2.1 GDP per capita annual growth (%); MENA—1969–2010. (Source: World Bank)

This period, which heralded the global neoliberal turn, was dominated by the idea that the command economy had failed to overcome underdevelopment and absorb the population explosion. The panacea, which before long would triumph across the board, had it that development should be based first and foremost on the private sector. The lessons of the history of capitalism down to the mid-twentieth century were blithely ignored. The assumption was once again that the market's "invisible hand" could ensure development much more efficiently than the state planners' heavy hand. Nothing of that happened in the Arab region: after the roller-coaster decline of the 1970s, the 1980s witnessed negative growth rates. Notwithstanding the pronounced slow-down in population increase relative to preceding decades, GDP per capita annual growth has since 1990 hovered between zero and five percent. So low a range cannot make up for the accumulated development lag; it confirms the downward trend that has produced the deplorable results reviewed in the preceding chapter.

THE PROBLEM OF INVESTMENT

There is nothing mysterious about this low rate of growth. The decline in GDP per capita growth has gone hand in hand with a decline in the ratio

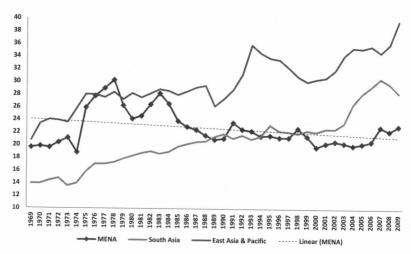

FIGURE 2.2 Gross fixed capital formation (% of GDP)

of investment, or gross fixed capital formation (construction, transport infrastructure, and industrial equipment), to GDP (Fig. 2.2). The curve of these rates for the MENA region shows the depressive effects of the 1967 and 1973 Arab-Israeli wars, which were followed by a jump in oil prices and a sudden increase in infrastructure investment, thanks to the increase in oil revenues. This increase did not benefit only exporting countries by boosting their budgetary resources; importing countries reaped benefits too, in the form of grants, loans, and direct investments from exporters. Between 1974 and 1988, MENA registered strong investment growth, culminating in 1978 in an investment rate of 30% of GDP. In the wake of the second oil crisis, precipitated by Iraq's 1980 attack on Iran, 1983 saw another peak in investment growth, up to 28% this time. Since 1985, however, MENA's curve has fluctuated within a narrow range of 19% to 24%, displaying a long-term downward tendency.

The contrast with South Asian and East Asian performances is striking. Although the curve of fixed investment as a percentage of GDP for South Asia set out from a much lower level than MENA's in 1969—14% as opposed to 19.6%—it exhibited an unmistakable rising trend thereafter, attaining a high of 30.6% in 2007, on the eve of the world economic crisis, as opposed to MENA's 23% the same year. As for East Asia's curve, it was initially quite close to MENA's (apart from a sharp dip in 1974 following the October 1973 Arab-Israeli war) but diverged from it after 1983, climbing steadily until it had reached more than

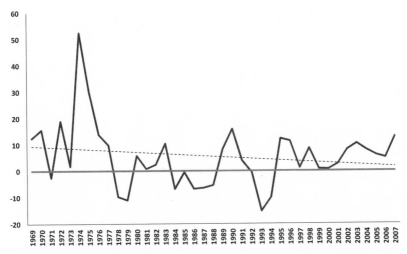

FIGURE 2.3 Gross capital formation annual growth (%); MENA without GCC—1969–2007. (Source: World Bank)

35% a decade later. After a drop induced by the 1997 Asian financial crisis, the ratio of fixed investment to GDP in East Asia started rising again at the turn of the century, climbing back up to 35% by 2004 and approaching 40% in 2009. In MENA, in contrast, it has since 1985 consistently fallen short of 24%.

With the exception of the six oil monarchies, for which annual statistics are not included in World Bank data, the annual growth rate of gross capital formation (including stocks variation) for the region showed a downward trend for the four decades between 1969 and the onset of the global Great Recession in 2007 (Fig. 2.3).

For the countries of the MENA region as a whole, the annual growth rate of gross capital formation was distinctly lower than that posted by all other developing regions of Africa and Asia in the 1990s. It was also distinctly lower than that of the other regions of Asia in the first decade of the present century (Fig. 2.4), although the MENA region was a net exporter of capital at a high rate.

PUBLIC AND PRIVATE INVESTMENT

Two crucially important points emerge when we examine the ratios of fixed investment to GDP more closely, comparing the MENA region's performances here—excepting, again, the GCC countries, for which World Bank data are unavailable—with those of "emerging" Asian

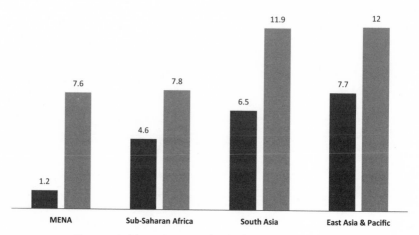

FIGURE 2.4 Gross capital formation annual growth (%); MENA without GCC—1969–2007. (Source: World Bank)

regions from 1995 to 2007 (the sole period for which we have relevant data for all three regions in question). The first point leaps to the eye: the rates of public gross fixed investment as a percentage of GDP are much higher in East Asia, where China is the dominant economy, than in MENA, notwithstanding their post-2004 decline (Fig. 2.5).[1]

East Asia's very high public investment rates are an index of the state's major role in this region, which boasts the world's highest economic growth rate, thus belying the basic assumptions of the neoliberal ideology that has held sway across the globe for more than thirty years. The fact is that China can in no sense be seen to illustrate the success of the export-oriented market economy model. As was recently pointed out in a special report on the Chinese economy published in *The Economist*,

> it is investment, not exports, that leads China's economy. Spending on plant, machinery, buildings and infrastructure accounted for about 48% of China's GDP in 2011. . . .
>
> A disproportionate share of China's investment is made by state-owned enterprises and, in recent years, by infrastructure ventures under the control of provincial or municipal authorities but not on their balance sheets.[2]

In MENA countries, in contrast, public investment in production and infrastructure has substantially decreased since *infitah* policies were

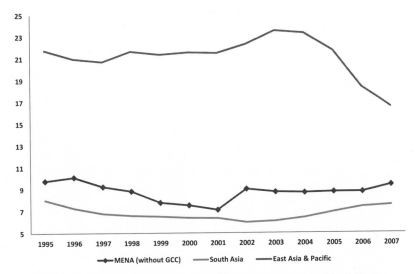

FIGURE 2.5 Gross fixed capital formation, public sector, 1995–2007 (% of GDP). (Source: World Bank)

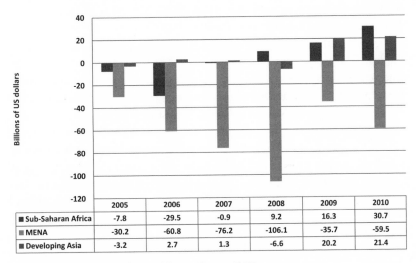

	2005	2006	2007	2008	2009	2010
■ Sub-Saharan Africa	-7.8	-29.5	-0.9	9.2	16.3	30.7
■ MENA	-30.2	-60.8	-76.2	-106.1	-35.7	-59.5
■ Developing Asia	-3.2	2.7	1.3	-6.6	20.2	21.4

FIGURE 2.6 Net official financial flows. (Source: IMF)

introduced in the 1970s and neoliberalism was imposed as the standard model here as in the rest of the world. This decline in state investment goes hand in hand with the fact that the region exports a much higher proportion of state funds than the other developing regions of Africa and Asia (Fig. 2.6).

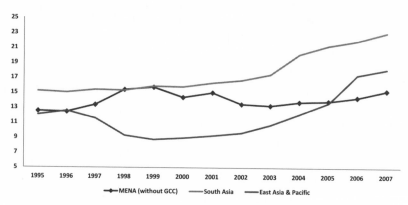

FIGURE 2.7 Gross fixed capital formation, private sector; 1995–2007 (% of GDP).
(Source: World Bank)

To be sure, South Asia has also experienced a steep relative decline in public investment over the past few decades: its public fixed investment rate as a percentage of GDP was even lower than MENA's in the period under consideration (see Fig. 2.5). South Asia—or, rather, India, the region's dominant economy—is likewise held up, with much greater justification than China, as evidence of the success of the neoliberal model, since the country has posted high rates of economic growth in the last few years, despite the contraction of the state's economic role. The reason for this growth is that, in India, private fixed investment has replaced public investment; the ratio of private investment to GDP appreciably exceeds MENA's. Private investment in East Asia, in contrast, was hard hit by the crisis that befell the region in 1997, with the result that, from 1997 to 2004, private investment relative to GDP was lower there than in MENA (Fig. 2.7).

The relative leveling off or decline in MENA public investment has not been offset by an increase in private investment. The private sector's contribution to gross fixed capital formation in MENA countries (except for the six GCC monarchies) essentially stagnated between 1982 and 2007, the period for which World Bank data were available at the time of writing. In that quarter century, the ratios of fixed private investment to GDP in MENA fluctuated within a narrow range between 12% and 16%. In contrast, they rose almost uninterruptedly in South Asia, climbing from only 9% of GDP in 1982 to 23% in 2007, on the eve of the international economic crisis. This ratio is nearly 50% higher than the peak ratio in MENA. As for East Asia, private investment as a proportion of GDP, after falling to 8.7% in the wake of the 1997 crisis, once again exhibited a distinct rising trend, reaching 22% in 2010, according to World Databank, the Great Recession notwithstanding.

Syria provides a good illustration of all that has just been said. Mohammed Jamal Barout has pointed out that the accelerated liberalization of the economy under Bashar al-Assad brought on a record fall in the rate of public investment, from 13% of GDP in 2005 to 8% in 2008, whereas the rate of private investments that were supposed to make up for the slackening public effort stagnated at 11% to 12%. In the same period, consequently, the overall rate of investment in the country fell from 25% to 20% of GDP, whereas the industrial public sector languished for lack of private buyers.[3]

Giacomo Luciani and Steffen Hertog lose sight of these realities when, in a 2010 study of the private sector's role in Arab economies, they celebrate the fact that

> business now is the main source of capital formation in the region, or at least on a par with the state, a radical shift from the 1970s when government capital formation dominated national investment even in the "liberal" GCC cases.
>
> While the share of private investment in total GDP is lower than in other emerging regions, notably East Asia, it has become much more important over time.[4]

In support of their claim, the authors cite only 2005–7 data, which is not sufficient warrant for a general conclusion (see Fig. 2.2 above). Even if we assume that we would observe an "important" increase in private investment as a percentage of GDP if data for GCC countries were taken into account, the significance of that observation would be seriously undermined by the ambiguity of the definition of the "private sector" in these countries. The authors themselves note this ambiguity:

> Our interpretation of the Saudi case—which in itself is the most important, as the Saudi economy is the largest in the GCC and in the broader Arab region—is very much contingent upon what exactly we consider private sector. Key government-initiated and majority-owned companies such as SABIC, the telephone company STC, and the electricity company SEC, are formally private corporations and have private minority shareholders. Substantively speaking, however, they fully belong to the public sector.[5]

The overall state of the private sector in MENA is well summed up in the 2005 World Bank regional report, due allowance made for the euphemisms traditionally employed in documents issued by international financial institutions:

The formal private sector remains underdeveloped in MENA, still emerging from the culture of decades of state-led growth and industrialization. On average, the private sector accounts for less than 50 percent of GDP in the region. Private sector activity is concentrated in a small number of large firms that have benefited from protective policies, along with a number of microenterprises that account for much of employment but have little access to formal finance, markets, or government support programs.

While most of the governments in MENA agree that the private sector needs to become the primary engine of job growth, the public sector remains a major source of job creation. It is estimated to account for almost a third of employment in the region, compared with 27 percent worldwide, and 18 percent worldwide excluding China. Public sector employment ranges from a low of 10 percent of total employment in Morocco to a high of 93 percent in Kuwait, and averages more than 70 among the GCC.[6]

Foreign direct investment (FDI), which had hovered at very low levels in MENA until the turn of the century, increased substantially after 2002, peaking in 2008 before falling off as a result of the economic crisis. Nevertheless, as the World Bank's September 2011 regional report points out, the bulk of this FDI went to the GCC states. It was concentrated in the Saudi kingdom and the United Arab Emirates, which together garnered 45% of total FDI in 2003–7 (this was, in part, FDI from other GCC member states). They were followed by countries with close links to GCC states, such as Egypt (12%), Lebanon, and Jordan.[7] We may generalize the conclusion that Mahmoud Ben Romdhane draws from the elimination of barriers to FDI in Tunisia—ranked, be it noted, as one of the economies offering the *best* conditions for foreign investment in the Arab region. "There has been no massive influx of foreign direct investment to Tunisia," Romdhane affirms. "FDI has stagnated, so to speak. It is only because of privatization of firms formerly in the public sector (cement plants and telecommunications) and the sharp rise in the international oil price that significant foreign investment has been attracted to the country."[8]

Taken together, the facts just mentioned and those discussed in the preceding chapter mandate the following conclusions: the low per capita GDP growth rates and record unemployment rates displayed by the MENA region, despite a slowdown in population growth, are natural corollaries of steadily declining growth in fixed investment. For more than three decades now, the overall ratio of gross capital formation to GDP in the region has exhibited a distinct downward trend (see Fig. 2.2). At the same time, the rate of private investment has displayed a

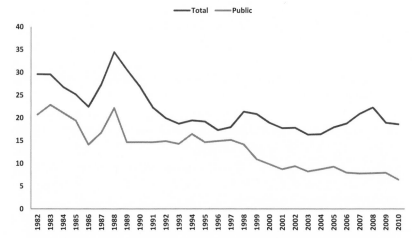

FIGURE 2.8 Gross fixed capital formation, total and public; Egypt—1982–2010 (% of GDP). (Source: World Bank)

cyclical pattern at a relatively low level since the early 1980s, confined to a narrow range with a stationary trend.

On the one hand, these facts suggest that most of the blame for the lamentable state of the region must be put on the drop in public investment induced by the change in economic paradigm at the regional and global levels. This is well illustrated in Egypt by the correlation between public investment and total investment (Fig. 2.8), if we disregard the exceptional 2007–8 jump in private (foreign) investment in the country, discussed below. On the other hand, the same facts lead us to ask why private investment has not climbed from levels too low to offset the withdrawal of public sector investment, a circumstance that authorizes Ray Bush to say that "the failure of Arab elites to invest locally or regionally is the biggest obstacle to sustained levels of economic growth."[9]

All in all, the results of the 1961–5 five-year plan in Egypt's "socialist" period under Gamal Abdel-Nasser were better than those of the Hosni Mubarak era from 1982 on, after the military and political vicissitudes of the Sadat years. Moreover, those results were achieved despite the Egyptian army's very costly involvement, from 1962, in a war in Yemen—an involvement that reached its height in 1966 and came to an end after the June 1967 Arab-Israeli war. Even the American authors of *Area Handbook for Egypt*, published in 1976 for use by US "military and other personnel," were forced to admit that "in spite of weaknesses the First Five Year Plan was a good first effort."[10]

Egypt's per capita GDP growth rate, 1.7% in 1961, the year the Nasser regime decreed sweeping nationalizations, reached a high of 6.5% in 1965, according to World Databank. This level was attained again and then exceeded only in 1975–7, as a result of the oil boom and the effect of offsetting the disastrous rates of the first Sadat years (1971–4), and again in 1980 and 1982, thanks to the second oil crisis and the financial support the United States and its allies extended to Egypt as a reward for signing a peace treaty with Israel (see Fig. 1.2, Chapter 1). The fact that the growth rate began rising again from the very low levels to which it had fallen in 2002 (0.5%), and that it continued to do so until 2008 (5.3%), was essentially due to increasing oil prices in this period. It resulted from both the direct effect of that increase on Egyptian exports and its induced effects (state or private capital from the oil monarchies, as well as remittances by Egyptian migrant workers).[11]

I demonstrated this in a 2009 critique of the IMF's 2007 assessment of Egypt's performance, which it described as an "emerging success story" due to 2004 reforms "geared to encouraging the private sector to become the engine of job-creating growth."[12] After refuting that claim, I concluded my examination of the IMF's evaluation as follows:

> Egypt's prospects are marred by such a high degree of social and political instability that the "success story" trumpeted by the IMF and the World Bank sounds like a very light-hearted tune indeed. . . . Rather than an unmitigated "success story," Egypt's situation should be regarded as quite worrying.[13]

It took the Arab uprising to make the IMF realize this eminently banal truth, obvious to anyone who had not been wearing blinkers. The admission came from the mouth of its managing director, Christine Lagarde:

> We all learned some important lessons from the Arab Spring. While the top-line economic numbers—on growth, for example—often looked good, too many people were being left out.
>
> And, speaking for the IMF, while we certainly warned about the ticking time bomb of high youth unemployment in the region, we did not fully anticipate the consequences of unequal access to opportunities. Let me be frank: we were not paying enough attention to how the fruits of economic growth were being shared.
>
> It is now much clearer that more equal societies are associated with greater economic stability and more sustained growth.[14]

The prescriptions for the Arab region that the international financial institutions' "experts" continue to hawk are nevertheless so hollow
as to be cause for consternation. Thus a World Bank report published
in April 2012 informs Arab governments how they can work nothing
short of "employment miracles." It's all very simple: "prudent macro-
economic management, sound regulation and good governance" and
"sound business regulations, as well as policies that facilitate trade."[15]
The report does, however, prudently add, putting itself beyond the reach
of Popper's falsification criterion: "However, when reforming, the devil
is in the details, and consistent implementation critical for success."[16]

These "experts" do not even dare suggest that Arab petrodollars be
massively redirected to job-creating investment in the region, Marshall
Plan–style, as Hillary Clinton herself has done.[17] The reason is that
Secretary of State Clinton's speech, delivered before the George C.
Marshall Foundation, was of no real consequence, whereas the international financial institutions cannot go so far as to suggest that the oil
monarchies stop investing their capital in Western economies, in particular in the United States, and transfer it to the Arab *governments*
instead, on the model of the aid that the United States provided its
European allies from 1948 to 1951.

In any case, wherever the required funds come from—external sources
or a mobilization of domestic resources—the path that will lead Arab
countries out of the vicious circle of underdevelopment runs through
the state and public investment. This is true in several respects.[18] We
have already seen, in Chapter 1, the impact that the relative fall in public sector investment has had on unemployment. It is a major cause of
the very high level of youth unemployment, especially graduate unemployment, as indicated by the 2004 World Bank study of unemployment
in the MENA region cited in Chapter 1.[19] Similarly, the 2004 World
Bank study on gender and development in the region observes that a
combination of social, cultural, and economic factors constitutes the
main impediment to female employment in MENA.[20]

The state's role is decisive in this regard. Along with legislative reform
and equality of educational opportunity, the most effective action that
can be taken by a government wishing to encourage women's liberation, if only to promote development, is to enhance women's employ-
ability by creating jobs open to them. Thus the condition of women in
MENA countries made considerable progress in the post–World War
II developmentalist phase, dubbed the Glorious Thirty Years, as they
did everywhere else. Since that phase came to an end, the trend has

run in the opposite direction, with powerfully regressive consequences for women:

> In most of the region, women have tended to participate heavily in public sector employment. Reasons include (a) the perception that public sector professions such as teaching and nursing are appropriate for women; (b) the public sector's egalitarian and affirmative action practices in hiring and wage setting; and (c) the favorable conditions of work in the public sector, including generous maternity leave benefits. With the share of public sector employment shrinking in many countries, the public sector will no longer remain an important source of jobs for women in the future.
>
> In the private sector, by contrast, women have faced significant disadvantages and fewer job opportunities. Often they work with lower wages and with little potential for growth.[21]

We find a similar diagnosis in the UNDP's *Arab Human Development Report 2005*, which focuses on women's condition.[22] While highlighting factors rooted in legislation and education, the report stresses the central role of the "mode of production":

> The extent to which women in Arab countries are empowered is significantly influenced by the political economy of the region. The mode of production in Arab countries is dominated by rentier economies and levels of economic performance marked by weak economic growth. The combination of these two characteristics results in weak production structures in the Arab economies and a paucity of means of expansion, laying the groundwork for the spread of unemployment and poverty. The overall result is a pattern of economic activity that has disastrous results for human economic empowerment, with other social circumstances multiplying the harshest results when it comes to women because of their economic weakness.[23]

A SPECIFIC VARIANT OF THE CAPITALIST MODE OF PRODUCTION

What features of the mode of production dominant in the Arab region account for the blockage of its development? The answer to this question will allow us to determine the nature of the current regional crisis as well as its significance on a global scale and, later, to define the conditions for overcoming it. This will put us in a position to judge whether there can be a successful short-term or medium-term outcome to the revolutionary process set in motion in December 2010 or whether it is, rather, inevitably destined to unfold over a period of several years, if not decades.

The MENA region has of course not escaped the worldwide domination of the capitalist mode of production. The modalities of this mode of production, however, vary widely from country to country and region to region. Many observers have hastily interpreted the social explosion rocking the Arabic-speaking region as a direct consequence of the current global capitalist crisis, manifested in the Great Recession that has since 2007 gripped the countries at the heart of the international economy: the United States, Europe, and Japan. The fact that the Arab explosion coincided with the international recession has inevitably spawned the temptation to take this analytic shortcut. Yet the fact is that MENA has suffered less from the global crisis than other regions in the Afro-Asian group. This is emphasized in a World Bank report on global economic prospects that was published in January 2011, at the very moment when turmoil began to engulf the region:

> The developing countries of the Middle East and North Africa region were less affected than other developing regions by the global recession, in part because of the region's limited financial integration, but also due to its export mix, which is concentrated in products (oil, materials and light manufactures) that were not as sharply affected by the crisis as capital goods—and, in turn, as the economies which produce them.[24]

That said, there can be no doubt that the multifaceted impact of the international economic crisis—especially the sudden 2007–8 jump in food prices—has exacerbated the discontent of the region's inhabitants. Thus, as the World Bank's regional report for 2008 did not fail to note,

> the sharp rise in the price of staple food grains such as rice and wheat had a varying impact on different countries, depending on certain risk factors. Low-income countries that are relatively big food importers (in terms of proportion of imports and consumption) have been at highest risk. . . . In the Republic of Yemen, food price inflation exceeded 20 percent in 2007, the highest in the region. Other risk factors include the extent to which food features in the spending patterns of the lowest-income groups in a country. Countries such as . . . the Arab Republic of Egypt, and the Republic of Yemen were among the most vulnerable, since the bottom two quintiles of their populations spend 50 percent or more of their household budgets on food. *It is not surprising that both Egypt and the Republic of Yemen experienced episodes of social unrest in recent months.*[25]

The report for the following year confirmed the gravity of the leap in food prices, especially as far as the most vulnerable rural populations were concerned. At the same time, it insisted that governments had taken important measures to mitigate its effects and ease social tensions before the 2008 fall in prices:

For the MENA region, the food price shock for rural poor populations amounted to a boost of 25.9% over the period, and with food taking up 64.5% of the consumption bundle for this group, purchasing power of households would have decreased by some 17% over 2 years in the absence of government support policies.[26]

To ease the burden of the food price crisis, MENA governments maintained food subsidies, imposed price controls and restricted exports. During 2008 rice suppliers in Egypt were constrained to export only up to the amount they could import. This "export ban" has been extended until further notice. Yemen started providing wheat at a subsidized price, while expanding and reforming a targeted cash transfer program. A second group of policy actions were targeted to ease the impact of high prices on households, with some governments cutting import duties on certain commodities deemed critical for households' food consumption. For example, Morocco reduced wheat tariffs and started subsidizing wheat importers.[27]

Moreover, sub-Saharan Africa experienced inflation rates higher than MENA's in the two years preceding the 2011 explosion: 10.6% and 7.4% in 2009 and 2010 respectively, against MENA's 6.6% and 6.9%.[28] Yet it has not witnessed a comparable uprising. In short, we cannot make the global crisis or higher food prices the determining cause of the Arab upheaval, just as we cannot, say, simply attribute the popular uprising in Syria to the exceptional droughts that have plagued the country, especially between 2006 and 2011.[29] In both cases, this would be to confuse an aggravating circumstance with an efficient cause—in other words, to confuse "structure with conjuncture," to borrow the terms Albert Soboul uses in his discussion of the debate about the causes of the French Revolution.[30] In the tradition of Marx and Jean Jaurès, Soboul distinguishes between, on the one hand, the basic, long-term contradictions that bring the development of the productive forces into conflict with political and social structures and, on the other, the conjunctural variations that exacerbate these basic contradictions:

The Ancien Régime's irreducible social contradictions had long since put revolution on the agenda. Economic and demographic fluctuations, which generated tensions and, in the conditions of the day, stubbornly resisted all governmental action, created a revolutionary situation. Confusedly or consciously, the overwhelming majority of the nation rose up against a regime whose ruling class was powerless to defend it. In this way, the point of rupture was reached.[31]

When it comes to the relationship between the worldwide crisis and the Arab upheaval, the distinction between conjunctural factor and structural cause is the more essential in that the impact of this crisis has varied from one country in the region to the next. This holds even for the countries that have experienced the biggest uprisings to date. As was just pointed out, the global crisis has hit other developing regions harder, without producing a revolutionary shock wave even remotely comparable to the one that has shaken the whole of the Arab region. Yet this region by no means comprises the world economy's "weakest link," if only because of its oil resources. We have seen, moreover, that the region's basic problems—especially unemployment and underemployment—have beset it for decades. These two circumstances require us to put the Great Recession's impact on the revolutionary explosion in the Arabic-speaking region into perspective: the hypothesis that the Arab crisis is basically just an avatar of the global crisis does not hold up under examination. The Great Recession has merely exacerbated the specific structural factors underlying the regional explosion.

To pursue the same comparative logic, the explanation of the sociopolitical explosion in MENA as a consequence of the general failure of neoliberalism is vitiated by the contrast between the region's poor economic performance and the good performances of other developing countries such as Chile, India, or Turkey, which have applied neoliberal prescriptions more consistently. For several years now, the international financial institutions have themselves been willing to concede that the results of their "Washington consensus" recipes depend on those charged with carrying them out. They have revised their doctrine to make room for the notion of "good governance," said to be a condition for the proper functioning of their economic model. Conveniently, this allows them to keep peddling the same neoliberal formulas in blithe disregard of sociopolitical contexts, while declining all responsibility for the consequences that adopting them has often had and continues to have. Thus, in an exercise in simplistic thinking that merely inverts the one that makes the Arab crisis an effect of neoliberalism without further qualification, the international financial institutions continue to claim that the Arab region is suffering from insufficient economic liberalization and that its current problems can be resolved only if it liberalizes still more.

While it is true that the Arab states are far from fully complying with the neoliberal model, the fact remains that economic and social policies inspired by the neoliberal paradigm have unquestionably had a major hand in precipitating the regional uprising. By exacerbating corruption on the highest rung of the social ladder while simultaneously producing disastrous results for the social strata on the lowest rungs, these policies have very obviously precipitated the explosion. Yet the way they have been implemented in Arab countries has been determined, in both its modalities and effects, by the sociopolitical character of the regimes already in place. At the same time, most of these countries have been hampered economically by heavy liabilities inherited from the extensive state capitalism established in the region in the 1960s and, albeit in contradictory fashion, from the 1970s with the nationalizations of oil. To determine the basic causes of the ongoing explosion, one should, rather, consider the specific constellation that has presided over the application of these economic and social policies.

We must therefore examine the specific modalities of the capitalist mode of production dominant in the Arab region in order to identify the underlying causes of the long-term economic blockage afflicting it. In the process, we shall be identifying the reasons for the revolutionary explosion that is now shaking the Arabic-speaking world to its core.

1. Rentier and Patrimonial States

The first unmistakable feature of capitalism in MENA is the one evoked in the UNDP report cited above: the role of state rents, for a significant share of MENA countries' state revenues derives from rents. In 2010, more than 60% of the inhabitants of the group of Arab countries lived in states that were net exporters of petroleum (Algeria, Iraq, Libya, Sudan, Syria, Yemen, and the GCC countries). If we take exports of natural gas into account, the proportion climbs, with Egypt, to 85%. If we include minerals, too, it may be said that virtually all the region's inhabitants live in countries in which the state obtains a more or less substantial part of its income from the export of (nonrenewable) resources extracted from the earth.

In 2007, exports of hydrocarbons—petroleum and natural gas—made up more than 80% of the exports of all Arab countries taken together.[32] These countries' exports exclusive of hydrocarbons represented, the same year, a mere 22.6% of the exports of just one country, Turkey. With hydrocarbons, their total exports were over six times greater than Turkey's. The GCC countries alone exported more than four times as much as Turkey in 2007.[33]

These exports provide the states involved with a "rent." In the broadest sense, the term designates regular revenue that is not generated by labor, whether performed by or hired by the beneficiary. The primary form of state rent in MENA is mining rent—oil, gas, and minerals. This is a subspecies of ground rent, that is, a source of revenue in hard currency produced by a land monopoly ("the monopoly by certain persons over definite portions of the globe," as Marx nicely puts it in *Capital*, *Volume 3*). Strictly speaking, mining rent is the surplus profit over and above the average profit on the capital (infrastructure, machinery, and labor) invested in the exploitation of a mineral resource. However, in World Bank data on the wealth of nations, the total profit (product price less production costs) is treated as "rent."[34]

Such rents make up a large proportion of most Arab states' GDP. To restrict ourselves to the countries in which this proportion exceeds 10%, the total rent derived from natural resources represented, in 2006—before the price peaks of energy commodities and raw materials—the following percentages of their GDPs: Algeria, 40.9%; Bahrain, 35.9%; Egypt, 21.8%; UAE, 28.5%; Iraq, 93.3%; Kuwait, 60.3%; Libya, 68.8%; Mauritania, 25%; Oman, 58%; Qatar, 48.3%; Saudi kingdom, 61.6%; Sudan, 20.8%; Syria, 28.5%; and Yemen, 38.5%.[35]

Besides mining rents, other rents also accrue to Arab states: geographical rents, such as transit fees or tolls (the Suez Canal, oil and gas pipelines, and so on); capitalist rents derived from financial and real estate investments or portfolio investments of sovereign wealth funds abroad, the source of a growing part of oil-exporting states' revenues; and, finally, strategic rents, that is, external funding that states receive in exchange for performing a military function or for other security-related reasons.

The last-named form of rent can be the reward for mercenary services: 84% of all US military subsidies went to the Near East in 2010. Israel alone received more than half the total, followed by Egypt (around 25%) and, in third place, Jordan.[36] Egypt and Jordan, together with other states such as Yemen, also reap big subsidies from the oil monarchies for participating in their regional security system under US suzerainty.[37] Another source of strategic rents is racketeering: for example, the moneys extorted from the oil monarchies over the years by predatory states such as Baathist Iraq or Syria. These states engage in political and/or military blackmail by invoking the "confrontation" with Israel or Iran, or simply by making unvarnished threats.[38]

Strategic rents from the oil monarchies are *derivative* rents, since they themselves stem from rentier revenue. Most rents in the Arab region, of whatever kind, are thus directly or indirectly linked to oil and gas. Hazem Beblawi was quite right to affirm in 1987 that

Arab oil states have played a major role in propagating a new pattern of behaviour, i.e. the rentier pattern. Oil as the primary source of rent in the Arab region has generated various secondary rent sources to other non-oil Arab states. To the first-order rentier oil states is thus added a second-order non-oil rentier strata. The impact of oil has been so pre-eminent that it is not unrealistic to refer to the present era of Arab history as the oil era, where the oil disease has contaminated all of the Arab world.[39]

Even if we ignore outright grants, and thus strategic rents, the available data show that the ratio of state revenue to GDP is far higher in the MENA region than in the rest of developing Africa and Asia. This holds above all for nontax revenues, in which rents represent the largest share (Fig. 2.9) even when we leave the GCC countries out of account; there, the ratio of state revenues and rents to GDP is much higher than in the rest of the region and the world, while the ratio of tax revenues to GDP is much lower. Thus, according to World Databank, Kuwait's state revenues accounted for 55.5% of the emirate's GDP in 2009, while its total tax receipts did not amount to even 1% of GDP. The corresponding figures for Bahrain in 2007 were 28.8% and 1.3% respectively.

An idea aired so often that it has become a cliché has it that the less governments depend on tax receipts, the less democratic they are. This contention is generally underpinned with a reference to a key slogan of the colonial protest movement against the British monarchy, the prelude to the American Revolution: "No taxation without representation." Thus it has been very correctly argued that governments whose budgets do not derive from taxes levied on the population feel little need to defer to a regime of representative democracy.[40] The rule finds its textbook illustration in the GCC's absolutist monarchies and, we may add, Libya's now defunct *Jamahiriyya* (state of the masses).

Common to all these states is the fact that rents accruing from the oil and gas sector account for the bulk of their revenues, which are high when measured against their economies as a whole. The rentier state thereby acquires maximum economic independence from the population. A good illustration is provided by the Saudi kingdom since it began receiving an oil rent, although, of all the states in question, it has by far the biggest economy and population. As Tim Niblock and Monica Malik have pointed out,

> there can be little doubt that the influx of oil revenues into the country after 1948, and particularly after the price rises of the early 1970s, freed the Saudi state from economic dependence on any social grouping in the country. Whereas in the pre-oil era, the state needed to raise money for its adminis-

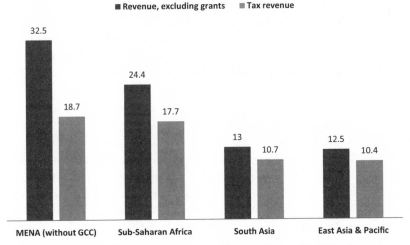

FIGURE 2.9 Public sector revenue, 2006 (% of GDP). (Source: World Bank)

tration and activities from taxation, customs duties, loans from merchants, etc., and all of these required political actions which maintained a form of economy that enabled the economy to produce the taxes and duties that needed to be raised, this was no longer the case by the 1970s. On the contrary, the state was now the provider, with no reason to raise money from the population.[41]

According to another oft-heard idea that has also become a cliché, the existence of a large "middle class" is a prerequisite for the proper functioning of representative democracy. This claim reflects the dominant nature of the demand for representative government raised, at the beginning of the democratic revolution, by the people from whom the European monarchies collected, in the form of taxes, the funds they needed to function: the bourgeoisie, called "the middle class" to distinguish it from the aristocracy and lower classes. To ensure its own representation, the bourgeoisie in various countries contented itself with one or another form of suffrage based on tax qualifications. Such selective suffrage was the rule until universal suffrage—universal male suffrage, to begin with, followed by that of both sexes—became the rule under pressure from mass movements, the workers' movement in particular.

The idea that the "middle class" is crucial to democracy might, at best, make sense in monarchies such as the Saudi kingdom, which are dominated by an aristocratic caste distinct from the business bourgeoisie. It makes little sense in republics in which no such aristocracy exists.

There is, of course, an officer caste in countries such as Algeria, Egypt, and Syria, but its interests are closely tied to those of the really existing bourgeoisie, which is, to a great extent, a "state bourgeoisie"—that is, a bourgeoisie deriving its economic power from the state, while functioning as private capitalism. We distinguish it here from the "market bourgeoisie." (Contrast the use of the term "state bourgeoisie" to designate a bourgeois bureaucracy presiding over a state capitalist economy with an enfeebled private sector, as in 1960s Egypt.)[42]

What is generally meant by "middle class" thus turns out to be a form of private capitalism independent of the state and dependent on the market. The idea that a properly functioning democracy presupposes a "middle class" encapsulates the real nature of representative democracy as it works in our times, in which elected governments are more deeply beholden to their capitalist sponsors and the market than to their voters. Nevertheless, when this idea is applied to the Arab region, it throws an undeniable truth into relief: here, what takes the place of the bourgeois democracy that is confused with democracy tout court is much *worse* than bourgeois democracy. Almost all Arab states take their places on a scale running from patrimonial to neopatrimonial regimes.

The definition of "patrimonialism" that we will be using here is basically Max Weber's, updated and adapted to the region that interests us. Patrimonialism is an absolute, hereditary type of autocratic power, which is, however, capable of functioning with an entourage of "kith and kin." The patrimonial power appropriates the state for itself, specifically (1) the armed forces, dominated by a praetorian guard whose allegiance is to the rulers, not the state as such; (2) the economic means at the state's disposal; and (3) the state administration.[43] The species of capitalism that tends to develop under this type of government, to the detriment of market capitalism, is "crony capitalism," dominated by a state bourgeoisie. The state bourgeoisie benefits from a rent-generating situation, granted by the political power. In return, it pays the rulers a rent in cash. The market bourgeoisie is often compelled to follow suit. The difference between the two is that the rent that the state bourgeoisie hands over is similar to payment to a partner, whereas that paid by the market bourgeoisie is more like money extorted by racketeers.

Neopatrimonialism is distinguished from patrimonialism of the type just described in that it is an institutionalized form of republican authoritarian power—in the sense that the exercise of power under neopatrimonial conditions has, in Weberian terms, a significant "rational-legal" bureaucratic dimension. To a greater or lesser extent, the neopatrimonial state enjoys autonomy vis-à-vis its rulers, who can always be replaced.[44] Nepotism nevertheless reigns in this type of regime as well. Corruption, in the sense of the venality of privileges, even tends to be more extensive in a neopatrimonial than in a patrimonial regime, since the rulers' relationship to the state is not a proprietary relationship, as in the patrimonial regime, but, rather, one of temporary usufruct. Once an autocratic neopatrimonial regime has achieved long-term stability, it tends to become a patrimonial regime, with hereditary or semihereditary (the autocrat designates his successor) transmission of power.

All the Arab monarchies—the GCC monarchies as well as Jordan and Morocco—are patrimonial regimes, as were the regimes of Iraq until 2003, Libya until 2011, and Syria down to the time of writing. The Jordanian and Moroccan monarchies have both created a neopatrimonial regime "by decree," granting it the right to operate at the level of political institutions (government and parliament); it is combined or coexists with royal patrimonialism. Before 2011, Egypt and Yemen were ruled by neopatrimonial regimes in the process of metamorphosing into patrimonial regimes. The regimes of Algeria, present-day Iraq, Mauritania, and Sudan are all neopatrimonial regimes, as was the regime of prerevolutionary Tunisia. Lebanon is a special case, with a system in which various interest groups with Mafia-like components hold central power by turns and thus share the spoils.

It goes without saying that, in a rentier state, the propensity for patrimonialism is accentuated. The more the state budget depends on rents, the greater that propensity and the more narrowly circumscribed the power of the market bourgeoisie. Nevertheless, even in Morocco, where the state rent is relatively low, the market bourgeoisie is confronted with a patrimonial regime in which the king is also the country's biggest property owner by far.[45] In Zine el-Abidine Ben Ali's Tunisia, where the state rent was still lower, the market bourgeoisie played a bigger role; but it, too, had to come to terms with the nepotism of a neopatrimonial regime emboldened by its access to external sources of funding.[46] In Lebanon, the role of the market bourgeoisie's various groupings depends closely on that of their respective foreign sponsors.[47]

Taken as a whole, the Arab region appears, in the final analysis, to be a vast concentration of patrimonial and neopatrimonial regimes in which the former preponderate to an extent unmatched in any other region of the world today. These sociopolitical corollaries of the predominance of the rentier state in the Arab region—a consequence, above all, of the region's rich reserves of oil and gas—are a heavier drag on its economic development than the "resource curse." Indeed, the "resource curse" is a typically tautological explanation of underdevelopment when it is brought to bear on the economy in isolation, without regard for the overall sociopolitical configuration. What fetters development is not the abundance of natural resources as such, but the uses to which resources are put under the prevailing type of social domination.

To be sure, patrimonialism and neopatrimonialism are not inherently antithetical to economic development, as many have pointed out in debates about institutionalism, citing the East Asian and Southeast Asian experiences.[48] The most convincing illustrations of the claim that neopatrimonial regimes can oversee successful economic development, however—South Korea and Taiwan, both Cold War outposts in East Asia—only confirm an observation that Max Weber made long ago about the potential role of patrimonialism in this regard. (There is no lack of examples in European history, either, from Colbertism in France to Bismarck's Germany.) The author of *Economy and Society*, after explaining that patrimonialism is not conducive to the development of forms of capitalism with extensive investments in fixed capital, adds this:

> The situation is fundamentally different only in cases where a patrimonial ruler, in the interest of his own power and financial provision, develops a rational system of administration with technically specialized officials.
>
> For this to happen . . . there must be a sufficiently powerful incentive to embark on such a policy—usually the sharp competition between a plurality of patrimonial powers within the same cultural area.[49]

Saddam Hussein's hegemonic ambitions in his "cultural area," conjoined with the technical and financial means at Iraq's disposal, would perhaps have provided an Arab example of capitalist development promoted by a patrimonial regime, had the dictator not brought his country to ruin by leading it into senseless wars. The same might have held for the shah of Iran, had his government not so sorely lacked popular legitimacy. Be that as it may, the historical exceptions to the rule just stated merely confirm another: neoliberal shibboleths notwithstanding, the state has a crucial role to play when it comes to boosting the development of countries lagging behind economically.[50]

2. A Politically Determined Capitalism: Nepotism and Risk

The more a state's budget depends on rents, the less that state depends on the domestic market and the freer it is to act without regard for that market's exigencies. This is a peculiar version of the problematic of "rationality and irrationality in the economy":[51] a more elementary version involving capitalist rationality as Max Weber synthetically defines it (while also essentializing it in ethnocentric fashion as "Western rationalism"). His definition appears in one of his last texts, the preface to a 1920 collection of his essays in the sociology of religion, in which he reissued his famous work *The Protestant Ethic and the Spirit of Capitalism*. Weber here summarily defines capitalism's distinguishing feature as "the striving for profit, in the course of continuous, rational, capitalist enterprise, for more and more profits, and for 'profitability.'"[52] Capitalism, he adds, is characterized by "rational business organization, based on the opportunities of the market for goods," with "separation of household and business" and "rational bookkeeping."[53]

When a state's revenues are guaranteed by a rent whose size depends only very slightly on its own activity (the size of the oil rent is of course determined by the fluctuations of the oil price on the international market) or, at any rate, when they do not depend on capitalist activity as defined above, the state's rulers are not compelled to respect the ideal-typical capitalist's economic rationality. This is especially true when they behave as if they owned the state, assimilating "business" to "household." Indeed, as a rule, such leaders act more like the feudal lords whose conduct Marx (a major inspiration for Weber's definition of the specific nature of capitalism) contrasts with the bourgeoisie's: "The bourgeoisie is too enlightened, it calculates too well, to share the prejudices of the feudal lord who makes a display by the brilliance of his retinue. The conditions of existence of the bourgeoisie compel it to calculate."[54]

The owner-rulers of the richest rentier states do not attend carefully to their bookkeeping. King, emir, sheikh, or colonel (Gaddafi), they spend money in a way that, from the standpoint of capitalist economic rationality, if not rationality tout court, is in large measure aberrant. Their rentier economic rationality asserts itself, not in the development of production, but in their striving to maximize the return on savings they invest abroad. Thus it is only natural that, of all their economic activities, the foreign portfolio investments of their semiprivate "sovereign wealth funds" and their formally private capital should be the ones that conform most closely, relatively speaking, to the rationality of capitalist calculation, even if such investments are also partly determined by their relationship to their protectors and overlords (first and foremost, the United States, followed by the United Kingdom and France, in most cases) or their foreign cronies (Muammar Gaddafi's relationship to Silvio Berlusconi is a case in point).

The oil monarchies' predilection for US Treasury bonds is conditioned by their relationship to their protector, even as it reflects their general predilection for government bonds issued by states that run no risk of going bankrupt (if only because the bankruptcy of one of them would entail the collapse of the whole system). This predilection is rooted in characteristic rentier logic as analyzed by Marx. The terms in which he describes the part that rentiers play in fanning financial speculation forcibly recall the pivotal role played by Arab sovereign wealth funds and other oil-related forms of rentier capital in the flowering of speculative capitalism that is typical of our neoliberal age:[55]

> As with the stroke of an enchanter's wand, [the public debt] endows unproductive money with the power of creation and thus turns it into capital, *without forcing it to expose itself to the troubles and risks inseparable from its employment in industry* or even in usury. . . . But furthermore, and quite apart from the class of idle *rentiers* thus created . . . the national debt has given rise to joint-stock companies, to dealings in negotiable effects of all kinds, and to speculation: in a word, it has given rise to stock-exchange gambling and the modern bankocracy.[56]

The development of ideal-typical productive capitalism, Weber insists, presupposes an adequate legal and administrative framework:

> Modern rational business capitalism requires both calculable technical tools as well as calculable law and administration conducted according to formal rules, without which no rational private economic business with standing capital and reliable calculation is possible, although adventure capitalism and speculative trading capitalism and all kinds of politically determined capitalism may be perfectly possible.[57]

This remark is especially germane to our subject. The absence of any real rule of law in virtually all Arab countries, due to the authorities' arbitrariness and also their venality (the problem called "governance" in the international institutions' jargon), fetters the development of the type of capitalism led by entrepreneurs willing to take risks of the sort implied by investment in fixed capital with long-term amortization. In contrast, speculative or commercial capitalism motivated by the pursuit of short-term profit thrives under such conditions. Such capitalism coexists and, often, combines with the state bourgeoisie's "politically determined capitalism."

By Weber's definition, the "political orientation" of capitalism of the latter type is a function of (1) "opportunities for predatory profit from political organizations or persons connected with politics," (2) "profit opportunities in continuous business activity which arise by virtue of domination by force or of a position of power guaranteed by the political authority," and (3) "profit opportunities in unusual transactions with political bodies."[58]

In patrimonial states, the "ruling families" tap state resources as they see fit, over and above the princely stipends collected by members of the ruling clans in the monarchies, or the substantial emoluments that they receive on various grounds in the "republics." (The term "ruling family" applies to certain republics of the Arab region no less than to its monarchies: whence a neologism, *jumlukiyya*, a cross between *jumhuriyya* [republic] and *malakiyya* [monarchy].) In patrimonial and neopatrimonial states, members of the ruling cliques and clans with a taste for business take advantage of the "position of power guaranteed [them] by the political authority" to accumulate sizable fortunes in the tradition of "politically determined capitalism." This includes the widespread practice of taking bribes and other "commissions."

Thus a dominant section of private capitalism in the Arab region must be classified as nepotism and crony capitalism, for which the state and its resources are a cash cow at the disposition of the autocrat as well as his familial entourage, friends, and henchmen.[59] The transformations wrought by neoliberalism have provided ideal opportunities for looting public property, thanks notably to the sale of land in the public domain to the rulers' relatives and friends at ludicrously low prices, either for their personal use or to commercial ends. (This was the fate of land in the Egyptian Sinai's tourist areas, for example.)

These facts are common knowledge in the region. They are at the heart of the protests accompanying the political uprisings and social movements set in motion since December 2010. The likes of Leila Trabelsi (Ben Ali's wife), Gamal Mubarak (Hosni's son) and Hussein Salem (a bosom friend of Hosni's), Saif al-Islam Gaddafi (Muammar's son), Rami Makhluf (Bashar al-Assad's maternal cousin), al-Walid bin Talal (grandson of the Saudi dynasty's founder), and many others of the same ilk have profited from their positions at the summit of the state to put their talents as wheeler-dealers to work. Some have built up veritable business empires as a result. The above-mentioned names are only the best known, those at the pinnacle of the pyramids of corruption and nepotism that are fettering the development of ideal-typical market capitalism by distorting the conditions of competition.

The massive capital flight (illicit financial flows) characteristic of the MENA region provides one indication of how extensive the corruption reigning there is. For 2008 alone, estimates are that the various forms of capital flight—bribery, kickbacks, embezzlement, tax evasion, and trade mispricing—came to $247.5 billion. Since capital flight frequently involves oil money, it rose at a 24.3% rate between 2000 and 2008, a period that saw a spectacular rise in oil prices and oil revenues; this increase in capital flight outstripped that in all other developing regions (Russia and China included). Of the ten countries in the world with the highest capital flight in this nine-year period, four were Arab states: the Saudi kingdom ($302 billion), the UAE ($276 billion), Kuwait ($242 billion), and Qatar ($138 billion).[60]

The specific variant of the capitalist mode of production that holds sway in the Arab region is "politically determined" in yet another sense, in a way that, once again, profoundly distorts the economic functioning of the market. The region is characterized by exceptional instability and political tension, and the kind of high economic volatility that this induces hardly encourages investors to tie down their capital for long periods of time. The clearest indication of the regional economic role of what might be called the *dominant political determination of the orientation of economic activity* (bearing in mind that the political is itself determined, in the last instance, by the economic) is the fluctuating price of the region's main export commodity, oil, which is intermittently subject to very abrupt swings linked to political tensions. Oil prices are, to be sure, determined by the play of supply and demand, which depends heavily on the overall state of the global economy. Political decisions, however, do much to determine them, even in periods of political stability, by virtue of their influence on the offer side. This is especially true in the context of the Organization of the Petroleum Exporting Countries (OPEC).

The sudden variations in oil prices caused by regional political events have, every time, tipped the balance of economic conditions on local markets one way or the other, creating a general impression of volatility that reinforces the misgivings and insecurity bred by the arbitrariness of administrative and political authorities—especially when potential investors lack the connections they need. These risk factors are further aggravated by the fact that, well before 2011, no regime in the region seemed immune to social, political, or military disruptions. There was no shortage of reasons for them: the Arab-Israeli conflict; international wars or smoldering, veiled, or declared civil wars in Algeria, Iraq,

Lebanon, Palestine, Sudan, Yemen, and the Saudi kingdom; the international tensions surrounding Iran; social tensions in Egypt, Tunisia, and Morocco; terrorism in virtually all the countries just named. The list could be extended at will. The precariousness of the monarchies in the rich countries' club known as the GCC has been thrown into sharp relief by the 1979 "Islamic Revolution" in Iran as well as Iraq's 1990 invasion of Kuwait.

The recruitment of migrant workers by GCC states provides another illustration of the "dominant political determination" mentioned above. Which migrant labor force is recruited is dictated not primarily by the "labor market," that is, by considerations of cost and/or quality, but by political considerations. A desire to punish the Palestine Liberation Organization (PLO) and the Yemeni government for their opposition to the US 1990 military intervention in Iraq led to the expulsion of 400,000 Palestinians from Kuwait and more than twice as many Yemenis from the Saudi kingdom. (Similarly, Gaddafi ordered the expulsion of tens of thousands of Egyptian, Palestinian, Sudanese, or Tunisian workers from Libya over the years, as his political moods dictated.) Again, the preference that the Riyadh government accorded Egyptians over other Arabs was eminently political: it was one manifestation of the Saudis' support for their Egyptian ally.

The Iraqi bid to annex Kuwait and the sympathy it had allegedly elicited among migrant Arab workers in the GCC states led to the massive replacement of Arab labor by labor imported mainly from South Asia, which seemed much less threatening to the monarchies concerned. Thus, between 1985 and 2002–4, the proportion of Arabs among migrant workers fell from 79% to 33% in the Saudi kingdom, from 69% to 30% in Kuwait, and, in the GCC countries as a whole, from 56% to 32%.[61] This has little to do with the low wages offered in the Gulf monarchies, which remain, despite all, just as attractive for Arab laborers as they do for others. There were nearly 12.5 million migrants in the GCC states in 2004: this figure provides some idea of the consequences that the turning point of 1990 had on employment levels and hard-currency income in the other Arab states.[62] Thus, whereas the proportion of Egypt's GDP represented by emigrant workers' remittances had oscillated between 8% and 13% in the 1980s, the corresponding range in the first decade of the present century was between 2.9% and the peak it reached in 2007, 5.9%.[63]

It follows from everything said so far that capitalism in the region is largely dominated by "adventure capitalism and speculative trading capitalism" and the concomitant pursuit of short-term profit. That is why the building trade, in particular, is a flourishing sector in the region. It stands at the intersection of land speculation, encouraged by the pursuit of safe-haven investments in real estate, and a commercial and tourist-oriented service economy heavily fueled by the regional oil rent—by both capital and consumers from the rentier states. This is, manifestly, the key to understanding an observation made in the World Bank's September 2011 report on MENA. The report examines the problems of growth and employment in light of the social explosions that had taken place in the preceding months in one Arab country after the next. Comparing the region to a series of middle-income developing countries, it observes that "manufacturing's employment share in the typical MENA country is smaller than the corresponding share in Turkey, Malaysia, Indonesia and Brazil, while the opposite is the case for construction."[64]

ILO data plainly substantiate this finding. In 2008, 2.6 million workers were employed in manufacturing in Egypt as opposed to 2.3 million in construction. These figures may be compared with the corresponding figures for Turkey: 4.2 million in manufacturing and 1.2 million in construction. In the same year, 517,000 people worked in manufacturing in the Saudi kingdom as opposed to 886,000 in construction. In 2004, again according to the ILO, there were 847,000 workers in manufacturing in Algeria and 968,000 in construction. Even in Tunisia, where manufacturing accounts for a greater share of employment than in the rest of the region, 598,200 people worked in manufacturing in 2010, only 36% more than the 440,500 who worked in construction. In the past few years, moreover, the growth rate of the segment of the Tunisian labor force employed by the building industry has sharply exceeded that of the manufacturing labor force.[65]

The World Bank report tries to explain the facts just noted in terms of "Dutch disease" for the oil-exporting countries and the underdevelopment of the financial sector for the region as a whole. This is very wide of the mark. Evocation of the Dutch disease—that is, declining competitiveness due to appreciation of the national currency—is all the more inappropriate in that the rich oil-exporting countries' economies import, at very low cost in US dollars, a labor force that can be exploited at will and goes without even the rudimentary rights accorded immigrant labor in other parts of the world. The lopsided distribution of this work force between the building and manufacturing industries is, rather, an expression of the tendency discussed above.

Indeed, the GCC countries offer an extreme illustration of the model in question. They have witnessed and continue to witness a veritable orgy of gigantic construction projects. The champion in this category was the Emirate of Dubai, until its speculative bubble burst in 2009 with the crisis of the emirate's investment-cum-land-and-real-estate-speculation company, Dubai World. Sheikh Mohammed bin Rashid Al Maktoum, monarch of Dubai and prime minister of the UAE, is Dubai World's majority shareholder—one example among many of the marriage of patrimonialism with private ownership of the country's resources. Between 2008 and October 2011, an estimated $958 billion worth of construction projects were canceled or suspended because of the UAE's economic crisis. The corresponding figure for the Saudi kingdom was $354 billion.[66]

One of Dubai World's subsidiaries has built the world's highest tower (2,717 feet, that is, more than half a mile high). It was to have been called Burj Dubai (Tower of Dubai) but was renamed Burj Khalifa in honor of the monarch of Abu Dhabi and president of the UAE, after His Highness Sheikh Khalifa agreed to bail out Dubai World. Not to be outdone, the Saudi al-Walid bin Talal is building a tower named Burj al-Mamlaka (Kingdom Tower) in Jeddah. It should, when finished, be 3,280 feet (0.62 miles) or more than a kilometer high. It was initially supposed to jut a full mile into the sky (and to be called Mile-High Tower); the target had, however, to be lowered for technical reasons. These huge towers are patent economic follies and ecological abominations (one need only consider the extreme temperatures in the Gulf region in the summer months). Their height is a good measure of their irrationality.

THE GENESIS OF THE SPECIFIC REGIONAL VARIANT OF CAPITALISM: AN OVERVIEW

The particularities of the Arab region's socioeconomic development stem from a mutation initiated in the 1970s at the heart of a regional system built up over the previous two decades. During this period, the monarchies that are today grouped in the GCC were de facto, and sometimes also de jure, colonial protectorates. The Saudi kingdom was de facto under the tutelage of the United States, while the other territories were de jure and/or de facto under the United Kingdom's. Fought over by various tribes and clans, these territories were thinly populated at first; they had archaic social structures and lacked even minimal attributes of statehood. London nevertheless created a whole constellation of such sham states, following the tried and true principle of *divide et impera*. This made it easier to dominate the territories in question while securing their allegiance to the British Empire, the only power capable of protecting them against the expansionist appetites of their much more populous neighbors.

The region's two tutelary powers, Britain and the United States, undertook to modernize other countries under their domination, establishing imitations—which were sometimes caricatures—of their own political and social institutions there. In the case of the oil monarchies, however, they carefully perpetuated the archaic tribal and patriarchal institutions of these clan-based sheikhdoms made over into monarchies. The reason for this conservatism, a striking departure from the "civilizing mission" that Western powers had arrogated unto themselves in the last decades of the nineteenth century, resided, very obviously, in the fact that the territories in question were rich in petroleum. Their archaism allowed the protecting powers to exploit their resources at leisure; the clan sheikhs contented themselves with oil royalties that were more than sufficient to satisfy their desire to amass conspicuous and often outlandish symbols of wealth.

The 1950s and 1960s witnessed the rise, in the Arab region, of a nationalism whose principal vector was the army; the means it usually employed to gain power was the coup d'état. The decay of Egypt's, Iraq's, and North Yemen's monarchies; the rise of anticolonial struggles in Algeria and South Yemen; the urgency of the agrarian question; the early phase of the blockage of capitalist development, illustrated by the atrophy of the industrial national bourgeoisie, confronted with an alliance of landowners and the comprador bourgeoisie, the commercial intermediary between its country and the tutelary power—the combination of all these elements spurred officer castes to replace faltering national bourgeoisies and their powerless political representatives, in order to lead their countries down a nationalist-developmentalist path.

The basic typological model for this political phenomenon is a variant sui generis of Bonapartism as analyzed by Marx,[67] one that has had considerable impact on the region: Kemalism. The sultanate-caliphate of the former Ottoman Empire, which had taken in the better part of the Arab region in the course of its history, was already in an advanced state of decay and under European domination by the time World War I came to an end. It was overthrown by a nationalist officer caste led by Mustafa Kemal, who set himself two main tasks: to modernize Turkey by following the example of Western Europe, even while throwing off European domination, and to develop his country's infrastructure and economy by means of vigorous state intervention. Turkey's effort to industrialize even drew part of its inspiration from the experiment under way in the neighboring Soviet Union, especially the Soviet five-year plan.

The type of Bonapartism that held sway in the 1960s in five countries of the Arab region—Egypt, Iraq, Syria, Algeria, and North Yemen—had its archetype in Gamal Abdel-Nasser's Egyptian regime. It diverged from the Kemalist model in two main respects. First, whereas, under Kemal, the Turkish army was confined to its barracks (although it would leave them again in 1960 in order to assert itself for almost fifty years as the supervisory power over Turkey's political authorities, even wielding power directly from time to time), Arab nationalist Bonapartism took the form, in the five countries just mentioned, of permanent military dictatorships. More precisely, it took the form of military/security-state dictatorships in which various intelligence services, the *mukhabarat*, played major roles. In the case of Saddam Hussein's Iraq, such intelligence services, together with the ruling party apparatus, had an even bigger part than the armed forces, somewhat as they did in Nazi Germany. Second, the state's economic role in Egypt, Iraq, Syria, and Algeria went well beyond that of the Kemalist precedent in its imitation of the Soviet model. Indeed, the state went so far as to largely substitute itself for the private sector by means of both far-reaching nationalization programs and massive public investment.

Arab nationalist Bonapartism became considerably more radical in the 1960s. Under the direct influence of the USSR, whose model of development often seemed attractive to Third World countries in this period, the Nasserite paradigm carried the substitution of the executive for the really existing bourgeoisie, the distinguishing characteristic of Bonapartism as analyzed by Marx, well beyond the political level. The Nasserite state replaced the bourgeoisie on the economic plane as well, subjecting it to extensive expropriations and establishing a form of state capitalism that it dubbed "socialism." Without legally abolishing private ownership of the social means of production, this state capitalism became heavily preponderant.

Over and above nationalization, public sector domination of the economy was guaranteed by large-scale infrastructural and industrial investments made by the state on the pattern of Soviet-style planning. At its height in the 1960s, the Nasserite model was not merely imitated by similar nationalist dictatorships, but also had an impact on other, more traditional Bonapartist experiments in the region. Thus Tunisia under Habib Bourguiba, an admirer of Mustafa Kemal, had its "socialist" phase, and even Lebanon took a stab at state planning under General Fouad Chehab.

Arab nationalist Bonapartism went into decline late in the same decade, despite 1969 Sudanese and Libyan coups d'état that briefly extended the Nasserite model to those two countries and despite nationalization of oil and natural gas in Algeria, Iraq, and Libya in the early 1970s. This model came up against its economic limits in the country in which it had first been introduced, Egypt, when it found itself confronting four big problems: (1) the population explosion that resulted from the significant improvement in health conditions achieved by the new regime; (2) the weaknesses of the Soviet model of industrialization, which privileged heavy industry and quantity at the expense of quality; (3) bureaucratic waste and corruption, which spread rapidly throughout the country, all the more easily because the regime stifled political freedoms; and (4) the burden of the external debt, which had been contracted to finance developmental and military projects.

All military dictatorships are, of course, bent on augmenting the means at their armed forces' disposal, but the genuine threats faced by most of the dictatorships in the Arab region subjected them to genuine pressure. Egypt, Syria, and Iraq, in particular, are all located in zones of high military turbulence. In the case of Egypt and Syria, this is due to the proximity of Israel; in that of Iraq, it is owing to tensions in the Gulf. In 1956, the recently established Egyptian military regime was attacked by France and Britain in alliance with Israel; in 1961, the military regime that had held power in Iraq since 1958 was threatened by Britain from Kuwait. Furthermore, the tensions between Iran and Iraq already existed in the Shah's day. Before the ruinous war with Iran, however, the scope of oil rent had alleviated the economic burden of debt in Iraq, as it had in Algeria and Libya too.

In this context of intensifying economic gridlock, Egypt's and Syria's crushing June 1967 defeat at the hands of Israel precipitated the decline of the two nationalist regimes that had undergone sharp left-wing radicalization in the preceding years. In this regard, 1970 was a decisive turning point in the contemporary history of the Arab region. When, in September 1970, Jordan's Hashemite kingdom bloodily crushed the Palestinian resistance, it eliminated the main counterweight to the 1967 defeat. Nasser's sudden death, coming at the end of the same month, brought the curtain down on an entire era. His successor, Anwar al-Sadat, firmly intended to take his country down the path of "de-Nasserization," a policy that included restoring land confiscated in a series of agricultural reforms to its former owners. In November 1970, Hafez al-Assad seized power in Damascus, sweeping aside the left-wing faction of the Syrian Baath party. Sadat and Assad lost no time introducing economic liberalization measures under the sign of *infitah*. This liberalization was all the more conducive to the development of nepotistic capitalism in that the dictatorial regime was left standing, despite the semiliberalization of the political sphere in Egypt.[68]

The turn initiated by these changes in Cairo and Damascus was greatly accelerated by the rise of the oil monarchies of the Arab-Iranian Gulf, which, in 1971, had joined the regional trend toward nationalizing oil and natural gas that had been inaugurated by Houari Boumediene's Algeria. They now suddenly found themselves in possession of enormous revenues thanks to the sudden increase in the price of oil that resulted from the gradual restriction of production and the partial export embargo decreed by the Arab oil countries during the October 1973 Arab-Israeli war. The Arab region thus lurched from the "socialist" Nasserite era into the ultrareactionary Saudi era. From then on, the Saudi kingdom enjoyed considerable financial means, to which were added those of the other Arab Gulf monarchies, which rallied to Saudi leadership. In these monarchies themselves, two factors paved the way for a spectacular expansion of nepotistic capitalism in the framework of the patrimonial state: the emergence, in the ruling clans, of a younger generation that was tempted by the chance to wheel and deal; and an influx, both from other countries in the region and from the rest of the world, of confirmed wheeler-dealers drawn by this new El Dorado. At the same time, the pace of similar developments in the nonoil monarchies quickened, with many ventures involving capital from the oil monarchies.

It was not long before *infitah* had spread to the other regimes descended from nationalist Bonapartism. This happened in Algeria under Chadli Bendjedid, who had succeeded Boumediene at his death in 1979,[69] and in Iraq under Saddam Hussein during the war with Iran.[70] The regime in North Yemen negotiated a radical right turn after the 1967 withdrawal of the Egyptian force that had intervened there, with the result that the country came under the Saudi kingdom's patronage. Nepotism was to mushroom in North Yemen under Ali Abdallah Saleh, who took office in 1978.[71] The Sudanese Gaafar al-Numeyri adopted

Sadat's post-Nasserite course in very short order, the more so as he had to battle a left-wing opposition in his first years in power. Ultimately, from 1981 on, he allied himself with the Muslim Brothers. The course charted by Muammar al-Gaddafi's Libyan regime was the most erratic of all. In the early 1970s, Gaddafi opted for an alignment with Sadat marked by powerful Islamic references; then, beginning in 1977, he made a "socialist" turn that was accompanied by very broad nationalization, while simultaneously reinforcing his personal power. Some ten years later, taking his cue from Mikhail Gorbachev, he undertook a new turn toward his own version of *infitah*—with a semblance of political liberalization accompanied by an economic liberalization that failed. The regime's more radical swing to the right at the turn of the century favored the rise of a patrimonial crony capitalism centered on Gaddafi's progeny.[72]

The 1970 turn also entailed stabilization of the region's autocratic regimes after the marked instability of the preceding decades.[73] The record holder in this department was Gaddafi, who ruled Libya for forty-two years, until the 2011 uprising. Sadat was assassinated in 1981, but his successor, Hosni Mubarak, clung to power for three decades, again until 2011. Hafez al-Assad ruled Syria for thirty years until his death in 2000. Saddam Hussein was driven from power, which he had taken in 1968, only by the US-led invasion of Iraq in 2003, that is, thirty-five years later. Ali Abdallah Saleh held power for thirty-four years before being forced to abdicate in 2012. Ben Ali seized power in Tunisia in 1987, after driving Bourguiba from the position of head of state that he had occupied since the country gained independence in 1956; Ben Ali remained in office until 2011, that is, for the next twenty-four years. The overthrow of the Libyan monarchy in 1969 was the last successful republican coup d'état, after the military coups staged in Egypt (1952), Iraq (1958), and North Yemen (1962). All the remaining Arab monarchies have survived to the present, and their monarchs have reigned, as a rule, to their dying day. (King Hussein of Jordan sat on the throne for forty-seven years.)

The longevity of the republican dictatorships did much to facilitate their evolution toward a neopatrimonialism that has increasingly gravitated, in the autocratic regimes—which is to say, in most cases, with the major exception of Algeria, where an officer caste has exercised collegial leadership since Boumediene's death—toward a patrimonialism resembling that of the monarchies. These dictatorships lacked none of the features of patrimonial regimes, hereditary transmission of power not excepted: Bashar al-Assad succeeded his father under grotesque circumstances, while Saddam Hussein had been grooming one of his sons to succeed him, like Gaddafi, Mubarak, and Saleh. The dominant groups in the countries in question—military/security castes and state bourgeoisies—acquired an increasingly Mafia-like character, a development that went hand in hand with the expansion of the nepotistic capitalism fostered by the application throughout the region of neoliberal prescriptions: trade liberalization, with nepotistic distribution of import licenses; prioritization of the private sector, with the expansion of business circles that were less hampered by restrictions the higher the rung occupied in the state apparatus by their accomplices; reduction of the public sector by means of privatization, which, as in Russia, is one of the dominant Mafia's favorite methods of enrichment, because it allows it to get hold of the most profitable public properties at derisory prices. The list could be easily lengthened.

In a context marked by a post-"socialist" continuity in dictatorial government in countries such as Egypt, Syria, Iraq, Algeria, or Libya, where old industrial, commercial, and financial bourgeoisies have been decimated, neoliberal recipes cannot but have the results we have been describing. A majority of the productive public sector firms brought into being by Soviet-style industrialization became less profitable the more trade was liberalized: the state found itself confronting a choice between continuing to operate factories at a loss or shutting them down. The social balance of power ruled out the option of massive layoffs. For the same reason, the state was unable to thin the ranks of the administrative bureaucracy or army as drastically as the international financial institutions were urging it to do.

If state bureaucracies had not absorbed at least part of the young workforce, especially graduates, the problem of unemployment in the region would have been even more explosive than it is today. For the same reason, the state was not able to apply "shock therapy" by abolishing price controls with the abruptness that Augusto Pinochet forced the Chilean people to accept after his bloody 1973 putsch, or by adopting measures like those that the international financial institutions have demanded of Eastern Europe after the collapse of the "communist" dictatorships there.

The fact of the matter is that the Arab regimes were aware of the potential for revolt smoldering in their populations. It was confirmed by the riots provoked by attempts to abolish subsidies for basic necessities in Egypt in 1977, Morocco in 1981, Tunisia in 1983, and Jordan in 1989. Unlike the populations of Eastern Europe, the great majority of those in the Arab region harbor no illusions about their chances of attaining a Western standard of living, illusions of the kind that might induce them to tighten their belts for a while—not to mention the fact that, for a significant segment of these populations, the belt can be pulled no tighter. The result of this local neoliberal dead end is that most of the region's economies have ended up marrying the disadvantages of a bureaucratic state capitalism that had reached the limits of its developmentalist potential with the disadvantages of a corrupt neoliberal capitalism—without the benefit of any of the purported advantages of statism or neoliberalism.

This peculiar modality of the capitalist mode of production—a mix of patrimonialism, nepotism, and crony capitalism, pillaging of public property, swollen bureaucracies, and generalized corruption, against a background of great sociopolitical instability and the impotence or even nonexistence of the rule of law—is dominant in the Arab region. It is this modality that is fettering the region's development. And it is this that cracked in Tunisia in December 2010, bringing the other links in the chain to crack in turn, one after the next.

In 2005, I concluded an examination of the *Arab Human Development Report 2004*, drawn up by the UNDP, with the following comment:

> However, the report has its shortcomings, due to the conditions under which it was produced and because it was published by an intergovernmental agency. It underestimates the fundamental contribution of satellite television, in particular the pioneering *al-Jazeera*, to the emergence of independent Arab public opinion. Its assessment of the political potential of Arabic-speaking peoples is consequently excessively gloomy. . . .
>
> Above all, the report appeals to governments and their subjects to implement the necessary changes. To avoid the "impending disaster" that would follow widespread revolt—which, it fears, would only lead to civil war—reformers in government and civil society must negotiate a redistribution of the political stakes in order to achieve "good governance." Given the reality of oppression in most Arab countries and the social make-up of their governments this seems remarkably unlikely.
>
> A report unfettered by institutional constraints would be more likely to conclude that democratic forces must unite and impose radical change from below. As history has shown often and recent events have confirmed, the larger the turnout, the less need for any bloodshed. It is impossible to consolidate democracy without a major redistribution of property and income. In the Middle East there are many patrimonial states where ruling families

still corner a large share of national agricultural and mineral riches. It is consequently foolhardy to suppose that concerted action in partnership with segments of the ruling classes will lead to the lasting establishment of civil liberties and democracy. There is no more chance of this working than with the absolute monarchies that once ruled Europe or the bureaucratic dictatorships of the former Soviet bloc.[74]

CHAPTER 3

Regional Political Factors

After Herodotus, who called Egypt a gift of the Nile, we might with equal justification call the current state of affairs in the Arab region a gift of oil. We would, however, have to add that it is a poisoned chalice. The Arab states alone held over fifty-six percent of the world's "proven" (that is, technically and commercially recoverable) conventional crude oil reserves in 2006, before the spectacular leap in Venezuela's proven reserves. Estimates in 2010 were that they still held nearly half of them (48.6%).[1] It is surely no accident that the First World War both catalyzed a quantitative and qualitative leap in oil's international economic and strategic importance and also gave Western imperialism an opportunity to complete the process that replaced the Ottoman Empire's domination of the Arabic-speaking region with its own, much harsher domination.

The Arab countries, which were the object, in the nineteenth century, of an Orientalist taste for the exotic, but also of ordinary colonial appetites, became the stakes of Great Power rivalry in the twentieth. The reason was oil. The Great Game that saw the nineteenth-century Czarist Empire vying with its British rival for control of Central Asia pales in comparison. In the vast region encompassing the Middle East and North Africa, the antagonism of the Great Powers first pitted the victors in World War I against each other. Later, it opposed the Axis powers and the Allies in a rivalry that culminated during World War II. Thereafter, the region became a major theater of the Cold War between the USA and the USSR. The rivalry persists today, in the framework of a new, postideological Cold War opposing Russia and China to the United States.[2]

THE OIL CURSE

Only one actor has stood permanently at the center of these antagonisms since the end of World War I: the United States of America. The oil century coincided with the "American century," and oil naturally took its place at the heart of the crusade for a "new American century" led in the first decade of the twenty-first century by the George W. Bush administration.[3] World War II completed both the process that hoisted the United States to the rank of the leading world power and the one that made petroleum the world's main strategic commodity. The Middle East very naturally became a priority for Washington, inasmuch as the United States dominated the international oil market. For Moscow, it was a privileged terrain on which to foil Washington, the more so as the radicalization of Arab nationalism offered the "socialist fatherland" precious allies. Daniel Yergin, in his monumental history of oil, has provided a good summary of the turn that this represented for Washington:

> Soviet expansionism—as it was, and as it might be—brought the Middle East to centre stage. To the United States, the oil resources of the region constituted an interest no less vital, in its own way, than the independence of Western Europe; and the Middle Eastern oil fields had to be preserved and protected on the Western side of the Iron Curtain to assure the economic survival of the entire Western world. . . .
>
> Saudi Arabia became the dominant focus of American policymakers. Here was, said one American official in 1948, "what is probably the richest economic prize in the world in the field of foreign investment." And here the United States and Saudi Arabia were forging a unique new relationship. . . .
>
> The special relationship that was emerging represented an interweaving of public and private interests, of the commercial and strategic. It was effected both at the governmental level and through Aramco [Arab-American Oil Company, originally a consortium of four US oil companies formed to exploit the kingdom's oil resources; the consortium was nationalized in stages between 1973 and 1980], which became a mechanism not just for oil development, but also for the overall development of Saudi Arabia—though insulated from the wide range of Arabian society and always within the limits prescribed by the Saudi state. It was an unlikely union—Bedouin Arabs and Texas oil men, a traditional Islamic autocracy allied with modern American capitalism. Yet it was one that was destined to endure.[4]

Rather than "unlikely," the union between the United States and the

Saudi kingdom may be regarded as a consequence of the "elective affinities" (combined with calculated interests) that induced King Abdul-Aziz Al Saud to join Washington in creating an "Islamic Texas" at the heart of the Middle East.[5] However that may be, it is an obvious fact that, since the end of World War II, the Saudi kingdom's first two pillars—the reigning Saudi dynasty and the "Wahhabi" religious establishment, so named after the ultrareactionary, ultrapuritanical eighteenth-century preacher Muhammad bin Abdul-Wahhab—have been reinforced by a third.[6] That third pillar is US tutelage, in the multidimensional form of economic, military, and political supervision. It was incarnated, in part, by a typically colonialist American presence, an enclave isolated from the world around it, which has overseen the "development" of the kingdom in such a way as to privilege preservation of the archaic sociopolitical system imposed and maintained by the other two pillars. What Yergin describes as respect for "the limits prescribed by the Saudi state" was in fact a deliberate US policy choice.[7]

The Saudi Arabian Kingdom was proclaimed on its present-day territory in 1932, after the 1925 conquest of Nejd and Hedjaz by the Ikhwan (the "Brothers," as the Wahhabi Bedouin forces under Ibn Saud called themselves).[8] The founding of the kingdom was an event crucial to the later development of the Arabic-speaking region in particular and the Islamic world in general. Its importance is widely underestimated, as I have argued elsewhere.[9] A few years after the new kingdom was founded, the political and religious influence that it had gained as a result of the conquest of Islam's Holy Places was substantially enhanced by the financial means guaranteed it by the 1938 discovery of immense oil wealth. The kingdom harnessed that influence and those means to the service of its privileged alliance (Yergin's "special relationship") with its suzerain protector, the United States. US protection has been all the more important for the kingdom for the reason that it has faced a number of major threats, embodied by its next-door neighbors (Iraq, Jordan, and Yemen); Nasser's Egypt from 1957 to 1967; Iraq from 1970 to 1990; and Iran from the 1979 "Islamic Revolution" to the present. To this must be added the need for protection from grave internal threats, such as the 1979 insurrection in Mecca or Al-Qaida's 1999 turnabout against the monarchy.

The Saudi kingdom's control over the religious center of gravity of two geopolitical groups, Arab and Muslim, has had an enormous impact on both. The Saudi state has no "constitution" apart from the Qur'an; instead of a parliament, it has a *shura* (consultative council) created as late as 1992, its members appointed by the king; it is coadministered by an ultrafundamentalist religious establishment; and its legislation explicitly identifies women as inferior to men. The fact that so reactionary a state holds the eminently strategic position it does is extremely serious. Mai Yamani describes the kingdom's institutional structure:

> The Wahhabi establishment controls not just the judicial system, but also the Council of Senior Ulama; the General Committee for Issuing Fatwas, Da'wa, and Irshad; the Ministry of Islamic Affairs; the Supreme Headquarters for the Council for International Supervision of Mosques; and the Committee for the Promotion of Virtue and the Prohibition of Vice. The latter includes the *mutaw'a* (religious police), whose head is a government minister. The Wahhabis also control all religious education, which comprises half of the school curriculum; Islamic universities in Mecca, Medina, and Riyadh; the Ministry of Hajj (pilgrimage); and the Ministry of Religious Endowments (*Awqaf*). Moreover, they influence the Ministry of Finance through control of *zakat* (the religious tax department), and control magazines, radio stations and websites, as well as exercising power over the military through religious indoctrination.
>
> ... the *shura* ("consultative council") is toothless, comprises more than 50% Wahhabis, and is headed by a Wahhabi cleric. Appointed by the king, the *shura* is unable to legislate, debate the budget, or discuss resource allocation and public expenditure, and will remain un-elected for the foreseeable future. [Then Saudi Crown Prince] Sultan confirmed that decision in 2005 in order to end a debate, initiated by liberal reformers, about the possibility of an elected *shura*, arguing "Saudi Arabia is not ready to have an elected parliament because voters might elect illiterate and unqualified candidates."[10]

Since its foundation, the Saudi kingdom has propagated the most fundamentalist, obscurantist, ultraright version of Islamic ideology in existence. The kingdom is the antithesis of freedom, democracy, equality, and women's liberation. During the Cold War, it was a bastion of reactionary resistance to the rise of nationalism and nationalism's subsequent socialist-leaning radicalization in alliance with the USSR. Furthermore, it has served as a regional relay for the neoliberal counteroffensive, has actively fostered corruption in its zone of influence, and has acted as choirmaster for the subset of Near Eastern Arab states aligned with Washington (until 2011, the GCC member states, as well as Jordan, Mubarak's Egypt, and Ali Abdallah Saleh's Yemen). As such, the Saudi kingdom bears a big share of the blame for the highly explosive economic and sociopolitical situation depicted in the preceding chapters.

The fact that a state as retrograde as this monarchy, which lacks all popular legitimacy and is the product of a singularly barbaric war of tribal conquest, managed to survive the upsurge of Arab nationalism that followed the 1948 Palestine War, is in very large measure due to US protection. The Kuwaiti state, for its part, owes its very emergence and, at an early stage, its survival to London. It was London which decided, at the outbreak of World War I, to make a separate emirate of the autonomous Iraqi province of Kuwait, which had been a British protectorate since 1899. In 1961, Britain granted Kuwait "independence," while protecting it against neighboring Iraq, which sought to reassert its control. Kuwait had a mere 320,000 inhabitants when it gained "independence." Its current population, 70% of which is comprised of "foreign residents," is estimated at ten times that number.

The other oil monarchies, too, owe their emergence and initial survival to London and British protection. They were proclaimed "independent" in 1971, after being administered by the British Residency of the Persian Gulf, founded late in the eighteenth century. The microstates ruled by the former Trucial Coast's tribal clans joined to form the United Arab Emirates (UAE) after having been British protectorates since 1892. In 1971, their total population was under 300,000; they have more than 5 million inhabitants today, some 80% of them "foreign residents." Qatar, officially a British protectorate since 1916, had been under de facto British control since 1878. It had some 120,000 inhabitants in 1971; it has 1.7 million today, 85% of them "foreign residents." Bahrain's ruling dynasty was placed under British protection before the others, at the turn of the nineteenth century; the country officially became a British protectorate in 1880. It had 216,000 inhabitants in 1971 and boasts more than 1.2 million today, 54% of them "foreign residents." Oman is the only one of these countries that has never had formal colonial status. The sultanate that rules the territory of contemporary Oman was nonetheless under London's protection until British troops intervened in Dhofar province in the early 1970s to put down the rebellion there. The country has 2.8 million inhabitants today, "only" 30% of them foreigners.

In the wake of Iraq's 1990 invasion of Kuwait, all these eminently artificial, highly vulnerable oil monarchies put themselves under the protection of the United States, which "liberated" the one that Saddam Hussein had foolishly attempted to reincorporate into the Iraqi state. The Baathist dictator in fact afforded Washington an ideal opportunity to station troops on a permanent basis in this highly strategic part of the globe. Thus the United States could award itself the lion's share of the broad set of economic advantages that accrue to the oil monarchies' protector. At the same time, Washington was able to inaugurate the "unipolar moment" of the post–Cold War years under its absolute supremacy, in the face of a USSR that was already in its death throes and would soon give up the ghost. In many respects, the first US Gulf War was indeed the defining moment of the "New World Order" that the elder George Bush proclaimed on that occasion.

Obviously, the massive US military intervention in the Gulf region in 1990–1, involving the deployment of more than half a million troops and impressive naval and air fleets, was exclusively motivated by the oil factor, as was the 2003 US occupation of Iraq. No convincing explanation that does not turn on a direct or indirect relationship to oil has been put forward by any of those who brand accounts based on the oil factor "simplistic." That claim is supposedly proof of sophistication—when it is not motivated by sheer hypocrisy. For "it is politically inconvenient to acknowledge what everyone knows: the Iraq war is largely about oil," as the former president of the US Federal Reserve Bank once put it.[11] In any case, whether motivated by pretensions to sophistication or bad faith, one can deny that oil is the stake of Western powers' intervention in the region only at the price of ignoring that stake's immense economic and strategic importance.

A few facts should suffice to illustrate the economic interest that oil represents. In 2011, according to a ranking published by the US magazine *Fortune*, the three biggest US oil companies (ExxonMobil, Chevron, and ConocoPhillips) were the country's second-biggest, third-biggest, and fourth-biggest firms. Of the world's twelve biggest firms, eight were oil companies. In 2008, with the OPEC reference price at less than $95 per barrel, the four richest GCC states' total oil exports (excluding Qatar's substantial natural gas exports) came to nearly $500 billion. Moreover, oil is distinguished by the fact that one can purchase it and get one's money back into the bargain: contrary to the popular adage, one can, in this domain, have one's cake and eat it. And there is a variety of ways to do so.

As estimated by the Washington-based Institute of International Finance, the GCC states' capital outflows amounted to $530 billion in the five-year period 2002–6. Of this total, $300 billion went to the United States and $100 billion to Europe; only $60 billion went to MENA, as much as went to Asia.[12] According to the same source, the GCC states' foreign assets tripled between 2002 and 2009, reaching $1,470 billion in gross assets and $1,049 billion in net assets by the end of 2009.[13] "Slightly more than half of these assets are in the form of Sovereign Wealth Funds (SWFs), and are largely invested in diversified portfolios of public equities, fixed-income securities, real estate and minority shares in big-name global companies."[14] Thus the group of oil-exporting countries is, after China and Japan, the world's third-biggest holder of US Treasury bonds. In other words, it is the US federal government's third-biggest creditor.

From 1950 to September 2010, the Saudi kingdom was the US arms industry's chief foreign client. By itself, it received nearly 17% of all US foreign military sales deliveries. It was followed by Egypt, with 7.3%, which received slightly more than Israel. The other Arab states, taken together, accounted for 32% of these arms deliveries; this was more than any other region of the world, including Europe.[15] Over the same sixty-year period, the Saudi kingdom was by far the biggest buyer of US military construction, accounting for 78% of total foreign military construction sales deliveries.[16] The Saudi kingdom also topped the list of countries that contracted to purchase US defense articles and services between 2007 and 2010, signing contracts worth $13.8 billion. It was followed by the UAE (10.4%) and Egypt (7.8%). Iraq came in sixth (5.6%).[17]

In 2010, Congress gave the Obama administration the go-ahead to close a military equipment and services deal with the Saudi kingdom involving a total of $60 billion. In question were, mainly, airplanes, helicopters, and maintenance services. This was the biggest arms export deal in US history. Vying with it for the title of biggest arms export deal ever was the Al-Yamamah transaction, initiated in 1985, between the United Kingdom and, again, the Saudis. The latter deal was, moreover, the occasion for a major scandal that offered a glimpse of the Saudi royal family's considerable corruption.[18]

In December 2011, in the framework of a 2010 agreement, the Saudi kingdom ordered eighty-four F-15SA Strike Eagle fighter jets, produced by Boeing, plus modernization of seventy F-15s already in the Saudi fleet. That deal, including equipment and maintenance, was worth a total of $29.4 billion. Finalization of another $25.6 billion helicopter contract is pending.[19] "The additional work is expected to keep Boeing's F-15 line open until at least 2017 or so, along with 600 suppliers in 44 states," *Defense Industry Daily* commented.[20] Comparing this contract with the many other options (France, Russia, United Kingdom) that the Saudis had, the *Daily* explained the kingdom's decision in terms that speak volumes about US interest in maintaining tensions in the region, especially with Iran:

The Saudis have long-standing relationships with America and its defense firms. That relationship frayed in the wake of 9/11. . . . Iran's nuclear weapons program, and its proxy wars to gain armed influence in the region, have helped paper over those wounds by putting the Saudis back on the front lines against a common foe. Saudi Arabia's own internal struggles with al-Qaeda have also represented a form of progress for its American relationships.

In a world where people often buy arms from you because they want you to be their friend, and a region where shiny new equipment is often meant as a message to neighbors, these political winds bode well for American arms sales to the desert kingdom.[21]

A recent report by the Congressional Research Service admitted this in the clearest possible terms:

The Persian Gulf crisis of August 1990–February 1991 was the principal catalyst for major new weapons purchases in the Near East made during the last twenty years. This crisis, culminating in a U.S.-led war to expel Iraq from Kuwait, firmly established the U.S. as the guarantor of Gulf security and created new demands by key purchasers such as Saudi Arabia, Kuwait, the United Arab Emirates, and other members of the GCC for a variety of advanced weapons systems. Subsequently, concerns over the growing strategic threat from Iran, which have continued into the 21st century, have become the principal basis of GCC states' advanced arms purchases. . . .

The United States ranked first in arms transfer agreements with the Near East during the 2004–2007 period with 30.3% of their total value (almost $20 billion in current dollars). The United Kingdom was second during these years with 26.5% ($17.5 billion in current dollars). Recently, from 2008 to 2011, the United States dominated in arms agreements with this region with almost $92 billion (in current dollars), a 78.9% share.[22]

Between 1991 and 2011, according to the Stockholm International Peace Research Institute (SIPRI), the Saudi kingdom was the world's fifth-biggest arms importer. The United States was its leading supplier, followed at a great distance by the United Kingdom and France. The UAE was the eleventh-biggest arms importer; its main supplier was the United States, closely followed by France.[23] These spectacular arms purchases by the GCC states, which lack the capacity fully to use what they buy, amount in large measure to prepositioning military equipment for their protectors' use. Above all, such deals help finance those protectors' arms industries, a contribution that is especially appreciated when economic crisis forces arms-exporting countries' governments to curtail domestic military outlays. In sum, the Middle East clearly appears as "central to a global process of accumulation based on finance, militarism and oil," as Ali Kadri puts it.[24]

It is, moreover, well known that the oil card is an invaluable strategic asset. Controlling access to oil, especially the biggest reserves in the Arab-Iranian Gulf, gives the United States a decisive strategic advantage in the battle for world hegemony, putting it in a position of dominance vis-à-vis both its greatest potential rival, China, and also its traditional vassals, Western Europe and Japan, all heavily dependent on oil imports from the region. The Saudi kingdom, a US protectorate, is, with Angola, one of the two main suppliers of petroleum to China, most of whose oil imports come from the Gulf (besides the Saudi kingdom, from Iran, Iraq, the UAE, and Kuwait). The situation is as paradoxical as the one that makes China the main holder of US Treasury bonds, that is, the US federal government's biggest creditor. Here we have two good illustrations of the two countries' economic interdependence, which contrasts starkly with their strategic rivalry.

Let us note, finally, that American oil interests are among the main reasons for the US government's military support for the State of Israel. Contrary to a widespread but false impression, the new state could by no means count on this support from the moment it was created, at least not in direct form. The first surge in US military credits for Israel, which were nonexistent down to 1958, came only in 1962: they rose from a few hundred thousand dollars to more than $13 million that year, before suddenly soaring to $90 million in 1966, a year before the Six-Day War. Washington's delivery of Skyhawk aircraft to Israel from 1966 on signaled the beginning of the conversion of the Israeli air force's equipment: materiel made in the USA now began to replace French goods. The change was accelerated after the 1967 June war. Cheryl Rubenberg offers a good description of this shift:

> When Kennedy assumed office in 1961, he initially took the position that peace in the Middle East was dependent on a balance of military power between Israel and the Arabs; however, he shortly began to perceive certain advantages in the idea of an Israeli Sparta acting as a U.S. surrogate. Kennedy thus initiated the concept of a "special relationship" with Israel and began the policy of providing the Jewish state with sophisticated American weapons. . . . In September 1962 Washington agreed to sell Israel short range Hawk missiles. That sale was followed by tanks in 1964 (under the Johnson administration) and Skyhawk planes in 1966. These sales marked the beginning of Washington's commitment to assure the absolute regional military superiority of Israel, which has continued to be a cornerstone of U.S.-Israeli relations and of American policy in the Middle East.[25]

This change of course followed a 1958 surge in Arab nationalism that saw the union of Syria and Egypt and the overthrow of the Iraqi monarchy. One consequence was that the United States had to abandon its Dhahran air base in the east of the Saudi kingdom in 1962 under pressure from both Egypt and Iraq.[26] This clearly shows why the idea of "an Israeli Sparta acting as a U.S. surrogate" became extremely appealing to Washington. Since then, Israel's strategic interest in Washington's eyes has depended heavily on how badly the United States needs the Zionist state as a military stand-in. It has needed Israel least, since the 1960s, during the administration of the elder George Bush, when US hegemony over the region peaked in the wake of the USA's first war on Iraq in 1991. Thus Yitzhak Shamir's government was first prevented from retaliating when Iraq launched Scud missiles against Israel and then strong-armed into participating in the "peace conference" that opened in late October in Madrid.[27] Since then, the situation has undergone another radical change. We shall return to it.

The importance of oil as the factor determining the Great Powers' foreign policy in the region is in fact underestimated, not overestimated, when it is not deliberately swept under the rug. Much more than a mere variation on the economic thesis of the "resource curse" discussed in the previous chapter, the oil curse is, first and foremost, a political phenomenon. Oil not only provides the bulk of the rent that, as we have seen, guarantees the states of the region broad autonomy from their societies; it also explains the special rapacity that characterizes Western powers' policy in the MENA region. Thus they have vied and continue to vie with powers ruled by undemocratic political regimes—the USSR yesterday, Russia and China today—in consolidating despotism in the region.

FROM "ARAB DESPOTIC EXCEPTION" TO "DEMOCRACY PROMOTION"

According to Samuel Huntington's historical periodization,[28] the "third wave" of democratization since the nineteenth century arose in the mid-1970s in Southern Europe (Portugal, Greece, Spain). It proceeded to engulf Latin America, sweeping away the "communist" regimes of Central and Eastern Europe in 1989–91 before breaking over parts of Africa and Asia. The rise of this wave coincided with the 1970s worldwide economic recession. Advocates of neoliberalism capitalized on the economic context of the recession to launch an offensive that rather quickly succeeded in imposing a radical paradigm change affecting the whole international capitalist system. The new paradigm governed the former Eastern Bloc countries' socioeconomic transformation.

The fact that these two upheavals occurred simultaneously spawned a neoliberal euphoria that, improbably, turned an essay written in 1989 by a member of the State Department's Policy Planning Staff, Francis Fukuyama, into an intellectual event of planetary proportions. In a spirited display of wishful thinking, Fukuyama announced the arrival of the "end of history" and the onset of "centuries of boredom," with "the universalization of Western liberal democracy as the final form of human government" and "the growing 'Common Marketization' of international relations."[29]

This ultraidealistic thesis drew admonitions from Huntington, the "realist," who warned his readers against Fukuyama's blind optimism. Huntington's book on the "third wave" includes a detailed analysis— a premonitory analysis that was largely substantiated in the following two decades—of the various factors that might well generate a "reverse wave" of authoritarianism in the context of a crisis of liberal democracy.[30] In the counterthesis on the course of history that he formulated thereafter, Huntington went on to place the post–Cold War period under the sign of the "clash of civilizations,"[31] explaining how democracy could clash with the Western model of liberalism in non-Western countries. He called this the "democracy paradox":

> Non-Western societies' adoption of Western democratic institutions encourages nativist and anti-Western political movements and gives them access to power. . . . Democratization conflicts with Westernization, and democracy is inherently a parochializing not a cosmopolitanizing process.[32]

The populations of the Arab region have more than one reason to be radically opposed to Western domination, which they quite rightly perceive as a factor inimical to their political self-determination and economic sovereignty. The Western powers have long since opted to prop up despotic regimes as guarantors of their own interests in this part of the world. The United States has pursued such a policy from the inception of its involvement in the Middle East.[33] The end of the Cold War changed nothing in this respect: its most spectacular consequence in the region was a massive deployment of US troops dispatched to protect the ultrareactionary Saudi kingdom and restore Kuwait's territory to its emir. The administration of the elder Bush, suspicious of the popular revolt that broke out in Iraq just after the 1991 war, preferred to keep Saddam Hussein in power in Baghdad. Worse, it gave Hussein free rein to crush the rebellion.

The official justification for the West's alliance with Arab regimes, antipodes to democratic, liberal values—particularly its alliance with the uncontested champion in this category, the Saudi kingdom—has traditionally turned on the hypocritical argument that "we have to respect their culture." This avatar of Orientalism—in the pejorative sense of the term popularized by Edward Said—implies that "Islamic culture," presumed to be archetypical here, is inherently incompatible with liberal democracy. Amos Perlmutter, an Israeli-American "expert" on Middle Eastern questions whose words carried weight in Washington both in the Reagan years and under the elder Bush, advanced this caricatural thesis in extremely categorical fashion in 1992, in an article intended for a broad public titled "Islam and Democracy Simply Aren't Compatible."[34] When this is one's basic postulate, it is easy to fob off collaboration with despotic regimes in countries with Muslim majorities as proof of respect for "cultural differences."

Like every other form of cultural essentialism, this postulate depends on fallacious reasoning. As Asef Bayat has rightly pointed out,

> the question is not whether Islam is or is not compatible with democracy or by extension modernity (however understood), but rather under what conditions Muslims can *make* them compatible. Because there is nothing intrinsic in Islam, and for that matter any other religion, which makes them *inherently* democratic or undemocratic. *We*, the social agents, determine the inclusive or authoritarian thrust of religion.[35]

As we have seen, the populations of the Arabic-speaking region must overcome particularly forbidding barriers to win the democratic rights that other countries with Muslim majorities, such as Indonesia, Senegal, or Turkey, have already secured. Those barriers are not limited to rentier states' domination of the Arab region, but also include international Great Power support for its tyrannical regimes, particularly support from powers that claim to be paragons of democracy and champions of human rights. Behind the "Arab despotic exception"—as it appeared when, at the end of the "third wave" of democratization, the Arab region figured as the last concentration of despotic regimes in a single geopolitical zone—stands a Western prodespotic exception.

Although the end of the Cold War led Western governments to abandon their support for "authoritarian" regimes, previously justified in the name of the struggle against "totalitarian communism," they carefully refrained from extending their advocacy of respect for democracy and human rights to the Arab region, aside from pro forma declarations that were, to boot, all but inaudible.[36] As Condoleezza Rice admitted in a March 2005 *Washington Post* interview, two months after being appointed secretary of state to replace Colin Powell, "people said, well, you talk about democracy in Latin America, you talk about democracy in Europe, you even talk about democracy in Asia or Africa, but you never talk about democracy in the Middle East. And, of course, they were right because this was the decision that stability trumped everything."[37]

The main motivation for this attitude was the rise and the anti-Western radicalization of Islamic fundamentalism in the Arab region. Western imperialism's two-bit ideologues lost no time branding such fundamentalism "the new totalitarianism." The hypocritical argument about respecting cultural differences was now shored up by another about the lesser of two evils. It is better, the line ran, to come to terms with "moderate," pro-Western despotic regimes than to have to face "extremist," anti-Western despotic regimes. Those who defended this position studiously ignored the fact that, measured by the standards of democracy and women's rights or the degree of obscurantism, the "moderate" Saudi kingdom is far worse than "extremist" Iran.

The long tradition of pursuing "realistic" US policies in the Middle East was to be abruptly repudiated by the George W. Bush administration and replaced by a crusade for "democracy promotion." The new crusade, however, did not last long. The neoconservatives happily promoted this sudden turnaround and basked in their hour of glory while it was still in the making, only to fall into disgrace when it failed. Until the turnaround, the Bush administration's policies had not really departed from tradition: George W. Bush and his vice president and mentor, Dick Cheney, had, in their first two years in office, steered a course between the neoconservatives, represented in the administration by Deputy Secretary of Defense Paul Wolfowitz and supported by Defense Secretary Donald Rumsfeld, and the "realists," represented by Secretary of State Colin Powell.

Seizing the chance provided by the terrible 11 September 2001 attacks and their profound impact on US public opinion, the Bush administration set out, waving the banner of the "War on Terror," on a sweeping campaign to expand Washington's imperial domain *manu militari*. The aim was to complete the globalization of the US Empire and consolidate the "unipolar moment" inaugurated by the Soviet collapse. This objective was to be attained by establishing a US presence in Central Asia (by invading Afghanistan and establishing a military presence in the former Soviet republics on its borders) while completing the process of bringing the Arab oil states of the Gulf under US tutelage (the invasion of Iraq). At the same time, the Bush administration gave Ariel Sharon's Israeli government a free hand to crush the second Palestinian Intifada by reoccupying the territories that the Israeli army had evacuated in compliance with the 1993 Oslo Accords.

The turn taken by the invasion of Iraq put a new face on things. The invasion was launched in March–April 2003 despite strong international opposition, in flagrant violation of international law, and on a false pretext: to eliminate the weapons of mass destruction ostensibly stockpiled by the Iraqi regime. The subsequent occupation of Iraq quickly turned into a disaster. The daft plan to transform Iraq into a permanent US protectorate, on the model of post–World War II West Germany or Japan, grew out of the illusion, nursed by the neoconservatives and their Iraqi cronies, that the Iraqi population would enthusiastically rally to this plan. It inspired an ill-advised decision (ill-advised from the standpoint of imperial US interests) to dismantle the Baathist state. This decision very rapidly precipitated a chaotic situation in a context in which the feelings manifested by the country's Arab population were divided between suspicion and frank hostility.[38]

The Bush administration found itself mired in a deep predicament a few months after the occupation began in spring 2003. It had become clear by then that it would be impossible to produce the least scrap of evidence that Saddam Hussein's regime had had weapons of mass destruction. This had been altogether foreseeable, inasmuch as Iraq had, since the 1991 war, been laboring under the most stringent set of sanctions and controls ever imposed on a country in the contemporary period. The Bush administration, now that its main alibi had crumbled, decided to put the accent on the other reason it had invoked to justify occupying the country: "democracy promotion." This had previously served only as a fallback, since it was hardly credible. The administration now espoused neoconservative rhetoric about the United States' Manifest Destiny to make the world over in its own image, a mission that the frontline neoconservative Michael Ledeen had propagated in the immediate wake of 9/11 under the label "creative destruction." "It is time once again," Ledeen had declared, "to export the democratic revolution."[39]

The administration's turn was announced in a programmatic 6 November 2003 speech that George W. Bush delivered to the National Endowment for Democracy, a bipartisan think tank created in 1983 on the Reagan administration's initiative. Its members convened in the

US Chamber of Commerce for the occasion. This speech was unusual enough to merit extensive quotation:

> [The Middle East] must be a focus of American policy for decades to come. In many nations of the Middle East—countries of great strategic importance—democracy has not yet taken root. And the questions arise: Are the peoples of the Middle East somehow beyond the reach of liberty? Are millions of men and women and children condemned by history or culture to live in despotism? Are they alone never to know freedom, and never even to have a choice in the matter? I, for one, do not believe it. I believe every person has the ability and the right to be free.
>
> Some skeptics of democracy assert that the traditions of Islam are inhospitable to the representative government. This "cultural condescension," as Ronald Reagan termed it, has a long history. After the Japanese surrender in 1945, a so-called Japan expert asserted that democracy in that former empire would "never work." Another observer declared the prospects for democracy in post-Hitler Germany are, and I quote, "most uncertain at best"—he made that claim in 1957....
>
> Many Middle Eastern governments now understand that military dictatorship and theocratic rule are a straight, smooth highway to nowhere. But some governments still cling to the old habits of central control. There are governments that still fear and repress independent thought and creativity, and private enterprise—the human qualities that make for strong and successful societies. Even when these nations have vast natural resources, they do not respect or develop their greatest resources—the talent and energy of men and women working and living in freedom....
>
> Sixty years of Western nations excusing and accommodating the lack of freedom in the Middle East did nothing to make us safe—because in the long run, stability cannot be purchased at the expense of liberty. As long as the Middle East remains a place where freedom does not flourish, it will remain a place of stagnation, resentment, and violence ready for export. And with the spread of weapons that can bring catastrophic harm to our country and to our friends, it would be reckless to accept the status quo.
>
> Therefore, the United States has adopted a new policy, a forward strategy of freedom in the Middle East. This strategy requires the same persistence and energy and idealism we have shown before.[40]

In February 2004, gearing up for a summit conference of the world's seven richest countries and Russia, the Bush administration improvised a "G8–Greater Middle East Partnership." It was seeking to sow the illusion that it had a comprehensive vision of the conditions required for the economic and social development of a vast zone, the definition of which was likewise improvised; it ran from Morocco through Turkey and Pakistan to Afghanistan.[41] This project was a patchwork of neoliberal clichés cribbed from the international economic institutions. It was retired in short order, at which point the

Bush administration fell back on the "democracy" section of the chapter on politics in its new battle ideology. The administration, however, after being thoroughly discredited by the hue and cry it had raised over Iraq's "weapons of mass destruction," had gone on to contradict its own democratic rhetoric by trying to force the Iraqis to accept a constituent assembly designated by the occupier. This attempt was foiled in January 2004, when Ayatollah Ali al-Sistani mobilized the Shiite population against it.

Intent on restoring its credibility, which had been seriously undermined by its appeals to a hodgepodge of threadbare pretexts, the Bush administration pressured its Arab partners into carrying out a semblance of reforms. Hypocritically, it claimed that its campaign to promote democracy had scored a success with the first, January 2005 Iraqi elections. Covered in depth by the Arab media, these elections, the first free, democratic ballot in the country's history, had been held in spite of the reigning climate of violence. They did, nevertheless, have a striking effect on people in the region.

Still more hypocritically, the Bush administration presented the election of Mahmoud Abbas as president of the Palestinian Authority, which took place the same month as the vote in Iraq, shortly after Yasser Arafat's death, as proof of the success of its "democracy promotion." In fact, Arafat had incessantly demanded, throughout the last years of his life, that Bush and Sharon authorize him to hold a presidential election, since he was certain he would win it hands down. In 2003, Washington had forced him to name Abbas as prime minister against the will of a large majority of the population of the Palestinian territories occupied in 1967. The Bush administration likewise took credit for the popular mobilization in Lebanon that followed the 14 February 2005 assassination of the country's former prime minister Rafic Hariri, a movement that compelled Syrian forces to withdraw from the country.

It must, however, be granted that three other components of what had already been labeled the "Arab Spring" were undeniably due to pressure from Washington. This plainly holds for the Saudi monarchy's willingness to organize elections in February–April 2005 for the first time since 1963. Needless to say, these elections did not bear on any of the country's central state institutions; they were municipal elections. More exactly, half the seats on the kingdom's city councils were put to a vote by the country's citizens—except for women, who could neither cast ballots nor run for office. The monarchy filled the other half of the seats by appointment, in a country in which, to top things off, political

parties are strictly outlawed. Of the exclusively male potential electorate, fewer than a quarter bothered to go to the polls. The data for the
capital are eloquent:

> People were reluctant to register and vote, as was clear in Riyadh (the Saudi
> capital and home to 2,692,780 citizens), where the number of registered vot-
> ers did not exceed 18% of those eligible to vote, i.e., 86,462 voters out of
> a potential electorate of approximately 470,000 persons—representing just
> two percent of the total population of the city.
>   The small number of registered voters was expected to lead to a relatively
> high rate of participation on election day (February 10, 2005). The rate of
> participation in the capital, however, barely reached 65 percent (i.e., a little
> bit more than one percent of the total population of Riyadh).[42]

The result was an unsurprising "landslide victory" for the "recommended" lists of "moderate Islamist" candidates—in other words, the
conservative fundamentalists—whom the ulama had pronounced faithful to the Prophet Muhammad's line.[43]

The second consequence of the Bush administration's pressure to
democratize was more significant. In May 2005, Kuwaiti women were
granted political rights and, for the first time, a woman was appointed
to a ministerial post. Both developments attest Washington's heavy
influence on Emir Jaber Al-Sabah, whom US troops had put back on
his throne.

The third consequence of the Bush administration's campaign, the
most far reaching of all, was that Hosni Mubarak consented to liberalize his country's electoral process somewhat in advance of the
autumn 2005 elections. Thus he had the constitution amended to make
it possible for people other than himself to run for president. However,
the amendment made who actually could run largely dependent on
Mubarak's whims. Under pressure from the United States and the
European Union, he authorized the liberal Ayman Nour to run against
him in the September 2005 presidential race: he had him let out of
prison for the purpose, after having stripped him of his parliamentary
immunity and incarcerated him on trumped-up charges earlier that year.

The high point of the Bush administration's democratic offensive
was the speech delivered by Secretary of State Condoleezza Rice at the
American University of Cairo on 20 June 2005. With staggering imperial arrogance, Rice indirectly took the Egyptian president to task in his
own country—even if it must be said that, in this case, her arrogance
was yoked to the service of unimpeachable principles. Her speech, like
Bush's, merits lengthy quotation:

For 60 years, my country, the United States, pursued stability at the expense of democracy in this region here in the Middle East—and we achieved neither. Now, we are taking a different course. We are supporting the democratic aspirations of all people. . . .

Now, here in Cairo, President Mubarak's decision to amend the country's constitution and hold multiparty elections is encouraging. President Mubarak has unlocked the door for change. Now, the Egyptian Government must put its faith in its own people. We are all concerned for the future of Egypt's reforms when peaceful supporters of democracy—men and women—are not free from violence. The day must come when the rule of law replaces emergency decrees—and when the independent judiciary replaces arbitrary justice.

The Egyptian Government must fulfill the promise it has made to its people—and to the entire world—by giving its citizens the freedom to choose. Egypt's elections, including the Parliamentary elections, must meet objective standards that define every free election.

Opposition groups must be free to assemble, and to participate, and to speak to the media. Voting should occur without violence or intimidation. And international election monitors and observers must have unrestricted access to do their jobs.[44]

Even before Rice delivered this oration, it had already become clear, as the author of these lines wrote at the time, that "by kicking the Arab anthill with the invasion of Iraq, followed by statements on promoting democracy, as a plausible replacement to destroying WMDs, the US has further undermined the stability of the region, bringing to the surface popular discontent, previously stifled by despotic rule."[45]

THE MUSLIM BROTHERS, WASHINGTON, AND THE SAUDIS

The anti-US agitation touched off by the occupation of Iraq, followed by the destabilizing effects of the Bush administration's campaign for "democracy promotion," very naturally profited the political and ideological current that has dominated Arab popular protest for the past quarter century: Islamic fundamentalism, in its multiple political manifestations.

With World War I, Arab societies entered a long period of recurrent crises. These took their place in the general crisis of colonial/imperialist domination combined with the major crisis that had broken out at the center of the world capitalist system. World War I and the revolutionary groundswell that followed it brought this twofold systemic crisis into the light of day. It was only thanks to the Second World War, far more destructive than the First, that international capitalism succeeded in overcoming this critical period, the most serious in its history, in its core zones. The partial blockage or slowdown of development in its peripheral zones, however, owing to the very structure of a world system dominated by imperialist economies, was to become an abiding feature of the system. Undeniably, the gravity of this process of "underdevelopment" varied from one country or region to another.

In the course of the twentieth century, this blockage of development generated various radical experiments to resolve it and accelerate industrialization. Revolutions led by communist intelligentsias abolished private ownership of the social means of production. These intelligentsias drew their support from the proletariat (that is, wage laborers and the broad mass of those who, since they do not own means of production, seek wage labor) and the poor peasantry; they led to the creation of diverse variants of a bureaucratic mode of production that made it possible to carry out basic industrialization. Such industrialization was doomed, by its very nature, to run up against the "problem of quality" mentioned at the outset of this book, except where it was combined with an exogenous capitalism. In those exceptional cases, however, capitalism inevitably sapped the very foundations of the bureaucratic system by generating, sooner or later, an endogenous capitalist dynamic. This has held in several instances, from the 1921–8 Soviet New Economic Policy to contemporary China.

Elsewhere, particularly in the Arab region, Bonapartist experiments that were usually conducted by nationalist, populist officer castes, but sometimes also by political parties or a combination of the two, tried to hasten industrialization in a state capitalist mode inspired by the bureaucratic model of the USSR. These Bonapartist regimes did not, however, abolish private ownership of the social means of production, especially petty proprietorship. Ultimately, the Bonapartist castes engendered new bourgeoisies that had incubated within them; these were combinations of the vestiges of the bourgeoisie of the old regime and a nepotistic state bourgeoisie. We surveyed the results of these experiments in the preceding chapters.

In addition to the various developmentalist responses to the crisis of dependent, atrophied, deformed capitalism, reactionary responses emerged in parts of the world in which urban and semiurban preindustrial societies had long existed—the central lands of Islam in particular. Such social formations had also long existed in the European heartland in which capitalism slowly came into being. In these European societies, the traditional middle urban strata—the strata comprising the petty bourgeoisie, which should not be confused with the "middle class" in the singular, a term that often designates the bourgeoisie itself—were impoverished as a result of the great capitalist transformation. Karl Marx and Friedrich Engels's famous *Communist Manifesto* describes this process, together with the political consequences of the middle strata's potential or actual social downgrading:

> The lower strata of the middle class—the small tradespeople, shopkeepers, and retired tradesmen generally, the handicraftsmen and peasants—all these sink gradually into the proletariat, partly because their diminutive capital does not suffice for the scale on which Modern Industry is carried on, and is swamped in the competition with the large capitalists, partly because their specialised skill is rendered worthless by new methods of production. . . .
>
> The lower middle class, the small manufacturer, the shopkeeper, the artisan, the peasant, all these fight against the bourgeoisie, to save from extinction their existence as fractions of the middle class. They are therefore not revolutionary, but conservative. Nay more, they are reactionary, for they try to roll back the wheel of history. If by chance, they are revolutionary, they are only so in view of their impending transfer into the proletariat; they thus defend not their present, but their future interests, they desert their own standpoint to place themselves at that of the proletariat.[46]

In the Arab region, the movement that espouses a reactionary ambition to "roll back the wheel of history" generally brandishes the banner of Islamic fundamentalism and advocates a return to the golden age of a mythologized Islamic history. It has its base among the traditional middle classes and also among intellectuals both traditional (especially religious) and organic (students, teachers, the lower and middle ranks of the liberal professions).[47] The Muslim Brotherhood, founded in Egypt in 1928, is the oldest political organization of a modern type with an Islamic fundamentalist program. It represented the first expression of this reactionary movement and remains, to the present day, its chief incarnation on the level of the Arab region as a whole.

In the aftermath of World War I, the fundamentalist movement began competing with the nationalist movement and communist left for hegemony over the middle social strata. The nationalists took power after the 1948 Arab defeat in Palestine. Thanks to their later 1960s radicalization, they succeeded in minimizing the influence of the fundamentalist movement, which they repressed. The failure of nationalism, however, had become obvious by the 1970s, while such credibility as "communism" had vanished with the crisis of the USSR. The ground was thus cleared for renewed expansion of the fundamentalist movement. The fundamentalists received help in the form of generous funding from the Saudi kingdom, which had, for its part, been immensely enriched by oil windfalls in the 1970s. Their movement was given another powerful boost at the end of the decade by Iran's "Islamic Revolution"; it was also promoted by various Arab regimes as an antidote to the left-wing radicalization that set in with the second, June 1967 Arab defeat at Israel's hands and continued until the 1970s.

Although certain regimes, often the very ones that had promoted the fundamentalist movements, later turned against and repressed them—subjecting them to partial, intermittent repression in Egypt and radical, violent repression in Libya, Iraq, Syria, Algeria, and Tunisia—the fundamentalists maintained their ascendancy over the region's popular protest movement for lack of credible competitors. Repression succeeds in marginalizing a political movement only when it is one component of an overall transformation that deprives that movement of its social base. This held for Islamic fundamentalism in the 1950s and 1960s. Since then, in contrast, the political and socioeconomic developments discussed in the previous two chapters have only reinforced the factors underpinning the fundamentalist movement's influence. At the same time, no viable new force capable of competing with it has sprung up.

Transformations of neoliberal inspiration, especially reduction of the state's social role, have not only reinforced the factors broadening the fundamentalist movement's potential social base; they have also fostered its expansion wherever it could operate openly as a substitute for the state. In Egypt, for example, the Muslim Brothers, made rich by moneys derived from the Arab oil economy, were able to provide some of the services no longer provided by the shrinking welfare state, in line with a logic of "charity" perfectly consonant with the neoliberal context.[48]

The breakthroughs that the Brothers have achieved every time with each political opening in Egypt, however slight, were eminently predictable. Hosni Mubarak knew what would be coming his way once he was forced to bow to the pressure from Washington. Hassan Abdul-Rahman, the head of Egyptian State Security, met with Muhammad Habib, first deputy to the Brotherhood's supreme guide at the time, in order to inform him that the government intended to hold "democratic" elections in 2005 and, accordingly, to work out an agreement covering the number of candidates the Muslim Brothers would be authorized to put up for election[49]—all under the label of "independents," since the Brotherhood had no legal status.

Thus the Brothers, who requested permission to run 200 candidates for the 444 seats up for election, were allowed to run 120.[50] They won 34 seats in the first round. As usual, few eligible voters went to the polls. The Brothers' success nevertheless encouraged more voters to vote in the second round, in which the Brotherhood took another 42 seats. During the third round, the infuriated regime bared its fangs; several people died and hundreds were injured as a result, and there were 1,700 arrests. In the end, the Muslim Brothers saw the number of their representatives in the People's Assembly rise from 17 in the outgoing assembly, elected in 2000, to 88 in the one returned by the November–December 2005 elections. This represented a little less than one-fifth of the total number of seats.

Mubarak had arranged for the Brothers to win enough seats to cause a stir in Western capitals, but not enough to cost him the free hand he enjoyed with the legislature. He calculated that the message thus sent would suffice to persuade Washington and its allies to stop pressuring him to democratize Egyptian politics. Ayman Nour, who had, despite everything, garnered seven percent of the vote in the presidential election, paid for what the enraged president regarded as an act of lèse-majesté: he was sent back to prison for five years in December. The move was perceived as a slap in Washington's face.

The Bush administration, too, was perfectly well aware that the Muslim Brothers would be the chief beneficiaries of a democratic opening in Egypt. However, Washington had begun to negotiate a new turn in its relationship with the Brotherhood, after a prolonged chill. The two parties had long maintained a cooperative relationship.[51] They had had the same enemies during the Cold War, communism and Arab nationalism, but, above all, Nasserism, perceived as the fruit of a cross between the first two. The break between Nasser and the Brotherhood dated to 1954, the year the Egyptian leader became prime minister. When, shortly thereafter, he broke with Washington, his two enemies very naturally started collaborating against him. They did so all the more readily in that they had the same friend and accomplice in their hostility to the Nasserite regime: the Saudi kingdom.

Hassan al-Banna, the founder of the Muslim Brotherhood in Egypt, established relations with the Saudi kingdom as soon as he had created his movement. His ideological inspiration, Rashid Rida, had collaborated actively with the Saudis from the kingdom's foundation to his death in 1935.[52] When the Egyptian monarchy dissolved the Brotherhood in 1948, Riyadh offered refuge to Banna, who was, nonetheless, murdered shortly thereafter. With the Brotherhood's rupture with Nasser and the onset of the large-scale repression to which it was subjected in Egypt, the kingdom opened its doors to the organization's members. Many settled there permanently and even acquired Saudi citizenship; some made fortunes.[53]

One of the instruments of the anti-Nasser, anticommunist alliance between the Saudi kingdom, the Muslim Brothers, and the United States was forged with the foundation of the Muslim World League in Mecca in 1962. The League brought together, under Wahhabi sponsorship, various Islamic groups and currents, among them the Egyptian Muslim Brotherhood and the other branches that the Egyptian Brothers had helped set up in various Arab countries and other parts of the world. From a very early date, Banna's son-in-law, Said Ramadan, played a leading role in setting up the Brotherhood's international network. Subsequently, he became a key leader of its activities in Europe and also helped found the Muslim World League.[54]

Anwar al-Sadat, who became president of Egypt on Nasser's death in September 1970, very naturally used religion as an ideological weapon in his battle against the Nasserites, the left, and the USSR, following the example of the United States and the Saudis, to whose camp he had rallied. It was to that end that he released the Muslim Brothers from Egypt's prisons and even allowed them to resume their activities, which were tolerated without ever being legalized. The executive bureau of the Muslim Brothers' international organization met in Mecca in 1973, in the presence of the Brotherhood's recently freed Egyptian leaders, in order to resume building its network.[55] A political central committee was formed in 1979, bringing together representatives of several branches of the Brotherhood, including Rached Ghannouchi for Tunisia.[56]

In the following years, the Egyptian Muslim Brothers, like the members of the Brotherhood's other Arab branches, enjoyed privileged access to employment (especially in education) and business in the Saudi kingdom, then in the midst of the oil boom, as well as in other oil monarchies. This circumstance did a great deal to promote and then accelerate the Brotherhood's bourgeoisification. The organization now underwent a veritable social mutation: increasingly, capitalists came to play an important role in it.[57] According to Khairat al-Shatir, himself a big businessman and currently the Egyptian Brotherhood's second in command, the Egyptian intelligence agency had identified 900 companies as belonging to members of the Brotherhood; it accused them of helping finance the association's campaign in the parliamentary elections of the year 2000. The capitalist Brothers were subjected to harassment by the Mubarak regime, which thus attempted to prevent other businessmen from following their example. However, again according to al-Shatir, the regime could not go so far as to confiscate their assets for fear of scaring off foreign investors.[58]

Yet the Brotherhood's social mutation did little to promote modernization of its program. This was in part because of the close ties between Muslim Brotherhood capitalism and the state with the most reactionary social and political structures in the world, the Saudi kingdom. A second reason was that that capitalism, predominantly commercial and speculative in nature, was fully integrated into the regional capitalist modalities sketched in the previous chapter. The Brothers' mutation did, however, undoubtedly help encourage the movement's political "moderation." A wait-and-see reformism now gained the upper hand over the radical fundamentalist tendencies, typified by Sayyid Qutb, that had developed in the years of its face-off with nationalism.[59]

The Brotherhood's modernists—those for whom Turkey's Party for Justice and Development (known by its Turkish acronym, AKP) constitutes the reference model—have been recruited, as a general rule, from the ranks of the "organic intellectuals" of the petty and middle bourgeoisie. These modernists are, for the most part, members of the liberal professions or students. We shall come back to the crucial difference between the Egyptian Brotherhood and the Turkish model.

The Muslim Brothers' first major disagreement with the Saudis and, behind them, the United States came with Iran's 1979 "Islamic Revolution." The Iranian upheaval gave Islamic fundamentalism a tremendous boost, both regionally and across the globe, in a context marked by the growing discredit into which both nationalism and communism had fallen. Whereas the Brothers hailed the birth of Khomeini's regime, the Saudi authorities regarded this antimonarchical, anti-US revolution with a deeply jaundiced eye. Their lack of enthusiasm was the greater for the fact that they themselves had to confront, in 1979, an ultra-Wahhabi revolt in Mecca and an uprising of Khomeinist inspiration among Shiites in the kingdom's Eastern Province.[60] The Brotherhood's dissonance with the Saudis was, however, quickly laid aside after the Soviet intervention in Afghanistan late in 1979, which revived the collaboration involving Washington, the Saudis, and the Muslim Brothers. It went on until Soviet troops pulled out of the country ten years later.

Iraq's 1990 invasion of Kuwait, followed by the massive deployment of US and allied troops on the Saudi kingdom's territory, precipitated the deepest and longest break in the relationship between the Brothers, on the one hand, and Washington and Riyadh on the other. In the Arab countries, Gulf monarchies excepted, most of the Brotherhood's branches and related organizations opposed the US-led coalition's intervention. They thereby aligned themselves with public opinion in their countries as well as with their own sociopolitical constituencies, both of which were generally hostile to the war against Iraq planned and led by Washington. Even the Brotherhood's Syrian branch took up cudgels for Iraq's Baathist regime. This was its way of reacting to the fact that Baghdad's *frère ennemi* and the Brotherhood's sworn enemy, Hafez al-Assad's Syrian Baathist regime, had joined the Washington-led coalition. The Saudis were so infuriated with the Brotherhood that when Said Ramadan died in 1995, they refused to bury his mortal remains in a grave in Medina, as he had wished.[61]

The fact that US troops were stationed in the Saudi kingdom in 1990 was the reason that Osama bin Laden and his organization, Al-Qaida, also turned against the Saudi dynasty and the United States. Until then, Al-Qaida had been a US auxiliary in the war against the Soviets and their allies in Afghanistan. Washington and Riyadh found themselves in the role of sorcerer's apprentice, as had, in an earlier day, Sadat, when he was driven to fight the radicalized fringe of the Islamic fundamentalism whose floodgates he had thrown open in 1971. Sadat was ultimately assassinated, ten years later, by a group belonging to precisely this fringe. Relations between Washington and the Muslim Brothers were strained until the 11 September 2001 terrorist attacks.

THE MUSLIM BROTHERS, WASHINGTON, AND QATAR

Meanwhile, another actor had arrived on the scene: the Emirate of Qatar. Qatar, a peninsula that the Saudi kingdom would certainly have annexed had it not been a British protectorate, has had an implausible history since becoming "independent" in 1971.[62] Two emirs have acceded to the throne since then, thanks to palace revolutions both times: the father of the current emir deposed his first cousin in 1972, only to be deposed by his own son in 1995! The son in question, Hamad bin Khalifa Al Thani, a ruler worthy of this comic-opera principality, with his three wives and (so far) twenty-four children, is distinguished from all his peers in the Gulf by a penchant out of the ordinary: rather than automobiles, weapons, or the hunt (the Gulf sheikhs' traditional pastimes), or even business (the postindependence generation's more recent hobby), he would appear to be enamored of foreign policy.[63]

Indeed, he must be, for there is no economic rationale for the fact that Al Thani spends part of the funds at his disposal to attain a regional, nay, international political stature altogether out of proportion to the size of the state over which he presides. That stature is certainly no source of profit; the opposite is quite clearly true. It might be supposed, at best, that Hamad bin Khalifa's aim is to endow the tiny emirate with a means of exercising political pressure that can make up for its small size, in view of Qatar's real or potential disputes with neighbors such as Iran or the Saudi kingdom. In any event, the emir's predilection for regional politics has led him to use the Qatari state's financial resources, which he can tap at will, to the aforementioned end. The resources in question are substantial: revenues of $43 billion—representing only part of the proceeds from the emirate's sales of oil and natural gas—were allocated to the 2010–1 budget of the government that rules this peninsula, with its fewer than 2 million inhabitants. State expenditures totaled $39 billion. (Compare Morocco's state budget for 2011: revenues of $33.4 billion and expenditures of $34.8 billion for a population of 32.5 million.)

Sheikh Hamad's foreign policy does not, however, defy the logic of rent or that of the middleman, both typical economic profiles for the capitalism of the region. Rentier logic makes itself felt in the way he hedges his bets. Hedging means, in the case at hand, cultivating relations with the whole gamut of regional forces that count, just as others invest in a basket of currencies so as not to depend on just one. The result is sure to surprise anyone looking for political logic, since it is exclusively a question, here, of *rentier* logic.

Thus the emirate has established friendly relations with Tehran and its regional allies, and has even been accused of maintaining a relationship with Al-Qaida. At the same time, it has, since 2003, hosted the US Combat Air Operations Center for the Middle East on its soil, as well as the operational command of CENTCOM (US Central Command, the unified command for US military operations in the zone extending from the Arab Middle East, including Egypt, through Iran, Pakistan, and Afghanistan to Central Asia). When the Pentagon had to evacuate its bases in the Saudi kingdom after the 2003 invasion of Iraq (so as not to expose the kingdom to the security risk entailed by a direct US military presence on its soil), the emir of Qatar welcomed the chance to demonstrate the valuable services he could provide his American overlord by making up for the failure of his neighbor and rival.

As if to point a paradox, Qatar provided significant financial support to the Lebanese Hezbollah in the wake of Israel's 2006 attack on Lebanon, although it had previously come forward as the sole GCC state to maintain official trade relations with Israel and accept the presence of an Israeli commercial delegation on its territory, as well as visits by Israeli leaders. These trade relations were suspended after Israel's 2008–9 onslaught on Gaza. In response to that aggression, Qatar held in January 2009, in its capital, Doha, a regional conference boycotted by Washington's traditional allies in the region. The stars in attendance were Iranian president Mahmoud Ahmadinejad, Syrian president Bashar al-Assad, and Khaled Meshaal, leader of the Palestinian Hamas.

As for Sheikh Hamad's exploits in the middleman's role, Allen Fromherz has drawn up an impressive list of the emirate's efforts along this line. Qatar mediated between Gaddafi's Libyan regime, on the one hand, and Washington and London on the other, leading the Libyan dictator to begin collaborating with the United States and Britain in 2003 (as its reward, Fromherz adds, Qatar received lucrative oil contracts). Qatar was likewise the mediator in negotiations between Sudan and Chad; between Washington and Saddam Hussein; between Hamas and the Palestinian Authority under both Arafat and Abbas, and between the Palestinians and Israel; between Lebanese factions; between Iran and the UAE; between Ali Abdallah Saleh's regime and the Houthi rebels in Yemen; between Omar al-Bashir's Sudanese regime and the rebels in Darfur; between the Moroccan monarchy and the Western Sahara's Polisario Front; and between various Arab dissidents and their respective countries' rulers (in Mauritania, Iraq, and Algeria).[64]

Today, however, the emirate's services as mediator in one particular set of relations appear to have been by far the most important of all: the relations between Washington and the Muslim Brothers. Even before the emir of Qatar had replaced his Saudi neighbors as host to US command centers, he had replaced them as the Brothers' sponsor. The commanding influence that the emirate now has over the Brotherhood derives not only from its utilization of the significant economic capital at its disposal, which allows it to lavish generous subsidies on the whole organization, but also from its equally important "symbolic capital," in the sense in which Pierre Bourdieu uses this concept, related to the Weberian notion of charisma.[65] The emir's symbolic capital is political-religious. It is embodied by the best-known Muslim preacher of our day, Yusuf al-Qaradawi.[66]

Falling halfway between the Weberian categories of charisma and rational-legal authority, Islamic preaching is a task entrusted to scholars, the ulama or *fuqaha*: men who know the religious corpus well (the Sunna, in the Sunnis' case) and can interpret it and are also familiar with religious law (the Sharia), with respect to which they provide consultations or fatwas. The symbolic capital here consists in a "charismatic" aptitude for communicating legal knowledge and interpretations of scripture with consummate didactic art. That aptitude, in turn, is conditioned by the public's perception that a preacher's personal conduct is in harmony with his teaching.

Born in 1926, Qaradawi has been active in the ranks of the Muslim Brothers in his native country, Egypt, where he has also spent time in prison. He settled in Qatar in 1961, teaching religion and eventually acquiring the privilege of becoming a naturalized citizen. An eminent officer of the Brotherhood in exile in the Nasser period, he helped reorganize its international organization, playing an active part in its executive bureau as the "representative from Qatar" from the late 1960s on.[67] Recognized in Egypt as a leading member of the Brotherhood after its public reemergence under Sadat, Qaradawi was on three occasions, according to his own testimony, invited to assume leadership of the organization, in 1973, in 1986, and again in 2003.[68] He turned the offer down each time, preferring the role of "guide and preceptor of the entire *Umma*" (the community of the faithful) to that of general guide of the Muslim Brothers of Egypt.[69]

The alliance between the emir and the preacher is a latter-day version of that between Muhammad bin Saud and Muhammad bin Abdul-Wahhab, the founder of the eighteenth-century religious-tribal movement to which the Saudi regime traces its origins.[70] It has played a pivotal role in Hamad bin Khalifa Al Thani's conduct of his country's foreign policy. Much as other tycoons acquire football teams, the emir has sponsored the Muslim Brothers, whom his Saudi neighbors had repudiated fewer than five years before he took power. He thus purchased the allegiance of a major force: a network of organizations that not only covers the whole Arab region, but also extends well beyond it, and has attained, in most Arab countries, a hegemonic position when it comes to channeling popular discontent.

The Saudis expected the Brotherhood to return penitently to the kingdom's fold after 1991. They could not imagine that a new emir at the head of their little neighbor Qatar would replace them as the sponsor of a network of this size, given the importance of the political stake and all the risks it entails. Vexed, the Saudis turned to the other regional fundamentalist current that they supported: the "Salafists" (a name that refers to the tradition of Islam's founding fathers).[71]

Whereas the Muslim Brothers are a political-religious movement of a modern type, rooted in the orthodox Islamic tradition and flexible enough to reconcile a fundamentalist religious program with certain political and social realities of modern times, the Salafists of our day are an outgrowth of Saudi-style Wahhabism; this applies even to their dress and accoutrements. Financed by the kingdom's Wahhabi institution, they are a pure product of the "Saudi era" spawned by the steep rise in oil revenues that began in the 1970s. Many of their regional branches are, moreover, led by men recruited from the ranks of immigrant Arab workers in the Saudi kingdom who have gone back to their countries to preach their new employers' doctrine.

Following the 11 September 2001 attacks, the emir of Qatar decided that the time had come to begin engineering a rapprochement between his fundamentalist clients and his imperialist protectors. As Husam Tammam quite rightly points out,

> contrary to what many people believe, the 11 September attack was the first factor to transform the American conception of the way politics had changed in the Arab region, and of the place the Islamists occupied in the equation that summed up this change. Of course, the Islamists whose image now changed in the Americans' eyes comprised the fraction of this movement that advocated peaceful political action and rejected violence, not the violent armed movements responsible for the blow dealt to Manhattan.[72]

Because the Bush administration had made the "War on Terror" its top priority in the aftermath of 9/11, it was duty-bound to spare no effort to isolate the new US Public Enemy No. 1, the Al-Qaida network. The very violence of the shock caused by the 2001 attacks made the "moderation" of the Muslim Brothers and their ideological family seem palatable in comparison. The Muslim "centrism" (*wasatiyya*) that Qaradawi had made his trademark[73]—and translated into acts, especially in his struggle against the radical tendency of the Muslim Brotherhood inspired by Sayyid Qutb[74]—became a precious ally of Washington in its battle against "extremism." Qaradawi appeared to be all the more attractive an option in that he maintained close relations with the Brotherhood's official leadership bodies and modernist members alike.

In November 2002, the Qatari government cooperated with the US Brookings Institution to organize a conference in Doha that was inaugurated by the emir in person. Among the participants were Qaradawi and Martin Indyk, vice president of the US think tank and head of its Saban Center for Middle East Policy.[75] Indyk was named to the latter post by the Israeli-American tycoon Haim Saban, a staunch Israel backer who has funded the center named after him since its foundation in 2002. Indyk was US ambassador to Israel in 1995–7, a member of the Clinton administration responsible for Near East affairs from 1997 to 1999, and again ambassador to Israel in 2000–1. Also taking part in the Doha conference was Martin Kramer, a leading member of the Washington Institute for Near East Policy that Indyk had founded in 1985, when he was working directly for the American Israel Public Affairs Committee (AIPAC), the pro-Israel lobby.

This first initiative eventually led to the creation of a standing forum patterned after the Davos World Economic Forum: the US-Islamic World Forum, a joint venture between Qatar and the Brookings Institution. It has since 2004 run an annual conference in Doha with from 160 to 200 participants, their expenses footed by the Qatari government.[76] The whole US foreign policy elite has put in an appearance at this forum, including VIPs such as ex-president Bill Clinton, Secretary of State Hillary Clinton, former secretary of state Madeleine Albright, the (at the time) commander of CENTCOM David Petraeus, and many others, Turkey's prime minister Recep Erdogan among them. Besides Qaradawi, other prominent leaders of the Muslim Brothers' regional network have attended one or another of the forum's meetings: the Tunisian Rached Ghannouchi (in 2006), the Egyptian Abdel Moneim Aboul-Fotouh (2008), and the Iraqis Fuad al-Rawi (2008) and Anas al-Tikriti (2010).

Two other major developments have strengthened this new orientation. The first was the rise of the AKP, founded a scant month after the 9/11 attacks. The AKP won the November 2002 Turkish parliamentary elections and has been the country's ruling party ever since, with Washington's blessing. Under the AKP, Ankara attaches more importance to its policy toward the Arab world than it has since Mustafa Kemal came to power—so much importance that this new orientation has been dubbed neo-Ottomanism in Turkey. Washington has responded by making Turkey an essential auxiliary in its pursuit of its own regional policy goals—a *political* auxiliary, that is, a role supplementing Turkey's much older role as a military auxiliary.

The second development was the US-led coalition's 2003 invasion of Iraq. The Muslim Brothers had struck an unmistakably refractory pose in 1990, precipitating a break with Riyadh and Washington. They changed their tone this time. For, this time, their fellow organization, the Iraqi Islamic Party, became the main Sunni force collaborating with the occupiers, in marked contrast to the great majority of Iraq's Arab Sunnis in the first years of the occupation. The Iraqi Muslim Brothers sat in the Iraq Governing Council established under the aegis of the Coalition Provisional Authority, the occupation authority headed by Paul Bremer. They then joined a string of collaborationist governments. The Brotherhood's other branches, especially the parent organization in Egypt, carefully refrained from publicly criticizing their Iraqi counterparts. The two men who, one after the other, held the position of general guide in Cairo in this period even declared that they would defer to the judgment of the Brothers in Iraq.[77]

Another major difference with 1990 is noteworthy. The Muslim Brothers' Syrian branch, which had vehemently opposed the first war that Washington had waged on Iraq with the Syrian regime's participation, took a different stance toward the 2003 invasion, since Damascus was now opposed to Washington's intervention. In view of the Bush administration's new hostility to Syria's own Baathist government, allied with Iran, the Syrian Muslim Brothers sought, at present, to establish relations with the United States, as they declared in the new political platform that they adopted in 2004.[78] Again, this position was not publicly criticized by the Brotherhood's other branches.

It was in the general context just sketched that relations between Washington and the Muslim Brothers became appreciably warmer, a development that peaked in 2005. The year before, the Bush administration had updated its 2003 *National Strategy for Combating Terrorism* with an appendix, titled "Muslim World Outreach," that defined a new political strategy toward the Muslim world. A *US News & World Report* journalist revealed the existence of this confidential document, which reflected the views of the new approach's real architect, Condoleezza Rice, then George W. Bush's national security advisor. One key element in the new strategy, the journalist reported, was "to make peace with radical Muslim figures who eschew violence." "At the top of the list: the Muslim Brotherhood," he added.[79] In the United States, this new policy met with opposition from the neoconservatives, who are known to be unconditional supporters of Israel.[80] The European Union, for its part, lost no time bringing its positions into line with Washington's, as usual.

The US feelers sparked a broad debate in the Brotherhood's international organization. It was prolonged in 2005 on the website IslamOnline, sponsored by Qaradawi,[81] and in a number of Arabic media of regional scope. While the organization's Syrian and Moroccan branches, for example, rejoiced at Washington's new approach and announced that they were inclined to give it a positive response, others, such as the Palestinian Hamas—which the Bush administration did not envision contacting in any case, for Israel's sake—voiced their distrust and disapproval. The Egyptian Brothers, for their part, struck a cautious, reticent stance; they avoided public contact with the United States, not only because they found themselves in a political quandary, but also because they feared their own government.[82]

Husam Tammam points to a series of events indicating, in his view, that the Brotherhood had begun to steer a new course in its relations with Washington in 2005.[83] In addition to the attitude adopted by its Iraqi and Syrian branches, discussed above, the Egyptian scholar notes two significant signals put out by the Brothers in November of that year, after the first two rounds of the Egyptian legislative elections had considerably beefed up their parliamentary delegation. The first was the publication in the London *Guardian* of an article by Khairat al-Shatir, who signed it in his capacity as "vice-president of the Muslim Brotherhood in Egypt"; it bore the title "No Need to Be Afraid of Us."[84] The second was a statement that General Guide Mohammed Mahdi Akef made to the Associated Press, in which he promised, on behalf of the Muslim Brothers, to respect all treaties that Egypt had signed with Israel.[85] Besides pointing out these two signs of a shift in position, Tammam cites a news report that appeared in the Egyptian press without eliciting comment or denials from the Brotherhood. The report claimed that the son of Mohamed Morsi, head of the Brothers' parliamentary group from 2000 to 2005 (and future Egyptian president), had declared, when he was arrested, that he was a US citizen and had demanded that the US ambassador be present at his interrogation.

The love affair between Washington and the Muslim Brothers was, however, short-lived. Hamas's victory in the January 2006 Palestinian legislative elections and the Western boycott that ensued, the relative moderation of Hamas's electoral program notwithstanding, poisoned relations between the Brotherhood and the United States. Once again, the organization's Palestinian branch turned out to be, because of Israel, the chief obstacle to a rapprochement between the Brothers and Washington. Their relationship deteriorated further when Israel attacked Lebanon that summer, and again when Washington supported Mahmoud Abbas's Palestinian Authority in its conflict with Hamas.

Capitalizing on the situation, Mubarak seized on a flimsy pretext to launch, in 2006, a vast wave of arrests in the Brotherhood's ranks. Only when Barack Obama took office was there a new thaw in relations between Washington and the Brothers. Yet it was not until the 2011 "Arab Spring" that signs of a radical turnabout in their relationship began to appear. Only then did the mediation between the two parties undertaken by the emir of Qatar, thanks to his costly sponsorship of the Brotherhood, pay off big. It proved to be a jackpot far beyond the emir's fondest hopes.

AL JAZEERA AND THE UPHEAVAL IN THE ARAB MEDIASCAPE

In taking over the space abandoned by his Saudi rivals, Hamad bin Khalifa Al Thani did not confine himself to accepting US bases in his country and standing godfather to the Muslim Brothers. He chalked up comparable accomplishments in the Arab mediascape. His Saudi neighbors had already constructed a media empire in the region. Its flagships were two Arabic daily newspapers and a group of satellite television networks known as MBC (the Middle East Broadcasting Center), all based in London. The MBC television networks were basically entertainment-oriented.[86] Another Saudi communications firm had tried to add a satellite news network to the group by working with the BBC to create an Arabic version of the British network. The undertaking soon folded because Saudi program content requirements were incompatible with the BBC programmers' need for freedom in this domain, the basic condition for the venerable British institution's credibility.

The emir jumped at the opportunity. In 1998, he made the spectacular announcement that official censorship had been abolished on his peninsula. He was perfectly well aware that, for well-paid employees with limited rights, the prospect of dismissal would suffice to impose a seamless self-censorship tailored to their employers' needs. After all, is this not how private and even public mass media work in democratic countries as well? The 24-hour satellite television news network Al Jazeera had gone into operation in 1996. Privately owned, in theory, by a mixed enterprise, it is in fact wholly dependent on the Qatari state, that is, on the emir, who uses state funds to subsidize it. It soon became the leading Arabic news network. Mohamed Zayani provides a good summary of the situation:

> If anything, the Emir's media venture corresponds with an interesting global trend favoring a marriage between media ownership and politics. For example . . . Silvio Berlusconi, Italy's Prime Minister, is a pioneer of commercial TV and publishing in Italy. In the Middle East, the Lebanese Prime Minister, business tycoon and media baron Rafiq Al Hariri, owns the satellite channel Future TV. Al Jazeera can be said to epitomize this new trend which is characterized by the politicization of media ownership.
>
> At the same time, Al Jazeera fits in with a deep-seated regional tradition. In the Arab world, the media in general, and satellite channels in particular, operate under a patron who is either the government or some rich owner who in many cases is associated, in one way or another, with the ruling elite or the government. Most television systems in the Arab world are subsidized by the government partly because they need a great deal of money and partly because Arab governments have a stake in the media.[87]

The network incorporated many members of the Muslim Brotherhood from a number of different Arab countries into its staff. Its reputation and audience grew, especially after the outbreak of the Second Intifada in September 2000, followed by the 11 September 2001 attacks on the World Trade Center towers and, two years later, the invasion of Iraq. In 2003, a journalist belonging to the Brotherhood, Wadah Khanfar, was even chosen to head the network. Khanfar had been a member of the Jordanian Muslim Brothers and, later, of Hamas's Information Bureau in Sudan.[88] At the same time, the emir took pains to diversify the political makeup of Al Jazeera's staff in the hope of establishing its credibility. The Muslim Brothers who dominated the staff thus found themselves working side by side with Arab nationalists and liberals. In the political domain, the network's journalists had a blank check as far as the Arab states went—with the exception of Qatar, of course, and, albeit to a lesser extent, its Saudi big brother, as well as the other GCC member states.

By providing a forum for the whole spectrum of oppositional forces in Arab countries—Islamic opposition of all stripes, Al-Qaida included, and nationalist, liberal, and even occasionally left-wing opposition—Al Jazeera succeeded in capturing a significant share of the audience interested in politics throughout the region and in the Arabic-speaking diaspora all over the world. Thus it worked a veritable revolution in Arabic news broadcasting, made possible at the technical level by satellite television. It is no exaggeration to say, in Marc Lynch's Habermasian terms, that the network initiated a "structural transformation of the Arab public sphere."[89]

Until Al Jazeera's arrival on the scene, the Arab states had held a monopoly on television news broadcasting in their respective countries. It had of course been possible to watch neighboring countries' broadcast (terrestrial) television programs, especially in border zones; however, respecting an unwritten code, the official networks of Arab regimes, even those at daggers drawn, rarely offered their respective opposition a forum and always ignored opposition movements independent of them. Their own (or their tributaries') contentious discourses had little credibility, in view of their official or semiofficial character. The "news" broadcast by such networks was deadening, like that diffused by all other dictatorships' television channels, which report the leaders' every public act and gesture, dishing up an ersatz for news in hackneyed political jargon.

Transcending all borders, satellite television has helped bring this chapter in mass media history to a close. Attempts to block the spread of satellite dishes were doomed to fail. The Saudi kingdom outlawed them in 1994, when there were fewer than 200,000 on its territory; the number had risen to a million four years later.[90] Al Jazeera, stepping into this new situation with substantial financial means at its disposal,[91] offered Arabic-language news broadcasts comparable in quality to those of its Western counterparts. Measured by the standards of the sterile television channels of the past, very few subjects were taboo. The new network even went so far as to give a broad range of political opponents of the existing Arab regimes a chance to air their views. Millions of viewers saw, for the first time, the faces of opponents of their governments who had been forced into exile. Some even learned for the first time of the existence of these dissidents, their compatriots.

It did not much matter, in Arab viewers' eyes, that Al Jazeera never expressed the least criticism of tiny Qatar: what it did reveal was infinitely more important and concerned incomparably greater numbers of people. The emirate, an eminently artificial state, could afford to take such liberties with most of its Arab counterparts. It had little reason to fear being given a taste of its own medicine in the form of news broadcasts: the potential opposition in Qatar was highly unlikely to take the risk of venting its grievances, whether the dissidents involved were immigrants who could be banished at will or natives susceptible to being locked up and/or stripped of their assets.

In 1998, the Washington Institute for Near East Policy published a perceptive study (a rather rare occurrence in the history of this propaganda mill) of the upheaval underway in the Arab mediascape. Its author, Jon Alterman, estimated that only ten to fifteen percent of Arabs in the Middle East had regular access to satellite television at the time, and that a much tinier minority had access to Internet. Alterman summed up three major transformations then under way:

> First, the efficacy of censorship will decline. With ever-growing amounts of information circulating at increasing speeds and decreasing costs, political systems predicated on restricting the information available to individuals will be sorely tested. . . .
>
> Second, the Arab media are likely to shape the emergence of a new kind of Arab identity in the coming years. New technology allows Arabs across the region and around the world to read, see, and hear the same information at the same time to a degree that is unprecedented. This will have a unifying effect on Arabs within the Arab world, and it may also reintegrate Arabs living in North America and Europe into the Arab intellectual life.
>
> Third, an exponentially expanding amount of information reaching Arab readers and viewers, combined with higher levels of education, will induce large numbers of Arabs to interpret information in new and more sophisticated ways. Governments will have to change how they interact with their citizenry, as on the one hand governments will have lost their monopoly over information, and on the other, they will have an increasingly difficult time convincing their publics to support ill-considered or ill-justified policies.[92]

Since Alterman wrote, there has been a steep rise in the penetration rate of FTA satellite television (free-to-air television, which broadcasts in unencrypted form) in households in Arab countries equipped with a television set. The poorer the offer in local broadcast (or cable) television programming and the stricter the political controls on it, the higher the FTA penetration rate is, where poverty does not hold it down. In 2008, according to a recent study, 89% of the households in Tunisia equipped with television sets had access to satellite television; the corresponding figures were 86% in the Saudi kingdom, 74% in Syria, 64% in Morocco, and 38% in Egypt (where broadcast television programs are more varied and of higher quality than in the other countries of the region, while the population is poorer than in most of them).[93] The number of FTA satellite television channels climbed from 100 in January 2004 to 450 in January 2009 and was estimated at 600 in 2010.[94]

Alterman, highlighting in 1998 what he called the "return of 'Arabism,'" stressed the originality of this new trend when compared with the preceding one, which had begun to wane in the late 1960s: "The 'new Arabism' tends to be Islamic-leaning rather than secular, and it emanates from the Persian Gulf rather than the Levant."[95] The satellite television mediascape fully substantiates this claim. In 2009, among the pan-Arab satellite television networks, religious networks were outnumbered only by general interest networks: there were 45 religious channels as opposed to 32 news channels and a mere 10 educational channels[96]—leaving aside the fact that most of the general interest and news channels offered religious programming as well.

Moreover, the most important Arabic Islamic religious program by far happens to be Al Jazeera's *Al-Shari'a wal-Hayat* (Sharia and life), and the star of the show is none other than Yusuf al-Qaradawi.[97] Launched in 1996, like the network itself, this program brings the sermons and fatwas that Qaradawi formerly delivered on Qatari national television to the pan-Arab mediascape. In the space of a few years, the program has garnered an extraordinarily big audience for programming in this category: estimates run from 35 million to 60 million viewers. Al Jazeera thus added considerably to the preacher's "symbolic capital," as Qaradawi himself is happy to acknowledge: "The benefit of Al Jazeera is that it has increased the size and breadth of my audience wherever they are. . . . Al Jazeera has provided me with millions of viewers; where my audience was once numbered in the thousands or tens of thousands, they are now in the millions."[98]

Lynch, assessing Qaradawi's influence, has rendered a verdict that can also be read as an overall judgment of Al Jazeera:

> Qaradawi may be a democrat but he is not a liberal. His fundamental orientations are to the social Islam of the Muslim Brotherhood and toward spreading a conservative Islamic way of life and way of thinking. While his orientation toward dialogue makes him a powerful proponent of a public sphere, this should not be misread as a commitment to liberal outcomes. For many critics, his pervasive influence on al-Jazeera suggests a wrong turn taken by the new Arab public: a turn away from liberalism and to something more populist, more conservative, more consumed by questions of authenticity and identity.[99]

Conversely, as Mahmoud Al-Sadi has shown,

> the evidence emerging from textual analysis of the channel's political discourse indicates that identification between the channel and the majority of the Arab masses does not signal a substantive, liberational rhetoric. Rather, identification signals a widely used rhetorical strategy that allows Al Jazeera to ultimately deflect the viewers' radicalism and channel it towards nonviolent political ideologies that are conducive to Qatari interests and policies. Furthermore, by indirectly connecting Qatar with the anti-establishment

viewers, Al Jazeera reinvents Qatari autocracy, depicting it as an acceptable form of governance.[100]

Let us add that the network, by profiling itself as a sounding board for criticisms of the US regional policy and for all varieties of Arab anti-Zionism, well and truly served—down to 2011—as the Al Thani dynasty's "supreme alibi in the face of the American grip on Qatar's sovereignty," to cite a phrase coined by René Naba, who knows the region's media well.[101]

Ultimately, Al Jazeera has turned out not only to have made a major contribution toward creating the political conditions for the Arab uprising, and even helping it unfold. The network has also served as the main vehicle for two strands of influence that have been woven together in this uprising, those represented by the Emirate of Qatar and the Muslim Brothers.

CHAPTER 4

Actors and Parameters of the Revolution

Let us return to our point of departure: Marx's thesis that revolutions are generated by the contradiction between the development of productive forces and the existing relations of production. Setting out from that basic thesis, we first established that such a fundamental contradiction does in fact exist in the region whose revolutionary explosion we are analyzing. In the process, we observed how complex the concrete manifestation of this contradiction is: first, by looking closely at the specific modalities of the mode of production holding back the region's development; second, by examining the structural and conjunctural developments as well as the political tendencies, regional and international, that have helped cause the explosion.

That complex tangle of determinations corroborates one of Louis Althusser's main contributions to the development of Marxist theory. Althusser's claim is that the fundamental contradiction defined by Marx is always "overdetermined." He borrows the concept of overdetermination from Freud's *The Interpretation of Dreams*, where it indicates that our dreams result from the convergence of many different determinations originating in various layers of our memory and unconscious.

OVERDETERMINATION AND SUBJECTIVE CONDITIONS

We can reread Althusser's discussion in the light of our exploration of the empirical conditions for the revolutionary break in the Arab region.

The extract that follows has been reduced to the passages in which he states the essence of his argument in the clearest terms. The historical illustration of overdetermination provided in the previous chapters of this book should, moreover, make the passage easier to read:

> If the general contradiction [the contradiction between the productive forces and relations of production] is sufficient to define the situation in which revolution is the "task of the day," it cannot of its own simple, direct power induce a "revolutionary situation," nor a fortiori a situation of revolutionary rupture and the triumph of the revolution. If this contradiction is to become *"active"* in the strongest sense[,] to become a ruptural principle, there must be an accumulation of "circumstances" and "currents" so that whatever their origin and sense . . . they *"fuse"* into a *ruptural unity*: when they produce the result of the immense majority of the popular masses *grouped* in an assault on a regime which its ruling classes are *unable to defend*. [These "circumstances" and "currents"] derive from the relations of production, which are, of course, one of the *terms* of the contradiction, but at the same time its *conditions of existence*; from the superstructures, instances which derive from it, but have their own consistency and effectivity, from the international conjuncture itself, which intervenes as a determination with a specific role to play.[1]
>
> What can this mean but that the apparently simple contradiction is *always overdetermined*?[2]

We have already seen how much the basic contradiction between the development of the productive forces and the relations of production that generates a revolutionary explosion has, in the Arab region, been "overdetermined" by particular historical circumstances and the development of regional political currents, and also by the international conjuncture, which plays a crucial role in this part of the world. We might complete Althusser's thesis by affirming that, in Marx, the basic contradiction between the development of the productive forces and the relations of production is always itself materialized in *specific modalities*, as we have tried to show. The generic essence of this contradiction, in contrast, belongs to the realm of theoretical abstraction.

Overdetermination should not, however, be understood as overdetermination of the revolution's *success*—that is, of the overthrow of the political powers that be and the shattering of what Marx calls, in the 1859 Preface that serves as the point of departure for this book, the "legal and political superstructure." Only the revolutionary explosion is overdetermined. It is overdetermined in the sense that the exacerbation of the structural blockage holding back the development of the productive forces, in combination with local, regional, and international conjunctural factors that contribute to heightening tensions, inevitably culminates in a popular revolt leading to a grave political crisis. If this popular uprising is to set a process of revolutionary change in motion, the rebellious masses must be capable of organizing to that end and acting effectively to achieve it. In other words, the transformation of a rebellious uprising into a revolution necessitates a subjective capacity. This subjective capacity cannot, for its part, be "overdetermined."

Shortly before the first of the passages just cited, Althusser explains overdetermination using 1917 Russia as his example. In his own words, overdetermination had here produced the "*objective conditions*" that Vladimir Lenin grasped in order to "forge its *subjective conditions*, the means of a decisive assault on this weak link in the imperialist chain."[3] Althusser here follows Lenin himself, indirectly citing his conceptualization of the dialectic of the objective and subjective in the revolutionary process. The founder of Bolshevism formulated this problematic in 1915. The passage in which he does so can contribute to our understanding of the Arab uprising and, for this reason, is worth quoting at length:

> To the Marxist it is indisputable that a revolution is impossible without a revolutionary situation; furthermore, it is not every revolutionary situation that leads to revolution. What, generally speaking, are the symptoms of a revolutionary situation? We shall certainly not be mistaken if we indicate the following three major symptoms: (1) when it is impossible for the ruling classes to maintain their rule without any change; when there is a crisis, in one form or another, among the "upper classes," a crisis in the policy of the ruling class, leading to a fissure through which the discontent and indignation of the oppressed classes burst forth. For a revolution to take place, it is usually insufficient for "the lower classes not to want" to live in the old way; it is also necessary that "the upper classes should be unable" to live in the old way; (2) when the suffering and want of the oppressed classes have grown more acute than usual; (3) when, as a consequence of the above causes, there is a considerable increase in the activity of the masses, who uncomplainingly allow themselves to be robbed in "peace time," but, in turbulent times, are drawn both by all the circumstances of the crisis *and by the "upper classes" themselves* into independent historical action.
>
> Without these objective changes, which are independent of the will, not only of individual groups and parties but even of individual classes, a revolution, as a general rule, is impossible. The totality of all these objective changes is called a revolutionary situation. Such a situation existed in 1905 in Russia, and in all revolutionary periods in the West; it also existed in Germany in the [1860s], and in Russia in 1859–61 and 1879–80, although no revolution occurred in these instances. Why was that? It was because it is not every revolutionary situation that gives rise to a revolution; revolu-

tion arises only out of a situation in which the above-mentioned objective changes are accompanied by a subjective change, namely, the ability of the revolutionary *class* to take revolutionary mass action *strong* enough to break (or dislocate) the old government, which never, not even in a period of crisis, "falls," if it is not toppled over.[4]

The three conditions that, according to Lenin, are indicative of a revolutionary situation are clearly present, albeit to varying degrees, in most Arab countries "from the [Atlantic] Ocean to the Gulf," as the Arabic expression goes. For anyone familiar with the situation in the region and possessed of a critical mind, this overdetermined explosion was eminently predictable; and it was, indeed, predicted. In the last few years, many observers warned that eruptions of popular rage might well break out in the Arab countries, like the hunger riots that occurred in Egypt in 1977, Morocco in 1981, Tunisia in 1983–4, and Jordan in 1989 or, again, the 5 October 1988 riots that occurred in Algeria at the height of the social struggles that had since 1980 been multiplying there. It was easiest to predict what would happen in the cases of Egypt and Tunisia, which had been theaters of major social struggles in the past few years.

Let us cite one example among others of these expectations, taken from an article published under the title "Memories of 1977" in the English-language Cairo periodical *Al-Ahram Weekly* on 24 January 2008—that is, exactly three years before the onset of the 25 January 2011 uprising in Egypt.[5] In interviews conducted by the author of the article, both the coordinator of the famous Kefaya protest movement, Abdel-Wahab Elmessiri (who died the year the interview took place), and Ammar Ali Hassan, director of Cairo's Middle East Studies and Research Center, pointed out the similarity between the social tensions of the day and those that had culminated in the January 1977 Bread Riots. Elmessiri even foresaw "a populist uprising in the form of a catharsis that could destroy everything." Hassan thought that Egyptians had been "more politicized" in 1977 but acknowledged that living conditions were "much worse" than they had been then. Elmessiri shared this view, while adding that the populace was in a process of repoliticization. In support of his claim, he pointed to the impressive wave of workers' strikes and the unprecedented strikes by civil servants then occurring in the country.

A few days after the 6 April 2008 general strike, the sociologist Dalal al-Bizri published a premonitory article. After describing the emergence of social struggles and pointing to the intersection between the workers' movement and young Facebook users, al-Bizri concluded with these lines:

> Will the first strike lead to convergence between the protesting groups, of different generations and different class and cultural backgrounds? Is it true that these isolated, ominous facts are precisely "a quantitative accumulation that will culminate in a qualitative change"? How? Will the rage today smoldering among the Egyptians suffice to touch off a long awaited mass movement, one last movement, before the effects of the very limited freedom introduced three years ago fade and disappear? All this—together with everything that is to be found in its margins, or is derived from it, or preceded it—heralds a new Biblical spectacle. Beware, beware of the anger of those who wait patiently. The Egyptians are masters of patience.[6]

A second example comes from Tunisia. After noting tendencies toward depoliticization, encouraged by the regime, the Tunisian dissident Sadri Khiari concluded his remarkable 2003 book on Ben Ali's regime with these very insightful lines about the "upsurge of the impromptu[, which] can touch off unpredictable bifurcations":

> This unexpected event could well come from the street.
>
> For there is an element of the aleatory in every popular movement. The rhythms of political maturation are multiple; they have to do, no doubt, with the differing rhythms of life. . . . Globalization puts Tunisia in an unprecedented tangle of spaces and temporalities. To cite just one example, the progress of technologies of communication and the sudden acceleration in the dissemination of information obviously go part of the way toward explaining the asymmetrical advance in oppositional activism and popular opposition. . . . Combining with the more or less slow, linear rate of formation of a critical public opinion at the national level are other rhythms that are more uneven, uncertain, and advance in leaps and starts. Telescoping ordinary rhythms, these are the rhythms of rage.[7]

Interviewed by the Reuters news agency in June 2008, at a time when popular riots were raging in the governorate of Gafsa in the country's midwest, Ahmed Najib Chebbi, a well-known figure in the opposition to Ben Ali's regime, declared: "This social explosion could very well spread to other regions."[8] He thus anticipated the explosion that broke out in the adjacent governorate of Sidi Bouzid in December 2010, spread to other regions of the country, and led to the overthrow of the dictator Ben Ali on 14 January 2011, less than a month later.

In Syria, Mohammed Jamal Barout, a reformist critic of the regime who was particularly well placed to take the measure of Syria's problems because he had supervised and carried out studies of the country for the UNDP, drew up, in 2005, an alarming balance sheet on the tendencies of the socioeconomic situation in Syria—low economic growth lagging behind population growth, low agricultural growth and industrial regression, a decline in productivity and per capita income—which he concluded with a prophetic warning:

> Should the present situation . . . persist until 2010 . . . the result will be a deepening of the abyss of unemployment and of poverty and the associated woes, with the dislocations and explosions that result from it in predictable fashion; a terrifying deterioration of justice in the distribution of wealth in a culturally diversified society, the cracks in which could be exploited by those who do not have Syria's welfare at heart. . . .
>
> Without going any further into the details of the projected indicators, sectoral or global, we can affirm in no uncertain terms and without the least hesitation that, in the present situation, Syria does not have multiple paths or choices before it. Only two paths remain, with no other options: a total, across-the-board reform—in politics, the economy, the administration, and human development—in conformity with democratic good governance of the political system and society, or catastrophe.[9]

I myself have systematically concluded a course on problems of development in the MENA region that I have been giving at SOAS, University of London, since 2008 by sketching the prospect of a sociopolitical explosion. In my course, I spoke, in this regard, about what I called "the four horsemen of the apocalypse" in the region: the question of development (growth and employment); the question of women's liberation; the question of democracy and basic freedoms; and, finally, the cultural question. I pointed out the role of satellite television and the Internet, and I identified, as the "agencies" of political and social change, the workers' movement, women's movement, and youth movement.

In a July 2009 interview that I gave Mustafa Bassiouny for the Cairo daily *Al-Dustur*, I stressed "the existence of great explosive potential in the [Arab] region" and made the following prognosis: "We are going through a period in which the fundamentalist movement's influence is waning, while a promising workers' movement is developing. It is a transitional period and, although there can be no foregone conclusions here, factors are accumulating that can put Egypt and, consequently, the whole region, on the road to major change."[10] Referring to the same tendencies, I concluded another interview that took place at roughly the same time and was published the following year in the Beirut journal *Al-Adab* with the words:

> This is, for the moment, only a beginning. But it is enough to fill me with some optimism for the first time in more than a quarter of a century, even

if it is a limited, cautious optimism. I have the feeling that we are on the threshold of a historical turning point, that we are near the end of the period that followed the collapse of the nationalist movement and, perhaps, on the verge of a new one.[11]

In sum, it was clear to a number of observers that countries such as Egypt or Tunisia, or even the region as a whole, were on the verge of exploding, and one could even hope that the explosion would lead to a historical shift.[12] However, what no observer could *foresee* with the least assurance, beyond the hope that manifests itself in *prognoses* like those I was led to make, was that the coming explosion would be crowned with success, unlike the explosions of 1977–89 mentioned above. The accumulation of objective conditions for an explosion was more than predictable; it was plain to see. But no one could confidently wager that a confluence of subjective conditions would make it possible for uprisings in (at the time of writing) Tunisia, Egypt, Libya, and, partly, Yemen to topple dictators who had been ensconced in power for decades, thereby transforming each "revolt" into a "revolution" or, rather, into a protracted *revolutionary process*.

The reason it was hard or even impossible to make such a wager was the state of the potential vectors of sociopolitical transformation: in other words, the state of the candidates for the role of the subjective factor in the revolutionary break. Let us review them, beginning with the *organized political forces*. Generally speaking, the political landscape in the Arab region was characterized by the historical attrition of its liberal, Marxist, and nationalist currents. In the liberals' case, this attrition is owing to their faintheartedness and their compromising image as allies of the West, if not of ultrareactionary regimes tied to the West, as many of them have indeed been in the past few decades.

The Marxist currents could marshal impressive forces in certain countries and periods in the latter half of the twentieth century (the Communists in 1950s Syria, Iraq late in the same decade, the Sudan of the 1960s, and the Lebanon of the 1970s, to which we must add the two decades, 1970–90, in which a Marxist force that emerged from the radicalization of the nationalist movement held state power in South Yemen). The general deterioration of these Marxist currents, which became acute after 1990, was due mainly to a combination of two factors: the particularly severe repression to which most were subjected and the pernicious influence that the Soviet Union had on their positions and political practices, an influence so pervasive that they collapsed when the USSR did. The nationalists, for their part, have been discredited as a result of the nationalist governments' bankruptcy and the abhorrent dictatorial practices that we have already had occasion to discuss. Only three regimes with roots in the nationalist movement were still in place on the eve of the Arab uprising, in Algeria, Libya, and Syria. Far from being potential sources of inspiration for revolutionary transformation, they were, rather, perceived as pillars of the established order to be overturned.

As we have already pointed out, the Islamic fundamentalist movement has, from the last quarter of the twentieth century on, established itself as the hegemonic force in the political protest movement on the level of the Arab region as a whole. However, as I suggested in the interview quoted above, the fundamentalist movement's influence had been ebbing in most of the region's countries in the years immediately preceding the 2011 explosion. That movement's most radical fringe had degenerated into a number of terrorist sects. The expansion of the whole constellation of groups around Al-Qaida, which extended and reinforced its regional network after the spectacular 11 September 2001 attacks and succeeded in establishing itself in Iraq's Sunni Arab regions in the wake of the US-led invasion of the country in 2003, was unmistakably brought to an abrupt halt after Al-Qaida's 2006 military defeat. In any event, the fact that Al-Qaida was a terrorist organization made it impossible for it to hoist itself into a position of leadership of a political mass movement. The regional fundamentalist movement's most traditional components, representing the great majority of its adherents, could far more credibly aspire to lead a regional sociopolitical transformation. They, too, however, were losing momentum in the years prior to 2011: although it had seemed, in the 1980s, in the aftermath of the Iranian Revolution, that these organizations were the potential vectors of an upheaval, they now no longer appeared capable of directly threatening the established order.

This was due to a combination of factors: the repression that crushed the fundamentalist movement in Algeria and Tunisia in the 1990s; Lebanese Hezbollah's close alliance with the Syrian dictatorship and its compromising participation in administering Lebanon's corrupt, neoliberal, confessional system; the unappealing regime that Hamas has imposed in the Gaza strip against a backdrop of corruption and the bullying inspired by its religious puritanism, notwithstanding the prestige it has acquired in the national struggle (like Lebanese Hezbollah); the severe crisis of the Iranian regime in 2009, which had a negative impact on the regional fundamentalist movement and put an end to the already waning positive impact of the 1979 Islamic "revolution"; the Muslim Brothers' spinelessness in the face of the Mubarak regime or the Jordanian and Moroccan monarchies, and that of the Al-Wefaq Society in the face of Bahrain's monarchy; the compromising connections between the Syrian Muslim Brothers and Washington or Riyadh, as well as the Iraqi Brotherhood's collaboration with the occupation authorities in Iraq.

In a word, of the region's organized political forces, no current seemed capable of leading a revolutionary transformation basically precipitated by socioeconomic contradictions. This prospect was all the more unlikely for the fact that the most powerful tendency, the fundamentalist movement, is in no sense hostile to neoliberal economic logic. Rather, it contents itself with denouncing corruption from a moralistic standpoint and preaching charity as a substitute for the kind of far-reaching social reform that would satisfy aspirations to social justice.

What *could* be predicted—indeed, this prediction had since the 1970s been commonplace, not to say ho-hum—was that the fundamentalist movement would, for as long as it maintained its hegemonic position in the popular protest movement, be the first to profit from a social explosion in the region. This prognosis was based on the experience of the 1977–89 social riots, in the wake of which Islamic movements had grown rapidly in the countries involved. The consequence was that, in the countries in which these movements had not been preventively repressed, they were finally put down with a savagery proportional to their expansion. It is, in part, for this very reason that it has been clear since the 1990s that the fundamentalist movement would be incapable of initiating a revolutionary upheaval—either because it is objectively not in a position to do so or because it is subjectively averse to taking the risk, for fear of repression, among other reasons.

Thus nothing, as far as the region's organized political forces are concerned, justified the prediction that the long-awaited social explosion would spawn a large-scale political transformation. Political formations, however, are by no means the only potential actors in revolutionary upheavals. No less important are the various components of social movements. I based the hopes evoked above, those I expressed in my courses and interviews, on such movements. Let us go on, then, to examine the "agencies" that I regularly identified as potential vectors of sociopolitical transformation.

THE WORKERS' MOVEMENT AND SOCIAL STRUGGLES

The *workers' movement* has been severely undermined in the Arab region, either by despotic conditions that rule out most manifestations of "civil society" or by the regimentation that official labor unions have imposed on it, standard practice in populist or totalitarian regimes. The only countries in the Arab region in which there exist relatively autonomous workers' movements (with, as a rule, low unionization rates) are Bahrain and Morocco, whose monarchies hold the labor union movement in check with repressive measures, as well as Iraq, Lebanon, and Mauritania, where feeble unions exist. (There are exceptions, such as the Federation of Oil Unions in Iraq). Nevertheless, two countries in the region stand out for their combative workers' movements, although we can point to no independent union movement in their recent history: Tunisia and Egypt.

In *Tunisia*, the Tunisian General Labor Union (known by its French acronym, UGTT) has had a singular history. The only national trade union center in the country, it joined Tunisia's independence struggle and then went on to become the major force of "civil society" that stood up to Habib Bourguiba's Bonapartist state.[13] The UGTT was, however, fiercely repressed after a series of major social confrontations that took place in 1978 and 1983–4. Its leadership was eventually co-opted under Ben Ali and remained under the regime's thumb until his fall. The result has been a dichotomy unique in the Arab world. On the one hand, the confederation's top leaders deferred to the state; the rank and file, on the other, was traversed by class-struggle currents. These currents were in many cases led by activists with a background in the left-wing student movement who managed, despite everything, to win election to the leadership bodies of local, regional, or sectoral unions (teachers' unions in particular).

This state of affairs sui generis has made the UGTT one of the main organized social protest forces in the whole of the Arab region, despite the hammerlock in which the regime held its central leadership. In the past few years, local UGTT activists and officials have often led social struggles in direct opposition to local or federal leaderships. This happened, notably, during the January–July 2008 revolt in the Gafsa mining basin, the biggest social eruption in Tunisia in the last twenty years and more. Adnane Hajji, secretary general of the elementary schoolteachers' union in the city of Redeyef, the stronghold of the revolt, has become the leading figure in a rebellion whose targets include the secretary general of the UGTT's regional leadership body. The latter was a deputy in the Tunisian parliament and a member of the central committee of the misnamed Democratic Constitutional Rally (known by its French acronym, RCD), the party of the dictatorship. He also owns subcontracting firms that, until recently, held a monopoly on recruitment for the Gafsa Phosphate Company. In that capacity, he was to blame for the nepotistic practices that touched off the explosion.[14]

In May 2008, taking the Gafsa demonstrations as their example, young unemployed graduates organized demonstrations in the cities of Magel Bel Abbès and Fériana in the governorate of Kasserine, which borders the governorates of Gafsa and Sidi Bouzid.[15] (An unemployed graduates' association had been created in Tunisia in 2007 on the model of a similar Moroccan association that has been in existence for more than twenty years.) Employment practices similar to the one in Gafsa were at the origin of yet another big mass protest, a February 2010 demonstration of young unemployed graduates in Skhira, a port city in east-central Tunisia. When the authorities tried to repress it, it turned into a riot.[16] UGTT activists were in the vanguard of this struggle, too. They also participated, side by side with unemployed graduates, in riots in Ben Gardane, a city in southeastern Tunisia near the Libyan frontier that is an important center for cross-border petty trade. Here it was the Tunisian authorities' attempt to outlaw this trade that set things off. It mobilized small traders and unemployed youths who themselves often had no prospects other than to engage in petty trade, an activity that falls, for the most part, in the "informal sector."[17]

The accumulation of revolts and struggles just sketched was to reach the point at which the desperate act committed by Mohamed Bouazizi in Sidi Bouzid on 17 December 2010 could spark a new revolt. Beginning in the city, it spread like wildfire through Tunisia's rebellious central region before engulfing the whole country and peaking in the capital.[18] A few months before Bouazizi, on 3 March 2010, another young man in a comparable social situation, Abdesslem Trimech, who made his living selling pancakes from a street-corner stand in the city of Monastir, had set himself ablaze under virtually identical conditions, in a desperate reaction to bullying by the municipal authorities. Two years before that, on 27 May 2008, during protests in Fériana, a young unemployed man had put an end to his days by throwing himself from a utility pole. Each of these acts had provoked expressions of anger, but the situation had not yet reached breaking point.

As Habib Ayeb has quite rightly pointed out,

while Bouazizi's suicide gave a boost to events that accelerated and made possible the rapid end of the dictatorship less than a month later, it would be quite wrong to suggest that the whole process started with this dramatic episode, and thus deny a build-up of a long series of political actions and workers' demands for rights, for example in the workplace and to health services.[19]

In *Egypt*, the Egyptian Trade Union Federation (ETUF) had been, since its creation in 1957, an institution subservient to the Nasserite state, on a model that prevailed in populist dictatorships taking their inspiration from the Soviet model. The ETUF's leaders belonged to the regime's nomenklatura and were members of the ruling party; their mission consisted in controlling and regimenting the working class far more than in defending its interests. The limited, carefully policed political liberalization that took place under Sadat and, later, Mubarak was accompanied by an extensive economic liberalization in the interests of capital and a notorious absence of trade union liberalization in the interests of labor. This provides further refutation of the ideology which has it that neoliberalism and democracy go hand in hand, the historical counterexample of Augusto Pinochet's Chile notwithstanding.[20]

That is why labor struggles in Egypt were for the most part "wildcat" actions that bypassed the official federation, in contrast with the situation in Tunisia, where Ben Ali's iron grip on the UGTT leadership failed to prevent the national trade union center's rank-and-file activists or local union officials from continuing to be deeply involved in social struggles. That was the case, notably, during the 18–19 January 1977 Bread Riots, the biggest social explosion in Egypt between the 26 January 1952 Grand Cairo Fire and the 25 January 2011 uprising. (January would definitely seem to be the month for major popular revolts in Egypt.) These mass riots were triggered and led by textile workers and steelworkers from Hilwan and Shubra al-Khayma.[21]

The brutal repression of the long 1989 Hilwan steel strike rang in a period in which labor struggles subsided. The downturn was accentuated by corporate restructuring and the privatization of public sector companies in the 1990s, developments that were accompanied by increasingly precarious working conditions and massive layoffs disguised as early retirement. The first decade of the new century, in contrast, saw an upsurge in militancy that generated, from 2004 to 2010, the biggest wave of workers' strikes in Egypt's history up until the 2011 uprising. The new wave of strikes was given a big boost by the victorious, widely publicized December 2006 strike of more than 20,000 textile workers in Mahalla (al-Mahalla al-Kubra).[22]

Their victory encouraged other sectors to join the battle.[23] The consequence was a significant escalation in labor conflicts. Real estate tax authority workers conducted another, much publicized, victorious struggle: tens of thousands of them organized sit-ins in several Egyptian cities in autumn 2007, culminating in a spectacular ten-day December sit-in in front of the Cairo office of the Council of Ministers.[24] This had been the first strike by state workers since the beginning of the Nasser era. Organized in exemplary democratic fashion, it led to the creation, in 2008, of the first independent Egyptian trade union in more than half a century, the Real Estate Tax Authority Union. After a hard fight, this union obtained legal recognition in 2009.

The first big increase in the total number of social protests in Egypt (strikes, mass meetings, sit-ins, and demonstrations) occurred in 2004: there were 266 such actions that year, as opposed to 86 the year before. The number leveled off at 202 in 2005 and 222 in 2006, then soared to a high of 765 in 2007. It dipped slightly in 2008, when there were slightly more than 700 protests, and pursued this relative decline in 2009 and 2010, with a concomitant fall in the total number of protestors in comparison with the 2007 peak (around 400,000 in 2007, against fewer than 300,000 in the following years).[25] These were, despite the post-2007 relative decline, impressively high levels of struggle, especially when we consider both the fact that the struggle was pursued in the face of steadily intensifying repression accompanied by massive dismissals, and the limited results of a general strike called for 6 April 2008. That general strike had been organized in solidarity with a new struggle by Mahalla workers. This time, it was severely repressed, yet it succeeded in obtaining promises from the government nonetheless.[26] Shaken by the blow, the workers' struggle eventually managed to regain its momentum.

Thus it can readily be seen that the general uprising set in motion by the events in Sidi Bouzid, Tunisia, in December 2010—both the Tunisian uprising itself and its extension, first to Egypt and then throughout the entire Arab region—did not come out of a clear blue sky. Quite the contrary: its objective conditions of possibility were spawned by a blockage of regional development overdetermined by the whole set of factors and circumstances that we have discussed in previous chapters. The expectation that the situation would explode was, certainly, greatest in the case of Tunisia and Egypt, as a result of the spectacular emergence of broad mass struggles there in the first decade of the present century. In both cases, the workers' movement decisively shaped their development. It was this characteristic of both Tunisia and Egypt—the relative strength of their workers' movement, the vector of mounting social struggles—that made them the "weak links" in the chain of Arab regimes. Other countries in the region, from Bahrain to Morocco, had experienced major working-class and popular struggles in the years preceding 2011; in these countries, however, the workers' movement has not had the same impact as in the two countries that have been the flagships of the regional uprising.

The piling up of objective conditions at the regional level had precipitated mobilizations in other socioeconomic sectors as well, those associated with the modern middle strata. Among them were the liberal professions—lawyers, engineers, physicians—and the related salaried strata, those working in the same professions, but for a salary. Also mobilized were teachers in higher education, journalists, and "white collar" workers (civil servants as well as people employed in commercial and financial services), and even small and medium entrepreneurs. Democratic struggles waged by lawyers, in particular, helped lay the groundwork for the 2011 uprising, in Egypt and Tunisia alike, as well as in other countries in the region. The same holds for the student movement. Throughout the first decade of the new century, political protest movements and mobilizations sprang up among these strata and categories of the population in various countries in the region. The protestors came together around democratic demands as well as in opposition to aggression perpetrated by Israel and the United States.[27] The best known instance is that of Egypt's Kefaya ("Enough!") movement.[28]

Women's movements also belong to the context just mentioned, that of mobilizations involving the middle strata. In the past few years, these women's movements have been the most active in Tunisia and Morocco, where they have also had the greatest impact. The Tunisian Association of Democratic Women, led by the courageous Ahlem Belhaj, has, apart from its feminist activities in the narrow sense, played a vanguard role in the democratic mobilizations against the Ben Ali regime and, consequently, the uprising as well. This may seem only natural, since Tunisia is reputed to be the Arab country in which women enjoy the most advanced status. Yet a women's association has also played an important part in one of the countries in which women's status is the most archaic, Yemen. Here, the organization Women Journalists without Chains (*Sahafiyyat bila Quyud*), founded by Tawakkul Karman, likewise distinguished itself in the democratic battle against the Saleh regime before going on to take an eminent role in sparking the 2011 uprising.[29] (Karman won the Nobel Peace Prize in 2011.) Women's movements in the Arab region are nevertheless beset by a problem that Islah Jad has called their "NGO-isation,"[30] meaning the fact that they have been professionalized in the form of internationally funded nongovernmental organizations (NGOs).

All in all, it may be said that none of the "agencies" described above satisfied the conditions required to bring about a "scale shift" in "transgressive contention," to employ the jargon of political sociology.[31] To put it differently, the state and the nature of the political and social movements we have so far described did not allow observers to predict either that there would be a generalization of the sociopolitical protest movement, the explosion of which was overdetermined, or that it would move in a political direction subversive of the established order. Still less did they authorize the prediction that it would succeed; this held even for the "weak links." What had been lacking was clearly the emergence of "new, self-identified political actors" and/or "innovative collective action."[32] Theoretically, independent self-organization of the workers' movement might have been possible, wherever that movement was objectively strong enough to undertake such self-organization, either by undermining, within the existing workers' organization, leaderships that deferred to the state (as in Tunisia, for example) or by inventing a new form of workers' self-organization in the heat of the action (as in Egypt).

In the contemporary era, we have become so used to the model in which subversive twentieth-century mass movements, whatever their sociopolitical nature, were led by charismatic figures—from Lenin to Hitler, Gandhi, Mao, or Castro to Khomeini—that many took the fact that the subversive Arab movements of 2011 were "leaderless" for an unprecedented historical novelty. Yet from the February 1917 revolution that overthrew Czarism in Russia to the 1989–91 revolutions that overturned the post-Stalinist regimes, there has been no lack of triumphant "leaderless" subversive movements, taking the word "leader" in the individual, charismatic sense. What is more, the paradigmatic revolution par excellence, the French Revolution of 1789, was itself "leaderless" at first (in contrast to its final phases, which differed from the earliest ones in the same sense in which the February and October 1917 Russian revolutions differed from one another).

NEW ACTORS AND NEW INFORMATION AND COMMUNICATIONS TECHNOLOGIES

Despite what has just been said, in both the France of 1789 and the Russia of February 1917 there existed political organizations and institutions, already established or forged in the thick of battle, that came together to provide the uprising with a collective leadership. Such were, in France, the Third Estate within the Estates General, or the political clubs, and, in Russia, the soviets as well as the revolutionary parties. In both cases, organized political forces played a determining role in the course of events. But we have already pointed out the absence, in the Arab region on the eve of 2011, of organized political forces capable of moving popular protest in subversive directions and leading it toward subversive goals. Those who would have liked to couldn't, and those who could have didn't want to.

If a situation of this sort was to be "disinhibited" so as to make it possible for collective protest to go through a "scale shift," the conditions defined by McAdam, Tarrow, and Tilly clearly had to be satisfied:

> By scale shift, we mean a change in the number and level of coordinated contentious actions leading to broader contention involving a wider range of actors and bridging their claims and identities. . . . The vast majority of contentious actions never outgrows the local, categorical, or institutional context in which it first emerges. But in major episodes of contentious politics, almost by definition, at least some degree of scale shift must occur. In all of our cases, we see new incidents following the outbreak of contention; new actors latching onto forms of conflict hazarded by their predecessors; broader claims and identities crystallizing out of the interactions among contestants.[33]

In the Arab uprising, new actors have emerged in a way very similar to the one depicted by the three sociologists: they have seized on new modes of action and established national coordinations by utilizing two different ways of diffusing information—interactive networks and also, for the purpose of establishing new connections between nodes in the protest movement, "brokerage." In question here, more concretely, is the role of youth networks forged through the Internet, improvising "coordinations" for struggles against established regimes and thus playing, in effect, the role of leaders of the uprisings.

Emboldened by the lack of inhibition typical of young people who can still "storm heaven," they have defied repression to this end, drawing on their technical expertise to foil police surveillance. Their determination has been strengthened by the fact that they are the primary victims of the socioeconomic blockage of the Arab region, as we have pointed out, while their access to globalized culture, far better than that of the older generations, makes them singularly intolerant of the cultural misery imposed by their countries' repressive regimes.

That is the subjective factor. There was no foreseeing the role that it effectively fulfilled and continues to fulfill, even if a retrospective reading of the course of events makes it possible, today, to identify the early signs of it.

At the heart of most of the protest movements that together constitute the broad regional uprising, whether in Tunisia, Egypt, Bahrain, Libya (in the first stage of the uprising), or Syria (the Local Coordination Committees) or, again, in the protests in Morocco (the February 20 Movement), we find comparable networks, made up of mostly young people using the whole range of social media (especially Facebook and YouTube and, to a lesser extent, Twitter) to ensure liaison, communication, and coordination as well as to disseminate information.[34] The exceptions to this rule, that is, the countries in which such networks have played a peripheral, not a central, role are those in which poverty levels sharply limit access to the Internet (Iraq, Mauritania, Sudan, Yemen) or organized political forces took control of the protests at a very early stage (Jordan, Mauritania, Yemen).

A number of observations about this phenomenon are called for here, in view of the various and sundry comments on the "Facebook revolution" that it has inspired. Thus it has been said that the prominent role of networks of young Internet users shows that the Arab uprising is being led by the "middle class," if not by the "golden boys" of whom Wael Ghonim is supposedly the archetype. Ghonim is the administrator of the Facebook page "Kulluna Khalid Sa'id" (we are all Khaled Said), named after a young man beaten to death by two plainclothes policemen in Alexandria on 6 June 2010. This tragedy vigorously fanned the anger that the younger generation felt toward the regime, a prelude to the demonstrations held on 25 January 2011, "National Police Day" in Egypt. Ghonim was the first person to call for that demonstration; he thus helped trigger the uprising.

Wael Ghonim certainly is a very affluent young bourgeois: he had settled in Dubai in 2010 in his capacity as Google's head of marketing for the MENA region. He is, however, much less representative of the majority of social media users than Khaled Said, a young man of such modest means that he did not even have an Internet connection of his own. Like the broad masses of young people of modest background, he surfed on the Internet in a cybercafe—such as the one in which he happened to be at the fateful moment when two policemen grabbed him. In fact, a majority of the young members of the social media networks who effectively coordinated the Arab uprising belong to their societies' middle or intermediate strata—which should not be confused with the "middle class." Very many of them are college students or former college students; we have seen how powerfully unemployment has affected these groups.

The ill-defined ideology of most members of these networks is a form of political and cultural liberalism wed to an acute sense of social justice. It is, in some sense, an Arab version of the programmatic "four pillars" defined by the Green Parties when the movement was getting under way in Europe around 1980 (the German Greens were a young, radical movement at the time). Three pillars are common to the Green movement and Arab social media networks: social justice, grassroots democracy, and nonviolence. The Greens' fourth pillar, the ecological principle, is replaced, in the Arab case, by a progressive nationalism opposed to Western and Israeli domination. At the heart of these aspirations is freedom of expression. As Hamid Dabashi puts it,

> they are expanding the public space they form as the modus operandi of the democracy they are demanding; this is not about the creation of an open market economy as the manifestation of democracy as we know it in North America and Western Europe. This does not mean that the uprisings are the work of socialist revolutionaries, but that paramount on the agenda is public space, not private property.[35]

Pace Tariq Ramadan, for whom the "Islamic reference" is the condition and manifestation of a nonaccommodating stance toward the "West" (the Turkish AKP, which Ramadan admires, is the best refutation of his own postulate),[36] the vast majority of these young people belong to a universal "culture" of emancipation. In their own estimation, they have closer affinities with the *indignados* of Spain's public squares than with the Salafists with whom they may have rubbed shoulders in the public squares of Arab towns. The *indignados*, in turn, have identified with them so closely as to find direct inspiration in their struggle.[37] What the great majority of them have in common is the fact that they are victims of the unemployment and insecurity engendered by contemporary capitalism.

By themselves, International Telecommunications Union data on

TABLE 4.1   PERCENTAGE OF INDIVIDUALS USING THE INTERNET (2010)

Algeria	12.5	Oman	62
Bahrain	55	Qatar	81.6
Egypt	30.2	Saudi kingdom	41
Iraq	2.5	Sudan	8
Jordan	27.2	Syria	20.7
Kuwait	61.4	Tunisia	36.8
Lebanon	43.7	UAE	68
Libya	14	West Bank & Gaza	42
Mauritania	4	Yemen	12.4
Morocco	49		

SOURCE: ITU

the percentages of Internet users clearly show that, in most Arab countries, the "Internet population" is by no means limited to young bourgeois. This is indicated by the available data for 2010, that is, the eve of the regional uprising (Table 4.1). These data bear on the proportion of individuals (the "penetration rate") belonging to statistical populations defined in accordance with the rules adopted by each country's competent institutions. For the Arab countries as a whole, according to the same source, the overall proportion of Internet users was 24.5% in 2010. This represents 87 million people, which indicates that the total population is virtually equal to the statistical population.[38]

According to *Arab Social Media Report*, there were 21.4 million Facebook users in Arab countries in December 2010, including 4.6 million in Egypt and 1.8 million in Tunisia (the penetration rate in Tunisia was 17.6%).[39] Seventy-five percent of the region's Facebook users were between fifteen and twenty-nine years of age. Since then, under the impact of events, their number has increased appreciably: in the first quarter of 2011 alone, it rose by around 30%, reaching 27.7 million by early April.[40] Like the television landscape, certainly, but to a lesser extent because it does not require the same financial outlay, the Information and Communication Technologies (ICT) landscape in Arabic is marked by an abundance of religious sites and themes; the frequency of the hits on these sites reflects the degree of "religiosity" of the societies involved. Thus the importance of religious themes in the Egyptian ICT landscape is hardly cause for wonder.[41] The novelty resides, rather, in the relative importance, in the region's overall ICT landscape, of sites and pages reflecting the aspirations just evoked.

The "despotic Arab exception" has done its work: just as it has done much to ensure the enormous success of satellite television in the region, so it also explains why rebellious young people have eagerly availed themselves of this new technology. With its help, they have managed to create antigovernment solidarity networks and exchange "subversive" ideas. Moreover, by developing a "citizen journalism" (in a day and age in which anyone with the right kind of mobile phone can shoot footage and then publish his or her video on the Internet), they have partially compensated for the fact that official media black out important developments in the social struggle or provide distorted information about them.

These networks did not wait until December 2010 to go to work. In Tunisia, for example, such networks relayed news and videos of the 2008 revolt in the Gafsa mining basin. In the same year in Egypt, the April 6 Youth Movement emerged from the same type of networks, which had tried to organize a general strike in solidarity with the Mahalla workers. Sami Ben Gharbia, the founder of Nawaat, a Tunisian protest site, and a veteran activist in the blogosphere, provided a very good definition of this phenomenon in a remarkable article posted on his site in September 2010:

> The digital activism field in the Arab world forms one of the most decentralized, unstructured, and grassroots oriented dynamics of change that even most of the cyber-savvy local NGOs and opposition parties have a serious trouble in "infiltrating" or exploiting for their own benefit. Consequently, this has made this movement independent, attractive, and resistant to any kind of control. But independence does not necessarily mean disconnection or isolation. Many digital activists in the Arab world do collaborate with opposition parties or movements. Most of these activists are also interconnected with each other; they collaborate during major events and rally to support each other's campaigns and causes. They are connected as well to the global digital activism movement through conference circuits and face-to-face meetings. Add to that the strong networking capability that social networking platforms have integrated in their daily web activity. Digital activists act, react, and interact in a multilayered context of activism that is local, regional, pan-Arab, and global.[42]

Ben Gharbia's formulation is apt: independence, but not disconnection or isolation. There is no denying that "cyber-activism" has played a crucial role in bringing about a "scale shift" in the struggle and transforming it into a general uprising. The new technologies have done much to facilitate and accelerate the creation of networks that repressive measures would otherwise have made it very hard to forge. These technologies have also promoted a form of democratic organization in step with modern times. Pastiching the Marx of *The Poverty of Philosophy*, we might say: "The printing press gives you centralized, hierarchical organization; the Internet, decentralized, egalitarian organization." But it would be quite simply illusory to imagine that "virtual" networks can by themselves organize revolutions. The effectiveness of such networks is directly proportional to the size of the real networks built up in mobilizations on the ground.

Without the intense experience of the struggles that occurred in Tunisia and Egypt in the years preceding the uprising, or the network of political and social movements that were constructed in these struggles and laid the groundwork for the social explosion, or, again, without the connection between "virtual" networks and real networks embodied by activists belonging to both spheres at once, the Tunisian and Egyptian insurrections would not have acquired, in a few short weeks, the extraordinary dimensions that they did acquire until the despots ruling the two countries were overthrown.

The contrast with the uprisings in Libya and Syria speaks volumes. In those two countries, the dictatorships were so harsh and the repression so fierce that they ruled out a Tunisian-style or Egyptian-style cumulative struggle over a space of several years. That is why the protest movements in Libya and Syria proved unable to—indeed, could not have—rapidly become so big and so widespread as to paralyze the Libyan and Syrian dictatorships or, at least, precipitate their disintegration. These dictatorships were accordingly able to bring murderous repression to bear on the protest movements, checking their spread and forcing them to take up arms in self-defense. This happened very quickly in Libya, where repression was, from the first, massive and bloody. It happened at the end of a protracted process in Syria, where the scope of the repression (but not its savagery) increased only gradually, in step with the protest movement itself. Conversely, in Yemen, where "virtual" networks have played a minimal role, real networks—both political and tribal—were responsible for the fact that the anti-Saleh mobilization rapidly pulled in considerable numbers of people. These differences do not explain everything, of course (we will assess other factors below), but they do nevertheless constitute one significant aspect of the problem.

Jillian York, an active defender of freedom of electronic expression, provides a very good summary of the situation in a blog posted in September 2010. It echoes Ben Gharbia's:

Digital activism has been construed as its own movement, a new [way] of organizing unique to the 21st century digital world. In fact, digital tools are complementary to "traditional" activism, for a number of reasons: They allow organizers to quickly mobilize large numbers of people; they help draw media attention to causes, and quickly; they allow for a centralized portal of information. . . .

Traditional activism is indeed enhanced by digital tools (sometimes greatly), while solely digital activities can be hampered by weak ties. . . .

In other words, "digital activism" alone is fairly useless, but the utilization of digital tools can make traditional activism infinitely stronger.[43]

Writing one year earlier from within the Saudi kingdom, Caryle Murphy concluded a November 2009 article on the Internet's political role in the region with this prophetic remark:

The Middle East is only at the beginning of the digital revolution, which has much more in store for all of us in terms of cyberspace experiences. But the changes that the Internet has already brought to the region in terms of social awareness, information access and grass-roots engagement all suggest that eventually and inevitably it also will usher in a new political world.[44]

The despotic Arab governments only dimly discerned the danger. They cracked down on the region's bloggers and Internet activists with such ferocity that, in August 2010, of the 253 Internet activists subject to repression worldwide, 103, or forty-one percent, were concentrated in the Arab region. These numbers are provided by Sami Ben Gharbia in the article cited above. Gharbia warned against interference by the United States and Europe and denounced the double standard that they applied when, defending basic freedoms, they condemned the repression of Internet users in Iran and China but said not a word about the harsher repression practiced by their Arab allies.[45]

The fact remains that neither governments nor cyberspace experts, neither scholars nor activists on the ground could foresee that the accumulation of the subjective conditions that we have so far inventoried—the experience of social and political struggles, the proliferation of Internet networks, the broadcasting of news on a very wide scale by satellite networks that thereby increase the force of an example a hundredfold—would combine with the exacerbation of the basic contradiction fettering the region's development, and the factors "overdetermining" it in such a way as to trigger a regional revolutionary process, one that, in both cases, overthrew at least two despots at an interval of less than a month. By virtue of its unprecedented nature, the "subjective change" of which Lenin spoke has caught everyone by surprise: the change that, in the Arab case, has engendered "the ability of the revolutionary *class* to take revolutionary mass action *strong* enough to 'break' (or dislocate) the old government" and make it "topple over" in certain countries in the region.

STATES AND REVOLUTIONS

The time has perhaps come to point out that there is a big unknown variable in Lenin's formula: How can we determine *which* mass actions are "strong enough" to topple a government? The question is further complicated when we consider that the Russian revolutionary leader indirectly points to *two* thresholds requiring definition: the one that must be crossed if a revolution is to shatter the institutions of the existing state—especially the hard core represented by the armed forces, as Lenin insists more forcefully than anyone else—and the threshold to be crossed by partial revolutions, which topple only a certain fraction of the people in power and "dislocate the old government" by partially reorganizing state institutions without shattering the basic structure of the state itself.

Plainly, if we have no definition of the conditions required for each of these two levels of revolutionary change, Lenin's formula threatens to become tautological: the actions that are "strong enough" are those that succeed in "toppling" the government, while those that are not strong enough are those that do not. To avoid a tautology of that kind, we have to enter into considerations that are much more concrete and complex than those Lenin mentions, considerations that he thought through in his capacity as strategist of the Russian revolution but could hardly take up in the very general, ad hoc remarks that we quoted above.

These considerations have to do with *two different dimensions of the state: its mass base, on the one hand, and its administrative apparatus and armed forces on the other.* These questions are relatively simple in the case of bourgeois democratic states that govern civil societies of the modern type. The picture is infinitely more complex in societies characterized by combined development, in which archaic social structures and categories are conjoined with a modern type of social stratification: archaic forms of domination welded to political institutions of modern inspiration. In one sense, certainly, every society is, to one degree or another, a product of combined development; there exists no society without a history, and none is completely free of survivals from the past. What is meant by combined development, however, goes beyond the pedestrian idea of the historical sedimentation of societies in general. Combined development refers, rather, to the combination of different social logics at the heart of a contemporary economic and/or political system.

Societies that may be considered underdeveloped when measured by the yardstick of capitalist industrialization all fall into the category of societies characterized by combined development. This holds even for those that have arisen from a colonization process that essentially eradicated their native archaic structures, insofar as colonization itself created specific institutions, survivals of which may have combined with ordinary capitalist structures. As for the more traditional survivals traceable to an underdeveloped society's precapitalist past, their importance varies according to the nature of that society's transition to capitalism: it depends on whether the springs of the transition were exogenous or endogenous, and how radical the transformations were in both the cities and the countryside.

The societies of the Arab region are among those that have emerged from a period of long historical stagnation extending into the comparatively recent past. Here the inertia of archaic structures and institutions is pronounced, precisely because they had existed for so long, undergoing relatively limited transformation until the latter half of the twentieth century. Combined development is, therefore, omnipresent in these societies. Even in Algeria, which was subjected to longer, more radical European domination in colonial-settler form than any other country in the region, French colonialism endeavored to assimilate only the "useful" part of the country. (It was Maréchal Hubert Lyautey, resident-general of the French protectorate of Morocco until 1925, who distinguished between "geographical Morocco" and "useful Morocco.")

In the Arab region, the main archaic survivals influencing the nature of political domination and the state are tribalism, sectarianism, and regionalism. These three factors are the legacy of periods antedating the bourgeois age, the characteristic ideology of which is the idea of the nation. They are relics of a past in which kinship and lineage structures were determinant (tribalism), religion was the political ideology par excellence (sectarianism), and the market had yet to unify the areas that were to become the territory subject to state sovereignty (regionalism).

To be sure, unlike ultra-archaic tribalism, which no longer exists in advanced capitalist societies, "sectarianism" survives in Northern Ireland. This "sectarianism" is, however, linked to the persistent anachronism of a colonial relationship in the heart of Western Europe that capitalist development has not succeeded in ending. Elsewhere, "sectarianism" survives, or has reemerged, as an expression of racism, a typical consequence of capitalist economic crisis. Regionalism, in contrast, is ubiquitous. The two modern versions of it found in advanced societies perpetuate its precapitalist forms. It makes itself felt either as a national question (the Basques, the Catalans, and so on) or as a result of unequal capitalist development (demands put forward by underprivileged regions versus the richest regions' "selfish" separatism). These modern dimensions of regionalism exist in the Arab states: the national Kurdish question in Iraq and Syria; the Amazigh "ethnic" question in the countries of the Maghreb, including Libya; regionalism due to socioeconomic factors almost everywhere.

Tribalism and sectarianism, in contrast, continue to perpetuate themselves in the region in their basically archaic forms. Their relative importance varies as a function of how long ago and how thoroughly each society was modernized. Tribalism is widespread, from countries where it forms the backbone of the existing sociopolitical formation, to others that include some provinces exhibiting a "tribalism without tribes," to borrow the term Mohammed Hachemaoui applies to Algeria.[46] As for sectarianism, it is at its height in the region today, wherever societies present a heterogeneous mix of religions and/or religious denominations.

The persistence of these archaic factors explains why Ibn Khaldun's theory of tribal, religious, or regional 'asabiyya (a term usually translated as "esprit de corps") is still considered pertinent, although he formulated it over 600 years ago. Ibn Khaldun argued that the comparative strength of a sociopolitical formation depends on how cohesive it is. In the past few decades, this theory has enjoyed great popularity among political scientists specializing in the Arab region.

The longevity of these factors is in no way due to some "cultural essence": the "Orientalist" explanation is no more valid here than when it is trotted out to justify a supposed incompatibility between Islam and democracy. The Arabs are no more forever doomed to tribalism and sectarianism than were the Europeans of the era of the gentes, Stämme, and tribes of all kinds, or the Europeans of the age of the wars of religion. The persistence of these factors in the Arab region, despite the capitalist transformation of Arab societies, is bound up with the penetration of the institutions specific to capitalism at an already advanced stage of those societies' evolution. Combined development is, quite simply, the product of this contemporaneousness, which explains how agents of modernization, foreign or native, could take advantage of these archaic structures to secure and consolidate their own power. We saw a case in point in discussing the way Western imperialist rule exploited preexisting archaic institutions in the Arabian Peninsula's oil-rich regions.

Another instructive example is provided by the exploitation of the three factors of tribalism, sectarianism, and regionalism in Iraq in the 100 years since the outbreak of World War I. They have been turned to account by, successively, British domination, the Hashemite monarchy, the Baathist dictatorship, and the US occupation authorities.[47] The continuous exploitation of these archaic factors by Iraq's successive governments has prevented their disappearance. They would have persisted even without the profound socioeconomic and cultural regression that Iraq has undergone since 1980, a consequence of the series of wars it has found itself fighting—especially the US-led coalition's devastating 1991 assault on the country and the disastrous twelve-year-long embargo that ensued. Far from gradually disappearing, they have been reinforced over the past few decades.

Basically, these factors affect an aspect of the state that determines the rulers' capacity to resist overthrow from without, which obeys conditions sharply different from those needed to overthrow from within, in "palace revolutions." This aspect is the state's *popular base* (which should be distinguished from its social base as defined in class terms). It goes without saying that wherever state power in an established regime depends on the allegiance that binds one or more tribes, minority religious communities, and/or territorial communities to the ruling group or family—an allegiance the government cultivates by granting all sorts of privileges to the popular minority comprising its special clientele—it becomes much harder to fulfill the conditions for a general uprising of the people.

As Fawwaz Traboulsi has correctly pointed out, one of the functions of the slogan "The people want," omnipresent in the Arab uprising, is plainly to "underscore national identity and popular unity in opposition to all the forms of belonging and identity exploited by despotic governments and external enemies."[48] Yet, except when the government itself alienates its own clientele by failing to satisfy its expectations, it is very hard to overcome that clientele's loyalty to the rulers by appealing to higher interests, whether they are democratic-national or class interests. An uprising by the majority, if it does not somehow meet this challenge, is likely to find itself confronting the hostility of the government's mass clientele, which, in the worst case, will throw in its lot with the regime or even rally to it in the kind of dynamic that culminates in civil war. In the most favorable case, particularly when the balance of forces seems to be overwhelmingly to the regime's disadvantage, that clientele will take refuge in a cautious wait-and-see attitude.

For lack of popular legitimacy—whether it is, in Weber's terms, democratic-legal (but, in that case, the government can by definition be recalled in an election), charismatic (Nasser), or traditional (the Moroccan Alawi dynasty, the only contemporary Arab monarchy that can claim long historical continuity)—the Arab regimes have tended to cultivate tribal, sectarian, and/or regional clienteles as a hedge against the risk of insurrection. In many such regimes, this type of clientele has been the government's backbone.

A glance at the regimes in place on the eve of the Arab uprising reveals that a majority of those with dynastic-familial governments—the Hashemite dynasty in Jordan, the Saudi dynasty in the kingdom of the same name, various monarchies in the other GCC states, Assad in Syria, Saleh in Yemen, Gaddafi in Libya—were based on loyalties of at least one of the types described above. Confronted by the insurgents' "The people want," the established regimes in Bahrain, Libya, Syria, and Yemen reacted by counterposing the will of "*their* people," that is, their tribal, regional, or sectarian clientele, thereby contesting the representative nature of the uprising.

In contrast, despite the existence of a moderate form of regionalism and the survival of a marginal form of tribalism in Tunisia and Egypt, together with a sectarianism that has been exploited to the detriment of Egypt's religious minority, the two flagship countries of the Arab uprising are characterized by a horizontal homogeneity of their social fabric that is much greater than in the countries mentioned above. In Egypt and Tunisia alike, it proved possible—and relatively easy, given the accumulation of protest movements and struggles already discussed—to unite the broad mass of the population in a tidal wave of protest big enough to cost the despised leader the support of much of the dominant class and state apparatus.

In both countries, the uprising was manifestly an "expression of the general will," to borrow a phrase of Rousseauist inspiration from the 1789 *Declaration of the Rights of Man and the Citizen*. Every rational member of the state apparatus not unconditionally loyal to the regime could see that it was pointless—or so risky as to be foolish—to oppose what "the people wanted." This became especially obvious after the great powers that had stood godfather to these regimes took their distance from their protégés, appealing for an "orderly transition" of power at the pinnacle of the state in order to maintain that state's overall cohesiveness.

Something else, however, was required. There had to be a *state apparatus* of which an essential segment, at least, was capable of taking its distance from its central leader. There had to be a state that was not the ruling group's private property, one whose supreme leader could not exercise power in arbitrary fashion because the state had an institutional existence independent of the individuals exercising central authority and was governed on the basis of a minimum of real, not purely fictive, constitutionality. In other words, there had to be, if not a fully fledged legal-bureaucratic state, then, at least, a neopatrimonial state closer to the ideal-typical legal-bureaucratic state than to the ideal-typical patrimonial state.

A decisive difference here has to do with the state's *armed forces*—its *military and paramilitary units* as well as its *police*—which comprise its hard core and main power bastion in critical situations. In patrimonial states, the armed forces' elite units—those that have a level of weaponry and training superior to the other troops' and enjoy various privileges (the air force is usually one such unit)—form the regime's praetorian guard. Their allegiance to the ruling group is truly guaranteed only when they are organically bound to it by ties of the kind that guarantee governments the firm allegiance of a popular base: tribalism, sectarianism, and regionalism.

From this standpoint, there is a big difference between the military-industrial complex of a country such as Egypt, which is more devoted to its own interests than the chief of state's and can therefore distance itself from him, and the "military-tribal complex" of countries such as the GCC monarchies, the Jordanian monarchy, Gaddafi's Libya, or Saleh's Yemen—to use Nazih Ayubi's typology.[49] The allegiance to the state leader displayed by the military-tribal complex or the military-sectarian complex of the kind found in Syria is such that they are willing to go to war against the majority of their country's populace to defend the regime. They know that the fall of the regime will bring the loss of their own privileges, if not the loss of their posts. It might even expose them to sanctions for their past actions in the regime's service.

When the factors already mentioned do not suffice to provide an absolutist patrimonial state with the military force it requires, it often falls back on mercenaries. Gaddafi, for example, recruited mercenaries from Mali, Niger, Sudan, and Chad. The Arab uprising induced the

UAE to follow suit; it hired the services of the founder of Blackwater, the US mercenary company that has earned itself a sorry sort of distinction in Iraq.[50] Although the loyalty of such troops is for sale, they have a big advantage from the rulers' point of view: nothing ties them to the majority of the people in the country, unlike the troops of a conscript army.

Finally, when a patrimonial government is basically a parasitic rentier government, it does not hesitate to hire other states' services to ensure its own protection. The oil monarchies know that they cannot count on the protection of their US sponsor and its Western allies at all times, if only because these countries' rulers are not always free to do as they wish. Hence they have often made use of Pakistani troops, as the Saudi kingdom did in the 1970s and 1980s until US troops returned to the Gulf in force. The Kingdom of Bahrain recently did the same thing.[51]

Similarly, the subsidies that the GCC monarchies grant Egypt have directly to do with the fact that the Egyptian army is an active component of the US military's panoply in the region. The United States finances Egypt's army because it is part of that panoply. The GCC's assumption was that the Egyptian armed forces could intervene to aid the Gulf monarchies more easily than American troops, which might be grounded as a result of US domestic politics. What is more, Egypt's army has an important advantage from the Saudi standpoint: like the Pakistani armed forces, it is made up of "Muslims."

In sum, a mass uprising, however big, stands little chance of peacefully overturning a patrimonial regime that is protected by a praetorian guard with tribal, sectarian, or regional loyalties. To overthrow such a government, an armed confrontation is required—either a general conflict (civil war) or one limited in time and space, depending on the relative weight of the praetorian guard in the armed forces. The state cannot be "reformed," "partially dislocated," or simply rid of its ruling family by peaceful means. Its hard core—its praetorian guard, above all—must be completely shattered by force of arms.

This is the idea to which Carmen Becker gave indirect expression in 2005, in remarkably insightful and premonitory fashion, at the end of an essay on the governmental transition in Syria:

> The personal interests of the PRE [politically relevant elite] are linked to Bashar al-Asad's survival. External pressure can influence regime stability if transmitted by credible local agents with a stable and reliable power base. This, however, is not the case in Syria. The other alternative, in the form of a foreign military campaign, is not in the interest of international advocates

of regime change in Syria, given the Iraqi example just across the border. In case the complex makeup of Syrian society breaks apart without having a new regulating and workable system at hand, the eruption of violence is very likely.[52]

In contrast, when a state has been institutionalized and displays long administrative continuity and a degree of constitutionality, even if it is a neopatrimonial state, a mass uprising can, when it is generalized and does not run up against a tribal, sectarian, or regional division in the population (all these divisions are present in Yemen), overthrow the regime by inducing the better part of the state apparatus to take its distance from the ruling group. Radical social transformation always presupposes, of course, that the state apparatus be completely "broken" so that it can be reorganized from top to bottom. To accomplish that, the uprising has to undermine the armed forces from within, first and foremost by gaining the sympathies of the "ranks," that is, privates and noncommissioned officers.

The parameters analyzed in this chapter map, broadly, the diverse routes charted by the Arab uprising. These routes are not a function of the decision of certain insurgents who, in some cases, ostensibly demonstrated their "wisdom" by limiting themselves to nonviolent struggle (which Barack Obama praised in a lyrical speech occasioned by the Egyptian uprising),[53] whereas, in other cases, they supposedly made the "mistake" of taking up arms, as has often been said in connection with the Libyan and Syrian uprisings.

CHAPTER 5

A Provisional Balance Sheet of the Arab Uprising

This last chapter but one attempts a comparative, cross-sectional analysis of the six major components of the Arab uprising up to the time this present book was completed (October 2012). We shall be looking at the six countries in which the mass movement has attained the proportions of a veritable popular rebellion against the established regime. These countries are, in the order in which their social explosions took place, Tunisia, Egypt, Yemen, Bahrain, Libya, and Syria. Our analysis will be concise, subject as it is to a twofold constraint: the scope of this book and the time available for writing it have been limited by both editorial requirements and the desire to make a timely contribution to the discussion during the uprising itself.

COUPS D'ÉTAT AND REVOLUTIONS

In a book that did much to establish his reputation as a political scientist long before he published his sensationalistic *Clash of Civilizations*, Samuel Huntington distinguishes two basic types of coup d'état. A "breakthrough coup" leads to a breakthrough in the political order and precipitates major social transformations that, as a rule, foster modernization. In a "veto coup," the armed forces set themselves up as guardians of the established order with the intention of calling a halt to a process of radicalization.[1] This very broad classification may be refined with the help of political concepts in general circulation.

Thus we may distinguish *four major categories of coup d'état*, taking our examples here from recent Arab history. *Revolutionary* coups aim radically to transform the political regime and call themselves "revolutions." Examples are the antimonarchical coups in Egypt in 1952, Tunisia in 1957, Iraq in 1958, Yemen in 1962, and Libya in 1969 or, again, the 1969 coup of Nasserite inspiration in Sudan and the 1989 coup of Islamic inspiration in the same country. *Reformist* coups d'état seek to "correct" or "rectify" (*tas'hih*) an established regime without causing radical discontinuity. Examples include the coups led by Houari Boumediene in Algeria in 1965, Ahmed Hassan al-Bakr and Saddam Hussein in Iraq in 1968, Hafez al-Assad in Syria in 1970, and Zine el-Abidine Ben Ali in Tunisia in 1987, as well as the various "palace revolutions" in the oil monarchies. *Conservative* coups come in reaction to political instability and aim to maintain the established order or to reestablish it in a transitional period. Most of the recurrent coups in Mauritania fall into this category. Finally, *reactionary* coups set out to repress a movement for radical change that has come to power or is about to. The 1992 Algerian coup provides an example.

Some have feared that the uprisings in Tunisia and, especially, Egypt might induce reactionary coups. Instead, both countries have witnessed conservative coups staged with Western complicity.

PROVISIONAL BALANCE SHEET NO. 1: TUNISIA

In Tunisia, Chief of Staff of the Land Army General Rachid Ammar refused to order his troops to help put down the uprising. He probably suspected that the fewer than 30,000 men in the army, faced with a rebellion as big as the one that had materialized in the country in the first few days of 2011, were likely to mutiny and fraternize with the popular masses to which most of them belonged, instead of confronting them. The bloody repression of the uprising by paramilitary forces and the police had simply roused people's anger. The UGTT had called for a "rotating" general strike accompanied by mass demonstrations in one region of the country after the next; the demonstrations were to culminate in the capital on 14 January. The lower classes no longer wanted "to live in the old way," and the upper class no longer could.[2]

Ben Ali thereupon proclaimed a state of emergency and entrusted the conduct of operations to the army. Convinced by information communicated to him by both French sources and the head of his presidential guard that a coup d'état was being prepared against him, he decided to play it safe and leave the country. The men occupying the two next highest positions in the state hierarchy, the prime minister and president of the chamber of deputies, were brought by night to the presidential palace *manu militari*.[3] The following day, the coup d'état officially terminating Ben Ali's presidency was completed with the declaration that there was a power vacuum in the country, despite the fact that Ben Ali had ordained that the prime minister should stand in for him. The president of the chamber of deputies was declared interim president of the republic.

The dictator had become too great a liability and had been abandoned by a majority of the Tunisian "power elite." This concept, elaborated by C. Wright Mills, designates the "triangle of power" in control of a state: the triangle constituted by the pinnacles of the military apparatus, political institutions, and capitalist class.[4] Although the concept was elaborated with reference to the United States of the Cold War years, it is even more apt and useful for oligarchic states in the strict sense, which is what virtually all Arab states are. The Tunisian power elite thought that if it got rid of Ben Ali and his wife, along with their inner circle and corrupt familial entourage, it could restore order and go back to business as usual.

The elite was also willing to sacrifice the ruling party (the traditional scapegoat for authoritarian regimes facing situations of this sort), while finding new positions for party members who belonged to the power elite's political faction. Elections were announced, and a transitional government was formed. It was headed by the outgoing prime minister, formerly one of Ben Ali's lackeys, and dominated by ex-members of the ruling party, the RCD. Three UGTT bureaucrats were included in the transitional government to throw sand in people's eyes, along with members of the legal opposition. As a concession, a few measures of political liberalization were adopted.

The elite had seriously underestimated the insurgent masses' determination to rid themselves of everything directly associated with Ben Ali's regime. In short order, the mass movement swung back into action throughout the country to protest this farce. The UGTT leadership, under heavy pressure from the rank and file from the first days of the uprising, had no choice but to call an end to its participation in the government and withdraw its support. A second transitional government was formed less than a fortnight after the first; it included no former members of either the RCD or of Ben Ali's entourage, except for the prime minister himself. Although the liberal parties and the union leadership (itself under great pressure to resign) threw their support behind the new government, the mass movement continued unabated. It demanded the departure of the prime minister himself and succeeded in having the ranking police officials of Ben Ali's regime removed from office.

Posturing by the military and rumors that a coup was in the offing failed to intimidate the mass movement or end the demonstrations. On the contrary: on 27 February, the demonstrations culminated in a tidal wave of popular protest in Tunis. That forced the regime to make more radical changes. The prime minister had to go; he was replaced by a member of Bourguiba's old guard. The outgoing regime's core political and repressive institutions were dissolved: the RCD, parliament, the State Security Department, and the secret police. The groundwork was laid for the election of a constituent assembly, one of the movement's principal demands.

In sum, the political component of the power elite, civilian and police officials alike, as well as members of the ex-dictator's immediate entourage in the power elite's capitalist component, had to be sacrificed in turn or, depending on the individual case, simply swept aside. The aim was to preserve the interests of the rest of the elite—capitalists and army officers alike. The fact that an eighty-four-year-old political "dinosaur" was chosen to head the government provided a clear indication of the bankruptcy of the political component and of the vacuum thus created at the pinnacle of state. The dictatorship had made it impossible to constitute any liberal bourgeois, or even Bourguibist, alternative to the regime.

A Constituent Assembly was elected on 23 October 2011. It proceeded to elect a new president and prime minister, and a new government was formed; thus the political personnel at the highest level of state were completely renewed. This brought the first stage of the Tunisian revolution to an end. Of the old regime's "triangle of power," the bulk of the political faction had been swept offstage, together with the fraction of the "politically determined capitalism" most closely associated with the ex–ruling family. Yet the capitalist class structure that had spawned the social crisis—the state and market bourgeoisies, combined in a neoliberal framework—survived the earthquake. The same is true of the state's repressive hard core, made up of the army plus the main corps of the paramilitary forces: the National Guard, as well as a variety of "brigades."[5]

PROVISIONAL BALANCE SHEET NO. 2: EGYPT

In Egypt, the uprising peaked on 10 and 11 February 2011, when the gigantic rallies and demonstrations intersected with a groundswell of working-class strikes and demonstrations. The whole world followed the former on its television screens, especially the huge rally on Cairo's Tahrir Square, which had become an international symbol of the struggles. The workers' strikes and demonstrations, in contrast, received much less coverage. Yet the weeks running up to 25 January, the day the uprising began, had seen a range of social mobilizations. As one observer rightly notes, "Whether these activities provided the impetus for mass participation in the uprising warrants further investigation, but at least these trends show that many signs of public discontent revolved around redistributive demands immediately before the uprising—[not to say] years before it."[6] The Egyptian government, at any rate, had made no mistake about the importance of the workers' mobilizations: trying to force things back to normal by reopening businesses and factories beginning on 7 February, when the cabinet met for the first time since the uprising, it announced a fifteen percent hike in public sector workers' wages and pensions.

This newfound generosity on the government's part merely encouraged the country's workers to organize yet more strikes and demonstrations. On 9 February, mobilizations spread like wildfire. They brought, by one estimation,[7] more than 300,000 workers together around objectives ranging from social and economic demands, to local demands for the resignation of ministers and directors that the government named to head public enterprises, to support for the universal demand for Mubarak's departure.[8] On 10 February, workers' struggles took on still bigger proportions. The next day, the daily *Al-Masry al-Youm* reported that "a new wave of worker sit-ins, protests, and demonstrations, involving hundreds of thousands, spread through both Cairo and the governorates yesterday. Social demands, demands for raises and better living conditions mingled with calls for political reform."[9] The new wave included a strike in Mahalla by the Misr Spinning and Weaving Company's 24,000 workers, whose victorious 2006 strike had given a powerful boost to the wave of social struggles traversing Egypt at the time. The same day, 10 February, even saw thousands of physicians and lawyers staging demonstrations.[10]

The mass meetings that mobilized millions of demonstrators in Egypt's cities fused with the working-class groundswell, dashing all hopes that, by making economic concessions, the regime could bring things "back to normal" without satisfying the uprising's main demand: Mubarak's departure. The combination of these mobilizations sufficed to convince the better part of Egyptian capitalism—the market bourgeoisie as well as most of the state bourgeoisie (except for the businessmen most closely tied to the Mubarak family), but also the military component of the power elite—that the time had come to get rid of a president who had, like his Tunisian counterpart before him, become too great a liability.

The army has been the backbone of power in Egypt since the revolutionary coup d'état of 1952. It assumed direct leadership of the country under Nasser, assisted by the political apparatus of the single official party. Under Sadat, thanks to the creation of a trilateral power elite with the president himself at its center, the army's role in managing the country's political affairs was reduced. The triangulation of power was made possible by the emergence of a new capitalism comprising the state and market bourgeoisies. It was to flourish under the *infitah* inaugurated by Sadat, himself a member of the military caste who had been named vice president by Nasser in 1969. The Nasserite military-bureaucratic dictatorship had consolidated by nationalizing the economy. It had taken its inspiration from the Soviet model, without going so far as to abolish the private sector. Instead of a fully fledged bureaucratic mode of production of the Soviet sort, the Nasserite government had gradually built up a public sector that became dominant in an economy that maintained avenues of communication between state capitalism and private capitalism.

Sadat, who advocated disengaging the state from the economy, sought to reverse Nasser's "socialist" process by expanding the private sector at the expense of the public sector. Thus he assigned private capitalism a leading role in the management of the country's affairs. To do so, he had to confront and eliminate the highest levels of the Nasserite political apparatus in a "bloodless coup d'état" that he called a "corrective revolution" (*thawrat al-tas'hih*). He then recomposed the political component of the power elite around a new ruling party, the National Democratic Party (NDP). The army supported him for two reasons. First, a segment of the military hierarchy aspired to make new careers in the private sector after years of active service (the officers of 1952 were twenty years older). Second, Sadat pledged not to tamper with the military-industrial complex (MIC) that had emerged under Nasser. The industrial wing of the Egyptian MIC, unlike that of the United States, where the term "military-industrial complex" was coined,[11] is not made up of private firms that supply the armed forces, but is itself owned by the "public" military sector.

Not only was the MIC not privatized; it was also allowed, under Sadat, to offset its declining profitability in the context of the overall liberalization of the economy by converting many military enterprises to nonmilitary production and creating new ones in widely varying sectors of the civilian economy: tourism, light industry, food products, pharmaceuticals, and so on. Thus the Egyptian MIC came to constitute a very peculiar sort of monster: an "economy within the economy," an ensemble of extremely diverse companies representing, today, one-third of the country's total economy on the generally accepted estimate.[12] As Zeinab Abul-Magd notes,

> in 2007, after fifteen years of neoliberal transformations, Mubarak amended the [post-Nasser 1971] constitution to remove Gamal Abdel Nasser's socialist articles.... Meanwhile, between 2004 and 2011, the "government of businessmen" formed by Gamal Mubarak's close circle of tycoons privatized dozens of state-owned enterprises. None of the military businesses were among them. Moreover, retired army officers were placed in prestigious positions (as high administrators and board members) in the privatized companies and factories.[13]

The triangulation of power cleared the way for a notorious intensification of personalized power in Egypt. The state lost the charismatic Bonapartist legitimacy that Nasserite "socialism" had enjoyed, taking on, instead, the character of a neopatrimonial class dictatorship. In 1973, Sadat, eager to promote an image of himself as the "hero of the crossing" [of the Suez Canal], sidelined Saad-Eddin al-Chazly, who had been chief of staff during the October war. This did not at all mean that the army had lost its influence. On the contrary, it underscored its importance. It is precisely because the army is the regime's backbone that Sadat could not let himself be overshadowed by a rival who had risen to prominence in its ranks. Nasser had had similarly strained relations with Abdel Hakim Amer, his defense minister and commander in chief of the armed forces from 1956 to 1967. In the wake of the Six-Day War, Amer was relieved of his duties and arrested on charges of preparing a putsch; he ultimately committed suicide, according to the official account of his death. In 1989, for the same reason, Mubarak got rid of Abdel-Halim Abu Ghazalah, defense minister and commander in chief of the armed forces. In 1991, he confided this post to the chief of the Republican Guard, Hussein Tantawi. Tantawi was nicknamed "the president's poodle" by middle-ranking officers, according to US diplomatic reports made public by WikiLeaks.[14]

The army gave up the direct exercise of political power without ever withdrawing completely from politics: both military men on active duty and reserve officers continued to hold important posts in one government after the next. This partial withdrawal from the political sphere went hand in hand with the development of paramilitary and police forces to deal with the mounting social tensions inevitably engendered by economic liberalization. The army wished to protect its image and had no desire to take a hand in day-to-day repression. It remained, nonetheless, the regime's backbone and hard core, as well as its weapon of last resort against the risk of insurrection—including insurrection by the paramilitary forces themselves, as Lieutenant Colonel Stephen Gotowicki has rightly pointed out:

> In two instances, the military has been called into the streets to respond to a domestic threat which could have endangered the government. The first occasion was the 1977 food riots, which broke out when the Sadat government proposed the elimination of various subsidies that would have raised the price of many common food items. Perhaps reflecting a corporate concern for Egypt's citizens, the Army reputedly refused to intervene in the riots unless the subsidies were reestablished. Sadat restored the subsidies. The second was the uprising of Central Security Force (CSF) conscripts in 1986. The conscripts rioted, setting fire to tourist hotels and nightclubs, when a rumor spread that their mandatory term of service was to be extended from 3 years to 4. Such an extension would have meant a significant hardship, considering that CSF conscripts were paid much less than those in the Army.... The military's performance in these crises has led to the public perception that the army is the ultimate safeguard of the regime. However, despite the effectiveness of the military in these crises, the Ministry of the Interior retains primary responsibility for domestic security.[15]

As in Tunisia, then, the hard core of the Egyptian state came to the conclusion, in early February 2011, that it was fast becoming necessary to jettison the president because he was too heavily compromised in the population's eyes. Its conviction was the stronger in that it was shared by the Egyptian army's financial backer, the United States, which urged the army to act in line with this perception of things (we shall return to this). Because, for reasons of amour propre, Mubarak was little inclined to leave the stage to the public's catcalls, the army went into action in a style highly reminiscent of a conservative coup d'état. The move had the *substance* of a conservative coup as well. On 10 February, the Supreme Council of the Armed Forces (SCAF)—a body that, in time of war or during states of emergency, is convened under the command of the president of the republic, who is also supreme commander of the armed forces—met in Mubarak's absence. Not even Director of General Intelligence Services Omar Suleiman, whom Mubarak had appointed vice president shortly after the uprising began, was present at the meeting.

In the best tradition of the classic military coup d'état, the SCAF issued its "Communiqué No. 1" at the end of this meeting. It was read out by an officer chosen for his theatrical voice. The military men had, as it were, appealed to themselves to arbitrate the situation and had decided to meet permanently until further notice. The tension at the highest level of the state became even clearer when a military source started circulating rumors about Mubarak's imminent resignation, and the president contradicted them in a speech delivered the evening of the same day. He declared that he was determined to remain in office until the end of his term in September, but he simultaneously delegated his powers to Suleiman. This speech merely drove popular frustration and anger to new heights, fanning the flames of the uprising, which was now pursued with greater intensity.

The next day, 11 February, the SCAF released its "Communiqué No. 2," promising political measures that, under ordinary circumstances, would have fallen within the president's prerogative. Thus the SCAF pledged to hold free elections and revoke the state of emergency that had been in force in Egypt since the end of the 1967 War. (Sadat had abrogated it in 1980, but it went back into force 18 months later, in the wake of his October 1981 assassination.) On the evening of 11 February, Hosni Mubarak was evacuated by air with his family, like Ben Ali before him. The difference was that Mubarak, who had a much more acute sense of honor and was sincerely convinced of his legitimacy, refused to leave the country. He was therefore conducted to his seaside residence in Sharm al-Sheikh in the Sinai while Suleiman read a short declaration on television on his behalf, in which Mubarak announced that he had stepped down and had charged the SCAF with "running the country's affairs." To save appearances, the military men even paid homage to their commander in chief after thus "resigning" him.

Mubarak's eviction was much more obviously a coup d'état than its Tunisian precedent; it brought a military junta to power, whereas, in Tunisia, the rudder of state had been handed to the power elite's political component. Yet the Egyptian mass movement distrusted the military less than the Tunisian movement distrusted Ben Ali's successors.

The Tunisian uprising would in all probability have massively rejected an outright putsch that brought the military to power; that is why there was not even a putsch attempt. This difference between the two uprisings reflects the fact that the Tunisian mass movement was more radical: the labor-union left played the leading role in Tunisia, whereas in Egypt, the Muslim Brotherhood constituted the strongest organized tendency. The Brothers, like the majority of the Egyptian mass movement, hailed the military as if they were witnessing a revolutionary coup d'état of the order of the 1952 Free Officers' coup.

Yet what took place in Egypt was quite clearly a conservative coup. The military, after serving notice that it was taking power for six months at most, dissolved the legislature and suspended the constitution. As in Tunisia, the most compromised figures in the political component of the power elite were tossed to the crowd, including the misnamed Ahmed Nazif (*nazif* means "clean"), Mubarak's last (and extraordinarily corrupt) prime minister before the uprising (2004–11). The military likewise sacrificed the most compromised members of the state bourgeoisie to the multitude, notably Ahmed Ezz, who had, moreover, like most of the others, made his fortune thanks to his participation in the political component. Yet it was not long before the mass movement had found its second wind and gone back on the offensive. It now targeted leaders and institutions closely associated with the fallen regime, without calling, as yet, for the military's departure.

Ahmed Shafiq, a man with a military background whom Mubarak had appointed to replace Ahmed Nazif, tendered his resignation in short order. He was replaced by a former minister of Nazif who had broken with the latter in 2005. The local headquarters of the State Security Investigation Service (*Mabahith Amn al-Dawla*) were invaded by demonstrators in various cities in the country, so the institution had to be officially dissolved on 15 March 2011. In reality, however, it was merely renamed Homeland Security (*Qita' al-Amn al-Watani*). The SCAF charged an ad hoc committee, whose members it designated itself, with establishing provisional constitutional articles that were submitted to a referendum and approved by a majority on 19 March. These articles were then integrated into an amended version of the constitution in force since 1971, which the military council promulgated by way of a "constitutional declaration." (This whole procedure would have stood little chance of success in Tunisia, where the election of a constituent assembly had been one of the movement's main demands.) The SCAF, which had from the outset called for an end to what it labeled "corporatist" strikes and social struggles, tried in vain to prohibit them in March, when it had the government adopt a law punishing such actions with prison terms and fines.

The popular movement's opposition to the SCAF grew more radical as the months went by and mass rally succeeded mass rally, compelling the authorities to adopt the movement's demands one after the next. In April, stricter sanctions were imposed on the old regime's political elite; the former ruling party was dissolved and Mubarak and his sons were arrested. They were soon indicted and tried. In October, the SCAF attempted to call a halt to the radicalization of the mass movement and to divert it from its path in particularly reprehensible fashion, by bloodily repressing a demonstration of Christian Copts. The Copts were protesting abuses visited on their community under circumstances that seemed all the more suspicious because it had come to light that similar abuses under the old regime had been orchestrated by the government.[16]

By November, the situation very closely resembled the one that had led to Mubarak's downfall. Bloody repression of rallies and demonstrations spawned bigger rallies and demonstrations, and the SCAF soon found itself with its back to the wall. A government was dismissed and a new prime minister was appointed: Kamal al-Ganzouri, who had already served as prime minister under Mubarak before breaking with the regime in 1999. The parliamentary elections held late the same month and again in December considerably reduced the size of the mass protests. Yet they continued into the early months of 2012, displaying ever more radical opposition to the military.

The two-round presidential election that took place in May and June 2012 ended this first stage of the Egyptian revolution. It had begun with mass rallies calling on Mubarak to resign; it culminated in anti-SCAF meetings protesting the SCAF's attempt to change the rules of the game to its advantage yet again by publishing a new "constitutional declaration" on 18 June, four days after the legislature was dissolved in accordance with the Constitutional Court's recommendation. The demonstrators warned against proclaiming Shafiq president, denouncing him as a representative of the old regime's "debris" (*fulul*). The Muslim Brothers declared that they had carried the election and announced, in advance, that they would reject any other result, which, in their view, could only constitute proof of electoral fraud. Their candidate, Mohamed Morsi, was proclaimed president on 24 June.

In Egypt, as in Tunisia, a broad segment of the political component of the power elite was swept aside, as was the fraction of "politically determined capitalism" most closely affiliated with the former ruling family. The structure of the capitalist class that was to blame for the social explosion—a state bourgeoisie and a market bourgeoisie in a framework of neoliberal inspiration—has nevertheless survived the earthquake. So has the state's repressive hard core: the army and the principal paramilitary corps.

PROVISIONAL BALANCE SHEET NO. 3: YEMEN

The revolutionary contagion from Tunisia infected Yemen—the poorest Arab country after Mauritania—even before it reached Egypt. Yet it was Egypt's example that allowed the Yemeni movement to take on the dimensions of an uprising. Ali Abdallah Saleh, who had observed events in Tunisia, attempted to fend off similar developments in his own country by proposing political reforms. But they fell far short of anything that could have defused the crisis, the more so because, in Yemen as in the other countries, its root causes were and remain socioeconomic.[17]

> Opposition protests began in Yemen's capital, Sana'a, on January 16, 2001. Using social media to organize, and motivated by images of revolt and repression broadcast prominently by Al Jazeera and other satellite television channels, Sana'a's university students comprised the bulk of the demonstrators, though they were led by more seasoned Yemeni democracy activists.[18]

As early as 19 January 2011, Aden—the former capital of South Yemen, the "Arab Cuba" until, exhausted by a civil war, it collapsed along with the Soviet Union and was absorbed by its northern neighbor in 1990—witnessed demonstrations against unemployment and poor living conditions. They were followed by clashes between demonstrators and the police. The next day, similar events occurred in the third biggest city in the country, Ta'izz, an industrial center plagued by heavy unemployment that is, like Aden, situated in the southern part of Yemen (although Ta'izz had not been part of South Yemen). Yemen even had its Mohamed Bouazizi, an unemployed youth who, like Bouazizi, set himself on fire.

Taking their cue from the beginnings of the movement in Egypt, the students and political opposition organized the first big demonstration in Sana'a on 27 January. But it was not until a few days later that the movement acquired the dynamics of an insurrection. Inspired by the 28 January "Friday of rage," the day of the first big jump in size of the Egyptian uprising, a "day of rage" was organized in Yemen on Thursday,

3 February. Tawakkul Karman was among those who had called for it. It was, however, only on 18 February that the country experienced its own "Friday of rage," with demonstrations occurring in several different provinces. As is well known, there were counter-manifestations, too, and violent clashes between the opposing sides. This peculiar feature of the Yemeni case requires explanation.

Of all Arab countries, Yemen is the most archaic. This is owing to its historical isolation, exacerbated by its geography (with the exception of the coastal regions) and dire poverty. Yemen is a country in which society is, for the most part, organized along tribal lines, with the exception of Aden and other urbanized zones in southern Yemen. The electoral constitutional regime established in North Yemen at the end of the civil war in 1970 was punctuated by a coup d'état and the assassination of two presidents before it was stabilized under Ali Abdallah Saleh. Saleh, an army officer who was first elected president by parliament in 1978, has been consistently reelected thereafter—first by parliament and then, from 1999 on, by popular suffrage, in the framework of a presidential personalization of power. The marriage between the parliamentary system and tribalism in Yemen was the stronger in that Saleh exploited this archaic social feature to the hilt to consolidate his neopatrimonial regime. Indeed, the regime's longevity went hand in hand with a tendency toward full-fledged patrimonialization.

The hard core of the Yemeni state is a military-tribal complex, as is true of the other states of the Arabian Peninsula founded on the perpetuation of archaic structures. Yet this structure itself stood in the way of Saleh's ambitions, since it was based, at least to some extent, on a collegial approach that forced the president to come to terms with tribal chiefdoms. Wishing to hand over power to his oldest son Ahmed, Saleh had devoted his efforts, in the past few years, to transforming the armed forces in such a way as to secure his extended family's grip on the command of the military-tribal complex, along the lines of the GCC's patrimonial monarchies. The transformation was even pursued to the detriment of the mighty Hashid tribal confederation, which is led by the powerful Al-Ahmar clan and includes the little tribe, the Sanhan, of which Saleh himself is a member.

The situation was nicely summed up by the *New York Times* a year before the outbreak of the Yemeni uprising:

> Mr. Saleh . . . has been spending less time in the past two years [more than two years, in fact] managing the complicated tribal and regional demands of fragile Yemen than trying to consolidate the power of his family, the ana-

lysts say. As Yemen's oil revenues erode and Mr. Saleh has fewer resources to spread around, the reach of the central government has been shrinking.[19]

Saleh accordingly put his son—a rich and very corrupt man, like most of the sons and other kith and kin of leaders in the rest of the region—at the head of the Republican Guard and the Special Forces, elite units of the Yemeni army. His half brother, who had held these posts before his son, was appointed chief of staff. Another of his half brothers had been commander of the air force for more than twenty years; a third half brother was the commander of the army's first armored division and the northwest military region. Saleh also named three of his nephews to influential posts: one was made head of the Central Security Forces and the Antiterrorist Unit; the second was named chief of the Special Guard, a unit attached to the Republican Guard; and the third was appointed director of National Security. A second circle of military leaders was made up of members of the president's tribe, the Sanhan. To take the full measure of the Yemeni state's patrimonialization, we must add that this organizational structure, rather more military-familial than military-tribal, was completed by a long list of firms belonging to these and other members of the same circles.[20]

This monopolization of military-political and economic power by Ali Abdallah Saleh and his entourage turned the Al-Ahmar family against him, along with most of the Hashid confederation that the Al-Ahmar leads. This constituted, in the last few years, the major Achilles' heel of Saleh's presidency. The "combined development" of politics in Yemen finds conspicuous expression in the fact that the Al-Ahmars also lead the political emanation of the Muslim Brotherhood's Yemeni branch: the Yemeni Congregation for Reform (Al-Islah), founded in 1990. Its tribal component aside, Islah brings together a set of Islamic currents running from Salafists to the modernist Tawakkul Karman.[21] These very peculiar Yemeni realities were to combine with others to produce the extremely heterogeneous constellation of the anti-Saleh opposition, which dominated the movement calling for his resignation.

The Yemeni uprising represented a conjunction of forces that issued from oppositions of all sorts—tribal, regionalist, religious, political, and social. These forces include the Bakil and Hashid tribal confederations, the biggest in the country; an alliance, itself extremely diverse, representing the organized political opposition (*al-Liqa' al-Mushtarak*) and encompassing the Islah party, the Yemeni Socialist Party (the former ruling party of the former People's Democratic Republic of South Yemen), and other nationalist (Baathist, Nasserite) or religious parties; the southern regionalist movement (*al-Hirak al-Janubi*), an alliance of separatist and federalist organizations with origins in the defunct state of South Yemen; the Huthi religious movement, a movement with a Shiite orientation that controls much of the northwestern part of the country and has Iranian support; a radical faction that has come out of the student movement, the Revolutionary Youth; and, finally, an amorphous set of social movements, NGOs, and youth networks.

These diverse forces converged in the uprising against Saleh, who, for his part, mobilized his tribal-political base. The upshot was a kind of "cold civil war" between mass demonstrations and meetings on the two opposed sides. This distinguishes the situation in Yemen from all the others[22]—including those in countries such as Libya and Syria, where established governments prohibited and bloodily repressed all antiregime demonstrations, while themselves organizing support demonstrations in which sincere partisans of the regime rubbed shoulders with a multitude of people demonstrating against their will, as is customary in totalitarian dictatorships. There were increasingly violent confrontations between mobilizations and counter-mobilizations, threatening to engulf Yemen in a veritable civil war. This dynamic was intensified when the division traversing the country appeared in the armed forces as well, such that the country was simultaneously the scene of military clashes and popular rallies.

Two factors, however, prevented civil strife from gaining the upper hand and forced Saleh to step down from the presidency. First, as the weeks went by, his tribal, military, and political base gradually crumbled; the growing patrimonialism of the regime had, in any case, considerably sapped the allegiance of that base in the last few years. Second, the president was heavily pressured to leave office by his Saudi sponsors, who were themselves under pressure from Washington. The GCC's potentates are terrified by the idea that Yemen, a neighbor with a population of more than 25 million, might plunge into civil war; so is the United States, whose fears stem from Al-Qaida's implantation in the country. The Saudis initially sent Saleh reinforcements: on 15 March, a Saudi ship unloaded 35 armored vehicles in Aden, accompanied by a military delegation.[23]

Later, however, the Saudis took a different tack. To forestall a collapse of the Yemeni state, from which both Iran and Al-Qaida could profit—Saleh had allowed Al-Qaida to gain ground in the southern part of the country in the belief that this would induce his sponsors to support him come what may[24]—they persuaded their Yemeni ally to accept an agreement regulating the transfer and redistribution of power. They had understood that to keep him in office at all costs was to risk plunging the country into a chaotic situation that would be very hard to get back under control. In Riyadh, on 23 November, Saleh, who had been critically injured in an assassination attempt, signed the agreement concocted by the GCC.

In exchange for immunity from prosecution for himself and his close collaborators, Saleh agreed to hand power over to ʿAbd Rabbuh Mansur Hadi, his vice president since 1994. A former officer, like Saleh himself, Hadi hailed from South Yemen, where he had served in the armed forces before fleeing to North Yemen in 1986. He formed a government of national unity that included loyalists to the regime (who received, notably, the portfolios for defense, foreign affairs, and oil) as well as the political-tribal opposition, while awaiting his election to a two-year term as the sole candidate in the 21 February 2012 presidential elections that put an official end to Ali Saleh's presidency. The Yemeni parliament voted to grant Saleh the immunity he had demanded. Not only did his son Ahmed remain in his post, but, one month after his father had signed the Riyadh agreement, he purged the Republican Guard of officers who had expressed sympathy for the opposition.

This agreement was a source of great frustration for the rebellion's most progressive political component, the Revolutionary Youth, which demonstrated against it, denouncing the collusion established between Islah and army officers opposed to Saleh in order to abort the Yemeni revolution. The continuity between the Yemeni state and its military-tribal complex had been maintained. The first stage of the Yemeni uprising had simply brought a reshuffling of posts within the Yemeni power elite between the Saleh regime's supporters and opponents. A new constitution is likely to ratify this redistribution of power. It will come by way of new legislative and presidential elections in 2014. The current legislature, controlled by Saleh's partisans, will remain in place until then. Needless to say, the country's socioeconomic structure has not been altered. Even the military-tribal complex at the heart of the state has hardly been shaken up. Only in August 2012 did Hadi muster up the courage to try to relieve Ahmed Saleh of his command of the Republican Guard by assigning his troops to other formations. Even that move sparked armed resistance from units loyal to the former president's son.

Ali Saleh continues to play a direct, central role in Yemeni politics as the leader of the majority party in parliament; his son still commands the Republican Guard, and his nephew is still director of National Security. Of all the victories of the great Arab uprising down to the time of writing, the Yemeni victory has, incontestably, been the most superficial. Not only has the change to which the uprising gave rise left the underlying causes of the explosion intact; it has not even gone far enough to usher in a period of temporary, relative stabilization before the revolution pursues its course—or the country sinks into chaos.

PROVISIONAL BALANCE SHEET NO. 4: BAHRAIN

Bahrain is a patrimonial state of the archaic type common to the Gulf tribal monarchies. It displays, however, a number of specific traits, determined by two features peculiar to the island/archipelago that make it the GCC's "weak link." First, Bahrain is the only Gulf monarchy—and, with Iraq, one of only two Arab countries—in which the absolute majority of the population is Shiite Muslim (around sixty percent in Bahrain, the same percentage as in Iraq). Second, the country is, in relative terms, not as rich in hydrocarbons as its neighbors. The oil rent comprises by far the greatest component of Bahrain's state revenues, yet the country's economy is, overall, better diversified than that of other GCC monarchies; it has a sizable industrial sector (notably an aluminum-producing industry that was founded more than forty years ago) and services of all kinds. The financial sector has been especially successful ever since it was decided to transform the island into a vast, ultraliberal offshore zone serving the whole region.

Because Bahrain's oil rent is relatively modest, its native population, albeit smaller than that of any other GCC state except Qatar, comprised a majority of the total population until 2008,[25] for the Bahraini state cannot afford to transform its subjects into idle rentiers. The fact remains that the tribal Sunni Al Khalifa dynasty, whose dominant position in the country was confirmed under the British protectorate in 1861, has always been a ruling minority facing a native Shiite majority. Moreover, because Bahrain was industrialized relatively early, an authentic organized workers' movement has managed to spring up there. So have oppositional political formations, running from sectarian-religious groups to left-wing organizations.[26] Their development has been fostered by a relatively liberal political climate.

Members of Bahrain's reigning family occupy the key posts in the state and its armed forces. The sectarian character of the government is reflected in the fact that Sunnis form a large majority of the components of the "elite" that is subordinate to the patrimonial state: the upper echelons of the military, political, and administrative hierarchy, as well as the big capitalists. Sunnis likewise compose the rank and file of the security forces and other armed forces, military or paramilitary. The armed forces and security services even include Sunni mercenaries, who come from various Arab countries and also Pakistan. The Bahraini parliament, which has sharply limited powers, compose two chambers, one of which is appointed by the king. In the elected chamber, blatantly unfair gerrymandering ensures that a majority of the deputies are Sunnis. Moreover, the monarchy has attempted to increase the proportion of Sunnis among the country's subjects by naturalizing Sunni immigrants from other Arab countries. By sustaining sectarian tensions, this flagrant discrimination allows the reigning dynasty to give its Sunni subjects the impression that they are privileged, while inculcating in them the fear that they in turn will suffer discrimination, should majority rule ever come about. This fear is naturally fanned by the proximity of Shiite Iran and compounded by the fact that Iran has long claimed sovereignty over the island.

The social inequalities among natives of Bahrain largely coincide with the sectarian divisions in the population: there is a disproportionate number of Sunnis among the rich and of Shiites among the poor and unemployed. Unemployment is an especially acute problem in the country, as a recent International Crisis Group report emphasizes:

> Unemployment, high since the 1990s, has been a major factor generating discontent among Shiites, particularly young working-age men. The government reported 16.5 per cent unemployment at the end of 2010, but according to unofficial estimates the true figure could be as much as 30 per cent. Levels of unemployment and underemployment are disproportionately high among Shiites. . . .
>
> In poorer, mainly Shiite, villages it is not uncommon for streets to be filled with unemployed or under-employed young men, many of whom express eagerness to work but are exasperated at being unable to find jobs that pay a living wage or losing them to foreign workers. Compounding the difficulties and frustrations is the almost total absence of a social safety net.[27]

This highly volatile society could not but join the general uprising that first broke out in Tunisia and was amplified in Egypt. On 14 February 2011, three days after Mubarak was toppled, the first demonstration took place in Bahrain. It had been called by the political opposition and youth networks. It was brutally repressed:[28] one demonstrator was killed and another died the following day at the funeral of the first. From the day of the funeral on, a nonstop popular rally occupied a square in Manama known as the Pearl Roundabout, Bahrain's "Tahrir Square." The monarchy mobilized its Sunni base in a counter-demonstration in an attempt to ensure that the conflict would have a sectarian character.[29] The repression grew fiercer over the next few days. Labor unions and the opposition organized a strike both to protest the repression of the movement and to press social and economic claims; it paralyzed parts of the island on 20 February. State violence only increased the demonstrators' numbers and resolve; their political demands became steadily more radical. Fewer and fewer demonstrators were now satisfied with the demand for a constitutional monarchy and called openly for abolition of the monarchy altogether. On 14 March, the General Federation of Bahraini Trade Unions (GFBTU) issued a call for a general strike. Joined by sixty percent of the workforce, it went on for a week. The strike led to the dismissal of almost 3,000 workers,[30] 300 of them in the oil sector.

The state's troops were overwhelmed by the scope of the uprising, the impact of which was considerably bolstered by the strike. The monarchy reacted by appealing to its fellow GCC monarchies for help. Beginning on 14 March, reinforcements made up primarily of Saudi units of the GCC's joint military force, the "Peninsula Shield Force," were dispatched to the island, which communicates with the Saudi kingdom via the King Fahd Causeway, a sixteen-mile-long string of bridges and dikes built in the early 1980s. A state of emergency was proclaimed. Over the following two months, the Bahraini monarchy intensively recruited mercenaries in Pakistan; in the era of the uprising, the Arab "market" for mercenaries was becoming too risky. According to one estimate, the number of troops in the National Guard and its antiriot division increased by fifty percent as a result.[31]

The popular protest movement was anything but daunted. At the time of writing, it continues to voice its grievances and demands in mass demonstrations. Nothing suggests that it is about to give up and go away, despite deadly repression (around 100 deaths in the eighteen months that have elapsed since 14 February,[32] thousands of injured, hundreds of arrests, and dozens of cases of torture) and the semblance of reforms and inquests staged by the monarchy for the benefit of its Western protectors.

To cope with a deterioration of the situation on the island, the Bahraini and Saudi monarchies, united in their fear of their Shiite populations, have decided to create a two-country "federation" (*ittihad*). The plan was publicly praised and recommended by the preacher of Bahrain's (Sunni) Grand Mosque as a trial balloon on 2 March 2012, less than a year after Peninsula Shield Force troops were stationed in the country.[33] On 14 May, at a GCC summit meeting, the project was officially approved; it was disguised as a first step toward a federation of the six GCC member states. Bahrain's Shiite opposition denounced the projected federation as de facto annexation and organized a massive demonstration to show its rejection of it on Friday, 18 May. The next day, the government orchestrated a demonstration of a few thousand Sunnis in support of the plan.

The main obstacle in the path of the Bahraini revolution—one potentially shared by protest movements in other Gulf monarchies, such as the predominantly working-class and social movement in Oman or the predominantly political movement in Kuwait—resides in the fact that it not only faces the local monarchy, but must square off with the GCC's mammoth, the Saudi kingdom, which will intervene to save its fellow monarchies whenever they are threatened by subversion—until the day when it is itself overwhelmed by a general uprising. Of all the Gulf monarchies, moreover, Bahrain is the reigning Saudi family's main source of anxiety. The island's Shiite majority is not merely the object of very special solicitude on the part of the Al Sauds' sworn enemy, the Islamic Republic of Iran; it is also in direct communication with a part of the Eastern Province of the Saudi kingdom on Bahrain's borders which, like the island, has a majority Shiite population that is also mistreated and oppressed.[34]

PROVISIONAL BALANCE SHEET NO. 5: LIBYA

In his unfinished biography of Stalin, Leon Trotsky remarks:

> "L'État, c'est moi" [I am the State] is almost a liberal formula by comparison with the actualities of Stalin's totalitarian regime. Louis XIV identified himself only with the State. The Popes of Rome identified themselves with both the State and the Church—but only during the epoch of temporal power. The totalitarian state goes far beyond Caesaro-Papism, for it has encompassed the entire economy of the country as well. Stalin can justly say, unlike the Sun King "La Société, c'est moi" [I am Society].[35]

The last phrase is clearly an exaggeration. Stalin was a terrible autocrat, to be sure, but he was, above all, the product of a gigantic bureaucratic apparatus, as Trotsky himself explains better than anyone else.

No Arab monarch could apply Louis XIV's formula to himself, to say nothing of the one Trotsky puts in Stalin's mouth. All Arab monarchs are obligated to respect traditional, religious, and institutional rules that limit their power over their states and societies. What the Saudi monarch can and cannot do, for example, is restricted by the collegial rule of the reigning family, the Wahhabi religious institution, and tribal custom, all the more so as the Saudi king exercises domination of a traditional type. Furthermore, the Saudi state does not encompass the country's entire economy, even if it heavily dominates it. The history books of the future will nevertheless affirm that, of all heads of state in modern times (and not just the Arabs among them), Muammar Gaddafi is the one who best exemplifies the Russian revolutionary's quip. In his case, *La Société, c'est moi* was not far from being a rigorous statement of fact.

Gaddafi took power in 1969 at the head of a revolutionary coup d'état that overthrew the monarchical regime established when Libya gained its independence in 1951. In a few short years, he forged a political regime that was, in Weberian terms, a cross between charismatic rule and absolute patrimonialism. In other words, Gaddafi did not content himself with de facto appropriation of the state and, simultaneously, the country's whole economy, but took the further liberty of radically changing course several times and, in the process, radically revising all of Libyan society's old and new rules as he saw fit, without blanching before the wildest extravagances. "For such is our pleasure," he might well have added, using the ritual formula that the kings of France appended to the bottom of their decrees. In Gaddafi's case, it was a question, rather, of desiderata, for the dictator had so thoroughly suppressed bureaucratic-legal rationality that, from 1979 on, he wielded arbitrary, absolute power in his "state of the masses" (*Jamahiriyya*), although he had no official position apart from his title of "Brother Leader and Guide of the Revolution." Under the same title, he also exercised the function of commander in chief of the armed forces.

Initially, Gaddafi imitated Nasser, like the rest of his colleagues of the Libyan Free Officers. Then, in the early 1970s, he one-upped Sadat's semi-Islamist right turn, decreeing that the Sharia was to replace the laws then in force in Libya. Still later, he took it upon himself to reform the Islamic faith itself. He recast himself as a radical socialist late in the same decade, to the point of imitating the Mao Zedong of the Chinese Cultural Revolution: he appealed to "the masses" to subvert existing institutions and turned out his own version of Mao's *Little Red Book*, the *Green Book*—green being the color of the Islamic banner. The major surge in the country's oil revenues that came with the 1974–5 oil boom had an especially powerful impact on Libya, which has a relatively small population and very big oil revenues: in 2010, this country of 6.6 million inhabitants exported $41.9 billion worth of oil. Contrast Algeria: with its population of 36.3 million, its oil exports netted it $38.3 billion the same year.[36]

This demonstrates, be it noted in passing, the stupidity of the argument put forward by Gaddafi's apologists, who, citing UNDP statistics, ballyhoo the fact that Libya enjoys the highest per capita income in Africa and that its Human Development Index before the uprising ranked it 64th of 187 countries—as if credit for that went to the regime. By the same yardstick, the Saudi kingdom, with four times as many inhabitants as Libya, has a distinctly better regime, because its HDI puts it in 56th place, with a per capita income almost twice Libya's.[37]

The 1970s oil boom raised Libya's state rent to such heights that Gaddafi believed he had been freed of all economic constraint and could simply disregard the rationality of economic calculation. He embarked on an outlandish nationalization campaign that encompassed the country's retail trade and even minor personal services such as hairdressing, persuaded as he was that the oil windfall would enable such an economy to function efficiently. In the process, he carried his totalitarian control of state and society to an extreme. This, naturally, necessitated reorganization of the state apparatus from top to bottom, particularly its armed hard core. (The reorganization was precipitated by coup attempts against his regime, including a military mutiny that commenced in the eastern part of the country in 1980.)[38] Gaddafi partially dismantled the regular army, which was transformed into a poorly trained, poorly equipped "people's army." In addition to mercenaries, he also relied on a network of military, paramilitary, and police apparatuses: various militias, elite forces, and a bloated security apparatus, all headed by members of his family and tribal entourage.[39]

Beyond the power-of-the-masses rhetoric, the reality of the Libyan state has been well described by Dirk Vandewalle:

In the Jamahiriyya, as during the monarchy, two separate sets of institutions retained the monopoly over the use of force: the regular armed forces, and a set of praetorian-guard-like organizations that were responsible for the physical survival of each regime. . . . Resembling the monarchy's earlier efforts to create a praetorian guard for its protection at the expense of a national army, real power was concentrated in a number of security apparatuses that came to dominate the intimate details of Libyans' lives, and of the country's formal political system, after 1969.[40]

As in most oil states, Libya's security sector remains governed in large part by the logic of patrimonialism, is not subject to civilian control, and remains the most privileged of any group inside Libya.[41]

The most important security organization during Gaddafi's reign was the "Leader's Information Office" (*Maktab Ma'lumat al-Qa'id*), at the top of the hierarchy of intelligence and security services. Crowning all these apparatuses and armed units was a coterie made up of Gaddafi's family and close friends as well as members of his tribe (the Qadhadhfa) and associated tribes (the Warfalla and Maqarha).[42] The Revolutionary Guard Corps, which acted as the regime's praetorian guard, was commanded by a cousin of Gaddafi. It comprised men recruited from the Qadhadhfa in the region around Sirte, Gaddafi's hometown, which received preferential treatment under his regime. In the past few years, the "Leader's" sons, now adults, were called on to do their share. Thus the 32nd Reinforced Brigade, the country's main elite armed force, was entrusted to Khamis and henceforth bore his name. As for Mu'tassim, who had also had a military education, he was appointed national security advisor and invested with broad powers.

The rationality of economic calculation recommended itself to Gaddafi's attention in the guise of the consequences of the 1980s "oil glut," the effects of which, exacerbated by US-imposed sanctions, were painfully felt by the Libyans. This inspired the "Leader" to imitate yet another statesman. This time it was Mikhail Gorbachev: Gaddafi aped perestroika and parodied glasnost. The Libyan *infitah*, arriving in a country in which power was exercised so arbitrarily, of course benefited only a "politically determined" capitalism on the periphery of the dominant state capitalism.

Libya's economic liberalization was nevertheless stepped up after the turn of the century. It went hand in hand with the increasing influence of Gaddafi's "reformist" son, Saif al-Islam, who was regarded as the country's de facto prime minister, although, like his father, he had no official functions. In 2008, the now infamous Dominique Strauss-Kahn, then director of the IMF, was pleased to note that his views on the Libyan economy were identical to those of "the Leader of Libya, Colonel Gaddafi," whom he had been "privileged to meet" in Tripoli.[43] In 2010, the IMF warmly congratulated the Libyan government for its "efforts to enhance the role of the private sector in the economy."[44] Neoliberalism is not fussy about who presides over the private sector, as long as it is "private." The adage that money never smells is fundamentally mistaken; it can, in fact, smell very bad indeed. Patrick Haimzadeh has provided an aperçu of the "private sector" in Gaddafi's Libya:

> Clientelism in its classic form has today been replaced by a predatory system centered on Gaddafi's sons and the security apparatus. This principle of familial favoritism now dominates every social domain, as is indicated by the handful of examples that follow, chosen from among the most lucrative fields of activity: red tuna fishing and the Gaddafi foundation for charitable associations (Saif al-Islam Gaddafi); the Adidas import license for Libya and the construction of a ring highway in Tripoli (Saadi Gaddafi); mobile telephones (Mohammad Gaddafi); maritime transport (Hannibal Gaddafi); the charitable association wa'tasimu ('Aisha Gaddafi); pleasure-boat construction (Naval Staff); the great Benghazi River retention pond (Benghazi Security Force Battalion); import-export, construction and civil engineering (battalions of the security forces).[45]

The Libyan military-tribal complex thus acquired another, military-industrial dimension on the Egyptian pattern. Economic liberalization did not, however, temper the ruling family's patrimonialism: the border line between their private property and state property remained eminently blurred. This is attested by the Gaddafis' relationship to the Libyan Investment Authority, a sovereign wealth fund that had been created under Saif Gaddafi's patronage in 2006 and managed tens of billions of petrodollars invested in various countries in extremely opaque fashion.[46] As in Yemen, the ruling family's usurpation and monopolization of political-military and economic power was one of the factors that cost it the allegiance of tribes other than its own Qadhadhfa tribe, as well as that of other members of the power elite excluded from the patrimonial coterie.

From the standpoint of ordinary people in Libya, which is very different from the IMF's, the results of economic liberalization offered considerably less cause for satisfaction. This is nicely summed up in a report issued by the African news agency afrol News on 16 February 2011, the eve of the day Libyans regard as the one on which their revolution began:

> Libya is the richest North African country. Counted in GDP per capita, Libya indeed is on an Eastern European level. But that does not reflect the real economy of the average Libyan, with around half the population falling outside the oil-driven economy. The unemployment rate is at a surprising 30 percent,[47] with youth unemployment estimated at between 40 and 50 percent. This is the highest in North Africa.
> Also other development indicators reveal that little of the petrodollars have been invested in the welfare of Libya's 6.5 million inhabitants.

Education levels are lower than in neighbouring Tunisia, which has little oil, and a surprising 20 percent of Libyans remain illiterate. Also, decent housing is unavailable to most of the disadvantaged half of the population. A generally high price level in Libya puts even more strains on these households.

But the key of popular discontent is the lack of work opportunities. . . . The few options for ordinary Libyans include the police or armed forces, construction works and petty trade. But even here, contacts and corruption are needed to have a chance. But how can this be in such a rich country? The answer is that the Libyan economy is totally driven by the oil sector, and that non-oil developments have focused on Mr Ghaddafi's megalomaniac projects. Both are dominated by foreign workers.[48]

Unemployment levels in general and youth unemployment in particular were higher in Libya than in most countries in the region, including two of Libya's immediate neighbors, Tunisia and Egypt, a fact of which even the IMF eventually took notice.[49] When we add that the Libyans had put up with an unbearable dictatorship for better than forty-one years, there is no reason to be astonished that the revolutionary wave that had already engulfed Libya's two neighbors soon broke over Libya itself. Indeed, it would have been surprising if it had not. Gaddafi himself had had a presentiment of what lay ahead: in a televised declaration made only a day after Ben Ali fled Tunisia, he criticized the Tunisians for getting rid of their president instead of letting him finish his term, declaring that they would not find a better one! There is likewise no reason to be astonished that, in an ultrarepressive country with no tradition of demonstrating against the regime and no authorized political or social organizations other than the state's, demonstrations should promptly have degenerated into skirmishes between demonstrators and the forces of repression or that they should have been accompanied by the multitude's attacks on symbols of power, as has frequently happened in other climes as well.

The Internet networks and the forces of the opposition in exile had from the beginning of February been calling for a "day of rage" set for the 17th of that month. Starting on 15 February, small demonstrations were held in Benghazi to protest the arrest of a human rights activist; demonstrators also took to the streets in other cities in disadvantaged regions. Repression quickly took murderous forms, resulting in more and more deaths daily from 16 February on. By 19 February, three days later, it had already caused between 100 and 200 deaths (estimates vary). Contrary to what had happened when previous Libyan explosions of popular rage were bloodily repressed, this state violence, far from deterring people from pursuing demonstrations, stiffened their resolve to take action. The result was that the number of demonstrators mushroomed. The Tunisian and Egyptian uprisings, which had triumphed despite the long string of protestors felled by the repressive forces' bullets, had served as an example and fueled new hopes throughout the region.

On 20 February, Benghazi, Libya's second biggest city, located in the northeastern part of the country, came under the control of a gigantic tidal wave of demonstrators. At the same time, the number of people killed grew exponentially. In several regions, individual soldiers and regular army units (half the soldiers in the regular army were draftees) rallied to the uprising. Before the week was out, it had spread to most of Libya's regions and cities, including the capital. The insurgents took control of several cities, including Misrata, the third biggest Libyan city, located in the northwest. The regime went to war against the rebels with all the military means it could muster, including armored vehicles and the air force. At the same time, it organized counterdemonstrations in Tripoli designed to show that it enjoyed popular legitimacy. In the Libyan case, these demonstrations brought together both real partisans and involuntary "partisans," in the best tradition of the demonstrations organized by dictatorships. On 27 February, a National Transitional Council (NTC) was formed in Benghazi. The country was now in a situation of *dual power* and *civil war*.

No one who was aware of what Gaddafi and his henchmen were capable of, and aware of the nature of the regime—especially the ruthlessness of its elite troops and mercenary units (reinforcements had been hastily recruited in Mali and Niger at stiff prices)—could harbor the least illusion that the regime might be overthrown relatively peacefully, as in Egypt and Tunisia. The elite units of the armed forces could by no means be expected to leave the ruling family in the lurch: they had been built up on the basis of tribal loyalties and appreciable privileges and were personally commanded by members of the ruling family. Gaddafi, for his part, could by no means be expected to give up without a fight. The man could only be overthrown by force of arms; the ineluctable precondition for his downfall was his military defeat. The only real choice was between civil war and allowing the uprising to be crushed, without fighting back.

Anyone in Libya who was nursing illusions on this score was soon disabused by the speeches of Gaddafi *père* and Gaddafi *fils*. On 20 February, Saif appeared on television to explain to the insurgents, whom he called drug addicts, that Libya was not Tunisia or Egypt and that, if they did not call a halt to their uprising, the consequence would be civil war and the partition of the country. He promised that he and his troops would fight to the last man and would never consent to hand the country over.[50] Two days later, Saif's father upped the ante in an extremely sinister, gruesome speech. The psychopathology of the personage had attained its apogee: he called the insurgents rats and drug addicts, threatening to "cleanse" Libya of such vermin "street by street, house by house." He invoked, among other massacres, those of Tiananmen Square (Beijing, 1989), Falluja (Iraq, 2004), and Gaza (2008–9), insinuating that he would not hesitate to stage the same sort of bloodbath.[51]

In early March, at a time when estimates of the number of those killed varied between at least one thousand and several thousand, the regime launched its elite troops, backed up by armored vehicles and aviation, on a vast offensive to regain control of the eastern part of the country, where the insurrection had its center of gravity. The main objective of the offensive was Benghazi, which had become the capital of the countervailing power. One week later, the campaign was clearly if laboriously gaining ground, and the insurgents began to demand arms and air cover. On 5 March, the NTC concluded its founding manifesto with a declaration of "its absolute rejection of any foreign intervention or military presence," even while calling on "the international community to meet its obligations to protect the Libyan people from the crimes against humanity to which the Libyan people is exposed as a result of the military imbalance between an armed regime and a people without arms."[52]

Over the next few days, the regime's offensive continued to gain ground in the eastern part of the country. On 12 March, the Arab League officially called on the UN Security Council to establish a no-fly zone over Libya. On the 15th, Gaddafi's forces attacked Ajdabiya, the last city on the road to Benghazi, capturing it the following day, while Saif Gaddafi promised that the insurrection would be put down within 48 hours. On 17 March, the Security Council—which had earlier called in vain for a ceasefire—adopted Security Council Resolution 1973, authorizing the creation of a no-fly zone as well as "all necessary measures . . . to protect civilians and civilian populated areas under threat of attack . . . while excluding a foreign occupation force of any kind on any part of Libyan territory."

On the evening of 18 March, Gaddafi's forces reached the outskirts of Benghazi. An invasion of the city was imminent. In response, NATO's and the GCC's aerial forces went into action. The French air force took the initiative of destroying on the ground the armored and transport vehicles that were threatening Benghazi. What happened next is well known: a civil war was fought on the ground in Libya, while NATO and its allies came to the aid of the rebel forces with long-range bombing until an insurrection broke out in Tripoli on 20 August. The insurrection led to the liberation of the capital and finally toppled the regime. Its downfall was an accomplished fact by October, when its last bastions were captured and Gaddafi himself was killed. On 7 July 2012, a General National Congress was elected in pluralist elections, the first such elections in Libya in forty years. One month later, the General National Congress replaced the NTC at the head of the country.

The dynamics of the Libyan uprising, dictated by the nature of the government, make it the only one of the Arab uprisings that, at the time of writing, had completely "broken" the state of the old regime. Comparing the three North African neighbors involved in the 2011 Arab uprising, Eberhard Kienle has observed that it is only in Libya that "the old regime, considered as an apparatus for exercising power, has completely disappeared."[53] This does not mean, however, that the Libyan social structure has been radically overturned.

Libya has, so far, undergone a radical political revolution but not a radical social revolution. The state superstructure and the ideological superstructure have been shattered and the armed forces have been dismantled and replaced by a host of militias formed in the course of the civil war; the changes have been so far-reaching and rapid that the prevailing situation is dangerously chaotic. It is undeniable that the socioeconomic structure has been more thoroughly shaken up than in the other countries of the Arab uprising up until the time of writing, since the patrimonial caste that presided over both state capitalism and private-sector capitalism in Libya, eliminated by the revolution, represented the heavily dominant section of the country's owning class. In Libya, however, as in the other countries of the Arab uprising to date, the economic context of neoliberal inspiration that has arisen from the developments of the past few years has not been altered.

The politically radical nature of the uprising resulted from the fact that the regime could not have been dislodged in any other way. The fact that the uprising was not equally radical at the social level was likewise due to the nature of the regime, which ruled out the accumulation of social struggles and the emergence of autonomous workers' organizations of any kind. That said, private capitalism is much weaker in

Libya than in neighboring countries, while popular demands are more energetic and assertive. The game is not over yet.

PROVISIONAL BALANCE SHEET NO. 6: SYRIA

In Syria, as in Bahrain—notwithstanding the difference between the two countries' political systems, one a tribal monarchy, the other a military-Baathist dictatorship—the government is based on a sectarian minority. Arab Sunnis, an institutionally privileged minority in Bahrain, are a majority in Syria, where they make up more than seventy percent of the total population on the estimate of demographer Youssef Courbage.[54] Syria's Alawite minority, which, again according to Courbage, comprises a little over ten percent of the population, is not institutionally and legally privileged. To codify Alawite privileges in that way, the Assad dynasty's regime would have needed to be even more tyrannical than it already is, given that Alawites represent a much smaller minority in Syria than do Sunnis in Bahrain.

While there is both de facto and de jure sectarian discrimination in Bahrain, the Syrian state is theoretically egalitarian as far as the country's Arab citizens are concerned. (Since the core of the Baath's official ideology is Arab nationalism, this official equality before the law does not extend to Syria's Kurds, many of whom were denied citizenship until the 2011 uprising. The Kurds, a large majority of whom are also Sunnis, constitute a national minority; they are oppressed in Syria, as they are in Turkey and Iran.) Indeed, Hafez al-Assad went so far as to conform to the Sunni faith in public, official practice, so as to accommodate the religious denomination of the majority of the population. The Syrian regime's sectarianism is based, not on religion, but on community, in the sense that the ruling clan, the extended Assad family, bases its power on the Alawite *'asabiyya*[55]—while simultaneously exploiting the various tribal *'asabiyyat* among the Alawites themselves—in order to make sure that it has the allegiance of the state's hard core: the elite troops and the regular army's officer corps.

The preponderance of Alawites among army officers, from noncommissioned officers to the highest levels of the military hierarchy, came about gradually in the course of the 1960s: it was not the result of a premeditated, organized operation, but stemmed from social and political factors that Hanna Batatu has studied in great detail in an excellent book.[56] Thus it precedes the 16 November 1970 reformist coup d'état, known as the "Corrective Movement" (*al-Haraka al-Tas'hihiyya*), in which Hafez al-Assad, then defense minister, seized power, purging the army and Baath party of the radical left faction to which Assad himself had once belonged. His putsch was, moreover, viewed much more positively by Sunnis, especially the Sunni urban bourgeoisie, than by his coreligionists.

The elder Assad was a shrewd Bonaparte—the most Machiavellian leader in contemporary Arab history, in both the positive and pejorative sense of the reference to the author of *The Prince*. He consistently saw to it that he was surrounded by well-placed Sunnis who had a direct interest in maintaining the government's stability for the sake of the material privileges that they derived from it. However, he kept them under his thumb or watched them closely to stifle any intentions they might have to take power for themselves. Among the Sunnis in his entourage were men such as his collaborator and old friend General Mustafa Tlass, army chief of staff at the time of the "Corrective Movement," who contributed to the coup and became Assad's defense minister; Abdel-Halim Khaddam, another old friend, who was Assad's foreign minister until 1984 and vice president thereafter; and Hikmat al-Shihabi, director of military intelligence until 1974, then army chief of staff until 1998.

When, for health reasons, Hafez al-Assad had to give up the active exercise of power for a few months in 1983–4, he created a six-man presidium, all of whose members were Sunnis, to run the country until his return.[57] This was because he knew that these men could never envisage turning against him, since they did not control the armed forces, unlike the ruling group's Alawite members, including Assad's own brother Rifaat. Rifaat fell into disgrace precisely because he had tried to transgress this presidential decision.[58]

It was in 1976–82, the most turbulent period of Assad's reign—both on the regional level and also domestically, since Assad was confronted by a Sunni armed rebellion led by the Muslim Brothers—that, according to Batatu, "Asad's dependence on his kinsmen and the 'Alawite brass and soldiery intensified and became the indispensable safeguard of his paramount power."[59] This development was very clearly reflected in the appointments made while Assad was president:

> Out of the thirty-one officers whom Asad singled out between 1970 and 1997 for prominent or key posts in the armed forces, the elite military units, and the intelligence and security networks, no fewer than nineteen were drawn from his 'Alawite sect, including eight from his own tribe and four others from his wife's tribe; and of the latter twelve, as many as seven from kinsmen closely linked to him by ties of blood or marriage.[60]

Apart from the special regime-shielding military formations, over which they had all along exclusive control, 'Alawite generals commanded in 1973 only two out of the five regular army divisions but in 1985 no fewer than six—and in 1992 as many as seven—out of the nine divisions now constituting Syria's regular army.[61]

The result of the thorough transformation of the Syrian armed forces undertaken by Hafez al-Assad has been described in a report on their current situation drawn up by the private intelligence agency Stratfor. The report paints an edifying picture:

> Syrian Alawites are stacked in the military from both the top and the bottom, keeping the army's mostly Sunni 2nd Division commanders in check. Of the 200,000 career soldiers in the Syrian army, roughly 70 percent are Alawites. Some 80 percent of officers in the army are also believed to be Alawites. The military's most elite division, the Republican Guard, led by the president's younger brother Maher al Assad, is an all-Alawite force. Syria's ground forces are organized in three corps (consisting of combined artillery, armor and mechanized infantry units). Two corps are led by Alawites. . . .
>
> Most of Syria's 300,000 conscripts are Sunnis who complete their two- to three-year compulsory military service and leave the military, though the decline of Syrian agriculture has been forcing more rural Sunnis to remain beyond the compulsory period (a process the regime is tightly monitoring). Even though most of Syria's air force pilots are Sunnis, most ground support crews are Alawites who control logistics, telecommunications and maintenance, thereby preventing potential Sunni air force dissenters from acting unilaterally. Syria's air force intelligence, dominated by Alawites, is one of the strongest intelligence agencies within the security apparatus and has a core function of ensuring that Sunni pilots do not rebel against the regime.[62]

Following Batatu, we may distinguish three echelons of the power pyramid in Syria beneath the all-powerful summit represented by the president himself, the level to which all others are directly subordinate. There is, first, an echelon made up of the heads of the four intelligence and security services: Military Intelligence, Air Force Intelligence, General Security, and Political Security. These are separate, rival institutions, as is usual under paranoid governments. Also part of this echelon are the heads of the regime's praetorian guard, the only troops authorized to set foot in the capital—the Republican Guard (led, in turn, by Assad's three sons, Bassel, Bashar, and finally Maher); the Fourth Armored Division (the former Defense Companies, now under Maher's command); and the Special Forces, such as the army's Fifteenth Division. The Baath party leadership comprises the next echelon of power. The third echelon is made up of members of the government and the high-ranking bureaucrats of the national and provincial administrations.[63]

The Republican Guard is the keystone of this structure and has, consequently, a claim on a share of the state's oil rent. According to information reported by Batatu, "this unit absorbs much of the revenue from the oil fields of the Dayr-az-Zur region—which, incidentally, is in large part not recorded in the country's budget."[64] More generally, people at the top of the military and security hierarchy have been able to accumulate large fortunes under Hafez al-Assad. Their wealth derives, in part, from the development of a military-industrial complex resembling Egypt's, although it is of lesser importance. They have also enriched themselves as obligatory partners of Syria's traditional market bourgeoisie and its state bourgeoisie—both of which have prospered under the regime's gradual *infitah*, the pace of which quickened in the 1990s—but also of Lebanon's market bourgeoisie and Mafiosi in the various business deals and trafficking that flourished thanks to the presence of Syrian troops in Lebanon for the thirty years between 1976 and 2005. Thus it is that a good part of Syria's military hierarchy has itself mutated into a Mafia that preys on the Syrian and Lebanese civilian economies, both licit and illicit.

The Syrian power elite, which was basically military and political in 1970, with a traditional bourgeoisie occupying a subaltern position, has seen its capitalist component expand over the years—the pinnacle of the state bourgeoisie.[65] Bashar al-Assad, after becoming president at his father's death in 2000 in a grotesque succession that provides a textbook illustration of the patrimonialization of power, significantly accelerated the liberalization of the economy. In contrast, he promptly called off the liberalization of politics that he had experimented with in the early phase of his presidency.[66] Neoliberal recipes and the denationalization carried out in an attempt to overcome the economic slump of the 1990s have led to the extremely rapid accumulation of big fortunes in Syria, as everywhere else. Thanks to the total absence of transparency characteristic of the Syrian regime, the new wealth has essentially gone to the Assad clan and its associates, thus completing the patrimonial metamorphosis of power. Bassam Haddad has described this process:

> After Bashar al-Asad succeeded his father in 2000, the architects of Syria's economic policy sought to reverse the downturn by liberalizing the economy further, for instance by reducing state subsidies. Private banks were permitted for the first time in nearly 40 years and a stock market was on the drawing board. . . . Again, the regime had consolidated its alliance with big busi-

ness at the expense of smaller businesses as well as the Syrian majority who depended on the state for services, subsidies and welfare. It had perpetuated cronyism, but dressed it in new garb. Families associated with the regime in one way or another came to dominate the private sector, in addition to exercising considerable control over public economic assets.[67]

This explains how Syria's ruling family, which had traditionally been at the command posts of the military apparatus, came to include the richest man in the country, Rami Makhlouf. Makhlouf is a son worthy of his father, Muhammad Makhlouf. The elder Makhlouf, the brother of Hafez al-Assad's influential wife, amassed a fortune by exploiting his high-ranking posts in the public sector and investing part of the proceeds in the private sector, while simultaneously taking advantage of the precedence in racketeering that came with his status as the reigning family's patriarch number two. Another of Muhammad Makhlouf's sons is one of the heads of General Security, charged with overseeing the capital, while a third is a ranking army officer. A fourth son helps Rami run his business affairs.

Initially, Rami Makhlouf was known above all for being the majority shareholder in the mobile phone company Syriatel. (In this typical sector of extremely corrupt and rapid enrichment, he worked together with two other magnates, the Egyptian Naguib Sawiris and the Lebanese Najib Mikati.) With a personal fortune estimated at $6 billion, Makhlouf owns or controls an impressive list of companies in a wide range of sectors:[68] banking, insurance, oil, industry, real estate, tourism, media, and so on.

Among the shareholders of the holding company Al-Sham, which Makhlouf completely dominates together with other members of his family, are local and émigré Syrian investors as well as owners of capital from the GCC (especially Qatar). The company controls sixty percent of all Syrian economic activity.[69] There are even members of the reigning family who directly combine business with jobs in the security apparatus: Dhul-Himma Shalish, for example, Hafez al-Assad's nephew and the chief of his presidential guard. Shalish is still involved in protecting the security of the Syrian president, his cousin Bashar, and helps direct operations outside the country as well; at the same time, he has, for several years now, been active in the business world and made a fortune in various enterprises, licit or illicit, in Syria, Lebanon, and elsewhere.

The very conspicuous enrichment of members of the ruling family has shaped popular perceptions of the regime in two ways. The presidency of Hafez al-Assad, or so it seemed, was characterized by a division of labor: military and political power was in Alawite hands, while economic power was left to Sunnis.[70] His son broke with this tradition. Under Bashar al-Assad's presidency, the third component of the power elite has come to be concentrated in the hands of an oligarchy belonging to the same Alawite clan.[71] Simultaneously, prominent Sunnis who had been part of the presidential entourage in his father's day were evicted from it. These combined developments have heavily accentuated an image of the regime as a band of usurpers milking the country in the interests of a religious minority. That image has been reinforced by deep suspicions that the Syrian regime played a role in the assassination of Lebanon's former prime minister, Rafic Hariri, a prominent Sunni.

The other consequence of the ruling family's stranglehold on the economy is due to the fact that the Assad clan's enrichment has coincided with a decline in living standards of the broad majority, under the impact of economic policies of neoliberal inspiration.[72] Rural Syria, in particular, long the regime's social base,[73] has been the chief victim of burgeoning unemployment. This has sped up the rural exodus and the growth of the "informal sector,"[74] swelling the ranks of the lumpenproletariat, among other groups. The *shabbiha*, the criminal militias that the regime is now utilizing against the uprising, are recruited from this stratum.[75]

A survey conducted for UNDP and the Syrian government by two Arab social scientists described a socioeconomic situation that is more than alarming. Published in 2005, the study revealed that the gross economic growth rate plummeted by more than half over a ten-year period, while the official unemployment rate more than doubled in the space of twenty years, climbing from 5% to 11.6%, to which must be added a 16.2% underemployment rate. The unemployment rate had reached 24% among young adults between twenty and twenty-four years of age. A large number of people, 11.4% of the population, lived under the lower national poverty line, while 30% lived under the upper line, the majority in rural areas. Finally, inequalities were growing.[76] In 2007, the numbers of the poor increased: 12.3% of the population lived under the lower line that year, 56% of them in the countryside, while 33.6%, equally divided between urban and rural zones, lived under the upper line. On the eve of the uprising,[77] according to official 2011 data, the unemployment rate had reached 14.9% of the total, with rates of 33.7% for those between twenty and twenty-four years of age and 39.3% for those between fifteen and nineteen![78]

The striking contrast between this impoverishment of the population and the enrichment of a clan distinguished by its conspicuous consumption—beginning with the president and his wife, whose lifestyle is a radical departure from the elder Assad's[79]—has heavily exacerbated social frustration. The accentuation of the regime's sectarian character has made the mixture especially explosive. Bashar al-Assad believed he could defuse these tensions by opening the door to the Islamization of Syrian society.[80] In fact, he heightened them.

The dictatorial legitimacy that Hafez al-Assad had been able to sustain in Machiavellian fashion was largely frittered away by his son, despite his efforts to cultivate his popularity by posing as an anti-imperialist. His opposition to the invasion of Iraq in 2003—an invasion to which Sunni Arab public opinion in Syria was even more hostile than Arab public opinion in general—was part of this effort. (It contrasted, be it noted, with the de facto acquiescence of Assad's Iranian allies.) The double game he played in the face of the subsequent occupation of Iraq (he facilitated the infiltration of jihadist Sunnis into the country, to the displeasure of Tehran's Iraqi Shiite allies), like his ostentatious support of Lebanese Hezbollah, moves that were very popular in Syria before the uprising, were ultimately not convincing enough.

Bashar al-Assad, however, was persuaded of the opposite. In the interview that he gave *The Wall Street Journal* in late January 2011, this was the only explanation he could find for the fact that Syria had not yet experienced—would not experience, he thought—an uprising or even demonstrations, as so many other Arab countries already had:

> We have more difficult circumstances than most of the Arab countries but in spite of that Syria is stable. Why? Because you have to be very closely linked to the beliefs of the people. This is the core issue. When there is divergence between your policy and the people's beliefs and interests, you will have this vacuum that creates disturbance. So people do not only live on interests; they also live on beliefs, especially in very ideological areas. Unless you understand the ideological aspect of the region, you cannot understand what is happening.[81]

This was wishful thinking. It was no more surprising than in the case of the other countries discussed here that the revolutionary wave that first arose in Tunisia should eventually reach Syria. Indeed, it was, rather, the relative lateness of the uprising that intrigued observers and spawned considerable conjecture about the supposed Syrian exception, in a way rather reminiscent of the thesis advanced by Bashar al-Assad himself. In reality, the only factor that retarded the explosion was fear of repression. The fact is that none of the other countries of the Arab uprising, not even Libya, had experienced an episode resembling the appalling massacre perpetrated under Hafez al-Assad in February 1982, when the regime's elite troops, commanded by his brother Rifaat, crushed the Muslim Brothers' insurrection in Hama, massacring, depending on the estimates, between 10,000 and 40,000 people in three weeks.[82]

Despite their fears, the Syrians, too, were encouraged by the Tunisian and Egyptian victories as well as the Libyan example and, especially, the worldwide attention that Libya attracted. They realized that the massacre that had been carried out in 1982 in a country closed to the outside world was no longer possible in 2011, in an age in which anyone at all can act as a reporter and send pictures taken with a cell phone camera around the world. The intervention of NATO forces in Libya from 19 March increased the Syrian protesters' courage and confidence: while they did not necessarily count on it being repeated in Syria, they had good reason to believe that this intervention would have a deterrent effect on the regime, ruling out a slaughter of the kind that had occurred in 1982. This calculation was not entirely wrong.

As in most of the other countries in the region, networks of young Internet users took the initiative of organizing the movement. Encouraged by the regional explosion, Syrian social networks started issuing calls to demonstrate in February. Modest gatherings of young and not-so-young people took place in Damascus; in a display of great courage, they expressed their solidarity with the Libyan uprising in hopes of generating a Syrian dynamic.[83] The first big protests of a local nature, however, were motivated by popular discontent in the country's poorest regions, the Kurdish northeast and the south. It was, moreover, a local explosion of popular anger that led to a conflagration in the country as a whole. It occurred in the city of Deraa in southern Syria in early March 2011, in reaction to the arrest of fifteen schoolboys who had scribbled the best-known slogan of the Tunisian uprising on the walls, the slogan that all subsequent uprisings took up: "The people want to overthrow the regime."

The authorities' brutal reaction—the arrest of the schoolchildren, their transfer to a prison in Damascus, and the insulting response served up to their parents, who were given to understand, when they demanded their sons' release, that they would never see them again—provoked an explosion of rage in the populace. It increased tenfold when the adolescents were released bearing marks of barbaric torture on their bodies. As the story spread like wildfire through the country, the demonstrations spread from Deraa to other cities, including the capital, from 15

March onward. The first "Friday" of the Syrian insurrection came on 18 March, baptized the "Friday of dignity" in reaction to the insulting attitude of the Deraa authorities, but also in coordination with the Friday of the same name in Yemen. Bigger and bigger demonstrations were held in several cities; they brought the first deaths due to the repressive forces' bullets. In Deraa itself, the rebellion was transformed into a local uprising.

The dynamic had been set in motion. A steadily increasing number of Syrians began to conquer their fears. People's patience had reached its limits. Escalating its repressive violence, the regime merely stiffened the protesters' resolve, even if it temporarily succeeded in deterring part of the population from joining the movement. As in Libya, and for exactly the same reasons, the protestors' slogans reflected, from the start, their desire to have done with the reign of the Assad family, which had been in power for more than forty years, only one year less than the Gaddafi family. As in Libya, the government organized huge counter-demonstrations in Damascus, mobilizing voluntary partisans and "partisans" despite themselves, so that it could claim that it enjoyed popular legitimacy.

There are, nevertheless, several major differences between the Libyan and Syrian dynamics. It is instructive to compare the two.

The *first difference* is that the Libyan uprising quickly took the form of a generalized explosion in most of the country and its principal cities, whereas the Syrian uprising developed gradually in regions with a Sunni majority, which comprise the better part of the country. It moved from the peripheral rural and semirural zones, the parts of the country hit hardest by poverty and unemployment, toward the big urban centers. In the urban centers themselves, it moved from the peripheral poverty belts toward the downtown areas.

In the first months of the uprising, when it seemed that the movement was confined to the peripheries, it was possible to argue that the commercial and industrial Syrian bourgeoisie supported the regime, whereas the popular strata did not. This division along class lines concerned the Sunni majority alone, the only religious community that did not react en bloc as a sect.[84] Another, more accurate interpretation distinguished between the state bourgeoisie, squarely in the camp of the regime, the source of its wealth, and the "traditional" market bourgeoisie, which had, in its spinelessness, taken refuge in a wait-and-see attitude, its aversion for the regime notwithstanding.[85] To explain the relative immobility of Aleppo and Damascus in the first months of the uprising, one should add that the array of repressive forces mobilized there was far more impressive and dissuasive than elsewhere, since the regime knew that its fate depended on those two metropolises.

Most Alawites backed the regime, some because they themselves or their families were on its payroll, others on sectarian reflex or out of fear of an uprising that the regime's propagandists had from the outset portrayed as the work of Sunni extremists motivated by religious hatred. A majority of Christians (5.3% of the population) and Druze (2%),[86] both susceptible to such propaganda, were favorably disposed toward the regime for this reason; however, they took refuge, as a rule, in a cautious wait-and-see attitude, like the Sunni market bourgeoisie, for they identified much less closely with the regime than the Alawites and were by no means as deeply implicated in its structures.

The *second difference* derives from the first: the Libyan uprising very early succeeded in taking control of the country's major cities, including the second and third biggest. The country was much more quickly divided into two geographic camps than Syria. The very great weakness of all organized political opposition in Libya, a consequence of the regime's despotism, was made up for by the fact that high-ranking state leaders, among them Justice Minister Moustafa Abdel-Jalil and the head of the National Planning Council Mahmoud Jibril, rallied to the insurrection early in the day. With a "capital" in Benghazi, the Libyan insurrection endowed itself with a leadership body on the ground in the form of the NTC. It was made up of men who had broken with the regime during the events, together with a few veteran dissidents and opponents as well as people representative of the country's regional and tribal diversity.

The Syrian uprising, in contrast, was for a long time largely reduced to staging furtive demonstrations, especially at night; bolder demonstrations were fiercely repressed. It was not even capable of taking and maintaining control of big cities such as Hama or Homs, and, after more than eighteen months of struggle, is still not. This limitation is compounded by the weakness of the political opposition organized on the ground, although it is not as weak as the Libyan political opposition was. Indeed, Syrian society is clearly more politicized than Libyan society as a result of its much stormier political history as well as the permanence of the Palestinian factor in all its diversity, thanks to the presence of Palestinian refugees, and the country's osmosis with Lebanon, the region's political agora thanks to the freedoms reigning there. The Assads' regime has intermittently tolerated the existence of opposition groups and currents, which were allowed conditional freedom as long as they posed no real threat to the regime. In the 1970s and again in the first decade of the present century, this held for the left-wing and liberal oppositions, but not for the (Sunni) Islamic opposition, which was regarded as the main threat to the regime, particularly because of the sectarian factor.

The *third difference*, which flows from the second, has to do with the absence of liberated zones and cities, the weakness of the opposition inside the country, and the absence of a significant fracture in the state apparatus capable of compensating for this weakness. These factors have had two important consequences for the leadership of the Syrian uprising.

First, the uprising was for a long time mainly led—and still is today, albeit to a lesser extent—by Local Coordination Committees [*lijan*] consisting, for the most part, of young people making heavy use of the Internet: Facebook for coordination between local committees and YouTube for the dissemination of information about the course of events. (Information work has been all the more crucial in Syria because it is extremely difficult and risky for international media to enter and/or circulate in the country.) The consequence of this feature of the uprising's leadership is that, of all the Arab uprisings in 2011–2, the Syrian rebellion has been the most democratically organized on the ground.

Second, however, a Syrian National Council (SNC) was formed in October 2011, after several months of arduous negotiations between diverse components of the opposition, with interference from Western governments (especially France and the United States) and regional governments (Turkey, Qatar, the Saudi kingdom). The SNC brings together three main components in exile: the Syrian Muslim Brothers, the Democratic People's Party (which originated from a split in the Syrian Communist Party, with this faction opposing the regime and the other participating in government), and a myriad of opposition figures and groups, political or ethnic (Kurds, Assyrians), including a few individuals known for their close relations with Washington or Paris. Unlike the Libyan NTC, which was formed in Benghazi, the SNC was created in Istanbul and continues to operate in exile. Hence its claims to representativeness and legitimacy are necessarily weaker than the NTC's were. They depend mainly on the fact that the Local Coordination Committees have recognized the SNC and are represented on it.

Other groups and individuals among the regime's nationalist and left-wing opponents have formed a National Coordinating Committee (*hay'a*). Their influence on the uprising is quite limited, all the more because some of them have an ambivalent attitude toward the regime. The NCC has been discredited by the fact that it long called for a "dialogue" with the government with a view to "reforming" institutions. Only later did it call for an end to the regime, while continuing to advocate a negotiated transition.

The *fourth difference* has conditioned the three just discussed. The situation of dual power in Libya and the rapid transformation of the insurrection into a generalized civil war were made possible by the contrast between the troops of the regular Libyan army, in which both the officer corps and the ranks reflect the makeup of the general population, and the forces of the old regime's praetorian guard, which were organically linked to it. The Libyan government was very distinctly superior to the uprising as far as its weapons, equipment, and professional troops were concerned, yet the insurrection very quickly won over a significant number of officers and ordinary soldiers. The most eminent military figure to rally to it was Major General Abdel-Fattah Younes, who resigned from his post as interior minister to join the rebels as early as 22 February 2011. He became the supreme commander of the Free Libyan Army created by the insurgency, subsequently renamed Army of National Liberation.

In Syria, every component of the armed forces was closely controlled and monitored by agents of the regime; moreover, the insurrection was not generalized from the outset, but increased in size and scope over a relatively protracted period. These circumstances had major consequences for the confrontation between the uprising and the regime.

To begin with, the Syrian uprising nursed the illusion for several months that it could carry the day while remaining "peaceful," the way the Egyptian uprising had. This explains why Syrian demonstrators chanted the slogan "*silmiyya, silmiyya*" (peaceful) in the first few weeks, and why the SNC initially adopted the same stance. This was a profound error of judgment, for all the reasons already stated. A concrete analysis of the nature of the regime and, especially, its armed forces could only lead to the conclusion that nothing but a civil war would topple the Syrian regime. In a June 2011 interview published in Beirut, three months after the uprising began, I myself said, "I see only two possibilities for Syria: either maintenance of the regime by means of bloody, still fiercer repression, or civil war. The regime could collapse as a result of the implosion of its armed apparatus. If that happens, there will be civil war."[87]

In fact, it was not long before activists on the local committees who had advocated a peaceful road to victory realized that the regime's forces were systematically firing on unarmed demonstrators in spite of their nonviolent slogans. The macabre daily body counts convinced them that it was impossible to steer this suicidal course. The uprising had only three options. It could admit defeat and give up—but this prospect, too, was suicidal. Michel Kilo, a well-known left-wing opponent of the regime, told me in October 2011 that activists in Syria were saying, "We continue to demonstrate because we are afraid to stop." In other words, these activists were perfectly well aware that, if the regime triumphed, it would exact a terrible revenge. Alternatively, the uprising could demand "international protection," as the local committees did from then on, inspired by the course of events in Libya, in order to prevent the regime's forces from continuing to kill and allowing the demonstrations to spread until the regime collapsed.

The latter prospect was more illusory still: it ignored the difference in nature between geographical and military conditions in Libya and Syria. This difference meant that, first, an intervention like the one in Libya would be far bloodier and more destructive for the country and more costly for NATO and its allies than had been the case in Libya and that, second, for the same reason, the Western states were little inclined to stage a repeat performance in Syria, as they did not fail to make known.[88]

It is no accident that military men understood before the rest of the opposition that the regime could only be overthrown by force of arms—the third, inevitable option. In July 2011, dissidents in the Syrian army, who, refusing to take part in repressing their people, had resolved to organize themselves in order to protect the towns and villages of the uprising, announced the creation of the Free Syrian Army (FSA). At first, they were repudiated by the SNC, which invoked its refusal to "militarize the revolution." Colonel Riyad al-Asaad, the FSA's commander, responded in a November 2011 interview in the daily *Al-Sharq al-Awsat* that "it is our duty to defend ourselves and our people; those who think that this Syrian regime will fall peacefully are nurturing illusions."[89] He might well have echoed the words of the French revolutionary Gracchus Babeuf, uttered in 1795:

> Civil war must be avoided, you exclaim? . . . But what civil war is more revolting than the one that puts all the murderers on one side and all the defenseless victims on the other? Can you accuse someone who wants to arm the victims against the murderers of committing a crime? Is a civil war in which each side can defend itself not to be preferred?[90]

The Syrian uprising's armament has improved considerably since summer 2011. In 2012, as a result, Syria plunged into a full-scale civil war.[91] What is known as the Free Syrian Army is made up, in part, of dissident officers and soldiers from the ranks of the regular army; many are draftees who comprise a majority of the regular army. (See the estimates of the size of the regular army above.) But the better part of the FSA is made up of reserve officers and former conscripts. (From the age of eighteen on, all men are subject to the draft in Syria; until 2005, they served for two and a half years, a term of service that has since been progressively reduced to eighteen months.) Like the Syrian uprising itself, this army is hardly centralized; it is even less centralized than the rebel Libyan army was. It consists, for the most part, of armed units that function on a local basis, although they coordinate their activities as best they can.[92] As in Libya, groups of jihadists have joined this force—including Al-Qaida, which has been able to link up with its network in Iraq. Their minority presence in the uprising cannot tarnish what is, in its overwhelming majority, an authentic instance of a people at arms.[93]

In November 2011, I pointed out that the main strategic challenge confronting the Syrian revolution was to combine peaceful demonstrations with armed struggle against the regime.[94] The Syrian uprising devised a strategy of this kind heuristically, in the heat of battle and in the absence of an overall strategic vision conceived by a political-military leadership equal to its tasks. Thus Hassan al-Ashtar, an FSA leader in Rastan, north of Homs, responded to a journalist who had asked him, in January 2012, how the regime could be defeated: "By the three pillars of the resistance: pursuit of the peaceful demonstrations, the Free Army, and civil disobedience."[95] The rebel army has evolved and the civil war has sharply escalated, while the mass Friday demonstrations that have been occurring since the beginning of the uprising continue to be held.

However, since there exists no political-military leadership equal to the task of the Syrian uprising, the sectarian dynamics of the conflict have inevitably intensified the longer it has gone on. The regime's increasingly blind, deadly violence and the accumulation of sectarian massacres perpetrated by its special forces or its *shabbiha* have begun to provoke reactions of the same general sort from Sunni fighters, who are, moreover, being egged on by the Saudi Wahhabis' sectarian propaganda. Such acts are being perpetrated despite the fact that both the Local Coordination Committees and the SNC, including the Muslim Brothers, have condemned them, as has the leadership of the FSA.

The armed Syrian uprising is confronted with two acute problems. The first is the marked superiority of the regime's military forces: they are better armed, better equipped, and better trained. The insurrection's arms consist above all, as in Libya, of material captured from the regime's army or constructed slapdash, as in other resistance movements in the region. This has been attested by *The New York Times'* specialist for military questions, C. J. Chivers, who has visited the scene of the fighting: "In many ways, the weapons gathered by the uprising here resemble those seen in the insurgencies fought against Western forces by Iraqis, or against Israel by Palestinians. This is in part, participants in the effort said, because they were able to model their weapons on those used in other Middle Eastern uprisings."[96]

Up to the time of writing, no direct international and/or regional military intervention has neutralized the superiority of the regime's forces in Syria, as happened in Libya; nor has it been neutralized by arms deliveries. Quite the contrary: the regime's military superiority is being maintained by outside support—political support and arms from Russia; financial support, arms, and fighters from Iran and its regional allies. Iranian financial assistance enables the regime to recruit more and more *shabbiha* and pay them at a level that is all the more tempting in that Syria's general economic situation is fast deteriorating. This is well illustrated by the remarks a Syrian business owner made to an Associated Press reporter in October 2012:

> If businesses fail, he warned, the new unemployed could further fuel the conflict. Already, 12 of his employees quit to work as "security" for the government.
> "I know what that means. They are Shabiha," he said, referring to the pro-Assad gunmen used in fighting against rebels and accused of killings of civilians. He said he paid the employees $200 a month, but the government pays Shabiha at least $300.[97]

The Western capitals, with Washington in the lead, continued to proclaim their opposition to militarization of the conflict until the civil war became a fait accompli on the ground. They never ceased to proclaim their unwillingness to intervene. As in Libya, they have refused to deliver weapons to the combatants out of fear that those arms will be directed against their interests in the medium or long term.

Only the Saudi kingdom and Qatar have come out in favor of providing the insurgents with arms. (The Saudis' support is strictly sectarian: it is absurd to accuse them of acting hypocritically in supporting a democratic insurrection when their own state is the very antithesis of a democracy, for they have never claimed to be riding to democracy's rescue.) Yet these two states' declarations of intention have not been followed up by arms deliveries, for the good reason that they have no delivery routes available to them. Both Jordan and Turkey have refused to allow the weapons to transit across their territory; that would be tantamount to direct military intervention in the conflict and would provoke retaliation by the Syrian regime.

Ankara fears that Damascus could react by arming the Kurdish Workers' Party (PKK), which has long been waging an armed struggle against the Turkish state; the Kurdish regions of Iraq and Syria serve the PKK as rear bases. As for Jordan, it is itself confronted with powerful social and political unrest, to say nothing of the fact that a majority of the kingdom's inhabitants are Palestinians who are subjected to discrimination and oppression there. Syria's remaining two neighbors are Lebanon and Iraq; the current governments of both are closer to the Syrian regime than to the insurgents. However, smugglers operate on the soil of both Lebanon and, above all, Iraq; they furnish the bulk of the weapons reaching the Syrian insurrection from outside the country. This brings us to the second acute problem with which the insurrection is faced: money.

The rule that has it that money is the nerve of war holds for wars of all kinds, civil wars not excepted. Money is needed to provision the Syrian combatants, as well as to provide them with the weapons that they cruelly lack. In this respect, the most privileged of all those fighting the Syrian regime are the fundamentalist Sunni groups: funds emanating from the Saudi government or the Wahhabi religious institution are reaching them. These funds give them an indisputable advantage over the networks of citizen-fighters who have declared allegiance to the FSA. They thus intensify the potential danger that these fundamentalist Sunni groups represent for the Syrian uprising as well as for the country's future in general. From this point of view as well, the sooner the Syrian regime topples, the better. The longer it lasts, the greater is the risk that the country will plunge into barbarism.

CHAPTER 6

Co-opting the Uprising

The proportion of partisans of "conspiracy theory"—the tendency to detect political plots everywhere—is naturally higher than average in two groups in particular: anti-imperialists and Middle Easterners. The fact that "conspiracy theory" generally derives from powerful distrust of the dominant powers explains why the proportion of its proponents is higher among people professing anti-imperialism. Those who continue to preach about the West's "civilizing mission" dishonestly exploit this fact in an attempt to discredit anti-imperialism across the board.

As for the Middle East, it is the region of the world that, in the twentieth century, became the object or theater of the greatest number of *real* conspiracies. From the secret agreement that Sir Mark Sykes and Monsieur François Georges-Picot concluded in 1916 for the purpose of dividing up the Ottoman Empire's Middle Eastern territories between Britain and France (while also catering to the interests of Czarist Russia and the Zionist movement) with blithe disregard for the promises that London had made the Arabs, to the very frequent intrigues and machinations of the Cold War era, the Middle East of the Oil Age was, and remains, the zone par excellence of conspiracies of all kinds. It is only to be expected that large numbers of its inhabitants should have a tendency to detect, systematically, shadowy intrigues behind events in the region.[1]

WASHINGTON AND THE MUSLIM BROTHERS, TAKE TWO

It is, naturally, the intersection of the two sets of people just evoked, anti-imperialists and Middle Easterners, that has provided the breeding ground for the idea that the "Arab Spring" was in fact engineered by the United States to achieve and consolidate its hegemony over the region while promoting Israel's interests. This idea reflects, all at once, a naive belief in the omnipotence of the United States, a skewed vision of the Arab uprising's impact on US interests and the Zionist state's, and, above all, deep contempt for the insurgent populations. Such contempt reflects a reactionary mentality, whatever its political pretensions in other respects.

The accusation is, however, propped up on a range of real elements running from the military intervention of NATO and its Arab allies in Libya to the subsidies and various training programs that US institutions liberally dispense to individuals and NGOs working in the region around issues of democracy and human rights. In Egypt, Washington has funded NGOs of this type, sometimes circumventing local laws by means of stratagems resembling those used to launder money, as the WikiLeaks cables have revealed.[2] Thus it has subsidized "democracy promotion" by strengthening "civil society" even in despotic states closely allied with it, allocating sums for this purpose that are derisory in comparison with those it spends on beefing up the repressive arsenals of the very same states. This will surprise only those who have not understood that electoral democracies engender manifold contradictions and tensions between the state and civil society (in the general sense of the term).

It is not just nationalist anti-imperialist circles, well known for their all-devouring predilection for conspiracy theory, that have attributed the popular revolts in the Arab region to an "imperialist" or even "Zionist" plot. A peculiar feature of the situation created by the Arab uprising is that such explanations have also been brandished—indeed, have perhaps been *primarily* brandished—by circles that have collaborated closely with the United States in the past. Faced with uprisings by their populations, many of those who, only yesterday, were counted among Washington's most faithful allies have unhesitatingly tried to turn public opinion back in their favor by exploiting popular aversion to the United States and its Israeli protégé in extremely demagogic fashion.

It was not just Bashar al-Assad who accused Washington and its

allies in the region of fomenting popular rebellion against his dictatorship. In his case, at least, Syria's alliance with two of Washington's foes
in the Middle East, the Iranian regime and Lebanese Hezbollah, lends
a semblance of rationality to conspiracy theory. Gaddafi, too, posed
as the victim of an imperialist plot against his regime. Yet documents
found in Tripoli when the city was liberated have made it possible to
demonstrate

> the degree of involvement of the United States government under the Bush
> administration in the arrest of opponents of the former Libyan leader, Muammar
> Gaddafi, living abroad, the subsequent torture and other ill-treatment of many
> of them in US custody, and their forced transfer back to Libya.
>   The United States played the most extensive role in the abuses, but other
> countries, notably the United Kingdom, were also involved.[3]

Moreover, did Ali Abdallah Saleh himself not have the unmitigated
gall to explain—in a speech delivered on 1 March 2011 before students of Sana'a University's medical school—that the Arab uprising was
"nothing more nor less than a media-made revolution directed by the
United States from an office in Tel Aviv?"[4] The grand prize in this category, however, goes not to Saleh, but to the Egyptian Fayza Abul-Naga,
minister of international cooperation under Mubarak, who continued
to exercise the same functions in governments formed under the SCAF's
regency. The minister endlessly harassed the NGOs specializing in questions of democracy after receiving the portfolio for international cooperation in Ahmed Nazif's government in 2004. Her battle against them
was an eternal bone of contention between Mubarak, intent on governing Egypt as he saw fit, and the US government, intent on justifying, before Congress and world opinion, the fact that it showers more
money on the Egyptian regime—particularly its armed forces—than on
any other, with the lone exception of its spoiled child, Israel.

Abul-Naga, who could not blame the Egyptian uprising itself on a
US plot because she was working for the SCAF, which claimed to represent the uprising's aspirations, accused Washington of trying to divert
the Egyptian revolution from its course. Although her military employers were financed by Washington to the tune of $1.3 billion annually,
she had the effrontery to criticize their sponsor for granting $150 mil-
lion to US NGOs operating in Egypt, drawing the money from the total
subsidy of $1.7 billion that it grants the country every year.[5] The unsub-
tle message that Abul-Naga was trying to get across was that Mubarak
had fallen victim to the intrigues that she had incessantly denounced,

and that his heirs and military successors, pursuing Mubarak's course, had in turn become targets of the same intrigues, the object of which was to drive them from power. In the same spirit, partisans of the *fulul* (debris) of Mubarak's regime accused Washington of maneuvering to prevent their candidate, Ahmed Shafiq, from winning the June 2012 presidential election.

Far from what is suggested by fantasies common to ultranationalists, who hate the Western powers for good reasons and bad, and those who, only yesterday, were collaborating with those powers, Western governments were by no means the instigators or even the dei ex machina of the Arab uprisings. On the contrary, they were, from the first, thrown into utter disarray by the explosion, and they continue to grope in the dark, amid the greatest possible uncertainty about the region's future.

Nicolas Sarkozy's French government initially reacted to the Tunisian uprising by offering Ben Ali, with whom successive French governments have for decades maintained very close relations, the support of its repressive forces. As late as 12 January 2011—that is, only two days before the Tunisian despot took to his heels—French Foreign Minister Michèle Alliot-Marie responded to opposition MPs, who had criticized the French government for saying nothing about the bloody repression of the Tunisian mass movement, that they should not "try to tell other people what to do" about the "complex" situation in Tunisia. Boasting that "the savoir-faire of [France's] security forces, recognized throughout the world, makes it possible to handle this kind of security situation," she announced that her government had offered to assist Algeria and Tunisia on security in order to bring the situation under control.[6]

As the pace of events quickened in the final forty-eight hours of Ben Ali's reign, Bernard Squarcini, director of the French intelligence agency (DCRI), spurred the dictator to leave Tunisia by informing him that a military coup was being prepared against him. This information was transmitted to Ben Ali by his son-in-law, the head of his presidential guard, according to the latter. His account matched that of the dictator's wife,[7] who likewise contended that her husband had been brought down by a plot. The training courses that "foreign governments" had offered bloggers were, in her view, evidence. The implicit target of her criticism was the United States.

Ben Ali's downfall deepened the disgrace into which Nicolas Sarkozy's government had already fallen, while France's image in Arab public opinion was seriously tarnished. This helps explain the unusual zeal Sarkozy subsequently showed over events in Libya when, wagering that Gaddafi was doomed, he sought to refurbish his government's reputation as a champion of human rights. His obvious hope was that France would be rewarded with a bigger share of the Libyan market, and also a bigger share of Libyan investments abroad—that is, a portion of the lion's share that the Italy of his doppelgänger Sylvio Berlusconi had enjoyed in the final years of Gaddafi's reign.

It is too early to tell what has been going on behind the scenes of the events unfolding in the Arab region since January 2011. It is certain that the United States was involved in Ben Ali's departure; the details, however, remain unclear. A 16 January 2011 bulletin from the Egyptian news agency MENA News quoted an officer of the Tunisian National Guard as saying that Washington urged Chief of Staff of the Land Army General Rashid Ammar to step in.[8] The part that the United States played in events in Egypt is clearer, thanks to Washington's much closer ties to Egypt and its armed forces. As a report by the Congressional Research Service pointed out, "the revolution in Egypt has put the Obama Administration in a major quandary."[9]

The administration was keenly aware of the problems in the Arab region, as diplomatic reports revealed by WikiLeaks show. It understood perfectly well that it would be highly counterproductive to oppose the uprising publicly, for both its own interests and its allies'. Rather, it would have to make a show of support for democratization of the region's states. From the very first days of the Egyptian uprising, a leitmotif ran through US leaders' speeches and official statements: "orderly transition." The formula was to be repeated verbatim and ad nauseam: by President Barack Obama and Secretary of State Hillary Clinton, separately, on 30 January 2011; by Obama, in his first public comment on the Egyptian situation on 1 February; by Clinton, in Munich, on 6 February; by a State Department spokesperson on 7 and again on 9 February; by the deputy national security advisor on 9 February; by the deputy secretary of state on 10 February; by Clinton again, on 17 and 22 February; and so on and so forth.

The mere use of the term "transition" confirmed the manifest disavowal of Hosni Mubarak that the US administration had publicly expressed the day the Egyptian uprising began, 25 January. On that date, a White House press release urged the Egyptian authorities to refrain from violence and respect the "universal rights of the Egyptian people." The press release included a list of the attributes of a government that defended "universal rights"; it contrasted glaringly with the nature of the Egyptian regime.[10] The same warning against resorting to violence and, in particular, against any army involvement in repressing the movement was doubtless issued to the Egyptian armed forces' Chief of Staff Sami Anan, who was on an official visit to Washington when the uprising erupted in his country.[11]

On the evening of 28 January, the day that saw the gigantic "Friday of rage" rally on Cairo's Tahrir Square, Barack Obama commented publicly on the events. He emphatically repeated his warning to the Egyptian government not to use violence and called on it to reestablish the avenues of communication (Internet, mobile phones, social media) that it had cut off. Adopting the tone that one state dares to use with another only when it is its financial sponsor, he declared that he favored "reforms that meet the aspirations of the Egyptian people" and a "government that is fair and just and responsive"; the implication was that Mubarak's was not.[12] What "orderly transition" meant was thus crystal clear: a peaceful regime change leading to a government that had issued from genuinely free elections. To the very last, Washington continued to believe that Omar Suleiman was the best man for the job.

The Obama administration's manifest irritation with Mubarak, which intensified when it became clear that the Egyptian president had still not understood that he had had his day, was in line with earlier practice: the previous US administration had showered Mubarak with advice on political reform. On this issue, the speech that Obama delivered at the University of Cairo on 4 June 2009[13] had distinctly echoed the one that Condoleezza Rice had given at the American University of Cairo four years earlier (see Chapter 3). The White House press release of 25 January, moreover, included direct quotes from Obama's speech. Thus, even before the world could familiarize itself with the secret diplomatic reports published by WikiLeaks, all indications were that the US government knew just how explosive the situation in Egypt was.

In the Egyptian case, the United States was well and truly intent upon "promoting democracy." This was not due to some sublime devotion to principles—it superbly ignores them when they contradict its oil-related interests in the absolute monarchies of the GCC—but, rather, because it fears that an explosion would jeopardize those interests, given Egypt's weight and pivotal regional role. Far from desiring the explosion, the previous two US administrations had spared no effort to forestall it, within limits dictated by the fact that they could not go too far in the direction of forcing Mubarak's hand without running the risk of hastening the explosion they feared and destabilizing the monarchies in question. That was the United States' dilemma. By no means did it reflect US omnipotence. On the contrary, it attested the precariousness of US interests and constraints on US power in the Arab region.

In fact, 2011 was the year in which Washington's hegemony over the region reached its lowest point since the peak of 1991. In that year, the United States had stationed troops on a permanent basis in the Arab-Iranian Gulf region after flattening Iraq under a carpet of bombs, in a gigantic demonstration, with live ammunition, of the capacities of its military technology. At the same moment, the USSR, its rival in the Middle East for the past thirty-five years, was in its death throes. Hafez al-Assad's Syria had joined the Washington-led coalition against his *frères ennemis* of the Iraqi Baath. Syria had likewise joined Egypt and the GCC monarchies in proclaiming, in March 1991, a "New Arab Order," obviously supposed to take its place in the "New World Order" proclaimed by the elder Bush. In the autumn, in Madrid, Washington initiated a "peace process" that, it hoped, would lead to an agreement defusing the Israeli-Arab conflict in ways that would consolidate and stabilize its regional hegemony, opposition to which had never been weaker.

Twenty years later, the picture was, from Washington's standpoint, gloomy indeed. The invasion of Iraq launched under the younger Bush had turned into so big a debacle that the United States was forced to withdraw its last troops from the country in 2011. It had not succeeded in subjugating Iraq politically or economically, although its objective had been to establish a massive permanent military presence there.[14] The loss of credibility was the greater for the United States in that Iran, its arch foe in the region, had managed to yank its chestnuts from the fire by imposing its hegemony on Iraq. The United States' other big enemy, Al-Qaida, enjoyed, after ten years of "War on Terror," a much more extensive territorial network in the Arab region (mainly in Iraq, Yemen, and the Maghreb) than it had had to begin with. Iran happily thumbed its nose at the United States. So did America's own ally, Israel, whose arrogant attitude toward the powerless Obama administration glaringly contrasted with its involuntary submission to the pressures that the elder Bush's administration had brought to bear on it in 1991.[15]

The Arab uprising exploded in this context, marked by the advanced decomposition of American hegemony over the region. What is more, it began by deeply destabilizing a pair of states that are US allies, one of which is also its principal Arab military partner. Two of the oldest Arab friends of Western governments fell. With movements springing up in virtually all the countries in the region, three more US allies had to face uprisings in their turn: Yemen, Bahrain, and Libya. The United States found itself in the position of a captain who has lost control of his ship in a raging sea. In such circumstances, it does no good to toil against wind and waves; one is better advised to go with the flow than to resist it at the risk of sinking the ship. That is what the Obama administration has done: rather than battling the revolutionary tidal wave, it has from the outset done what it could to create the impression that it stands shoulder to shoulder with the uprising, by echoing the demands for freedom and democracy raised by demonstrators from one end of the region to the other. The echo has been now loud, now soft, depending on the case.

Even in the case of Bahrain, where Washington cannot afford to allow the regime to fall—no more than it can accept the overthrow of any of the other GCC monarchies, from which it exacts immense financial and strategic advantages in its capacity as their protector—the Obama administration paid very hypocritical lip service to its ostensible principles by condemning repression of the movement. The "universal rights" that it had demanded for the Egyptian people were not, however, mentioned in connection with its Bahraini counterpart, for good reason. For the sake of appearances, Washington prevailed on the king to play along by setting up a commission of inquiry into the "excesses" committed by his repressive forces. Then, in May 2012, it resumed arms shipments to the monarchy. Indignant over this flagrant hypocrisy, the revolted population of Bahrain has not failed to demonstrate its resentment of the United States.[16]

In short order, the Obama administration decided to come to terms with the political force that, it knew, was best placed to profit from the new situation at the regional level: the Muslim Brotherhood. Washington once again adopted the same attitude it had had when it was allied with the Brotherhood against left-wing Arab nationalism and the communists; it decided that it was high time to revive the dialogue begun by the Bush administration and then broken off in 2006. This renewed flirt was facilitated by the emir of Qatar, the Brotherhood's sponsor, whose day of glory was now at hand, along with that of his protégés. Wherever the Muslim Brothers play a significant role, Washington has seen fit to treat them as a major dimension of its regional policy.

The Obama administration has regularly manifested its opposition to prolongation of the Egyptian military's interim rule, just as it has systematically condemned the military's repressive excesses. At the end of the six-month transitional period announced by the SCAF, Washington repeatedly signaled it was losing patience with its protégés and was well disposed toward the Muslim Brothers.[17] Its preference for the Brotherhood's presidential candidate, Mohamed Morsi, was thinly veiled in the second round of the election. For its part, the London review *The Economist*, a mouthpiece for British capitalism, went so far as to title an editorial released on the eve of round two "Vote for the Brother."[18] When the Presidential Elections Commission proclaimed Morsi the victor on 24 June 2012, the sighs of relief in Washington indicated just how single-mindedly the United States had set its hopes for a restoration of order in Egypt on the Muslim Brothers, at the end of a "transition" that had been rather more chaotic than "orderly."

In the same spirit, Washington had welcomed the Ennahda movement's accession to power in Tunisia in the wake of the October 2011 Constituent Assembly elections. Ennahda is, de facto, the Muslim Brotherhood's Tunisian branch, although it has never publicly clarified its relationship to the Brotherhood. The US Embassy had established contact with the movement after Ben Ali's downfall in January 2011:

> In May, with help from the US embassy in Tunis, Ennahdha party leaders quietly visited Washington for talks at the State Department and with congressional leaders, including Sen. McCain of Arizona, according to organizers. US officials described the visit as an opportunity to build bridges with a moderate Islamist party that could serve as a model for groups in other countries in the region.[19]

In Yemen, too, an emanation of the Muslim Brothers' local branch has played a key role: Islah, the party through which the Brotherhood operates. Islah was a crucial partner in the agreement concluded under GCC auspices, with Washington's support, in an attempt to defuse the crisis: it endorsed the "compromise" that prevented the Yemeni uprising from achieving its minimal objective, which was to topple the regime and bring Ali Abdallah Saleh to trial. Two intermediaries stepped in to make the agreement possible: the Saudis, who interceded with Saleh, and Qatar, which intervened with Islah.[20] If, in spring 2012, Washington advocated a "Yemeni solution" for Syria—in which Bashar al-Assad's Russian sponsors were supposed to play the part Saleh's Saudi sponsors did[21]—it was most assuredly in the hope of getting the Muslim Brothers, who have representatives in the Syrian National Council, to endorse such a solution under pressure from Qatar and Turkey.

NATO, LIBYA, AND SYRIA

The flagrant contrast between Western attitudes toward Syria on the one hand and Libya on the other is not at all surprising. It has not, however, prevented some from denouncing US intervention in both countries as if the same sort of intervention were involved, thus creating a pretext, if not for supporting the Syrian regime, then at least for denigrating the popular insurrection in Syria, just as they had earlier denigrated the popular insurrection in Libya.

The problem is not new. It is as old as the establishment of communist rule in Russia and the formation of the Soviet Union. Thereafter, the concrete exercise of a people's right to determine its own future was denied time and time again, whenever it was asserted against Moscow. Leon Trotsky elaborated the line of argument justifying this in 1922, before the rise of Stalinism and the unconditional support of the USSR characteristic of it. To legitimize the previous year's invasion of the Democratic Republic of Georgia by the Red Army, which he commanded, Trotsky contended that the right to self-determination was subordinate to the interests of "proletarian revolution" and the fight against imperialism.[22] Fidel Castro, in a speech delivered on 23 August 1968, invoked the same argument about the priority of the interests of the "socialist camp" and anti-imperialism over the right of the people, to justify his support of Warsaw Pact troops' invasion of Czechoslovakia (which ended the "Prague Spring").

It was with apparently even stronger anti-imperialist reasons that, forty-three years later, Castro reiterated by supporting the Libyan despot against, first, the Libyan people and, later, the imperialist powers' military intervention. The Venezuelan Hugo Chávez and the Nicaraguan Daniel Ortega followed suit. Thereafter, the same three leaders proclaimed their support for Bashar al-Assad against the popular insurrection in his country, dismissed as an imperialist conspiracy. Chávez went so far as to describe the Syrian despot as a socialist and humanist (one would be hard put to say which adjective is more grotesque when applied to Assad). The same threesome had already demonstrated its solidarity with the despotic Iranian regime after its repression of the mass protests in Iran in 2009. Segments of the international anti-imperialist movement shared these attitudes, notably in the Americas.

Two different issues are at stake here. The first is ethical. Of anti-imperialism and the right of the peoples, which value determines the other? If one opposes imperialism because, by definition and as a general rule, it violates the peoples' right to self-determination, one will prioritize defense of that right, even in the exceptional cases in which, for purely opportunistic reasons, imperialism, too, defends certain peoples' exercise of it. It was inadmissible to qualify, in any way whatsoever, recognition of the Czechoslovak people's right freely to decide the kind of political regime it wished to establish. A fortiori, it was inadmissible to deny it that right on the pretext that the United States expressed support of it (simply because it was asserted against Moscow).

If, on the other hand, one considers anti-imperialism as such to be the supreme value, one will unhesitatingly endorse the crushing of peoples who assert their right freely to choose their own future, if only imperialism opportunistically supports them, or if one considers the despotic regime oppressing them to be "anti-imperialist." This is the dismal logic that has it that "the enemy of my enemy is my friend" and, conversely, that "anyone who benefits from the friendship of my enemy is my enemy." Such logic is self-defeating. The best service that anti-imperialists can render imperialism is to demonstrate that they attach no more importance to the right of the peoples than it does.

The second problem is related to the first: the question of the motivations for the imperialist powers' stance. Only those who are politically very simple-minded indeed can fail to understand that the maxim "my enemy's enemy is my friend" is precisely the maxim that guides imperialist policy. The sole "values" motivating such policy are the ones negotiated on the stock market. The proof is the whole of the imperialist powers' history for the last century and a half. The preceding pages have underscored the hypocrisy of the Western powers that swear by democracy, human rights in general and women's rights in particular, while cultivating close relations with the very antithesis of democracy or human and women's rights: the Saudi kingdom. Their attitude toward events in Libya and Syria was no exception to that rule.

Let us begin with Libya. There is no further need to explain why the notion that Muammar Gaddafi's regime was "anti-imperialist" in 2011, and that that is why the Western powers attacked it, is an untruth attesting its partisans' profound ignorance of the situation—in the best of cases. The secret documents discovered when Tripoli was liberated show that the collusion between Western powers, beginning with the United States, and Gaddafi's regime was even deeper than had been known or suspected (see the first quote of this chapter). Anyone who has the most cursory acquaintance with politics in the Middle East knows about the "Leader's" political turnabout of 2003.[23]

In December of that year, Gaddafi came to Bush's and Blair's political rescue, declaring that he had decided to renounce his programs to develop weapons of mass destruction. This was a badly needed boost for the credibility of the claim that Iraq had been invaded to halt WMD proliferation. Gaddafi was transformed overnight into a respectable leader and warmly congratulated for his accomplishments; Condoleezza Rice cited him as a model.[24] One after the other, Western leaders flocked to Libya to visit him in his tent and sign lucrative contracts.

The Western leader who developed the closest relation with Gaddafi was the racist, hard-right prime minister of Italy, Silvio Berlusconi. His friendship with Gaddafi was not only very fruitful economically: in 2008, the two men concluded one of the dirtiest deals of recent times, agreeing that poor boat people from the African continent intercepted by the Italian navy while trying to reach European shores would be handed directly over to Libya, rather than being taken to Italian territory and screened for asylum.[25] This agreement was so effective that the number of such asylum seekers in Italy fell from 36,000 in 2008 to 4,300 in 2010.[26] The deal was condemned by the UN high commissioner for refugees, to no avail.

The idea that Western powers intervened in Libya because they wanted to topple a regime hostile to their interests is simply preposterous. Equally preposterous is the claim that they were trying to get their hands on Libyan oil. In fact, the whole gamut of Western oil and gas companies was already active in Libya: Italy's ENI; Germany's Wintershall; Britain's BP; France's Total and GDF Suez; the US companies ConocoPhillips, Hess, and Occidental; Spain's Repsol; Canada's Suncor; Norway's Statoil; British-Dutch Shell; and so on.[27]

As Ethan Chorin says very well in the most complete and best informed book to appear so far on the relations of the United States and its Western partners with Gaddafi's Libya from 2003 until the regime's downfall,

> while the US preached "good governance" under the administration of George W. Bush, it was simultaneously an egregious violator of these same principles, selling arms (or, practically as bad, allowing arms to be sold) to Libya, and worse, literally delivering individuals to Gaddafi's front door with all but the weakest caveats against torture—without really knowing much about these people or their motives. The fact that so many weapons were sold with zeal by the West to Gaddafi in the lead-up to the revolution, and that the US, the UK, and other countries actually participated in a program to deliver some of Gaddafi's enemies to him on a plate for torture, should by rights be cause for far greater outrage by the American public than has hitherto been the case.

As the Libyan revolution unfolded, many argued that the United States had no business intervening militarily in Libya. Few, however, were aware of the scale on which "we," the West had been intervening in support of Gaddafi for the previous seven years.[28]

Why, then, did the Western powers intervene in Libya? The fact is that this was far from being the first time that they turned against a country that had been an ally only yesterday. Were the United States and the United Kingdom not compelled to break with the South African apartheid regime and impose sanctions on it in a fairly recent past? Was the United States not forced to break with Philippine dictator Ferdinand Marcos or Indonesian dictator Suharto and back popular rebellions against their regimes? If so, it is no wonder that the same powers should have turned against Gaddafi, with whom their alliance was far newer than the ones just evoked. Moreover, had the United States not abandoned, only weeks earlier, Ben Ali and, in short order, Mubarak as well?

To be sure, a military intervention took place in Libya, but not in Tunisia or Egypt. In the two last-named countries, however, where repression was incomparably less severe than in Libya, no one was calling for military intervention. In contrast, the Libyan insurrection insistently demanded international protection in the form of air cover, while categorically rejecting any intervention by ground troops. This demand was raised, above all, by the population of Benghazi—and the closer Gaddafi's troops came to the city, the more urgent it became. It was relayed by the League of Arab States on 12 March 2011: the Arab leaders, with the GCC monarchs in the lead, were not about to pass up a chance to feign concern about the fate of the masses at Gaddafi's expense—if not, indeed, taking their cue from the emir of Qatar, to pretend to have joined the revolutionary camp. Gaddafi, be it recalled, had in the course of his long reign had a bone to pick with all of them at one time or the other.

The psychopathological speech that the Libyan despot delivered on 22 February, coming on top of the murderous violence of his praetorian guard, especially the troops under his son's command, justified fears of a large-scale massacre in Libya's second biggest city (with a population of over 600,000 that had recently been swollen by throngs of displaced people fleeing the regime's advancing troops). The world powers, including Russia and China, could not have been unaware of the fact that the city of Hama had been laid to waste in 1982 (it had had a population of 200,000 at the time) by Hafez al-Assad's praetorian guard under his brother's command. This caused the deaths of more than 10,000 people in three weeks—25,000, on the most common estimate, or as many as were killed by Adolphe Thiers's troops when they put down the Paris Commune during the "Bloody Week" in May 1871.

It was fear of butchery on this scale that induced the Western powers to act in extremis. The same fear was responsible for the fact that Russia and China preferred to abstain rather than veto Security Council resolution 1973, which gave NATO forces the green light to intervene. Thus it was Russia and China who made adoption of the resolution possible on 17 March 2011. No member of the Security Council voted against it: none was ready to assume moral responsibility for a highly probable bloodbath.[29] NATO forces went into action on 19 March, at the moment when the Gaddafi regime's troops had reached the outskirts of Benghazi. These troops had ignored the ceasefire, ordered by the United Nations, that the Libyan government had pretended to accept to buy time.

Western powers have allowed untold massacres to happen; they let hundreds of thousands, if not millions, of people, notably in sub-Saharan Africa, perish every year, victims of wars, epidemics, and famine. Why, then, did they mobilize to rescue the Libyans? A first response leaps to the eye: for the same reason that galvanized them to fly to the defense of Kuwait's "sovereignty" after Iraq invaded the country in 1990. That reason is, of course, oil. As Noam Chomsky likes to repeat, if Kuwait exported nothing but dates, the United States would never have gone to war to "liberate" it. In the Libyan case, three objectives go to make up the "oil factor": redistributing shares in the exploitation of the country's oil and natural gas (present and future contracts and concessions); winning shares in a profitable, potentially important market (the development of infrastructures, but also the reconstruction made necessary by wartime destruction); and, last but not least, attracting the billions of petrodollars in Libya's sovereign wealth fund.

The one-upmanship in which Nicolas Sarkozy's French government engaged on the Libyan issue led all the Western governments to rally to Sarkozy's cause—even the most reluctant, such as the German and Italian governments. No one could ignore the lesson of Iraq: Jacques Chirac's France, which had opposed the 2003 coalition led by Washington and London because France had major economic ties with Saddam Hussein's regime, ultimately sustained big losses, including the contracts for prospecting and exploitation granted it by Hussein.

What is more, inaction on the part of the Western powers would have had two adverse consequences in the event of a Libyan massacre. First, public opinion in various parts of the world, beginning with the Arab region, would surely have attributed their inaction to an actual connivance with Gaddafi's regime. More generally, the credibility of the ideology of the "right of humanitarian intervention" would have been ruined, irreparably. Second, Gaddafi's regime would once again have become a pariah, and Western powers would have had no choice but to impose sanctions on it. In a situation marked by a structural tendency toward rising oil prices against a backdrop of global economic crisis, an oil embargo on Libya would have had very negative economic consequences. This particularly applies to Europe, for which Libyan oil and natural gas present the additional advantage of relative proximity.[30]

The NATO states' intervention took place for all these reasons. But there was one more, which considerably amplified the others: the fear that chaos would become the status quo in Libya—that the Libyan situation would develop the way the Somalian situation had, allowing Al-Qaida and Co. to proliferate. The ultimate result would have been a disruption of the international oil market as far-reaching as the one an embargo would have caused. Western intervention on the side of the Libyan insurgents was a "marriage of convenience" between partners, each animated by patent suspicion of the other. The Libyans' suspicion found expression in their rejection of intervention by foreign ground troops. NATO's found expression in the way its member states conducted their intervention.

In this regard, let us first note the striking difference between the United States' absolute preeminence in the two wars against Iraq and the war in Afghanistan, on the one hand, and its back-seat, low-profile posture in the bombardment of Gaddafi's forces in Libya on the other. The United States' setbacks in the region, and also the decline of US dominance at the international level, have given rise to what pundits have dubbed the "Obama doctrine." It is summed up in a phrase attributed to one of the president's advisors: "leading from behind." Cited in *The New Yorker*, the anonymous advisor had clearly explained the reasons underlying this new doctrine. "It's a different definition of leadership than America is known for," he was quoted as saying, "and it comes from two unspoken beliefs: that the relative power of the US is declining, as rivals like China rise, and that the US is reviled in many parts of the world."[31]

The NATO states serenely violated the letter and spirit of Security Council Resolution 1973 in one respect and, in another, followed it as if it were a binding rule. While the resolution merely authorized UN member states "to take all necessary measures . . . to protect civilians and civilian populated areas under threat of attack," the NATO states and their Arab allies became full-fledged participants in the civil war under way in Libya. They served as an air force and a long-range strike force for the insurgents until their final victory. On the other hand, the same states took the embargo that the Security Council had imposed on the dispatch of arms to Libyan territory as a pretext for refusing to deliver the insurgents weapons. The insurgents continued to demand them, declaring that they themselves would see to it that Gaddafi's troops were defeated if only they were provided with adequate weaponry. Except for the ad hoc, limited arms shipments from Qatar and France, especially to combatants in the western part of the country, the bulk of the Libyan rebels' armament consisted of weapons that they managed to capture or fabricate locally.

Untold statements by Western leaders testify to their suspicion of the Libyan insurgents and their fear that the arms circulating in Libya would fall into the hands of people whom Western governments deemed dangerous. NATO's intervention in the Libyan civil war went hand in hand with an attempt to steer it from a distance, at the cost of prolonging the conflict: NATO restricted itself to a bombing campaign of low intensity in comparison with the aerial campaign it had waged over Kosovo, to say nothing of the bombardment of Iraq in 1991 and again in 2003.[32] It is true that this made it possible to limit the number of "collateral" civilian deaths due to NATO air strikes[33] (while increasing the number of victims of the more deadly civil war). The real objective, however, was to negotiate an "orderly transition" with the regime's men, especially Gaddafi's son Saif, the darling of Western circles until the uprising. Western powers sought to maintain the better part of the Libyan state apparatus without Muammar Gaddafi at its head, while also organizing elections that would usher in political institutions that could lay claim to democratic legitimacy. In other words, the Western powers were seeking a "Yemeni solution" *avant la lettre*.

Andrew Mitchell, the UK international development secretary, revealed the plan on 28 June:[34] the fifty-page "stabilization document" concocted by a UK-led international "stabilization response team" (including Turkey) contained a post-Gaddafi scenario that turned on the assumption that the King of Kings (the title that Gaddafi had arranged to have bestowed on himself by African tribal chiefs who were duly rewarded for their tribute) would step down or be removed. The overarching objective of this UK-led NATO road map was to avoid a repetition of the catastrophic US-led handling of the situation in post-invasion Iraq. There, the Bush administration had faced the choice of co-opting the better part of the Baathist state or dismantling it wholesale. It took the latter option, advocated by Ahmed Chalabi and the neocons, with their absurd blueprint for a minimalist US client state in Iraq.[35]

Thus the Libyan road map was inspired by a CIA-sponsored scenario that had been rejected in Iraq. As Mitchell explained, it was based on "the recommendation that Libya should not follow the Iraqi example of disbanding the army, which has been seen by some officials as a strategic mistake that helped fuel the insurgency in the sensitive and volatile circumstances after Saddam Hussein's overthrow."[36]

This was exactly what Western capitals, Washington in the lead, had wanted from the very start of the Syrian uprising. Their preference found a direct echo in an October 2012 declaration by Abdulbaset Sieda, president of the Syrian National Council. Sieda was, beyond a doubt, acting under Western pressure, like members of the Libyan NTC who had made similar declarations during the civil war in their country:

> The leader of Syria's main opposition group said Monday that he would not oppose a role for members of President Bashar Assad's ruling Baath party in the country's political future as long as they did not participate in killings during the uprising. . . .
>
> Sieda said the Syrian opposition will not repeat a policy carried out in Iraq years ago when members of Saddam Hussein's Baath party were forced to leave their jobs after his government was overthrown during the 2003 U.S.-led invasion. . . .
>
> "We will not repeat the failed experience of de-Baathification," Sieda said. "We will just remove all its (Baath party's) illegitimate privileges and officials who committed crimes will be put on trial," he added. "The Baath party will practice its activities in accordance with the democratic process. We will not have a revenge policy and we will preserve state institutions," he said.[37]

The big difference here is that the reasons given above to explain the NATO states' military intervention in Libya do not apply in the Syrian case. In Syria, unlike Libya, the economic stakes are meager. The Syrian uprising was repressed at a distinctly slower pace than the one in Libya, and it was several months before it turned into a civil war. Bashar al-Assad's regime was careful not to threaten its opponents with a second Hama, and when the scope of the killing increased, it was in the framework of a civil war in which the rebel camp was presumably capable of fighting back, at least to a certain extent.

Furthermore, the cost of an intervention in Syria—the economic cost for Western states, given the extensive means required to intervene in the country, and, for Syria, the cost as measured in destruction and civilian lives—would be significantly higher than in Libya. There are several reasons for this: the nature of the terrain, the fact that Syria's military is much better equipped and trained than Libya's, and the support that the Syrian regime receives from Russia and Iran, and even from Iraq and Lebanese Hezbollah. Contrast Libya, where the regime was completely isolated, apart from the African mercenaries it was able to recruit thanks to its dollars.

For all these reasons, then, the Western powers are disinclined to intervene in Syria. It might be supposed that, for the very same reasons, they would be inclined to deliver weapons to the insurgent Syrian fighters, who have been demanding them incessantly—the more so because Iran and Russia have not hesitated to replenish the Syrian regime's supply of arms and ammunition. What has stood in the way of arms deliveries to the insurgents up to the time of writing is the same fear that prevailed in the Libyan case: the possibility that weapons will contribute to creating a chaotic situation in Syria, on the Iraqi rather than the Somalian pattern. The resulting situation might allow Al-Qaida to extend its network and link up with Iraq in a regional sectarian war that would be extremely dangerous for the world economy. France and Turkey, as well as the GCC monarchies, have, with Washington's blessing, urged the Syrian insurgents to unify their forces under a single leadership, in the hope that this will bring the situation on the ground under control if the regime collapses. The Syrian groups participating in these initiatives hope they will persuade the Western powers to arm them and give Turkey the go-ahead to let arms transit its borders.

In the present situation, this is improbable. For, besides all the reasons listed above, there is a major consideration known as Israel. Western powers do not want arms to proliferate in the hands of Syrian groups that could use them against the Zionist state. That prospect is the more likely in that Israel has since 1967 occupied a slice of Syrian territory, the Golan Heights, which it went so far as to annex, de facto, in 1981. It is likewise owing to the Israeli factor, among all the other reasons already named, that it was and still is a grave error on the part of the Syrian insurgents to call for direct international intervention of the kind that occurred in Libya (as opposed to calling for arms, which is a perfectly legitimate demand).

The intervention in Libya destroyed most of the country's military stock. Western arms merchants will be delighted to sell weapons to the new Libyan authorities to replace these losses in the medium term, the more so as the Libyans do not lack the means needed to buy them. Intervention in Syria would destroy the country's military capacity with no reason to think that the West would help build it back up. The more likely prospect is that pressure would mount on Syria to follow Egypt's lead and conclude a peace treaty with Israel on ignominious terms.

Even if, for the reasons stated, there is no direct military intervention, the same result could be attained by refusing to furnish the insurgents with the weapons they need to put a rapid end to the conflict—in other words, by prolonging the fighting. This explains why the combatants of the Syrian uprising are increasingly convinced, as were their Libyan counterparts, that they are the victims of a "conspiracy." Instead of the US plot against Bashar al-Assad denounced by those for whom the worst dictatorships need only proclaim themselves "anti-imperialist" in order to be decked out in humanist and socialist virtues, it is a question of a "conspiracy" aiming to destroy Syria's military resources by denying the insurgents the wherewithal to achieve a swift victory. 'Abdul-Qadir Salih, commander of the combatants of the Free Syrian Army's Tawhid Division in Aleppo, has explained this in the clearest possible terms:

> We think that there is an international conspiracy against the Syrian people. We all hear, day after day, the statements calling on Assad to resign, without any concrete action, and we wonder: What is preventing them from supporting us, arming us, or protecting us?
>
> The world regards us as a free army fighting the regime's army. We are not, however, an army; we are brigades of revolutionaries who are capturing the regime's arms and using them to fight the regime. It seems that the world wants the war to drag on so that the country's infrastructure will be destroyed. This conspiracy against our people will go down in history.[38]

Western powers in general, and the United States in particular, have reaped no gratitude whatsoever from the populations of the region for their show of "support" for their aspirations. No one has been fooled, not even the Libyans, who are perfectly well aware that the West intervened because of their oil and their petrodollars, not for love of Libya. The contrast between the Western attitudes toward Bahrain, Yemen, Libya, and Syria is flagrant. Hostility toward the United States is as strong in the Arab region as it has been for decades, and the Israeli government has taken it upon itself to keep the flame of this hostility burning bright, should it ever begin to dim. The balance sheet of the Arab uprising is already very negative for Washington, despite all its efforts to contain the damage.

The idea that NATO's intervention in Libya meant that this country would come under its control, like Kosovo or Afghanistan, could arise only in minds that are prey to an extreme form of "idealism," whether they profess "materialism" or not. How can anyone believe for even a moment that NATO could control Libya without boots on the ground, when the United States has not managed to control Iraq after stationing as many as 170,000 soldiers there (the peak attained in September 2007), not counting the troops of its coalition partners?

The truth of the matter is that Libya's ties to the United States are plainly more fragile today than they were in the last years of Gaddafi's reign, if only because the new Libyan institutions, which are incomparably more transparent and democratic than their predecessors, make the kind of secret cooperation that previously existed between the intelligence agencies of the two countries harder to achieve. The fact that the new Libyan power elite includes people who have suffered terribly under the previous regime makes that kind of cooperation all the more unlikely. A well-known example is Abdel-Hakim Belhadj, the former military commander of Tripoli during the insurrection; the CIA turned him over to Gaddafi's regime in 2004, on the grounds that he was a jihadist militant. The new Libya is so utterly "under NATO's thumb" that the London *Economist* recently deplored what it called the Libyans' "ugly xenophobic traits," while trying to convince itself that the Libyan operation was a success "despite everything":

> The outgoing ruling council decreed that no candidate for prime minister should have either a foreign passport or a foreign spouse, thus forcing a series of prominent returnees either to withdraw their candidacy or to disavow a second nationality. The issuing of visas to foreigners is also fraught, with Islamists in the relevant ministries suspected of being loth to welcome Westerners.[39]

The strongest sign of the decline in Washington's influence in the region is the admission by Barack Obama himself that relations between Egypt and the United States have become "work in progress" and that some of the new Egyptian government's positions "may not be aligned with our interests." The president of the United States even added: "I don't think we would consider them an ally, but we don't consider them an enemy. They are a new government that is trying to find its way."[40] Obama's words are, at the same time, a good indication that the rapprochement between Washington and the Muslim Brothers cannot make up for the fact that the United States has lost dependable, relatively docile allies such as Mubarak, Ben Ali, or Saleh—to say nothing of the danger that the destabilization of the region represents for Western interests as a whole.

THE "ISLAMIC TSUNAMI" AND THE DIFFERENCE BETWEEN KHOMEINI AND MORSI

It was in September 2012, while coming to terms with the wave of violent attacks on institutions representing the United States in the Arab countries that had been triggered by a provocative anti-Muslim film so stupid as to defy the imagination, that *The Economist* tried to reassure itself that the enthusiasm for the "Arab Spring" that it had been voicing since January 2011 was well founded—"despite everything." The venerable review thus confirmed Karl Marx's characterization of it more than 150 years ago as an "optimist conjurer of all things menacing the tranquil minds of the mercantile community."[41]

Conversely, we have also witnessed the rapid proliferation of birds of ill omen exploiting the resources of Islamophobia to announce that the "Arab Spring" would culminate in totalitarian Islamic dictatorships that would make everyone regret the fallen regimes.[42] In one of the many incongruous convergences spawned by the Arab uprising, even certain leftists who, only yesterday, had been lambasting Islamophobia as a racist ideology fell back on the worst sort of Islamophobic arguments to denigrate the Libyan and Syrian uprisings, if not the Arab uprising as a whole. Certain liberals, for their part, went from wild enthusiasm for the revolution to melancholic depression.[43]

What shall we say—from the standpoint of the democratic, secular values that underpin this book—about the undeniable upsurge of Islamic fundamentalist forces throughout the Arab region? The first thing to point out here is that there is nothing astonishing about it. Those who imagine that they have demonstrated their gift for prophecy by "predicting" Islamic forces would be the Arab uprising's main beneficiaries have in fact only pushed on wide-open doors. For several decades now, a majority of those observing the region have predicted that militant Islamic forces would gain the upper hand in the event of a political upheaval. This prediction has been the main argument that Western governments, beginning with the United States, have used to justify their collusion with the region's despotic governments, as we have already noted.

In the aftermath of Iran's 1979 "Islamic Revolution," there was reason to fear that the scenario I described in 1981 as a "permanent revolution in reverse" might be repeated in other countries in the region. The reference was to a hypothesis formulated by Marx and Engels in 1850 to the effect that a bourgeois or petty bourgeois democratic revolution could mutate into a socialist revolution under proletarian leadership.[44] I accordingly said about the Iranian revolution that, setting out from the terrain of a national democratic revolution, it had undergone a "reactionary regression" under an Islamic fundamentalist leadership personified by Ayatollah Khomeini.[45] Although the popular aspirations of the February 1979 revolution were profoundly democratic at first, the revolution was diverted from its course and culminated in the establishment of a socially reactionary clerical dictatorship, thanks to the hegemony that the very charismatic Ruhollah Khomeini and the majority of the Shiite clergy who had rallied to his leadership succeeded in gaining over the mass movement.

Since the 1990s, however, the Sunni Islamic fundamentalist current in the Arab region has not produced a charismatic, radically populist leadership capable of conducting a mass movement toward the revolutionary overthrow of the established order. The Islamic Salvation Front in Algeria was the last potential manifestation of such a leadership. It was crushed by the 1992 coup d'état. That, and the terrible civil war that ensued, created a lasting trauma. It reactivated the one that has haunted the Muslim Brothers since they were repressed in Egypt, beginning in 1954. Together, these traumas go a long way toward explaining the Brotherhood's faintheartedness before the established governments of most of the countries in the Arab region. The populism of a Hassan al-Banna and the radicalism of a Sayyid Qutb, carried to an extreme, eventually went their separate ways, after having been united for a time in one and the same movement. What is today labeled jihadist Salafism, a movement initially confined to small groups on the margins of society, has found a mass echo with bin Laden and his Al-Qaida network. Yet, because of its terrorist nature, Al-Qaida has not succeeded in winning popular support and organizing a mass movement.

The impasse to which Sunni fundamentalism's revolutionary road eventually led explains why the first phase of the Arab uprising was initiated and organized by new actors, the networks of young Internet users discussed in Chapter 4. This is a crucial difference from the 1979 Iranian process. The fundamentalist movements that have gained prominence thanks to the uprisings in the region have all joined a movement started by others.

The part that youth networks and left-wing activists, especially activists from the UGTT, played in the Tunisian uprising down to the overthrow of Ben Ali was much more important than Ennahda's, the more so as the Islamic movement had been harshly put down in the country in the early 1990s. This movement has nevertheless succeeded in cultivating its influence by using the most powerful propaganda tool in existence: television. Ennahda and its main leader, Rached Ghannouchi, have benefited immensely from the television network Al Jazeera, which was created only a few years after the onset of the repression of which he and his movement were the victims. That is why, albeit physically absent from the local scene because of repression, Ennahda was able to acquire a reputation and influence greater than that of all the other components of the Tunisian political opposition put together.

That is also why the movement, exploiting freedoms won by the uprising, could very quickly rebuild, bringing together a wide range of Islamic tendencies running from admirers of AKP-style Turkish Muslim conservatism to fundamentalists faithful to the Muslim Brothers' tradition (more precisely, to one or the other of its two currents, moderate or radical). Financial support from Qatar also helped. The result of this support was, from the outset, quite as conspicuous as the "external signs of wealth" that, in other climes, would excite the suspicions of the tax inspectors who look into "inexplicable enrichment." Ennahda's headquarters, a new building in Tunis, is designed to impress while providing a visible symbol of the movement's strength and respectability. This strategy is effective, as long as one does not ask where the money comes from. According to the Syrian foreign minister, the emir of Qatar ordered, in the minister's and Ghannouchi's presence, that $150 million be disbursed to Ennahda to finance its campaign in the elections for the Constituent Assembly.[46]

Thus it comes as no surprise that the Tunisian Islamic movement carried these elections, above all because the competition was, by and large, derisory and dispersed. It is, moreover, no coincidence that the one surprise of the Tunisian elections was provided by a list headed by a businessman with a shady reputation, the owner of a television channel that has an audience in Tunisia and benefits from Saudi funding. After the fall of Ben Ali, with whom he had colluded, he launched the "Popular Petition" (the short form of the organization's name and the one it is known by). The Popular Petition represented one of the main attempts to recuperate what remained of the networks of the RCD, the former ruling party. In the elections, it came in fourth in the popular vote and third in terms of seats. It ran against a host of parties and groups of all kinds, only four of which obtained more than five percent of the votes cast.

Of these four, only Ennahda received more than 10%: it garnered 37% of the votes cast and 41% of the seats in the Constituent Assembly. We must, however, make due allowance for the fact that fewer than half of the eligible voters actually went to the polls. In other words, the results obtained by all the parties were even scanter than is suggested by the percentage of the vote they won. Thus fewer than 19% of all eligible voters cast their ballots for Ennahda. This is one indication of how close Ben Ali's dictatorship had come to reducing the field of Tunisian politics to a wasteland.[47]

As for the Egyptian Muslim Brothers, they had, over the years, repeatedly broken ranks with the anti-Mubarak opposition. This behavior took its place in their tradition of kowtowing to a government that, since Sadat, had allowed them only conditional freedom under constant surveillance, jailing them whenever they exceeded the limits of its tolerance. The Brotherhood's most recent capitulation dates to barely two months before the outbreak of the uprising. Although represented in the National Association for Change—the liberal-dominated coalition that had been created in February 2010 with, as its figurehead, Mohamed El-Baradei, former director of the International Atomic Energy Agency and a Nobel Peace Prize laureate—it ignored the call issued by the liberal and radical oppositions to boycott the November–December 2010 parliamentary elections as undemocratic.

The Muslim Brothers participated in the first round of the elections, held on 28 November. They hoped to induce the government to renew, as a reward for their cooperative stance, some of the eighty-eight seats that they had won in 2005 thanks to the electoral liberalization that Washington had forced on Mubarak.[48] As usual, they reassured the regime by limiting themselves to running candidates for only thirty percent of the seats up for election. The regime, however, rigged the vote so grossly and vengefully that the Brotherhood had no choice but to boycott the second round. It found itself without a single deputy in the newly elected assembly.

When youth networks issued a call for a demonstration on 25 January 2011 that was subsequently endorsed by most parties and groups opposed to the regime, the Brotherhood decided not to associate itself with either the call to demonstrate or the demonstration itself, although it did authorize young people in its ranks to participate. Only on the fourth day, 28 January or the "Friday of rage," did the Muslim Brothers join the uprising and throw their organized strength into the protest. Simultaneously, their leaders made sure to sing the army's praises, aware that it might take it upon itself to resolve the situation. Then, when Mubarak appointed the head of his intelligence agency, Omar Suleiman, to the post of vice president and Suleiman called for "dialogue" with the opposition, the Muslim Brotherhood's leadership agreed to meet with him. Their decision elicited a broad wave of condemnation in the protestors' ranks.

The Brotherhood maintained a deferential attitude toward the SCAF up to the eve of the June 2012 second round of the presidential election, when the military itself broke the rules of the game, attempting to seize power rather than hand it over to the president-elect. The Muslim Brothers began by reassuring it, and also Washington,[49] pledging to run candidates for only half of the seats up for vote in the parliamentary elections and consenting not to put up a candidate in the presidential elections. They also approved the antidemocratic procedure for the revision of the constitution by an ad hoc committee designated by the SCAF. An eminent member of the Brotherhood participated in the committee.

The Brothers next ran an enthusiastic campaign for a yes vote in the 19 March 2011 referendum on the constitutional revisions, whereas both the liberal and left-wing oppositions had called on Egyptians to reject them. The revisions were approved by a seventy-seven percent majority of the votes cast, after a campaign distinguished by both the extreme religious demagoguery of all the Islamic parties and the substantial means they mobilized. Thus they did not hesitate to declare that a vote against the referendum was a vote against God and Islam, while spreading the lie that the stake of the constitutional referendum was Article 2 of the existing constitution, which stipulated that "the principles of the Sharia" should be the "principal source of legislation."[50] Given the nature of the campaign for a yes vote, the sole cause for wonder is that, despite everything, nearly one-quarter of the voters (twenty-three percent) rejected the constitution.

Like their sister organization in Tunisia, the Egyptian Muslim Brothers have constantly benefited from the largesse of the emir of Qatar as well as the influence of his television network, Al Jazeera. The network's impact increased after Mubarak's downfall, with the creation of a local Al Jazeera associate, *Al-Jazeera Mubashir-Misr* (Al Jazeera direct Egypt), which Egyptian wags have renamed *Al-Jazeera Mubashir-Ikhwan* (Al Jazeera direct Brothers).[51] While there is no denying that Al

Jazeera's coverage of the Arab uprising, its first two phases in Tunisia and Egypt in particular, played a pivotal role in spreading the revolt, it is just as obvious to anyone who has followed the satellite network's reporting that it has everywhere and at all times privileged the Muslim Brothers and their vision of things in its coverage of events.

Yet, unlike Ennahda, which was outlawed on Tunisian territory until the uprising, the Muslim Brothers have, since Sadat, been able to reconstruct and then develop their network in Egypt for forty years running, albeit under close surveillance. Their strategy of building a movement in the form of a "counter-society," as big mass parties, notably workers' parties, have also done in the course of European history,[52] has been partly based on the provision of social services, a way of compensating for the terrible inadequacy of public services in Egypt.[53] The Brotherhood's strategy also proceeds from its ability to provide a spiritual refuge (religion as the "opium of the people," to cite the early Marx's famous phrase) to victims of socioeconomic oppression and all those suffering from the anomie due to economic liberalization together with local and international political upheavals.[54]

Availing itself of the freedoms acquired by the 25 January 2011 uprising, in addition to the advantages just mentioned, the Brotherhood very quickly emerged as a formidable political machine. With great fanfare, it opened new headquarters in Egypt's every nook and cranny, while also organizing congresses in five-star hotels. In addition to the social and political base that it had built up for itself over four decades, it has attracted, since the uprising, a throng of opportunists drawn by its status as the country's main political force, even before it became both the party of the new government and the new governing party. The coincidence between the Muslim Brothers' and the military's interests made itself felt once again during the first stage of the parliamentary elections, set for 28 November 2011—a year to the day after the previous elections, held under Mubarak.

As it had in those elections as well, the Brotherhood proceeded to betray the rest of the opposition to the fallen regime. The country was going through a "second revolution" that saw the biggest mobilizations since February 2011; they were directed, this time, against the SCAF and were violently put down by the military. The liberal and left-wing oppositions both called for postponing the balloting and for adopting, before elections were held, a constitution different from the "constitutional declaration" that was supposed to govern the electoral process. The Muslim Brothers, in contrast, went massively to the polls on 28

November. The famous Egyptian feminist Nawal el-Saadawi passionately expressed the revolutionaries' bitterness in an article written the day before:

> In this second Egyptian revolution, the forces opposed to the first have tipped their hand: the transitional government, led by a minister of the Mubarak era who has parachuted into the revolution like the Salafist religious current, as well as the SCAF, the Brothers, and the *fulul* (debris) of the regime. All these forces have collaborated, both secretly and openly. Blood is flowing in the streets, while they, for their part, insist that elections be held on the scheduled date. What is the explanation for this stubborn defense of the 28 November elections? Might it be a secret agreement concluded by the *fulul*, the military, and the Brothers to divide the seats in parliament up among themselves? . . .
>
> This second revolution has succeeded in unmasking the forces that trade in religion, exposing their ties to the military and Mubarak's *fulul*. It has also demonstrated the opportunism and hypocrisy of the old and new parties alike, which have again tried to co-opt the January revolution and make deals with the people in power while the blood of young people flows in the streets. They insist, today, on holding artificial elections before the adoption of a new constitution. All they want is to take the reins of government, even if the people are massacred and the country destroyed.[55]

As in Tunisia, the opposition to the old regime, with the exception of the Muslim Brotherhood, was characterized by fragmentation and organizational weakness, despite the much greater latitude for political action in Mubarak's Egypt than in Ben Ali's Tunisia. Under these circumstances, the Brothers easily emerged from the first elections held in the post-Mubarak period as the big winners. They obtained, hands down, a plurality of the seats in the People's Assembly, which was elected in three stages between November 2011 and January 2012. The coalition they headed included Islamist-leaning and liberal parties, and even Hamdeen Sabahy's Nasserite party, Karama (dignity), which stumbled into this misadventure out of sheer electoral opportunism. The coalition received 37.5% of the 27 million ballots cast, in a country in which an estimated 50 million people are eligible voters.[56] The Freedom and Justice Party, a political organization that the Brotherhood created so as to preserve its character as a purely religious movement, won nearly 42% of the seats in the People's Assembly. The only surprise the parliamentary elections held, a big one, was the score of the Salafists of the Islamic Bloc, led by the Nur Party; it came in second in the voting, garnering 27.8% of the ballots cast.

From the 1990s on, the Mubarak regime, which was closely allied with the Saudi overlords of the Salafists' Wahhabi sponsors, had facilitated the Salafists' expansion as a counterweight to the Muslim Brothers. The Salafists took advantage of the reigning anomie to lure troubled minds toward a form of religious withdrawal from the world that was outrageous in its outward aspects; they preached a political quietism based on a doctrine of submission to the powers that be. Once Mubarak was toppled, they promptly converted to political activism.[57] This change of heart was liberally subsidized by the Saudis: having lost their Egyptian accomplice, they wanted a margin of political maneuver vis-à-vis the Muslim Brothers, who were allied with their neighbor and rival, Qatar, and funded by it. When various Islamic fundamentalist movements held big antisecular demonstrations on Friday, 29 July 2011, known as the "Friday for the Application of the Sharia," Saudi flags were raised in the Salafists' ranks. This came as a shock to many.[58]

With close to 60% of the vote going to fundamentalist parties, the Egyptian parliamentary elections looked far more like an "Islamic tsunami" than did the elections to the Tunisian Constituent Assembly. Yet the Muslim Brothers' procrastination and compromising attitude toward the SCAF (typical of the rest of the Islamic fundamentalist current dominating the People's Assembly), their inability to incarnate the aspirations of the Egyptian revolution, their repeated failure to honor their commitments, especially their promises to limit their role in the elections, culminating in their decision to run a candidate for president—all this was reflected in a massive drop in the "Islamic vote."

In the first round of the presidential elections on 23 and 24 May 2012, in which 23.7 million ballots were cast, the Muslim Brothers' candidate, Mohamed Morsi, received only 24.8% of the vote, that is, 5.8 million votes as opposed to the more than 10.1 million that had gone to the coalition led by his party in the parliamentary elections. The only other Islamic candidate to emerge from the pack was Abdel-Moneim Aboul-Fotouh, who belongs to the Muslim Brothers' "modernist" tendency. Long a member of the Brotherhood's highest leadership body, Aboul-Fotouh had left it after the uprising, expressing a wish to run for president at a time when the Brotherhood was promising not to wage that battle. Trying to please everyone, he was endorsed by a broad range of tendencies that went from the main force within the Salafist current, the Nur party, to a fringe of the radical Egyptian left convinced that the Egyptian people is incapable of rallying massively to any non-"Islamist" (a variant of "Orientalism in reverse").[59]

Aboul-Fotouh won 17.5% of the votes cast, or a little over 4 million votes. Even if one puts all these votes in the "Islamic" camp, which is unwarranted, the total of fewer than 10 million votes that Morsi and Aboul-Fotouh together obtained was far lower than the 17.7 million votes that had gone to the two Islamic blocs in the parliamentary elections. In the second round of the presidential elections, held on 16 and 17 June, Morsi was the only candidate still in the running against Ahmed Shafiq, the candidate of the partisans of the old regime. He accordingly captured the votes of a majority of those who did not wish to see the country turn back the clock, including a radical left-wing group advocating the politics of the "lesser evil." Morsi nevertheless obtained just 51.7% of the ballots cast (13.2 million votes), fewer than a million more than his adversary.

The third election organized in a country turned upside down by the Arab uprising was held in Libya on 7 July 2012. Up for election were the 120 seats of the General National Congress (GNC); this body was to replace the NTC, which had presided over the uprising. Eighty percent of those eligible, or 2.9 million voters, registered to vote. Twenty-two coalitions or parties entered the lists, and 1.8 million ballots were cast, representing 62% of all registered voters. The party founded by the Muslim Brotherhood's Libyan branch, the Party of Justice and Construction (PJC), was heavily handicapped by the Brothers' negative image, which was due to several factors: its compromising dealings with Saif Gaddafi prior to the uprising; the fact that it was in the Egyptian Muslim Brothers' orbit and thus seemed to be a tentacle of the Big Brother to the east; and its association, along with the rest of the Brotherhood, with the Emirate of Qatar, fiercely resented in Libya for its meddling in Libyan politics.

The PJC won a mere 10.3% of the ballots cast, that is, less than a quarter of the 48.1% that went to the National Forces Alliance, a coalition dominated by liberals that played the card of Libyan independence. That coalition's figurehead is Mahmoud Jibril, the first person to have been designated as prime minister by the NTC in March 2011, a capacity in which he had served until he was replaced in October of the same year. (Only 80 of the 200 members of the GNC are elected by a party-list, proportional voting system; the election of the other 120 is based on a majoritarian voting system in their electoral districts.)

According to Moussa Grifa, a scholar working at the University of Tripoli, the poor results of the Islamic parties in the Libyan elections are due to the following factors: the moderate, apolitical character of the dominant strain of Libyan Islam and the fears provoked by the Salafists' attacks on sites of "popular Islam"; the population's reaction to the Islamic parties' arrogance and their attempt to take control of the new institutions in the aftermath of the revolution; a perception of the Islamic parties as vehicles for outside influences (that is, those of the oil monarchies), especially in light of the financial means at their disposal; and the mobilization of women in reaction to the fundamentalist discourse of the Islamic parties, a mobilization reflected in the election of 31 women representatives to the GNC.[60]

In Bahrain, Syria, and Yemen, the forces behind the uprisings are by no means exclusively Islamic. In all three countries, left-wing forces are playing a prominent role in the movement. In Yemen, the most archaic of the six countries of the Arab uprising discussed in these pages, the famous jihadist Salafist preacher 'Abdul-Majid al-Zindani, founder of the local branch of the Muslim Brotherhood and president of Islah's Consultative Council (*Majlis al-Shura*), published, together with other ulama, a fatwa that condemned the concept of the "civil state" and democracy as Western and advocated the creation of an "Islamic State." In response, the young revolutionaries who had organized the uprising decided to name a day of planned mobilizations, 15 July 2011, "the Friday of the civil and democratic state."

On 15 July, huge groups of demonstrators gathered on the squares of Sana'a and several other towns in Yemen beneath billboards on which the uprising's organizers had blazoned those words. At the same time, several dozen intellectuals, journalists, and political and human rights activists published a declaration sharply criticizing Zindani. They called his tendency "extremist-jihadist"; it was, they said, an "obscurantist tendency that strikes fear of Yemen's talibans into everyone's hearts." They demanded that the Islah party take "a clear, unambiguous position on Zindani's and his group's positions and acts." They branded it "a group that jeopardizes the revolution and constitutes an obstacle on its road to victory."[61]

What this overview suggests is that while the earthquake of the Arab uprising has certainly caused an "Islamic tsunami," as was only to be expected, it was, all in all, limited in size and scope. We would, moreover, do well to spin the metaphor out to the end. A tsunami is a transitory phenomenon; it rarely engulfs stretches of land for good. In time, we may very well discover that the "Islamic tsunami" was both the high point of the resurgence of Islamic fundamentalism that has been under way since the 1970s and also the point of departure for a new political cycle in the Arab region, one determined by the long-term revolutionary process that was set in motion on 17 December 2010 in Sidi Bouzid, Tunisia.

Conclusion:
The Future of the Arab Uprising

Al-Nahda, an Arabic word meaning "awakening" that is used in the sense of "renaissance," is both the name of the movement that came to power in Tunisia in 2011 and the title of the Egyptian Muslim Brothers' electoral platform, on which the new Egyptian president, Mohamed Morsi, ran for office. Islamic fundamentalism lite, that is, a relatively moderate fundamentalism striving to project an image of itself as modernist, has taken the commands in the two countries that initiated the Arab uprising. Is it truly capable of presiding over a regional "renaissance"?

THE DIFFERENCE BETWEEN ERDOGAN AND GHANNOUCHI . . .

Both movements, Tunisian and Egyptian, like to evoke the experience of Turkey's AKP, the Party for Justice and Development. Founded in 2001, the AKP came to power a year later, after a resounding victory in the legislative elections. Since then, it has racked up success after success in various fields: electoral successes, for the party has been twice reelected, in 2007 and 2011, after winning, each time, both more votes and a larger percentage of the vote than in the previous election; respectability in the West, which the AKP enjoys as the ruling party of a member state of both NATO and the OECD (the Organisation for Economic Co-operation and Development, the club of the economically developed countries); a reform of Turkish institutions, accompanied, notably, by the end of the armed forces' tutelage over politics; and, above all, Turkey's economic performance under its leadership, marked by vigorous growth and a moderate public debt ratio that contrast with the state of most European economies, hard hit by the recession. These successes are the main aspects of the "Turkish miracle." Some take it for a miraculous manifestation in the literal sense.

The Arab Islamic parties, especially those belonging to the family of the Muslim Brothers, like to think that the AKP's success is directly related to the fact that its founders, too, came from the Islamic movement. This magical conception of things ignores socioeconomic realities that are much more important than the Turkish party's religious affinities. A political party's character is not primarily determined by the nature of its general ideological references or the type of ethical "values" it propagates. It is determined, above all, by the nature of the social categories to which its leadership is organically tied and the way in which the party's real governmental program gives concrete expression to those social categories' views, interests, and aspirations.

The AKP is a product of Turkey's neoliberal transformation, launched under Turgut Özal, the country's prime minister and then its president from the 1980s until his sudden death in 1993. One of the main consequences of this period was the enrichment of the middle bourgeoisie (small and medium enterprises) of the country's peripheral zones. That bourgeoisie finds organized expression in the Independent Industrialists' and Businessmen's Association (MÜSIAD), founded in 1990. The AKP is basically a political outgrowth of MÜSIAD. And it is heir less to an Islamic tradition like the Muslim Brotherhood's, which was represented in Turkey by Necmettin Erbakan, than to that of Özal's Motherland Party (ANAP). In fact, the AKP's founders broke with Erbakan to form their own party.[1]

The AKP engineered a convergence, at the highest levels, between this peripheral Turkish capitalism—the "devout bourgeoisie," to use Sebnem Gumuscu's phrase[2]—and the majority fraction of Turkish big capital. The context for that convergence was a community of interests combining neoliberalism and a European orientation. This consolidation of capitalist power that has mobilized traditionalist populism to secure firm hegemony over Turkish society has made Bonapartist military control over civilian authorities superfluous. Such control had been established and maintained for decades in Turkey in reaction to sociopolitical instability. The AKP was able to do away with it at the price of an ideological mutation: breaking with Erbakan, its reformist founders espoused the principle of the separation of religion and state in order to forge an Islamic version of European Christian democracy. And, in fact, the AKP belongs to the European People's Party, founded by the continent's Christian democratic parties.

The Turkish economy has been characterized by marked dynamism since 2002, in the context of a radical neoliberal restructuring carried out under IMF supervision after the serious crisis that shook the Turkish economy in 2001. Its newfound dynamism finds its explanation in the combination of Turkey's industrial base (its infrastructure and technological know-how) with advantages that facilitate export (cheap labor, a sharp devaluation, and access to the European market). This is a combination that lends itself remarkably well to the neoliberal model of export-oriented industrialization. By 2000, Turkey had already gone a long way down this path: its manufacturing industry accounted for 81.2% of its total exports of goods, as opposed to 38.4% for Egypt and 9.8% for the Arab states overall.[3]

Tunisia went down a similar path under Ben Ali's dictatorship: its own manufacturing industry accounted for 77% of its total exports of goods in 2000. The big difference between the two countries appears in their growth and employment levels the same year: Tunisia's GDP per capita rose a mere 3.1%, with an unemployment rate of 15.7%, whereas Turkey boasted growth of 5.2% and had an unemployment rate of 6.5%. Ten years later, the GDP per capita growth rate had fallen to 1.9% in Tunisia, while soaring to 7.8% in Turkey. In Egypt, in the same period, GDP per capita growth stagnated: it was 3.5% in 2000 and 3.3% in 2010, far below the corresponding Turkish figure.[4]

Ennahda's and the Egyptian Muslim Brothers' problem is that, appearances notwithstanding, they have little in common with the AKP. In Tunisia, industrialization proceeded under the stewardship of Ben Ali's neopatrimonial dictatorship. Most of Tunisian capitalism adapted to the dictatorship as best it could. If we are to believe the 2010 *Global Competitiveness Report* of the World Economic Forum (the Davos Forum), drawn up by Columbia University's Xavier Sala-i-Martin on the basis of interviews with business executives, the hundred participating Tunisian executives' degree of satisfaction with their country's public institutions[5] put Tunisia in 20th place in this category, ahead of France (26th) and far ahead of Italy (88th). The most surprising rankings had to do with ethics and corruption in public institutions (Tunisia 18th, France 29th), diversion of public funds (Tunisia 20th,

France 25th), public trust of politicians (Tunisia 15th, France 31st), the transparency of government decisions (Tunisia 20th, France 28th), and even favoritism in decisions of government officials (Tunisia 12th, France 32nd)! As far as public institutions are concerned, France fared better than Tunisia in just one category: irregular payments and bribes (Tunisia 33rd, France 29th).[6]

By 2011, Tunisian public institutions had slipped back to 40th place in the opinion of the country's business executives. In 2012, the World Economic Forum decided temporarily to omit Tunisia under the new, Ennahda-dominated government from its report "because an important structural break in the data ma[de] comparisons with past years difficult."[7]

In line with the Muslim Brothers' general profile, Ennahda finds its basic source of support in the Tunisian petty bourgeoisie, self-employed workers, and traditional small urban and rural entrepreneurs, but also in one segment of the modern middle classes, especially members of the liberal professions and office workers. People in these social categories are attracted by Ennahda's traditionalist religious populism, but also by the self-image it grooms by presenting itself as a "centrist" movement representing the "golden mean."

After denouncing the old regime's corruption and despotism, the Ennahda government, adopting the same tone its predecessors had, harshly upbraided the wage laborers and unemployed youth who maintained their struggle in pursuit of social and economic demands; it blamed the country's economic woes on them.[8] Similarly, Ennahda took up a position halfway between modernists who demand freedom of cultural and artistic expression and the Tunisian Salafists, who have made such freedom their main bugbear. The modernists denounce its accommodating attitude toward the Salafists, accusing it of failing to repress their machinations and attempting to intimidate others so as to create a situation in which it can pass off regressive measures as compromises.

In the past, Ennahda did not enjoy much support among Tunisia's capitalists. This was a natural consequence of the fact that, under the dictatorship, the movement was strictly outlawed and repressed. Hardly had it taken the reins of government than it sought to reassure Tunisian employers, as the blogger Emna El-Hammi points out:

> Ennahdha kept faith with its liberal political vision by meeting with the business community as soon as its victory [in the elections to the Constituent Assembly] had been announced. One meeting took place at the headquarters of the Tunisian Union of Industry, Trade, and Handicrafts (UTICA). Another

was held at the Tunisian stock market, for the purpose of reassuring investors in the Tunisian capital market. Ennahdha also engaged in dialogue with firms active in the tourist industry with an eye to developing this key sector of the Tunisian economy.[9]

Ennahda professes the Islamic version of the neoliberal credo, which looks to private initiative for economic development and substitutes the activity of religious charitable organizations for welfare rights guaranteed by the state. The fact is, however, that really existing Tunisian capitalism, which constitutes the unsurpassable horizon of Ennahda's vision, is incapable of solving the economic and social problems at the origin of the Tunisian uprising.

Tunisian capitalism was rather relieved when it was freed of the onerous burden of control by Ben Ali's clan. Under the dictator, the Tunisian bosses' boss, the head of UTICA, offered a good résumé of the nature of the regime in his person: Hedi Jilani became the organization's president in 1987, the year Ben Ali seized power. Jilani was a member of the RCD leadership and a parliamentary deputy; one of his two daughters is the wife of a nephew of the fallen dictator, while the other is married to Ben Ali's brother-in-law, Belhassen Trabelsi, a Mafioso of the first rank. Jilani was forced to step down shortly after Ben Ali fled.

The fact remains that, for the export and tourist industries, which are the Tunisian economy's main sources of foreign exchange, the old regime's despotism and nepotism represented "transaction costs" (to borrow the expression of institutionalist economists) that were, all in all, deemed acceptable in view of the profits that the dictatorship's seeming stability and its positive image in the West allowed those industries to rake in.

Indications are that the Tunisian economy's performance under the Ennahda government, in contrast, will be worse than under the dictatorship. This is due to a number of factors: the instability of postdictatorial Tunisia; Ennahda's incompetence when it comes to capitalist management; Tunisian capitalism's mistrust of a populist, petty-bourgeois movement of religious inspiration that includes a hard-core fundamentalist component and has taken an accommodating stance toward the Salafists; and, above all, the movement's inability to forestall the intensification of social struggles whose protagonists have been emboldened by the uprising's victory.

To put it another way, the growth deficit responsible for sizable, steadily rising unemployment rates under Ben Ali, especially among youth, will only get worse, exacerbating the country's social problems as it does. At a time when unemployment is already significantly higher than in 2010, Tunisian employers are warning against the country's "deteriorating investment climate."[10] The "entrepreneurial strategy of self-limitation"[11] that was dictated by fears of arbitrary despotism in Ben Ali's day will, for the reasons just stated, only be reinforced under Ennahda.

Far from mobilizing the country's domestic resources by means of determined state intervention from a developmentalist perspective, Ennahda, with its typically neoliberal, rentier vision, is looking beyond the country's borders for ways to solve this crisis. Thus it has solicited subsidies and investment from Qatar and other GCC monarchies, while praying that the economy of its Libyan neighbor will recover and once again thin the ranks of Tunisia's unemployed. It has also sought assistance from European countries and the United States and taken out a new loan from the World Bank. All this comes at a time when the country is already staggering under the weight of the debt it contracted under Ben Ali.[12] This economic strategy has very little chance of pulling the country out of the quagmire.[13]

That is one reason that the Tunisian government designated by the Constituent Assembly elected in October 2011 has adopted so accommodating a stance toward the repressive apparatus bequeathed it by the dictator. This indulgence, laced with a heavy dose of cowardice, has attained levels such that even international human rights organizations have seen fit to deplore it. The highly revelatory occasion for their protest was a trial, held in the town of Kef, of twenty-three ranking members of Ben Ali's security forces (including the dictator himself, in absentia). They were charged with ordering subordinates to fire on demonstrators during the December 2010–January 2011 uprising. Of the 132 people who died as a result of the repression, 23, according to an official report published in May 2012, fell in the cities of Thala and Kasserine on 8 and 9 January 2011:

> Amnesty International deplored that several officers charged with the killing of protesters have not been suspended and continue to carry out their duties, compounding the fears of the families of victims that they will not be held accountable for their actions.
>
> One of the defendants, Moncef Laajimi, was the director of the riot police ("Quwat al Tadakhol") in the northern region of Tunisia, including the towns of Thala and Kasserine, during the uprising. He has been charged for giving the orders to shoot protesters in the region. The families of victims resented that he remained free and was even promoted following the uprising to become the General Director of that police force. On 28 December, in

the only court session he has attended so far for questioning, he was escorted by a large number of security officers who according to lawyers and others present threatened to storm the court if Moncef Laajimi was detained.[14]

The second transitional government—between March and October 2011—in March appointed one of the accused, Moncef Krifa, who had been regional director of Anti-Riot Police in Kasserine [known by their French acronym, BOP], to be director of the Presidential Guard.

Likewise, after his indictment, the same government promoted Moncef Laajimi, a defendant who had been head of the Anti-Riot Police in Tala, to be director general of the Anti-Riot Police. On January 10, 2012, the new interior minister, Ali Laaridh, removed Laajimi from his position. However, under pressure from the Anti-Riot Police union, who threatened a general strike, he later retracted his decision and appointed Laajimi deputy chief of cabinet at the Interior Ministry.[15]

As for the Tunisian army, it is cultivating an image as arbiter of the situation by posing as a state institution above all the others, under the direction of Chief of Staff of the Land Army General Rashid Ammar, who was promoted to the post of chairman of the joint chiefs of staff in April 2011. After profiling himself as the nation's savior, Ammar has been posturing as the supreme overseer of the country's government and has not hesitated to issue the occasional warning. Moreover, the Kef trials are being conducted by military tribunals, a circumstance that guarantees that there will be no investigation of the army's real role in, and responsibility for, crushing the uprising.[16]

When Ayoub Messaoudi, a young advisor to Tunisian President Moncef Marzouki, resigned in protest over the way Ammar had circumvented Marzouki to extradite the former Libyan prime minister in June 2012, publicly denouncing this violation of democratic principle, the chief of staff had him brought before the military tribunal. Messaoudi has explained the situation in terms that provide an excellent summary of the situation in Tunisia:

> The Ennahda party is plainly being confused with the state, as the RCD was confused with the state before Ben Ali's downfall. So I publicly explained what was happening. I mentioned the commander of the army, Rashid Ammar, by name, as well as Defense Minister Abdelkarim Zbidi, and I called this extradition an act of state treason.
>
> On 20 July, the government issued a communiqué condemning my statement and threatening me with legal prosecution. My friends started calling me to warn me not to return from France, where I was spending a little time with my wife and children, who live there. My place, however, was in Tunisia, and I returned to the country on 9 August, the day when the social movements began in Sidi Bouzid. I went to that city on the 11th to try to understand what was going on and, on the 12th, I published an article enti-

tled "Sidi Bouzid and the Mafia" in which I explained that the deep state had not been overthrown on 14 January [2011], since the roots of the system had been preserved. Only the tip of the regime—the Ben Ali clan—had been sacrificed.

I think that the fact that I come from the system spawned fears that my words would have greater impact on the population. On 15 August, the political bureau of the party I belonged to, the CPR [the Congress for the Republic, the party of Tunisian interim president Moncef Marzouki], convened in order to suspend my membership; Rashid Ammar testified before the military tribunal; and, the same day, the judge decided to forbid me to travel abroad.[17]

. . . AND THE DIFFERENCE BETWEEN ERDOGAN AND MORSI

Mohamed Morsi has apparently done better. On 12 August 2012, the new Egyptian president sent the SCAF's two most eminent members into retirement. Both of these military men had been close associates of Hosni Mubarak: Hussein Tantawi, the commander in chief of the armed forces and minister of defense without interruption since 1991, and Sami Anan, chief of staff since 2005. This operation was orchestrated with great fanfare in order to make the very colorless Morsi out to be a forceful and, to boot, "revolutionary" president, since he was supposedly fulfilling what had become the popular movement's main demand throughout the year preceding his election: that the army go back to its barracks.

The Muslim Brothers promptly mobilized to sing the praises of the president—a loyal follower of the Brotherhood's leadership, just as the Tunisian prime minister is a loyal follower of Ennahda's chief and Tunisia's real president, Rached Ghannouchi. Presenting Morsi as the man who has fulfilled the "revolution's" wishes is all the more grotesque for the fact that he has named the chief of military intelligence, Abdul-Fattah al-Sisi, to replace Tantawi. Sisi had distinguished himself in June 2011 by justifying the "virginity tests" that the SCAF had inflicted, among other humiliations, on seventeen female demonstrators who had been arrested on Tahrir Square in March. (Sisi's declarations were such an embarrassment that the SCAF was forced to publicly disavow him.)

In actual fact, of all the dismissals of military leaders punctuating the history of the Egyptian republic, the one for which Morsi was responsible is the least dramatic. Compared with the dismissals of Amer, Chazly, or Abu Ghazalah, engineered by Morsi's three presidential predecessors,[18] his dismissal of Tantawi and Anan appears as an act of broad consensus, so broad, indeed, that even those relieved of their commands approved of it. The novelty, undoubtedly, is that Morsi is the first Egyptian president not to have come from the army's ranks. This fact has been thrown into sharp relief by untold commentators who seem to have forgotten that the Egyptian uprising cheated another civilian of the presidency: Gamal Mubarak, Hosni's son. Yet it is clearly because Morsi is a civilian lacking prestige and professional authority in the military's eyes that he took care to confer with the upper echelons of the armed forces, in order to secure their full approval before deciding on dismissals, promotions, and appointments from their ranks, as has been attested by both the military men themselves and numerous observers.

Tantawi and Anan had to go in any case. Born in 1935, the SCAF's former chief had long since passed the age limit for the exercise of high military functions. As for Anan, born in 1948, he had lingered in the post of army chief of staff for seven years, although it is traditionally rotated every four years in Egypt. The man had been closely associated with Mubarak. Even before the Egyptian president was toppled, an Egyptian expert with intimate knowledge of the country's military hierarchy had predicted that Anan was "too close to Mubarak to stay," should the president himself step down.[19] Mubarak and Tantawi were both deeply resented by Egyptian army officers, as is attested by the 23 September 2008 secret report of the US Embassy in Cairo revealed by WikiLeaks:

> Recently, academics and civilian analysts painted a portrait of an Egyptian military in intellectual and social decline, whose officers have largely fallen out of society's elite ranks. They describe a disgruntled mid-level officer corps harshly critical of a defense minister they perceive as incompetent and valuing loyalty above skill in his subordinates. However, analysts perceive the military as retaining strong influence through its role in ensuring regime stability and operating a large network of commercial enterprises. . . .
>
> Since Abu Ghazalah, X noted, the regime has not allowed any charismatic figures to reach the senior ranks. "(Defense Minister) Tantawi looks like a bureaucrat," he joked. X described the mid-level officer corps as generally disgruntled, and said that one can hear mid-level officers at MOD clubs around Cairo openly expressing disdain for Tantawi. These officers refer to Tantawi as "Mubarak's poodle," he said, and complain that "this incompetent Defense Minister" who reached his position only because of unwavering loyalty to Mubarak is "running the military into the ground."[20]

Thus it was obvious that Tantawi and Anan could not cling to their posts very long after presidential power was handed over, as has been confirmed by Mustafa Higazi, another Egyptian specialist on the military:

> In an interview with *Aljazeera.net*, Higazi described Egyptian president Mohamed Morsi's decisions about the SCAF's leaders as being, in some sense, a change of generations. Higazi said that this change had long been under discussion in Egyptian army circles and that the name of Egypt's current Defense Minister, General Abdul-Fattah al-Sisi [born in 1954], had been seriously advanced. . . .
>
> According to this analysis, Higazi thinks that the military has the same power it always has, despite the changes, with the difference that the new leadership does not assert this power as crudely as previous leaderships may sometimes seem to have.
>
> To illustrate his analysis, Higazi points to the way Tantawi and Anan were honored by, among other things, being named [presidential] advisors, besides being given high distinctions. He also points to the appointment of the previous chief of the military police to the post of Egyptian military attaché in China, and cites the fact that the military has maintained its economic interests and control over its own affairs.[21]

Tantawi's and Anan's exit thus took place under very favorable conditions for the two men: rather than being judged for crimes committed by the repressive forces while the SCAF was overseeing Egypt's government, as the revolutionaries of Tahrir Square and other strongholds of the Egyptian uprising had repeatedly demanded (but then every member of the SCAF would have had to face judgment, including the new commander in chief of the armed forces and defense minister appointed by Morsi), they obtained de facto immunity from persecution for their past acts. Indeed, the president thanked them, decorated them, and even offered them sinecures! Describing that as a "revolutionary" deed, if not a "coup d'état," is one symptom of a very advanced case of political myopia—if it is not simply a question of bad faith intended to deceive the people.

The army's power and privileges have by no means diminished under Morsi in comparison with what they were under Mubarak. Egypt has seen nothing even remotely resembling the events in Turkey, where heads in the military hierarchy rolled one after the next, dozens of high-ranking officers were put on trial, and the members of the armed forces' joint staff went into "voluntary" retirement, ceding their posts to successors named by the AKP government—developments that put a real end to the military's tutelage over the Turkish political authorities. The difference between Morsi and Erdogan is considerable here, like that between the Muslim Brothers and the AKP.

Unlike their sister organization in Tunisia, the Egyptian Muslim Brothers had the leisure to establish ties with a fraction of Egyptian capitalism, for reasons explained in Chapter 3. Released from prison by Sadat in order to serve as a counterweight to both stalwarts of the Nasserite tradition and the post-1967 student New Left, the Muslim Brothers had enjoyed a wide margin of maneuver in the fields of public morality and culture as zealous contributors to Egypt's Islamization, the main ideological stratagem of Nasser's successor. Tolerated under tight surveillance where their political activity was concerned, they were much less severely restricted when it came to promoting the new Islamic moral order that the regime deemed useful. Thus Sadat, like Mubarak after him, fit perfectly into the Saudi era inaugurated by the boom in oil revenues after Nasser.

The *infitah* in Egypt, in conjunction with the old and new Egyptian emigration to the Saudi kingdom, had facilitated the emergence of a "devout bourgeoisie." Members of this bourgeoisie soon assumed leading positions in the Muslim Brotherhood. They are represented there by the organization's second in command, Khairat al-Shatir, a very wealthy businessman.[22] Some have even seen the 2007 trial of several businessmen accused of belonging to the Brotherhood as stemming from

> competition between two groups of people who controlled capital in Egypt: Gamal Mubarak's, and the Brothers'. All of the accused were rich businessmen who belonged to the Brotherhood, beginning with Khairat al-Shatir. . . .
>
> Which companies the Muslim Brothers own and how far they have penetrated Egypt's economic structure remain secrets, like everything else involving the Brotherhood. It is impossible to determine the number of firms that belong to it, or how many millions or billions of Egyptian pounds they earn. However, we do, at least, have a public list of enterprises confiscated from them during the 2007 court martial . . . seventy-two companies engaged in commercial or rent-producing activity, selling consumer goods to the Egyptian upper and middle classes . . . the Al-Farida clothing stores; the Sanabil trade firm; Al-Shihab in automobile sales; Virginia in tourism; Misr in construction; and so on.[23]

This brief overview of the segment of the Egyptian "devout bourgeoisie" that has rallied to the Brothers suggests that it does not differ qualitatively from the rest of the Egyptian or Arab *infitah* bourgeoisie, which is chiefly engaged in commerce, construction, or speculation. The Muslim Brothers also include industrialists in the domestic consumer goods sector in their ranks or immediate entourage. Thus they reflect the overall makeup of Egyptian market capitalism. This crucial difference between Egyptian capitalism and its Turkish counterpart, dominated by industrial export-oriented capital, is not sufficiently taken into account in Sebnem Gumuscu's otherwise interesting comparison between the Turkish and Egyptian Islamic political movements:

> Economic policies in Egypt enabled the state to construct a new winners circle mostly composed of big business and state bourgeoisie, pushing small and medium entrepreneurs and the middle and lower classes to the sidelines. As a result, the devout bourgeoisie emerged divided and ineffective. Small devout businessmen have never found the opportunity to expand, given the unfavorable economic environment for small-scale manufacturers. Only big businesses owned by devout families could grow in this economic environment and could do so heavily dependent on the state. . . . [24]
>
> Second, continued state dominance in the economy combined with ongoing confrontation with the Islamists had significant consequences for the activity of [the] devout bourgeoisie within political movements. Because of high costs associated with political Islamic activity, many devout businessmen have remained apolitical, whereas some parts of the devout bourgeoisie [have] stayed closer to the moderate and less confrontational line of the Wasat Party. This ultimately left the [sic] mainstream political Islam under the dominance of lower-middle classes whose interests have been hurt by economic reforms and who demand an Islamic state to replace the existing corrupt and exclusionary regime.[25]

Gumuscu is doubtless right to emphasize that the petty bourgeoisie and middle strata have greater weight in the Egyptian Muslim Brotherhood than in the AKP. However, whereas the Turkish party— after constituting itself in a break with the reactionary populist tradition embodied by Erbakan—has succeeded in achieving hegemony, its nearest equivalent in Egypt, the Wasat (center) Party, created by Brotherhood dissidents, has remained on the sidelines; it is even more typically confined to the modern middle strata, especially the liberal professions, than the Brotherhood itself. On the other hand, the Brotherhood includes representatives of big capital among its members and even in its leadership and has come forward as a representative of the market bourgeoisie's interests against the corrupt state bourgeoisie's.

In a sense, the Muslim Brothers' economic credo of free enterprise unhampered by state interference is more closely consonant with neoliberal doctrine than was the form of capitalism dominant under Mubarak. This holds in particular for the version of that credo articulated by Khairat al-Shatir, the Brotherhood's very capitalist number two after the *murshid* (guide), and a representative of its most conservative wing, or by Hassan Malek, an extremely wealthy, eminent member of the Brotherhood who, after making his debut in the business world in a partnership with al-Shatir, today manages, with his son, a constellation of enterprises in textile, furniture, and trade employing more than 400 people. The portrait of Malek painted by *Bloomberg Businessweek* could well have been titled *The Brotherhood Ethic and the Spirit of Capitalism*, so faithfully does it seem to paraphrase Weber's classic:

> [The Maleks] are part of a generation of religious conservatives ascendant in the Muslim world, whose devotion to God invigorates their determination to succeed in business and politics. As Malek says, "I have nothing else in my life but work and family." These Islamists pose a formidable challenge to secular governance in countries such as Egypt—not only because of their conservatism but because of their work ethic, single-minded focus, and apparent abstention from sloth and sin. They're up for winning any contest. . . .
>
> "The core of the economic vision of Brotherhood, if we are going to classify it in a classical way, is extreme capitalist," says Sameh Elbarqy, a former member of the Brotherhood.[26]

This "extreme capitalism" makes itself felt in the choice of economic experts in the assembly charged with drafting a new Egyptian constitution. The assembly is heavily dominated by the Muslim Brothers and Salafists and has for that reason been boycotted by the liberal and left opposition:

> Tareq El-Dessouki is a businessman and now MP with the [Salafist] Nour Party. Heading the economic committee in Egypt's new parliament, among his duties are settling disputes with Saudi investors in Egypt.
>
> Hussein Hamed Hassan, 80 years old, is an expert in Islamic finance who has held executive posts at the Islamic International Bank, Dubai Islamic Bank, Al-Sharja National Islamic and the International Union of Islamic Banks.
>
> Maabed Ali El-Garhi is head of the [International Association for Islamic Economics] and an ally of Salafist Sheikh Mohamed Hassan. [He also holds high-ranking posts in the Emirates Islamic Bank and the Dubai stock market.]
>
> Ibrahim El-Arabi is a businessman close to the Muslim Brotherhood and a member of Cairo's Chamber of Commerce.
>
> Hussein El-Qazzaz is director of a business consultancy and a friend of the recently-announced Brotherhood presidential candidate Khairat El-Shater.
>
> In contrast to the pro-business group in charge of drafting economic policy, the entire 100-member constituent assembly proposed by the Freedom and Justice Party (FJP) [the party created by the Brotherhood] includes only three workers' representatives:
>
> Abdel-Fattah Khattab, [the head of the Tourism and Hotel Workers Union] under Mubarak.
>
> Khaled El-Azhari, a member of the FJP and former member of the dissolved Trade Union Federation.
>
> Maher Khezema, also a FJP member and ex-member of the Trade Union Federation.[27]

The former Muslim Brother interviewed by *Bloomberg Businessweek* asked the right question. What is in doubt is clearly not the Brotherhood's allegiance to the neoliberal capitalism of the Mubarak era, but its capacity to shed its worst traits:

> What remains to be seen is whether the crony capitalism that characterized the Mubarak regime will change with pro-business Brotherhood leaders such as Malek and el-Shater in charge. Although the Brotherhood has traditionally worked to alleviate the conditions of the poor, "the working people and farmers will suffer because of this new class of businessmen," Elbarqy says. "One of the big problems with the Muslim Brotherhood now—they have it in common with Mubarak's old political party—is the marriage of power and capital."[28]

In any case, this marriage of state power and capital removes the main obstacle to Egyptian capitalism's collaboration with the Brotherhood pointed out by Gumuscu: the repressive harassment of the Brothers under Mubarak. The Muslim Brothers are today assiduously emulating the Turkish experience by creating an association of businessmen, EBDA (Egyptian Business Development Association), which addresses itself, in particular, to small and medium enterprises. It has been constructed on the model of MÜSIAD, with the direct help of that Turkish association.[29] Like the AKP and Erdogan's government, however, the Brotherhood and Mohamed Morsi pose as representatives of the common interests of all categories of Egyptian capitalism, big and small, not excluding the segment of it that collaborated with the old regime—a sizable segment of its uppermost levels in particular, as might be expected. Only the corrupt capitalist faction that was the most closely associated with the Mubarak clan is missing from this family portrait, for it accompanied the Mubaraks in their fall from power and was dragged before the courts; some of its members even found themselves behind bars.

Morsi's government has, moreover, maintained Decree no. 4 of 2012, issued by the last SCAF government and passed into law by the parliamentary majority dominated by the Muslim Brothers before parliament was dissolved. This decree exonerates entrepreneurs guilty, under Mubarak, of corruption or diversion of public funds from criminal or administrative prosecution, by offering them the opportunity to settle such matters amicably with government commissions.[30]

The makeup of the delegation of eighty businessmen that joined Morsi on his August 2012 trip to China nicely illustrates the Brotherhood's capitalist syncretism. The new president wants to play the role of traveling salesman for Egyptian capitalism, in the style of Western heads of state. The members of the delegation were chosen by Hassan Malek, who formed a committee charged with organizing communications between business circles and the president's office. Invited to make the trip were several business executives who had belonged to the former ruling party, the NDP, and collaborated with the old regime. Among them was Mohamed Farid Khamis, chairman of Oriental Weavers, which boasts that it is the biggest producer of machine-made rugs and carpeting in the world. Khamis was a member of the NDP's political bureau and of parliament as well. Another member of the former ruling party's political bureau included in the delegation, Sherif El-Gabaly, was reputedly a close associate of Gamal Mubarak. El-Gabaly is on the board of the Egyptian Federation of Industry and chairman of Polyserve, an industrial group that makes chemical fertilizers.[31]

Basically, Morsi has taken up a position resembling Erdogan's, at the point of convergence of various capitalist fractions in his country and squarely on the path that Egyptian capitalism overall had already been following. There is, however, a major difference here between the Muslim Brothers and the AKP—and, therefore, between Morsi and Erdogan. As mentioned earlier, it resides less in the differing relative weight of the petty bourgeoisie and middle strata in the two organizations than in the very nature of the capitalism whose interests each represents: in the Turkish case, a form of capitalism dominated by the export-oriented industry of an "emergent" country; in the Egyptian case, a rentier state, and a capitalism that is dominated by commercial and speculative interests and heavily marked by decades of neopatrimonialism and nepotism. This difference has certainly not escaped Gumuscu's attention,[32] but she has not drawn all the consequences as far as Egypt is concerned.

The trip to China was, to be sure, meant to promote Egyptian exports and reduce the $7 billion–plus Egyptian trade deficit in exchanges between the two countries. The Egyptians also sought to convince the Chinese leaders to invest in their country, albeit with little success. Morsi's basic continuity with Mubarak, however, appears in Egypt's manifest dependency on GCC capital—with the difference that Qatar has replaced the Saudi kingdom as the new regime's main source of funding, as is only natural in light of the Muslim Brothers' relationship with the emirate. Qatar has granted Egypt a loan of $2 billion and pledged to invest $18 billion over a five-year period in industrial and petrochemical projects, as well as tourism and real estate; it is also considering acquiring Egyptian banks. Moreover, Morsi's government has applied for a $4.8 billion loan from the IMF, making it clear that it is entirely disposed to comply with the IMF's conditions as far as budgetary austerity and other neoliberal reforms go.

A note on the MENA region drawn up by the IMF for the May 2011 G8 summit offers a preview of these conditions:

> About 700,000 people enter Egypt's labor market every year. Absorbing them and reducing the number of the currently unemployed will require a more vibrant economy. Achieving this requires bold actions, many of which will have to be implemented by the government that will emerge from the general elections later this year. Key reform challenges include enhancing competition so that markets become more contestable for domestic and foreign investors; creating a business environment that attracts and retains private investment and supports small businesses; reforming labor markets; and reducing the fiscal deficit, including by reducing waste through general subsidies. . . . To avoid excessive reliance on the domestic borrowing and leave sufficient space for private sector credit growth, continued external financing will remain desirable for several more years, including from the private sector.[33]

These new loans will exacerbate Egypt's already very onerous debt burden: one-quarter of the country's state budget expenditure, which exceeds receipts by thirty-five percent, currently goes to servicing its debt. The decision to borrow more, in compliance with neoliberal logic, means that the government will have no choice but to cut public sector salaries as well as the subsidies and pensions that go to the neediest. Morsi, moreover, promised a delegation of businessmen on a September 2012 visit to Egypt organized by the US Chamber of Commerce that he will unhesitatingly carry out drastic structural reforms to put the country's economy back on its feet.[34] Given these economic orientations, the regime will inevitably have to prepare to repress social and working-class struggles. The new government's effort to suppress labor union freedoms won as a result of the uprising, like the spiraling dismissals of labor union activists, are harbingers of things to come.

Morsi, his government, and, behind them, the Muslim Brothers are leading Egypt down the road to economic and social catastrophe. Neoliberal prescriptions, applied in the country's present socio-economic environment, have already provided ample proof that they cannot help Egypt break out of the vicious circle of underdevelopment and dependency. Quite the contrary: they have plunged it even deeper into the quagmire. The profound political and social instability engendered by the uprising only make the prospect of growth led by private investment still more improbable. And one has to have a strong dose of faith to believe that Qatar will make up for the penury of public investment in Egypt, particularly in a climate of uncertainty about the country's future.

In Mubarak's day, the only recourse the poor had was to charity, combined with "the opium of the people." "Islam is the solution," the Muslim Brothers have been promising them for decades, masking, with this empty slogan, their incapacity to draw up an economic program fundamentally different from the government's. The hour of truth has now come. As Khaled Hroub has stressed,

> in the period just ahead of us, these two questions or logics—the slogan "Islam is the solution" and the discourse in the name of religion—will, with their ideological burden, face the test of a public, mass experiment conducted in the laboratory of popular consciousness. The experiment may last a long time, devouring the lives of an entire generation. It seems, however, that the Arab peoples must inevitably traverse this historical period, so that their consciousness can make a gradual transition from an exaggerated obsession with their identity to an awareness of political, social, and economic reality—in other words, so that the consciousness of the peoples and public opinion can negotiate the passage from a utopia that consists in founding one's hopes on illusory ideological slogans to confrontation with reality and evaluation of parties and movements as a function of the real, concrete programs they present on the ground.[35]

Those who traffic in "the opium of the people" have now become the government. The soporific power of their promises has inevitably waned as a result, the more so as—this is another difference between Khomeini, on the one hand, and Ghannouchi and Morsi, on the other—they do not have the advantage of a big oil rent with which to buy the consent or resignation of a large segment of the population. Maxime Rodinson posed the issue very well more than a quarter of a century ago:

> Islamic fundamentalism is a temporary, transitory movement, but it can last another 30 or 50 years—I don't know how long. Where fundamentalism isn't in power it will continue to be an ideal, as long as the basic frustration and discontent persist that lead people to take extreme positions. You need long experience with clericalism to finally get fed up with it—look how much time it took in Europe! Islamic fundamentalists will continue to dominate the period for a long time to come.
>
> If an Islamic fundamentalism regime failed very visibly and ushered in an obvious tyranny, an abjectly hierarchical society, and also experienced setbacks in nationalist terms, that could lead many people to turn to an alternative that denounces these failings. But that would require a credible alternative that enthuses and mobilizes people. It won't be easy.[36]

CONDITIONS FOR A GENUINE SOLUTION

The great poverty of the Egyptian Muslim Brothers' program is attested by their main slogan: "Islam is the solution." Further proof of it is provided by the *Project for the Nahda* (*Mashru' al-Nahda*), subtitled *An Egyptian Nahda Based on Islam* (*Nahda misriyya bi-marja'iyya islamiyya*), which the Brotherhood published amid great fanfare in April 2012 as it was gearing up for the presidential election campaign. The socioeconomic chapter of this "program," which, the introduction tells us, is the fruit of fifteen years of effort, consists of a collection of hollow slogans adorned with verses from the Qur'an. Similarly inspired, the Brotherhood's supreme guide was led to announce, in a discussion of agriculture, that surat Yusuf (the section of the Qur'an named after the prophet Joseph) offers "a marvelous way to make the Egyptian economy thrive and to avoid droughts."[37]

This unabashed sort of "magical thinking" informs even the main slogan itself, which is more incantation than rational argument. Given the fact that a majority of Muslim countries are in crisis, it might seem rather more reasonable to suppose that "Islam is the problem." It is, to be sure, a stock idea typical of "Orientalist" thinking that the Muslim countries' problems can be chalked up to the Islamic faith. In fact, Islam is neither the problem nor the solution. Religion may seem to play a bigger role in countries with majority Muslim populations than elsewhere; yet it is a question here not of a cause, but of an effect of those countries' socioeconomic condition. Factors such as those analyzed in the first chapters of this book are far more decisive than religion.

Mohamed Morsi's *Presidential Program*, published in May 2012, was concocted on the basis of a *Project for the Nahda* shorn of references to the Qur'an, but not of a goodly number of invocations of the divine will. The same collection of clichés and truisms that litter the *Project* is to be found in the *Program* as well. Whereas the private sector is described as "the true propeller of sustainable human development," the "state's economic role" is reduced to four components. Topping the list is the fight against corruption. It is followed by the tasks of setting financial, monetary, and commercial policy; exploiting natural resources in optimal fashion; and, finally, absorbing the parallel (informal) economy in the formal economy. This minimalist definition of the state's economic role, consonant with neoliberal dogma, is the exact opposite of what Egypt and the other countries of the Arab region need to extricate themselves from the swamp they are in.

The reader will perhaps pardon me for quoting a talk that I gave on 18 December 2011 in Sidi Bouzid at the invitation of the Committee for the Commemoration of the First Anniversary of the 17 December 2010 Revolution:

> The forces that dominate the electoral scene all espouse neoliberal principles prioritizing the market, private sector, and free trade, the very principles that led our countries into the quagmire they are in today. The grave problem of development afflicting our societies stems from the kind of capitalism that prevails in our countries, together with the dominance that oil rent exercises over our economies. It is a capitalism of quick profits, with no interest in making long-term productive investments capable of inducing intensive job growth, the more so as the capitalists are alarmed by the instability characteristic of the Arab region. The truth is that the revolutionary conditions that are developing in our region, together with the corresponding rise in social demands, will only increase the reluctance of the dominant form of capitalism to engage in job-creating investment.
>
> The undeniable truth is, therefore, that reliance on private capital will not give us economic development. If we are to develop, we must break sharply with the neoliberal model in order to put the state and public sector back in command of development, and we must focus the country's resources on this crucial priority by means of progressive taxation and nationalizations.
>
> For all their drawbacks, the developmental policies put in practice in our region from the 1950s to the 1970s had a more positive impact and more positive social effects than the neoliberal policies that followed. What is required today is a return to the developmental policies of that period, without the despotism and corruption that accompanied them. The regimes that replaced them have simply done away with developmentalism, while maintaining despotism and taking corruption to a much higher level.
>
> The fact that the masses have become accustomed to making their voices heard in the streets and public squares since the revolution began in Sidi Bouzid is the crucial condition for popular democratic control of a concentration of the nation's potential in state hands. This condition is indispensable if the Arab world is finally to take the path of development without corruption, after having experienced, from the 1950s on, first, development with corruption, and then corruption without development.[38]

There is a much more solid sociopolitical basis for such a project in the Arab region than is suggested by the results of the various parliamentary elections held there since the historic December 2010 turn. The simple fact is that the forces comprising this basis, those at the head and heart of the Arab uprising, were absent during the elections, or were pushed to the margins of the electoral arena. This was the case even in the two countries that pioneered the uprising, where genuinely free elections took place. As Rashid Khalidi has observed, one thing that's obvious is that the kind of forces that organized the revolution do not have the skills to run in elections. . . .

One of the reasons that the revolution succeeded is that it was not organized hierarchically—it was organized in terms of a network and it didn't have any real formal structural organization. That enabled them to elude the surveillance of the Mukhabarat (secret services). And it's why the revolution was so wildly successful. That's why they eluded the secret police of various Arab countries.

But elections are not won by enthusiasm or networks . . . elections are won by pyramid-like structures with money and organizations; elections are won by machines. Anybody who didn't think that the Muslim Brotherhood would do well in these elections, especially once the National Democratic Party was disqualified, was not looking at reality.[39]

I have already underscored the fact that the effectiveness of the "virtual" networks built up with the resources of the Internet depended to a great extent on the connection between those "virtual" networks and the real ones forged by political and social activism in the countries involved (Chapter 4). The young people responsible for the rapid progress of the uprisings in Tunisia and Egypt had neither the material means nor the organizational resources required to participate effectively in electoral campaigns. The horizontal, anarchic pluralism characteristic of the way a virtual social network functions is hard to transfer to the type of organizational mechanism needed to carry out a real electoral campaign in a country in which nothing can replace door-to-door electioneering—if only because Internet penetration remains quite partial there—unless one happens to own a television station.

A project for progressive change could have carried the elections only if it had found its base of support in the workers' movement and the associated political forces. Anyone familiar with Tunisia knows that the chief organized force there, after the collapse of the party of the dictatorship, was and remains the national trade union center UGTT. In a context marked by the shattering and dispersal of the forces of the political left, the UGTT provided, over the years, a unifying framework for the activists of the left forces engaged in social struggles. There can be little doubt that if the UGTT had participated as such in the parliamentary elections, it would have won, defeating Ennahda by a large margin.

This is not an original or unprecedented perspective. The UGTT, which has always had a political dimension over and above its basic identity as a labor confederation, participated in Tunisian parliamentary elections on three occasions, in 1956, 1981, and 1986. To be sure, it did so each time in an alliance with Bourguiba's party, the ruling party after the country won its independence in 1956, yet it maintained real autonomy. In 1956, relations between the UGTT and Neo Destour, as Bourguiba's party was called at the time, were marked by rivalry.[40] Shortly before the two other electoral periods in which it was allied with the ruling party, in 1978 and again in 1983–4, the national trade union center again found itself in a situation of confrontation with the government. It is to be hoped that the forces of the Tunisian left succeed in establishing a lasting unity and work together to convince the UGTT to enter the electoral arena as, this time, an independent class force.

In Egypt, no force already in existence was capable of successfully battling the "Islamic tsunami" in the parliamentary elections. Only after Mubarak's fall did an independent trade union federation come into being—for the first time since the 1957 creation of an official trade union confederation under Nasser. The first independent Egyptian union, the Real Estate Tax Authority Union (RETA),[41] founded in 2008, played a key role in organizing the Egyptian Federation of Independent Trade Unions (EFITU), which today claims 2 million members, three-quarters of whom joined in the very first phase of its creation. Left-wing activists are prominent in the leadership of both RETA and the EFITU. Among them are members of the Nasserite party Karama (dignity), whose most charismatic representative is Hamdeen Sabahy, a parliamentary deputy between 2000 and 2010. Kamal Abu Aita, a leader of the Karama Party who served as president of RETA, is currently president of the EFITU.

Sabahy has manned his post in every battle against the Sadat and Mubarak regimes. He was active in the 1970s student movement, emerging as one of its leading figures in 1977; decades later, he played a prominent role in the Kefaya movement, which he helped found. He is also on familiar terms with Egyptian prisons, since he has frequently spent time in them. Sabahy provided the big surprise of the 23 and 24 May 2012 first round of the presidential elections. He had been all but dismissed by the preelection opinion polls. Yet, in a field defined by two Islamic candidates (Morsi and Aboul-Fotouh) and two men of the old regime (Shafiq and Amr Moussa), all of whom had incomparably bigger campaign treasuries and better media coverage, he came in third after Morsi and Shafiq, garnering more than 20% of the ballots cast (more than 4.8 million votes). His score in the country's and the uprising's two main urban centers was a still bigger surprise: here he out-polled all the other candidates, taking 27.8% of the votes in Cairo and 31.6% in

Alexandria. In Port Said, Egypt's fifth biggest urban area, he captured 40.4% of the vote!

Sabahy proclaims his allegiance to the ideals of Nasserism without defending the Nasserite regime's dictatorial nature. His electoral program included measures for consolidating democracy that were much more radical than his competitors', especially as far as the security forces, local democracy, and trade union freedoms were concerned. Simultaneously, he advocated "strategic planning for development," a "revival of the state's role in development, and increased spending on developmental investment," to be financed, notably, by raising taxes on profits.[42]

Sabahy's election results demonstrate the existing left's potential even in a profoundly "Islamized" country such as post-Nasser Egypt, and even in a city such as Alexandria, supposedly an impregnable bastion of the Muslim Brothers. He gives the lie, in the clearest possible fashion, to all those who take it for granted that a left that defends socialism has become a negligible quantity, if not a repellent, for Arab public opinion. Since the elections, Hamdeen Sabahy has founded a broad movement, the Egyptian Popular Current (*al-Tayyar al-Sha'bi al-Misri*), which brings together other personalities and groups on the Egyptian left. The creation of the new movement was announced on 22 September 2012.

The Arab uprising's basic aspirations found expression in the very first slogans proclaimed by demonstrators in Tunisia and Egypt: "Employment is a right, you pack of thieves!" in Tunisia; and in Egypt, "Bread, Freedom, Social Justice!" and "Bread, Freedom, Human Dignity!" where the notion of dignity refers, above all, to social conditions that give the unemployed or small peddlers the feeling that their dignity has been trampled underfoot. If the path leading to the realization of these basic aspirations is to be found, left forces such as the UGTT in Tunisia or the combination Popular Current–EFITU in Egypt will have to grow and triumph. For as long as those fundamental demands—for jobs and better living conditions—are not satisfied, over and above the conquest and consolidation of freedoms constantly threatened even in the countries in which they have already been won, there can be no end to the revolutionary process which, touched off by the spark in Sidi Bouzid, set the whole Arab-speaking prairie ablaze, even if that process continues for many years.

Unless there is a radical turn in the region's political trajectory, one capable of erasing the reactionary developments of the last few decades and reviving progressive social projects on a profoundly democratic basis, the whole region runs the risk of plunging into barbarism.[43] The Salafists who emerged with the Arab uprising are the very antithesis of the values it incarnates; their alliance with the Muslim Brothers could engender fundamentalist dictatorships generalizing the worst aspects of the Pakistani, Saudi, and Sudanese regimes. The course of events in Egypt has already swept away the fond illusions of the upholders of the "post-Islamism" thesis who believed that the Muslim Brothers were going to reproduce the model of Turkey's AKP in the Arab region.[44] Samir Amin has rightly excoriated this vision of things:

> "Western" opinion (if that term has any meaning) all too easily believes that there is no alternative to political Islam for the countries concerned. Fear of falling into the trap of Islamophobia makes it all too easy to "accept" this sad alternative—when it is not one. A number of works published in Great Britain and in the United States . . . put the argument that "the Islamisation of power and of society"—in this case, Iran—is not incompatible with "progress." It is constantly repeated that in Islamic Iran, the marriage age of girls has been raised, as has the number of women at work, illiteracy has been reduced as well as infant mortality, while the number of students has increased, etc. However, these statistics, certainly not without importance, also apply almost everywhere (Egypt, for example) and they only mean that no society can completely escape from certain minimum requirements of the "evolution of the modern world." But they do not mean that there has been a general systemic evolution that is equal to the challenge.
>
> The failure of Iran to impose itself as an "emerging" power is not unrelated to the Islamist ideology that cannot imagine an economic system other than that of the existing market—an insignificant version of the "bazaar." . . . It is not very different with the Muslim Brothers in Egypt. This "market economy, miserable and dependent" is perfectly compatible with an equally lamentable interpretation of the sharia, reduced to implementing brutal forms of forced submission on women and the application of penal law. The battle for secularism conditions, in the Muslim world as elsewhere, the possibilities of social and democratic advances, which are themselves the condition for a sustainable emergence of the nations and peoples concerned.[45]

The consolidation of democracy itself presupposes the existence of a strong workers' movement independent of the state. This criterion is a determinant, albeit often neglected by traditional political science. Much more than the "middle class," the workers' movement has historically spearheaded the struggle for egalitarian democracy, as opposed to suffrage based on tax qualifications, from the Chartist movement in nineteenth-century Britain through Solidarnosc in Poland and the National Council of Trade Unions in South Korea to the African National Congress in late twentieth-century South Africa. The real touchstone for determining the extent to which a country has been democratized is the real freedom its labor unions enjoy. The Arab region provides a good illustration of this rule.

Just as the Arab uprising has been a source of inspiration for youth and workers' struggles in Europe and the United States, its evolution will be influenced by the fate of developing struggles in its neighbor, Europe, against all attempts to resolve neoliberalism's acute crisis at the expense of laboring populations—by imposing more neoliberal reforms on them. In the 1950s and 1960s, socialist-leaning developmentalism arose in conjunction with the dominance of the Keynesian paradigm at the core of the international capitalist economy. The reversal of the civilizing process that the triumph of partisans of the most reactionary neoliberalism would bring—the significant regression observable in the United States under George W. Bush has given us a foretaste of it— would inevitably encourage, in the Arab region, parallel attempts to impose the crudest neoliberal prescriptions in the context of dictatorships "with an Islamic reference." Conversely, victories in one region will not fail to influence struggles in others, as has already happened more than once in our information and communication age.[46]

So far, the Arab uprising's main achievement is that the peoples of the region have learned to *want*. That is already a great deal. They have learned to express their democratic will in the most radical way: not only the will that periodically finds expression in balloting at intervals set by the powers that be, but also the one that is expressed in the streets, whenever *the people want*. The workers, the unemployed, and the students of the Arab region have learned that "power is in the streets" and that this power is an indispensable complement and corrective to the one that comes from the ballot box, even when the vote has not been rigged. As Mona El-Ghobashy has aptly put it, with regard to Egypt,

> street demonstrations are participatory politics by other means. They don't compete with or undermine standard democratic procedures; they deepen democracy by enabling more forms of participation and ensuring that more conventional forms of participation are effective. Now that the uprising is over, Egyptians will not confine their politics to the ballot box. They will enthusiastically vote if elections are free and fair, but they will continue to take to the streets to keep their new rulers in check.[47]

The Egyptians continue to fight for their demands in the streets, and so do the Tunisians and Libyans, in spite of the elections. The Egyptian Center for Economic and Social Rights (ECESR), drawing up a balance sheet of the struggles that took place during the first 100 days of Mohamed Morsi's presidency, observed that the number of social protests and strikes had increased. In that period, the ECESR counted 1,591 actions of all sorts (mass meetings, demonstrations, strikes, roadblocks, and so on) carried out by people in a vast range of socioprofessional categories in various sectors of the economy.[48] Managerial and state authorities reacted to this resurgence of struggles with repressive measures, including a sizable number of individual and collective dismissals.

But none of this has been or will be any use, for a simple reason that Maha Abdelrahman has summed up well:

> After all, the millions of Egyptians who have taken to the streets for over a decade, during the mass uprising of January 2011 and in its continuing aftermath have not been protesting, taking huge risks, and sacrificing their lives so that one variety of crony capitalism is replaced by an untrammelled neoliberal capitalism which is determined by a national elite in consort with Western governments and international financial institutions. With no measures to redress their lived injustices, long ignored demands and ever deteriorating living conditions, it is hard to imagine how those millions could be convinced to go back to their homes and give up their fight for both political and economic justice.[49]

The Arab uprising is just beginning. "The future lasts a long time," as Charles de Gaulle wrote in his war memoirs.[50] That is a lovely formula of hope.

Notes

INTRODUCTION

1. Translated from the Arabic by the author of the present book with the assistance of the translator.

2. On the comparative etymology of *thawra* and *inqilab*, see Bernard Lewis, *Islam in History*, Chicago: Open Court, 1993, pp. 319–20 and 343. See also Azmi Bishara, *Fi al-Thawra wa al-Qabiliyya lil-Thawra*, Doha: al-Markaz al-'Arabi lil-Abhath wa Dirasat al-Siyasat, 2012, pp. 25–30.

3. Hyppolite-Adolphe Taine, *The Origins of Contemporary France*, vol 2, *The French Revolution*, vol 1, book 1, trans. John Duran, New York: Henry Holt, 1890—Book 1st, Chapter 1, I—Kindle edition, <http://www.amazon.com/French-Revolution-1-ebook/dp/B0082XLEIY/ref=sr_1_1?s=books&ie=UTF8&qid=1351938648&sr=1-1&keywords=taine#reader_B0082XLEIY>.

4. In the same vein, François-René de Chateaubriand, in his *Mémoires d'Outre-tombe*, vol 3, book 31, chap. 8, recounts the thoughts that the beginning of the three days of July 1830 known as the *Trois Glorieuses* inspired in him: "I saw the three-coloured flag of the revolution fluttering in the wind; I concluded that what was under way was not a riot, but a revolution."

5. Taine, *Origins*, as above (emphasis in the French original).

CHAPTER 1

1. Leon Trotsky shrewdly judges the Soviet regime's potential for development as well as its historical limits in *The Revolution Betrayed*: "The Soviet regime is passing through a *preparatory* stage, importing, borrowing and appropriating the technical and cultural conquests of the West. The comparative coefficients of production and consumption testify that this preparatory stage is far from finished. Even under the improbable condition of a continuing complete

capitalist standstill, it must still occupy a whole historical period." "There was, thus far, no question of any new wor[k] in the sphere of technique, science, or art. It is possible to build gigantic factories according to a ready-made Western pattern by bureaucratic command—although, to be sure, at triple the normal cost. But the farther you go, the more the economy runs into the problem of quality, which slips out of the hands of the bureaucracy like a shadow." Leon Trotsky, *The Revolution Betrayed: What Is the Soviet Union and Where Is It Going?*, trans. Max Eastman, New York: Pathfinder, 1980, pp. 20, 276.

2. Karl Marx, Preface to *A Contribution to the Critique of Political Economy*, in *Marx Engels Selected Works*, London: Lawrence & Wishart, 1991, p. 174.

3. Albert Soboul, *La Civilisation et la Révolution française*, Paris: Arthaud, 1988, p. 43.

4. A good critical introduction to the many different dimensions of the question of neoliberalism may be found in Alfredo Saad-Filho and Deborah Johnston, *Neoliberalism: A Critical Reader*, London: Pluto, 2005.

5. These data are taken from UNICEF, *The State of the World's Children 2012: Children in an Urban World*, New York: UNICEF, 2012.

6. See Youssef Courbage and Emmanuel Todd, *A Convergence of Civilizations: The Transformation of Muslim Societies Around the World*, New York: Columbia University Press, 2011, esp. chap. 5. This book provides a good refutation of the religious explanation of demography, but it also illustrates the limits on attempts to explain history by demography.

7. Let us note with regard to the disparity in population growth rates that the same holds for urbanization. This is why urbanization cannot by itself explain the Arab uprising. To see why, we need only compare statistics on the six countries that have seen the biggest upheavals (up to the time of writing). Urbanization rates for 2010 and the growth rates of the urban population in 2005–10 (the latter rate is in parentheses) were, expressed in percentages, Bahrain 88.6 (2.12), Libya 77.9 (2.2), Tunisia 67.3 (1.6), Syria 55.7 (3.3), Egypt 43.4 (1.8), and Yemen 31.8 (4.7). UN-Habitat, *The State of Arab Cities 2012: Challenges of Urban Transition*, Nairobi: UN-Habitat, 2012.

8. In 1990, the real price of crude oil (base 1973) was three times higher than in 1970—$7.05 per barrel as opposed to $2.36 per barrel (in prices adjusted for inflation and exchange rates). The price in 2008 ($16.40) was more than twice the 1990 price; in 2009, the real price ($10.95) was still one and a half times the 1990 price. OPEC, *Annual Statistical Bulletin 1999*, Vienna: OPEC, 2000 and *Annual Statistical Bulletin 2009*, Vienna: OPEC, 2010.

9. OPEC, *Annual Statistical Bulletin 2009*.

10. See François Lequiller, "Is GDP a Satisfactory Measure of Growth?" *OECD Observer*, no. 246–7, Dec. 2004–Jan. 2005, <http://www.oecdobserver.org/news/fullstory.php/aid/1518/Is_GDP_a_satisfactory_measure_of_growth_.html>.

11. UNDP, *Human Development Report 2011*, New York: UNDP, 2011, pp. 130, 168–9.

12. Ibid.

13. For 2005: Bangladesh -47%, Philippines -41%, China -39%, India

-37%, and so on; Mexico +10%, Nigeria +27%, and so on. See Branko Mila-novic, *Global Inequality Recalculated: The Effect of New 2005 PPP Estimates on Global Inequality*, Policy Research Working Paper 5061, Washington, DC: World Bank, 2009, p. 6.

14. For one example among many others, see "The Upheaval in Egypt: An End or a Beginning?" *The Economist*, 3 Feb. 2011.

15. World Bank, *World Development Indicators 2012*, Washington, DC: World Bank, 2012.

16. Ibid.

17. UNDP, AFESD, *Arab Human Development Report 2003: Building a Knowledge Society*, New York: UNDP, Regional Bureau for Arab States, 2003, p. 139. See also Ray Bush, *Poverty and Inequality: Persistence and Reproduction in the Global South*, London: Pluto, 2007.

18. UNDP, *Arab Human Development Report 2009: Challenges to Human Security in the Arab Countries*, New York: UNDP, Regional Bureau for Arab States, 2009, pp. 112–3.

19. UNDP, *Arab Human Development Report 2009*, p. 114. For a discussion of the estimates regarding Tunisia, see the study presented in 2009 by Ghazi Boulila, Chaker Gabsi, and Mohamed Haddar, "La pauvreté régionale en Tunisie," GDRI DREEM, May 2009, <http://gdri.dreem.free.fr/wp-content/d1-2boulila-chaker-haddar-la-pauvrete-regionale-istalbul-2.pdf>. According to Boulila, Gabsi, and Haddar, the rate of multidimensional poverty in Tunisia varied between 22.4% and 26.9%, depending on the approach taken.

20. Sarah Sabry, *Poverty Lines in Greater Cairo: Underestimating and Misrepresenting Poverty*, London: IIED, Human Settlements Programme, Working Paper 21, 2009, p. 10. See also Ray Bush and Habib Ayeb, eds, *Marginality and Exclusion in Egypt*, London: Zed, 2012.

21. Al-Jihaz al-Markazi lil-Ta'bi'a al-'Ama wa al-Islah, "Mu'ashshirat al-Faqr Tibqan li Bayanat Bahth al-Dakhl wal-Infaq wal-Istihlak," <http://www.capmas.gov.eg/pdf/studies/pdf/enf1.pdf>.

22. UNDP, AFESD, *Arab Human Development Report 2003*, pp. 139–40. On regional inequalities in Egypt, see MNSPR, *Arab Republic of Egypt—Reshaping Egypt's Economic Geography: Domestic Integration as a Development Platform*, 2 vols, Washington, DC: World Bank, June 2012.

23. World Bank, *World Development Indicators 2012*.

24. UNDP, *Arab Human Development Report 2009*, p. 116.

25. The rate of conversion of one US dollar into Egyptian pounds was 2 in PPP rates and 5.54 at market exchange rates in 2008. World Bank, *World Development Indicators 2010*, p. 278.

26. Hernando de Soto, "The Free Market Secret of the Arab Revolutions," *Financial Times*, 8 Nov. 2011.

27. Roberta Gatti, Diego Angel-Urdinola, et al., *Striving for Better Jobs: The Challenge of Informality in the Middle East and North Africa Region*, Washington, DC: World Bank, 2011, p. 6.

28. Ibid., p. 8.

29. Ibid., p. 12.

30. Ibid., p. 18.

31. ILO, LABORSTA Internet, <http://laborsta.ilo.org/applv8/data/c2e. html>. It is explicitly stated that "for operational purposes, the notion 'some work' may be interpreted as work for at least one hour."

32. Ibid., <http://laborsta.ilo.org/applv8/data/c3f.html>.

33. ILO, *World Social Security Report 2010/11: Providing Coverage in Times of Crisis and Beyond*, Geneva: ILO, 2010, Table 22a, pp. 245–50.

34. George Corm, *Labor Migration in the Middle East and North Africa: A View from the Region*, Washington, DC: World Bank, ca. 2006, p. 8. On emigration from the region, see also Christophe Schramm, *Migration from Egypt, Morocco, and Tunisia: Synthesis of Three Case Studies*, Washington, DC: World Bank, ca. 2006. These two studies are among the contributions that spawned an interesting World Bank report, *Shaping the Future: A Long-Term Perspective of People and Job Mobility for the Middle East and North Africa*, Washington, DC: World Bank, 2009.

35. Arab Monetary Fund, ed, *Tahwilat al-'Amilin fi al-Kharij wal-Tanmiya al-Iqtisadiyya fi al-Duwal al-'Arabiyya, Al-Taqrir al-Iqtisadi al-'Arabi al-Muwahhad 2006*, Abu Dhabi: Sunduq al-Naqd al-'Arabi, 2006.

36. Arab World Initiative, "Research: Broad-based Youth Programs Needed," 15 Jan. 2011, World Bank, <http://arabworld.worldbank.org/content/awi/en/home/featured/youth_programs.htm>.

37. ILO, *Global Employment Trends for Youth: 2011 Update*, Geneva: ILO, 2011.

38. UNICEF, *The State of the World's Children 2012.*

39. For a good critique of the theory of the Youth Bulge, see Anne Hendrixson, "Angry Young Men, Veiled Young Women: Constructing a New Population Threat," *Briefing 34*, Dorset, UK: The Corner House, Dec. 2004.

40. Graham Fuller, "The Demographic Backdrop to Ethnic Conflict: A Geographic Overview" in CIA, *The Challenge of Ethnic Conflict to National and International Order in the 1990s, Geographic Perspectives: A Conference Report*, Washington, DC: CIA, 1995, pp. 151–4. Fuller was national intelligence officer for Near East and South Asia at the CIA between 1982 and 1986, before becoming vice chairman of the CIA's National Intelligence Council until 1988; from 1988 until 2000, he worked for the Rand Corporation, which is located at the interface between the military industry and the US government.

41. Samuel Huntington, *The Clash of Civilizations and the Remaking of World Order*, New York: Touchstone, 1997, p. 259.

42. Gunnar Heinsohn, *Söhne und Weltmacht: Terror im Aufstieg und Fall der Nationen*, Zurich: Orell Füssli Verlag, 2003. See Göran Therborn's critique, "NATO's Demographer," *New Left Review*, II, no. 56, March–April 2009, pp. 136–44.

43. Graham Fuller, *The Youth Factor: The New Demographics of the Middle East and the Implications for U.S. Policy*, Washington, DC: Brookings Institution, 2003.

44. Gunnar Heinsohn, "Ending the West's Proxy War Against Israel," *Wall Street Journal Europe*, 12 Jan. 2009.

45. For a critique of the Youth Bulge theory as applied to the Arab region,

see Youssef Courbage, "The Demographic Youth Bulge and Social Rupture" in Samir Khalaf and Roseanne Saad Khalaf, *Arab Youth: Social Mobilisation in Times of Risk*, London: Saqi, 2011, pp. 79–88.

46. ILO, *Global Employment Trends 2012*, Geneva: ILO, 2012.

47. Pierre Bourdieu, *Masculine Domination*, trans. Richard Nice, Cambridge, UK: Polity, 2001, p. 82.

48. Ibid., p. 83. Bourdieu adds that such a history "must also take note of and explain . . . the hierarchical dispositions . . . which lead women to contribute to their own exclusion from the places from which they are in any case excluded."

49. World Bank, *Gender and Development in the Middle East and North Africa: Women in the Public Sphere*, MENA Development Report, Washington, DC: World Bank, 2004.

50. Ibid., pp. 10, 94–8.

51. Ibid., p. 1.

52. Stephan Klasen and Francesca Lamanna, "The Impact of Gender Inequality in Education and Employment on Economic Growth in the Middle East and North Africa," Washington, DC: World Bank, 2003, p. 17, n. 25.

53. The figure in today's dollars is taken from the World Bank's online data base. It has been converted into 1996 dollars on the basis of the US inflation rate (CPI).

54. UNESCO Institute for Statistics, *Global Education Digest 2011: Comparing Education Statistics Across the World*, Montreal: UNESCO Institute for Statistics, 2011.

55. Ghazi Ben Jaballah, "Graduate Unemployment in the Maghreb," *Policy Brief*, Washington, DC: German Marshall Fund, Nov. 2011.

56. See Pierre Blavier, "La révolution tunisienne: chômage, expansion scolaire et fracture régionale?" *Actes de la Recherche en Sciences Sociales* (forthcoming in Sep. 2013).

57. World Bank, *Migration and Remittances Factbook 2011, 2nd edn*, Washington, DC: World Bank, 2011, p. 29.

58. Idarat al-Siyasat al-Sukkaniyya wal-Hijra, *Al-Taqrir al-Iqlimi li Hijrat al-'Amal al-'Arabiyya: Hijrat al-Kafa'at al-'Arabiyya, Nazif am Furas 2008*, Cairo: Arab League, 2009, p. 49.

59. World Bank, *Migration and Remittances Factbook*, p. 10.

60. World Bank, *Unlocking the Employment Potential in the Middle East and North Africa: Toward a New Social Contract*, MENA Development Report, Washington, DC: World Bank, 2004, p. 92.

61. ILO, *Global Employment Trends 2012*.

62. Karl Marx, *Grundrisse: Foundations of the Critique of Political Economy*, trans. Martin Nicolaus, London: Penguin, 1993, pp. 749–50 (emphasis added). The questions of the population reduced to unemployment and "overpopulation" are at the heart of Marx's description of the contradictions inherent in the mode of capitalist production in "The General Law of Capitalist Accumulation," *Capital Volume 1*, trans. Ben Fowkes, Harmondsworth: Penguin, 1976, chap. 25, pp. 762–870.

CHAPTER 2

1. The ratio of public investment to GDP has been calculated on the basis of World Bank data by subtracting the ratio of private sector investment to GDP from that of total investment.

2. Simon Cox, "Pedalling Prosperity" in "Pedalling Prosperity, Special Report: China's Economy," *The Economist*, 26 May 2012. The same argument had already been put forward in an editorial published in the same review four years earlier: "An Old Chinese Myth," *The Economist*, 3 Jan. 2008.

3. Mohammed Jamal Barout, *Al-'Aqd al-Akhir fi Tarikh Surya: Jadaliyyat al-Jumud wal-Islah*, Doha: al-Markaz al-'Arabi lil-Abhath wa Dirasat al-Siyasat, 2012.

4. Giacomo Luciani and Steffen Hertog, *Has Arab Business Ever Been, or Will It Be, a Player for Reform? ARI Thematic Study*, Oct. 2010, Mubadarat al-Islah al-'Arabi / Arab Reform Initiative, <www.arab-reform.net>, p. 2.

5. Ibid., p. 5.

6. World Bank, *Oil Booms and Revenue Management, MENA Economic Developments and Prospects 2005*, Washington, DC: World Bank, 2005, pp. 54–5.

7. World Bank, *MENA Economic Developments and Prospects September 2011: Investing for Growth and Jobs*, Washington, DC: World Bank, 2011, p. 23.

8. Mahmoud Ben Romdhane, *Tunisie: Etat, économie et société. Ressources politiques, légitimation, régulations sociales*, Tunis: Sud Editions, 2011, p. 129.

9. Ray Bush, "Marginality or Abjection? The Political Economy of Poverty Production in Egypt" in Bush and Habib Ayeb, eds, *Marginality and Exclusion in Egypt*, London: Zed, 2012, p. 68.

10. Richard Nyrop et al., *Area Handbook for Egypt*, Washington, DC: The American University, 1976, p. 256.

11. On the GCC monarchies' investments in the Arab countries, see Adam Hanieh, *Capitalism and Class in the Gulf Arab States*, New York: Palgrave Macmillan, 2011.

12. IMF, *Regional Economic Outlook: Middle East and Central Asia*, Washington, DC: International Monetary Fund, 2007, pp. 32–3. On similar assessments of Egypt by the international financial institutions from the 1990s on, see "Dreamland" in Timothy Mitchell, *Rule of Experts: Egypt, Techno-Politics, Modernity*, Berkeley, CA: University of California Press, 2002, pp. 273–303.

13. Gilbert Achcar, "Stability and Instability in Egypt: A Closer Look at Recent Egyptian Growth," <http://eprints.soas.ac.uk/10365/>. Published in Spanish translation: "Estabilidad e inestabilidad en Egipto: una mirada de cerca al reciente crecimiento económico" in ICEX, ed., *Claves de la Economía Mundial 2009*, Madrid: Instituto Español de Comercio Exterior, 2009, pp. 455–61.

14. Christine Lagarde, "The Arab Spring, One Year On," IMF, 6 Dec. 2011, <http://www.imf.org/external/np/speeches/2011/120611.htm>.

15. World Bank, *MENA Region: A Regional Economic Update, April 2012: Enabling Employment Miracles*, Washington, DC: World Bank, 2012, p. 32.

16. Ibid.

17. "Secretary of State Hillary Rodham Clinton's Remarks on Receiving the George C. Marshall Foundation Award," George C. Marshall Foundation, 2 June 2011, <http://www.marshallfoundation.org/SecretaryClintonremarksJune22011.htm>.

18. International financial institutions' prescriptions for solving the unemployment problem contrast starkly with the International Labour Organization's recommendations, centered on the role of public effort. See ILO, *Employment for Stability and Socio-Economic Progress in North Africa: Strategy for North Africa 2011–2015*, Cairo: ILO, 2012.

19. World Bank, *Unlocking the Employment Potential in the Middle East and North Africa: Toward a New Social Contract*, MENA Development Report, Washington, DC: World Bank, 2004.

20. World Bank, *Gender and Development in the Middle East and North Africa: Women in the Public Sphere*, MENA Development Report, Washington, DC: World Bank, 2004.

21. Ibid., p. 8 (see also pp. 79–86).

22. UNDP, AFESD, AGFUND, *The Arab Human Development Report 2005: Towards the Rise of Women in the Arab World*, New York: UNDP, Regional Bureau for Arab States, 2006.

23. Ibid., p. 20.

24. World Bank, *Global Economic Prospects January 2011: Navigating Strong Currents*, Washington, DC: World Bank, 2011, vol 2, p. 95.

25. World Bank, *MENA Economic Developments and Prospects 2008: Regional Integration for Global Competitiveness*, Washington, DC: World Bank, 2009, p. xiv (emphasis added). On the global food crisis, see Derek Headey and Shenggen Fan, *Reflections on the Global Food Crisis: How Did It Happen? How Has It Hurt? And How Can We Prevent the Next One?* Washington, DC: International Food Policy Research Institute, 2010.

26. World Bank, *MENA Economic Developments and Prospects 2009: Navigating through the Global Recession*, Washington, DC: World Bank, 2009, p. 5.

27. Ibid., p. 22.

28. IMF, *World Economic Outlook April 2012: Growth Resuming, Dangers Remain*, Washington, DC: IMF, 2012, p. 198.

29. For an overview of the question of drought in Syria, see Francesco Femia and Caitlin Werrell, "Syria: Climate Change, Drought and Social Unrest," The Center for Climate & Security, 29 Feb. 2012, <http://climateandsecurity.org/2012/02/29/syria-climate-change-drought-and-social-unrest/>. On the problem of food security in Syria as an antecedent to the uprising, see Mohammed Jamal Barout, "Tahaddi al-Amn al-Ghaza'i: Ru'yat Mashru' 'Suriyya 2025,'" *Buhuth Iqtisadiyya 'Arabiyya*, nos. 43–4, Summer–Autumn 2008, pp. 175–91.

30. Albert Soboul, *La Révolution française*, Paris: Presses Universitaires de France, 1965, pp. 10–30.

31. Ibid., pp. 27–8.

32. These calculations are based on World Bank, *Economic Integration in the GCC*, Washington, DC: World Bank, 2010, pp. 28 and 32.

33. Ibid. The figure for Turkey is taken from World Bank, *World Development Indicators 2009*, Washington, DC: World Bank, 2009, p. 218.

34. World Bank, The Changing Wealth of Nations, <http://data.worldbank.org/data-catalog/wealth-of-nations>.

35. World Bank, World Databank, <http://databank.worldbank.org/data/home.aspx>.

36. US Department of State, Foreign Military Financing Account Summary, 23 June 2010, <http://www.state.gov/t/pm/ppa/sat/c14560.htm>.

37. On the Jordanian aid rent, see Warwick Knowles, *Jordan Since 1989: A Study in Political Economy*, London: I.B. Tauris, 2005.

38. Lebanon was subsidized under joint Syrian-Saudi tutelage until 2005, in order to forestall the emergence of a chaotic situation there that would inevitably have affected the entire region. Some authors include migrant workers' remittances as part of the "rent" of the countries from which they have emigrated. This makes little sense, since such remittances go, not to the emigrants' states, but to their families. At most, the share of these remittances accruing to the state in the form of taxes or bank fees may reasonably be considered state rent.

39. Hazem Beblawi, "The Rentier State in the Arab World" in Beblawi and Giacomo Luciani, eds, *The Rentier State*, London: Croom Helm, 1987, p. 62. For an update and refinement of the concept of rentier state as applied to the GCC monarchies, see Matthew Gray, *A Theory of "Late Rentierism" in the Arab States of the Gulf*, Qatar: Center for International and Regional Studies—Georgetown University, 2011.

40. For a sample of the most conventional analyses of the lack of democracy in Arab countries, see Ghassan Salamé, ed, *Democracy Without Democrats? The Renewal of Politics in the Muslim World*, London: I.B. Tauris, 1994. For a good critique of the theories of the rentier state utilized in traditional political science, see Mohammed Hachemaoui, "La rente entrave-t-elle vraiment la démocratie? Réexamen critique des théories de 'l'État rentier' et de la 'malédiction des ressources'" in *Revue française de science politique*, vol 62, no. 2, 2012, pp. 207–30.

41. Tim Niblock with Monica Malik, *The Political Economy of Saudi Arabia*, Oxon, UK: Routledge, 2007, p. 21. On the Saudi kingdom, see also Kiren Aziz Chaudhry, *The Price of Wealth: Economies and Institutions in the Middle East*, Ithaca, NY: Cornell University Press, 1997 and Steffen Hertog, *Princes, Brokers, and Bureaucrats: Oil and the State in Saudi Arabia*, Ithaca, NY: Cornell University Press, 2010. Hertog's book revisits the concept of the rentier state as applied to the Saudi case. On the evolution of the role of the kingdom's bourgeoisie, see also Said Khalid Scharaf, "Institutioneller Wandel und die Rolle der Bourgeoisie in Saudi-Arabien" in Ulrike Freitag, ed, *Saudi-Arabien. Ein Königreich im Wandel?* Paderborn: Ferdinand Schöningh, 2010, pp. 279–301.

42. Hassan Riad [pseudonym of Samir Amin], *L'Egypte nassérienne*, Paris: Minuit, 1964. See pp. 223–49 for the thesis that the "bourgeois bureaucracy" itself was transformed into a "state bourgeoisie" and a "new bourgeoisie." Amin was reacting to a thesis developed by Anouar Abdel-Malek in *Egypt, Military Society: The Army Regime, the Left, and Social Change under Nasser*, trans.

Charles Lam Markmann, New York: Random House, 1968 (French original published in 1962), which located the army at the heart of the transition from capitalism to socialism, in line with the "Soviet Marxist" thesis of the "noncapitalist path of development." A more precise delimitation of the concept, which distinguished the bureaucracy, the bourgeoisie, and the army, may be found in Nazih Ayubi, *Bureaucracy & Politics in Contemporary Egypt*, London: Ithaca, 1980.

43. Max Weber, *Economy and Society*, 2 vols, Berkeley: University of California Press, 1978.

44. For a good clarification of recent debates on the concept of neopatrimonialism in the light of the experience of sub-Saharan Africa, see Gero Erdmann and Ulf Engel, "Neopatrimonialism Revisited—Beyond a Catch-All Concept," Hamburg: GIGA Working Papers, no. 16, Feb. 2006.

45. See Moumen Diouri, *A qui appartient le Maroc?* Paris: L'Harmattan, 1992; see also Catherine Graciet and Eric Laurent, *Le Roi prédateur*, Paris: Seuil, 2012.

46. The foreign relations cultivated by Ben Ali's Tunisian regime gave rise to what Steffen Erdle calls a "semi-rentier state" in a lengthy work on Tunisia based on a PhD thesis, *Ben Ali's 'New Tunisia' (1987–2009): A Case Study of Authoritarian Modernization in the Arab World*, Berlin: Klaus Schwarz, 2010. On Tunisia, see also Olfa Lamloum and Bernard Ravanel, eds, *La Tunisie de Ben Ali. La société contre le régime*, Paris: L'Harmattan, 2002; Sadri Khiari, *Tunisie: le délitement de la cité. Coercition, consentement, résistance*, Paris: Karthala, 2003; Béatrice Hibou, *Force of Obedience: The Political Economy of Repression in Tunisia*, Cambridge, UK: Polity, 2011; Christopher Alexander, *Tunisia: Stability and Reform in the Modern Maghreb*, Oxon, UK: Routledge, 2010; and Ben Romdhane, *Tunisie: Etat, économie et société*. According to Béatrice Hibou, Ben Ali's regime, albeit repressive, benefited from popular consent thanks to a "security pact" that guaranteed the population social and economic advantages. Hibou's thesis has been subjected to a vigorous critique by Mahmoud Ben Romdhane, who describes it as "Orientalist" in Edward Said's sense, notwithstanding her own critique of the most stereotypical culturalist theses.

47. See Hannes Baumann, *Citizen Hariri and Neoliberal Politics in Post-War Lebanon*, PhD dissertation, London: SOAS, University of London, 2012.

48. See esp. Mushtaq Khan and Jomo Kwame Sundaram, eds, *Rents, Rent-Seeking and Economic Development: Theory and Evidence in Asia*, Cambridge, UK: Cambridge University Press, 2000; see also David Kang, *Crony Capitalism: Corruption and Development in South Korea and the Philippines*, Cambridge, UK: Cambridge University Press, 2002.

49. Weber, *Economy and Society*, vol 1, p. 240.

50. See Ha-Joon Chang, *Kicking Away the Ladder: Development Strategy in Historical Perspective*, London: Anthem Press, 2003, and Robert Wade, *Governing the Market: Economic Theory and the Role of Government in East Asian Industrialization*, 2nd edn with a new introduction by the author, Princeton, NJ: Princeton University Press, 2004.

51. Maurice Godelier, *Rationality and Irrationality in Economics*, trans. Brian Pearce, New York: Monthly Review Press, 1973.

52. Weber, "Prefatory Remarks to *Collected Essays in the Sociology of Religion*," in *The Protestant Ethic and the "Spirit" of Capitalism and Other Writings*, London: Penguin, 2002, p. 359.

53. Ibid., p. 362.

54. Karl Marx, *Wage Labour and Capital*, in *Marx Engels Selected Works*, London: Lawrence & Wishart, 1991, p. 85.

55. On the role of GCC capital in the formation of international neoliberal capitalism, see Hanieh, *Capitalism and Class in the Gulf Arab States*. As Hanieh quite rightly says, "class formation in the Gulf did much to underpin the ascendancy of US power in the postwar era. Simultaneously, Gulf capitalism was wrought in the world market formed by this very same ascendant power and its careful assurance of the systemic drives of internationalization and financialization. Whatever the future course of world politics, there will continue to be a close interlacing of the needs and outlook of the ruling elites of the Gulf region with those of global capitalism" (p. 186).

56. Marx, *Capital Volume 1*, trans. Ben Fowkes, Harmondsworth: Penguin, 1976, p. 919 (emphasis added).

57. Weber, "Prefatory Remarks," p. 365.

58. Weber, *Economy and Society*, vol 2, pp. 164–5.

59. For the Egyptian case in particular, see the edifying picture painted in Amr Adly, *Mubarak (1990–2011): The State of Corruption, ARI Thematic Studies*, Mubadarat al-Islah al-'Arabi / Arab Reform Initiative, <www.arab-reform.net>, March 2011 [actually March 2012]. See also Mahmud 'Abdul-Fadil, *Ra'smaliyyat al-Mahasib: Dirasa fil-Iqtisad al-Ijtima'i*, Cairo: Dar al-'Ayn, 2011, and 'Abdul-Khaliq Faruq, *Iqtisadiyyat al-Fasad fi Misr: Kayfa Jara Ifsad Misr wal-Misriyyin 1974–2010*, Cairo: Maktabat al-Shuruq al-Dawliyya, 2011. The reports of US diplomats revealed by WikiLeaks are filled with information about corruption in various Arab states. For an example, see "Corruption in Tunisia: What's Yours Is Mine," dated 23 June 2008, <http://tunileaks.appspot.com/>.

60. The preceding data is taken from Dev Kar and Karly Curcio, *Illicit Financial Flows from Developing Countries: 2000–2009*, Washington, DC: Global Financial Integrity, Jan. 2011. On MENA capital flight from the 1970s to 2002 and its relationship to oil revenue, see Abdullah Almounsor, "A Development Comparative Approach to Capital Flight: The Case of the Middle East and North Africa" in Gerald Epstein, ed, *Capital Flight and Capital Controls in Developing Countries*, Cheltenham, UK: Edward Elgar, 2005, pp. 234–61.

61. Andrzej Kapiszewski, "Arab Versus Asian Migrant Workers in the GCC Countries," Beirut: EGM, Population Division, Department of Economic and Social Affairs, United Nations Secretariat, 15–17 May 2006, p. 9.

62. Ibid., p. 4.

63. World Bank, World Databank.

64. World Bank, *Investing for Growth and Jobs*, pp. 40–1.

65. Al-Ma'had al-Watani lil-Ihsa', *Al-Mas'h al-Watani hawl al-Sukkan wal-Tashghil 2010*, Tunis: Wizarat al-Takhtit wal-Ta'awun al-Dawli, June 2011. For the period 2000–7, see also Fakher Zaibi, "Evolution du marché de l'emploi en

Tunisie", n.d., <http://www.emploi.gov.tn/fileadmin/user_upload/PDF/928081.PDF>.

66. UNCTAD, *World Investment Report 2012: Towards a New Generation of Investment Policies*, Geneva: UNCTAD, 2012, p. 48.

67. Karl Marx, *The Eighteenth Brumaire of Louis Bonaparte* in *Marx Engels Selected Works*, London: Lawrence & Wishart, 1991, pp. 91–171.

68. On the political economy of Egypt after Nasser, see, in addition to the works cited above, the voluminous opus that 'Adil Husayn produced on the Sadat years in Egypt while he was still writing from avowedly Marxist positions: *Al-Iqtisad al-Misri min al-Istiqlal ila al-Taba'iyya 1974–1979*, 2 vols, Beirut: Dar al-Kalima, 1981. See also Nazih Ayubi, *The State and Public Policies in Egypt Since Sadat*, Reading, UK: Ithaca, 1991; Eberhard Kienle, *A Grand Delusion: Democracy and Economic Reform in Egypt*, London: I.B. Tauris, 2000; and Vincent Battesti and François Ireton, eds, *L'Egypte au présent. Inventaire d'une société avant révolution*, Paris: Sindbad/Actes Sud, 2011, esp. chap. 3, pp. 403–647. On the Hafez al-Assad years in Syria, see Michel Seurat, *L'Etat de barbarie*, Paris: Seuil, 1989; Volker Perthes, *The Political Economy of Syria under Asad*, London: I.B. Tauris, 1995; Raymond Hinnebusch, *Syria: Revolution from Above*, London: Routledge, 2001; and for Syria under Assad *père* and Assad *fils*, Bassam Haddad, *Business Networks in Syria: The Political Economy of Authoritarian Resilience*, Stanford, CA: Stanford University Press, 2012. An instructive picture of socioeconomic transformation in Syria is drawn in a work cited above: Mohammed Jamal Barout, *Al-'Aqd al-Akhir fi Tarikh Surya*. The political component of this study is, in contrast, much more open to question, since Barout's political perspective is shaped by his preference for a negotiated solution with the Syrian regime and its president. On this issue, see Husam al-Din Darwish's noteworthy detailed critique of Barout's book, *Munaqasha Naqdiyya li-Abhath Muhammad Jamal Barut 'an al-Thawra al-Suriyya*, Doha: al-Markaz al-'Arabi lil-Abhath wa Dirasat al-Siyasat, 2012. For a comparison between the processes of economic liberalization in Egypt and Hafez al-Assad's Syria, see Raymond Hinnebusch, "The Politics of Economic Liberalisation: Comparing Egypt and Syria," in Hassan Hakimian and Ziba Moshaver, eds, *The State and Global Change: The Political Economy of Transition in the Middle East and North Africa*, Richmond, UK: Curzon, 2001, pp. 111–34.

69. On the Chadli Bendjedid years, see Abderrahim Lamchichi, *L'Algérie en crise. Crise économique et changements politiques*, Paris: L'Harmattan, 1991. An edifying description of the accelerated corruption of the Algerian regime after Boumediene is provided by Hocine Malti, *Histoire secrète du pétrole algérien*, Paris: La Découverte, 2010.

70. See Issam al-Khafaji, "State Incubation of Iraqi Capitalism" in *Wealth and Power in the Middle East*, MERIP, no. 142, Sep.–Oct. 1986, pp. 4–9 and 12, which should be read together with Hanna Batatu, "State and Capitalism in Iraq: A Comment," ibid., pp. 10–12.

71. See Charles Schmitz, "Politics and Economy in Yemen: Lessons from the Past" in Kamil Mahdi, Anna Würth and Helen Lackner, eds, *Yemen into the Twenty-First Century: Continuity and Change*, Reading, UK: Ithaca, 2007, pp. 31–49. See also Chaudhry, *The Price of Wealth*.

72. Dirk Vandewalle, *Libya Since Independence: Oil and State-Building*, Ithaca: Cornell University Press, 1998, and *A History of Modern Libya*, New York: Cambridge University Press, 2006. See also Patrick Haimzadeh, *Au Coeur de la Libye de Kadhafi*, Paris: J-C Lattès, 2011.

73. See Roger Owen, *The Rise and Fall of Arab Presidents for Life*, Cambridge, MA: Harvard University Press, 2012.

74. Gilbert Achcar, "Arab Spring: Late and Cold," *Le Monde diplomatique*, July 2005.

CHAPTER 3

1. Percentages calculated on the basis of data found in OPEC, *Annual Statistical Bulletin 2010/2011*, Vienna: OPEC, 2011.

2. I developed the concept of a New Cold War in my book *La Nouvelle guerre froide. Le monde après le Kosovo*, Paris: PUF, 1999, published in English translation in the form of two contributions to Tariq Ali, ed, *Masters of the Universe? NATO's Balkan Crusade*, London: Verso, 2000: "The Strategic Triad: USA, Russia, China" and "Rasputin Plays at Chess: How the West Blundered into a New Cold War," pp. 57–144.

3. It is well known that the Bush administration was top-heavy with people who had been associated with the Project for the New American Century, among them Abrams, Armitage, Bolton, Cohen, Khalilzad, Libby, Perle, Rodman, Rumsfeld, Wolfowitz, and Zoellick. On US strategy in the Middle East from the First World War and, in particular, what it has to do with oil, see my "U.S. Imperial Strategy in the Middle East" in *Eastern Cauldron: Islam, Afghanistan, Palestine and Iraq in a Marxist Mirror*, New York: Monthly Review Press, and London: Pluto, 2004, pp. 9–45.

4. Daniel Yergin, *The Prize: The Epic Quest for Oil, Money and Power*, 3rd edn, London: Simon & Schuster, 2008, pp. 409–10.

5. This is the thesis I uphold in *The Clash of Barbarisms: The Making of the New World Disorder*, 2nd edn, London: Saqi Books, and Boulder, CO: Paradigm Publishers, 2006.

6. On the two pillars, esp. the religious pillar, which he calls the "Wahhabi Vatican," see Anwar 'Abdullah, *Al-'Ulama' 'wal-'Arsh: Thuna'iyat al-Sulta fi al-Sa'udiyya*, London: Mu'assasat al-Rafid, 1995.

7. On the history of US-Saudi relations, with special emphasis on military relations, see David Long, *The United States and Saudi Arabia: Ambivalent Allies*, Boulder, CO: Westview, 1985, and, with special emphasis on Aramco, Anthony Cave Brown, *Oil, God and Gold: The Story of Aramco and the Saudi Kings*, New York: Houghton Mifflin, 1999. Brown's book is partly based on the private archives of an Aramco employee who was an Arabist.

8. On the history of the Saudi kingdom, see Madawi al-Rasheed, *A History of Saudi Arabia*, 2nd edn, Cambridge, UK: Cambridge University Press, 2010.

9. See chap. 4 of my *The Arabs and the Holocaust: The Arab-Israeli War of Narratives*, trans. G. M. Goshgarian, New York: Metropolitan/Picador, 2010; London: Saqi, 2010; 2nd edn, 2011.

10. Mai Yamani, "The Two Faces of Saudi Arabia" in *Survival*, vol 50, no. 1, Feb.–March 2008, pp. 146–7.

11. Alan Greenspan, *The Age of Turbulence: Adventures in a New World*, New York: Penguin Press, 2007, p. 463.

12. Institute of International Finance, *Economic Report: Gulf Cooperation Council Countries*, Washington, DC: IIF, 16 Jan. 2008, p. 10.

13. Institute of International Finance, *GCC Regional Overview*, Washington, DC: IIF, 13 May 2010, p. 16.

14. Ibid.

15. Security Cooperation Agency, *Historical Facts Book as of September 30, 2010*, Washington, DC: Department of Defense, 2010.

16. Ibid.

17. Richard Grimmett, *U.S. Arms Sales: Agreements with and Deliveries to Major Clients, 2003–2010*, Washington, DC: Congressional Research Service, 16 Dec. 2011.

18. See Saïd Aburish, *The Rise, Corruption and Coming Fall of the House of Saud*, London: Bloomsbury, 1994.

19. Amy Butler, "Saudi, U.S. Finalize F-15SA Sale," *Aviation Week*, 2 Jan. 2012.

20. *Defense Industry Daily*, "2010–12 Saudi Shopping Spree: F-15s, Helicopters & More," 9 March 2012.

21. Ibid. For an analysis of the context preceding the 2010 US-Saudi deal, see Nadim Hasbani, "The Geopolitics of Weapons Procurement in the Gulf States," *Defense & Security Analysis*, vol 22, no. 1, March 2006, pp. 73–88.

22. Richard Grimmett and Paul Kerr, *Conventional Arms Transfers to Developing Nations, 2004–2011*, Washington, DC: Congressional Research Service, 24 August 2012, p. 14. One of the figures cited is obviously mistaken and has been corrected in the light of the tables appended to the report.

23. SIPRI Database, <http://armstrade.sipri.org/armstrade/html/export_top list.php>.

24. Ali Kadri, "Accumulation by Encroachment in the Arab Mashreq" in Ray Bush and Habib Ayeb, eds, *Marginality and Exclusion in Egypt*, London: Zed, 2012, p. 50.

25. Cheryl Rubenberg, *Israel and the American National Interest: A Critical Examination*, Chicago: University of Illinois Press, 1986, p. 91. See also Mitchell Bard, "The 1968 Sale of Phantom Jets to Israel," *Jewish Virtual Library*, <http://www.jewishvirtuallibrary.org/jsource/US-Israel/phantom.html>.

26. Long, *The United States and Saudi Arabia*, pp. 39–40.

27. My own analysis of the evolving relationship between the United States and Israel may be found in Achcar, "U.S. Imperial Strategy in the Middle East."

28. Samuel Huntington, *The Third Wave: Democratization in the Late Twentieth Century*, Norman, OK: University of Oklahoma Press, 1991.

29. Francis Fukuyama, "The End of History," *The National Interest*, Summer 1989, available online at <http://www.wesjones.com/eoh.htm>.

30. Fukuyama responds indirectly in his *The End of History and the Last Man*, New York: Avon Books, 1992, in which he repeats his prognosis about the expansion of liberal democracy and its putative corollary, economic liberalism.

31. Samuel Huntington, *The Clash of Civilizations and the Remaking of World Order*, New York: Touchstone, 1997. Huntington here develops the thesis that he had advanced in an essay published in Summer 1993 in *Foreign Affairs*. I subject Huntington's argument to a critical examination in *The Clash of Barbarisms*.

32. Huntington, *The Clash of Civilizations*, p. 94.

33. See Rashid Khalidi, *Sowing Crisis: The Cold War and American Dominance in the Middle East*, Boston, MA: Beacon, 2009.

34. Amos Perlmutter, "Islam and Democracy Simply Aren't Compatible," *New York Times* and *International Herald Tribune*, 21 Jan. 1992.

35. Asef Bayat, *Islam and Democracy: What Is the Real Question?* ISIM paper 8, Amsterdam: Amsterdam University Press, 2007, p. 10.

36. See my "The Arab World: Absence of Democracy," *Le Monde diplomatique*, June 1997; rpt. under the original title "The Arab Despotic Exception" in *Eastern Cauldron*, pp. 69–74.

37. Condoleezza Rice, "Interview with The Washington Post Editorial Board," 25 March 2005, <http://2001-2009.state.gov/secretary/rm/2005/43863. htm>.

38. I describe the circumstances under which this decision was made in "Self-Deception and Selective Expertise: Bush's Cakewalk into the Iraq Quagmire," *Counterpunch*, 5 May 2004, <http://www.counterpunch.org/2004/05/05/bush-s-cakewalk-into-the-iraq-quagmire/>. For an analysis of the way the situation in Iraq has evolved under the occupation, see Noam Chomsky and Gilbert Achcar, *Perilous Power: The Middle East and U.S. Foreign Policy*, ed Stephen Shalom, 2nd edn, Boulder, CO: Paradigm Publishers, 2008.

39. Michael Ledeen, "Creative Destruction: How to Wage a Revolutionary War," *National Review*, 20 Sep. 2001, <http://old.nationalreview.com/contributors/ledeen092001.shtml>.

40. George W. Bush, "Remarks by the President at the 20th Anniversary of the National Endowment for Democracy," Washington, DC: White House, Office of the Press Secretary, 6 Nov. 2003, <http://georgewbush-whitehouse.archives.gov/news/releases/2003/11/20031106-2.html>.

41. See my "Fantasy of a Region That Doesn't Exist. Greater Middle East: The US Plan," *Le Monde diplomatique*, April 2004.

42. Pascal Ménoret, "The Municipal Elections in Saudi Arabia 2005: First Steps on a Democratic Path," *Arab Reform Brief*, Mubadarat al-Islah al-'Arabi / Arab Reform Initiative, <www.arab-reform.net>, n.d., p. 2.

43. Hendrik Jan Kraetzschmar, "Electoral Rules, Voter Mobilization and the Islamist Landslide in the Saudi Municipal Elections of 2005," *Contemporary Arab Affairs*, vol 3, no. 4, Oct.–Dec. 2010, pp. 515–33.

44. Condoleezza Rice, "Remarks at the American University in Cairo," Washington, DC: Department of State, 20 June 2005, <http://2001-2009.state.gov/secretary/rm/2005/48328.htm>.

45. Achcar, "Arab Spring: Late and Cold," *Le Monde diplomatique*, July 2005.

46. Karl Marx and Frederick Engels, *Manifesto of the Communist Party* in *Marx Engels Selected Works*, London: Lawrence & Wishart, 1991, pp. 41–4.

47. See my 1981 "Eleven Theses on the Current Resurgence of Islamic Fundamentalism," rpt. in *Eastern Cauldron*, pp. 48–59. I develop the theses put forward there in *The Clash of Barbarisms*.

48. See Salwa Ismail, *Political Life in Cairo's New Quarters: Encountering the Everyday State*, Minneapolis: University of Minnesota Press, 2006.

49. According to remarks made by Muhammad Habib on the Egyptian television channel CBC as reported by the Cairo daily *Al-Masry al-Youm*, 22 March 2012.

50. Further remarks made by Muhammad Habib, reported in Samar al-Jamal, "Khayrat al-Shatir wa Abul-Futuh, Farasa al-Rihan min Rahm al-Ikhwan," *Al-Shuruq*, 7 April 2012. Also conducting the negotiations for the Brothers were the Brotherhood's guide, Mohammed Mahdi Akef, and Khairat al-Shatir.

51. See Robert Dreyfuss, *Devil's Game: How the United States Helped Unleash Fundamentalist Islam*, New York: Henry Holt, 2005. Dreyfuss would have been better advised to restrict himself to studying the United States' relations with Islamic fundamentalism, rather than attempting to analyze the history of this current, for which he lacks the required competence. Taking his basic inspiration from Elie Kedourie, he presents, at the beginning of his book, an account of the origins of Islamic fundamentalism that is more yellow journalism than investigative reporting. On the collaboration between Washington and the Muslim Brothers in Europe during the Cold War, see also Ian Johnson, *A Mosque in Munich: Nazis, the CIA, and the Rise of the Muslim Brotherhood in the West*, New York: Houghton Mifflin Harcourt, 2010.

52. On Rashid Rida, see my *The Arabs and the Holocaust*, Metropolitan, pp. 105–8; Saqi, 2nd edn, pp. 104–7.

53. On relations between the Muslim Brothers and the Saudi kingdom, see Husam Tammam, "Al-Ikhwan wal-Sa'udiyya: Hal Daqqat Sa'at al-Firaq?" in Tammam, *Tahawwulat al-Ikhwan al-Muslimin: Tafakkuk al-Idiyulujiya wa Nihayat al-Tanzim*, 2nd edn, Cairo: Madbuli, 2010, pp. 100–8. The Egyptian scholar Husam Tammam, whose knowledge of Islamic movements was unrivaled, died at an early age in Oct. 2011.

54. In 1958, Said Ramadan convinced Faysal bin Abdul-Aziz, then heir apparent to the Saudi throne, to finance his efforts to create an Islamic propaganda network in Europe. Ramadan then settled in Switzerland to carry the project out. See Johnson, *A Mosque in Munich*, as well as Abduh Mustafa Disuqi, "Al-Duktur Sa'id Ramadan, al-Sikritir al-Shakhsi lil-Imam Hasan al-Banna wa Zuj Ibnatihi" in the Muslim Brothers' online encyclopedia *Ikhwan Wiki* (in Arabic), <http://www.ikhwanwiki.com/>. On the Muslim Brothers' international organization, see the same author on the same website, "Al-Tanzim al-'Alami lil-Ikhwan al-Muslimin. Al-Nash'at wal-Tarikh."

55. On the Muslim Brothers' international organization, see Alison Pargeter, *The Muslim Brotherhood: The Burden of Tradition*, London: Saqi, 2010, pp. 96–132, the best available study on the Brothers' international network.

56. Disuqi, "Al-Tanzim al-'Alami lil-Ikhwan wal-Nash'at al-Thaniyat," *Ikhwan Wiki*.

57. See Tammam, *Tahawwulat al-Ikhwan al-Muslimin*, pp. 82–6.

58. Cited in Hesham al-Awadi, *In Pursuit of Legitimacy: The Muslim Brothers and Mubarak, 1982–2000*, London: Tauris Academic Studies, 2004, pp. 186–7.

59. On the Muslim Brothers' political mutation, see Mona El-Ghobashy, "The Metamorphosis of the Egyptian Muslim Brothers" in *International Journal of Middle East Studies*, vol 37, no. 3, August 2005, pp. 373–95. There is an extensive literature on Qutb; see esp. Olivier Carré, *Mystique et politique. Lecture révolutionnaire du Coran par Sayyid Qutb, Frère musulman radical*, Paris: Presses de la FNSP and Cerf, 1984; Sharif Yunis, *Sayyid Qutb wal-Usuliyya al-Islamiyya*, Cairo: Dar Tayyiba, 1995; Adnan Musallam, *From Secularism to Jihad: Sayyid Qutb and the Foundations of Radical Islamism*, Westport, CT: Praeger, 2005; and John Calvert, *Sayyid Qutb and the Origins of Radical Islamism*, New York: Columbia University Press, 2010.

60. See Yaroslav Trofimov, *The Siege of Mecca: The Forgotten Uprising in Islam's Holiest Shrine and the Birth of al Qaeda*, New York: Doubleday, 2007.

61. "Al-Duktur Sa'id Ramadan," *Ikhwan Wiki*. Ramadan was buried in Egypt.

62. See Allen Fromherz, *Qatar: A Modern History*, Washington, DC: Georgetown University Press, 2012.

63. Allen Fromherz devotes most of chap. 6 of his book to providing a general overview of Emir Hamad's very dynamic foreign policy. The subtitle of the relevant section of the chapter is "Hamad's Qatar and the World—A Diplomacy of Stealth and Wealth," pp. 86–110. See also Hugh Eakin, "The Strange Power of Qatar," *New York Review of Books*, vol 58, no. 16, 27 Oct. 2011.

64. Fromherz, *Qatar: A Modern History*, pp. 88–90.

65. Pierre Bourdieu, *Practical Reason: On the Theory of Action*, Cambridge, UK: Polity, 1998, p. 102.

66. See Bettina Gräf and Jakob Skovgaard-Petersen, eds, *Global Mufti: The Phenomenon of Yusuf al-Qaradawi*, London: Hurst, 2009.

67. Yusuf al-Qaradawi, "Ma' al-Tanzim al-'Alami lil-Ikhwan," *Qaradawi .net*, 19 Sep. 2011, <http://qaradawi.net/life/8/5194-2011-09-20-12-41-14 .html>.

68. Qaradawi, "Al-Qaradawi Yanfi Talaqqi 'Ard min al-Ikhwan li-Khilafat al-Hudaybi," *Aljazeera.net*, 12 Jan. 2004, <http://www.aljazeera.net/news/ pages/558d374a-bc05-4639-b537-85c220dd7e50> and "Al-Isti'fa' min al-'Amal al-Tanzimi fi al-Ikhwan," *Qaradawi.net*, 22 Sep. 2008, <http://qaradawi.net/ life/8/940-2011-09-29-12-22-50.html>.

69. Qaradawi, "Al-Isti'fa' min al-'Amal al-Tanzimi fi al-Ikhwan."

70. Let us note in passing that the Qatari dynasty itself adheres to Wahhabism.

71. On Salafism and the various meanings of the term, see Roel Meijer, ed, *Global Salafism: Islam's New Religious Movement*, New York: Columbia University Press, 2009, esp. Meijer's introduction, pp. 1–29.

72. Tammam, *Tahawwulat al-Ikhwan al-Muslimin*, p. 141.

73. See Bettina Gräf, "The Concept of *wasatiyya* in the Work of Yusuf al-Qaradawi" in Gräf and Skovgaard-Petersen, eds, *Global Mufti*, pp. 213–38.

74. See the series of seven articles on the relationship between Yusuf al-Qaradawi and the Muslim Brothers published by Husam Tammam in the Cairo

daily *Al-Shuruq* from 22 to 27 August 2011 under the title "Al-Qaradawi wal-Ikhwan. Qira'at fi Jadaliyyat al-Shaykh wal-Haraka."

75. The Brookings Project on U.S. Policy Towards the Islamic World, *An Agenda for Action: The 2002 Doha Conference on U.S. Relations with the Islamic World*, Washington, DC: The Brookings Institution, 2003. See also Husam 'Abdel-Hamid, "Mu'tamar al-Dawha. Khutwat Ula li-Hiwar Islami Amriki," IslamOnline (originally), 4 Nov. 2002, <http://www.onislam.net/arabic/newsanalysis/analysis-opinions/europe-north-america-australia/85660-2002-11-04%2000-00-00.html>.

76. The US-Islamic World Forum's website may be consulted at <www.dohanetwork.org>.

77. Tammam, *Tahawwulat al-Ikhwan al-Muslimin*, p. 147.

78. Pargeter, *The Muslim Brotherhood*, p. 90.

79. David Kaplan, "Hearts, Minds, and Dollars," *US News & World Report*, 17 April 2005, <http://www.usnews.com/usnews/news/articles/050425/25roots.htm>.

80. For a sober presentation of the terms of the debate on the relation between "democracy promotion" and "Islamists," see the study conducted for the US Congress by Jeremy Sharp, *U.S. Democracy Promotion Policy in the Middle East: The Islamist Dilemma*, Washington, DC: Congressional Research Service, 15 June 2006.

81. Bettina Gräf, "IslamOnline.net: Independent, Interactive, Popular," *Arab Media & Society*, no. 4, Winter 2008, <http://www.arabmediasociety.com/?article=576>.

82. In 2005, when the US ambassador sought to meet with him, Mohammed Mahdi Akef, then the Egyptian Brotherhood's general guide, answered that he could see the ambassador only if a representative of the Egyptian government was present at the meeting.

83. Tammam, *Tahawwulat al-Ikhwan al-Muslimin*, pp. 148–9.

84. Khairat el-Shatir, "No Need to Be Afraid of Us," *The Guardian*, 23 Nov. 2005.

85. Associated Press, "Egypt's Muslim Brotherhood Chief: We Don't Recognize Israel, but Won't Fight It," *Haaretz*, 27 Nov. 2005.

86. Only in 2003 did MBC launch the network Al Arabiya, Al Jazeera's chief competitor.

87. Mohamed Zayani, "Al Jazeera and the Vicissitudes of the New Arab Mediascape" in Zayani, ed, *The Al Jazeera Phenomenon: Critical Perspectives on New Arab Media*, London: Pluto, 2005, p. 14. This collection offers a panorama of the many different facets of the Qatari network.

88. Wadah Khanfar resigned his post in 2011. His departure was attributed to a scandal sparked by WikiLeaks documents that showed that he had cooperated with US authorities in connection with Al Jazeera's coverage of the Iraq war.

89. Marc Lynch, *Voices of the New Arab Public: Iraq, Al-Jazeera, and Middle East Politics Today*, New York: Columbia University Press, 2006. See also Naomi Sakr, *Satellite Realms: Transnational Television, Globalization and the Middle East*, London: I.B. Tauris, 2001.

90. William Rugh, *Arab Mass Media: Newspapers, Radio, and Television in Arab Politics*, Westport, CT: Praeger, 2004, p. 220.

91. The Qatari government allocated Al Jazeera annual operating costs of $137 million in the network's first five years of existence (ibid., p. 221).

92. Jon Alterman, *New Media, New Politics? From Satellite Television to the Internet in the Arab World*, Policy Paper no. 48, Washington, DC: The Washington Institute for Near East Policy, 1998, p. xii.

93. Dubai Press Club, *Arab Media Outlook 2009–2013*, Dubai: Dubai Press Club, 2010, p. 44.

94. Ibid., p. 46.

95. Alterman, *New Media, New Politics?* p. 76.

96. Dubai Press Club, *Arab Media Outlook 2009–2013*, p. 47. Let us point out, in passing, that there are many pornographic Arabic-language satellite networks. This source does not list them separately, but they undoubtedly comprise a significant proportion of the 40 "interactive" and 22 "specialized" networks listed.

97. See Ehab Galal, "Yusuf al-Qaradawi and the New Islamic TV" in Gräf and Skovgaard-Petersen, eds, *Global Mufti*, pp. 149–80.

98. Abdallah Schleifer, "Interview with Sheikh Yusuf al-Qaradawi," *Transnational Broadcasting Studies*, no. 13, Fall 2004, <http://www.tbsjournal.com/Archives/Fall04/interviewyusufqaradawi.htm>.

99. Lynch, *Voices of the New Arab Public*, p. 88.

100. Mahmoud Al-Sadi, "Al Jazeera Television: Rhetoric of Deflection," *Arab Media & Society*, no. 15, Spring 2012, <http://www.arabmediasociety.com/?article=786>.

101. René Naba, *Les Révolutions arabes*, Paris: Bachari, 2011, p. 104.

CHAPTER 4

1. Louis Althusser, *For Marx*, trans. Ben Brewster, Harmondsworth, UK: Penguin, 1969, pp. 99–100.

2. Ibid., p. 106.

3. Ibid., p. 98. The essay from which these passages are drawn—"Contradiction and Overdetermination (Notes for an Investigation)"—was written in 1962. It assigns a decisive place to the "subjective factor," even going too far in the direction of personalizing this factor (Lenin's role). A few years later, at a time when the structuralist paradigm reigned supreme in France, leaving its mark on every field of thought, Althusser—in writings such as his contribution to *Reading Capital* (1965) or his worst text, "Reply to John Lewis" (1972)—went to the extreme of proposing the theory of the "process without a subject," which tended to banish the "subjective factor" from the historical process altogether, reducing history to a structural mechanism.

4. Vladimir Lenin, "The Collapse of the Second International," in *Collected Works*, 21, Moscow: Progress Publishers, 1964, pp. 213–4.

5. Mohamed El-Sayed, "Memories of 1977," *Al-Ahram Weekly*, no. 881, 24–30 Jan. 2008, <http://weekly.ahram.org.eg/2008/881/eg5.htm>.

6. Dalal al-Bizri, "Laysa Ghadab al-Sabirin ka Kul Ghadab, wal-Misriyyun Sadat al-Sabirin . . . ," *Al-Hayat*, 20 April 2008.

7. Sadri Khiari, *Tunisie: le délitement de la cité. Coercition, consentement, résistance*, Paris: Karthala, 2003, pp. 195–6.

8. Ingrid Melander, "Interview—Tunisia Must Open Up or Risk Unrest—Opponent," *Reuters*, 10 June 2008.

9. Mohammed Jamal Barout, "Suriyya 2010: al-Islah aw al-Karitha," *Al-Tajdid al-'Arabi*, 2 June 2005, <http://arabrenewal.info/>. Not only did the warning fall on deaf ears, but the neoliberal reforms against whose consequences the author had warned were accelerated from 2005 on. See International Crisis Group, *Popular Protests in North Africa and The Middle East (VI): The Syrian People's Slow Motion Revolution*, Middle East/North Africa Report no. 108, 6 July 2011, pp. 15–6.

10. Mustafa Bassiouny, "Gilbert al-Ashqar, Ustadh al-Tanmiya fi Jami'at London: al-Nizam al-Masri Jama'a Sayyi'at Nizam al-Suq wa Nizam al-Shumuliyya wa Taraka Hasanatahuma," *Al-Dustur*, 11 Aug. 2009.

11. Gilbert Achcar (al-Ashqar), "Al-Yasar al-'Arabi: Hiwar Ajrahu Wa'el 'Abdul-Rahim," *Al-Adab*, no. 4–5, 2010, p. 49.

12. The neoconservative Walid Phares likewise had the presentiment that a regional explosion was in the offing—in *The Coming Revolution: Struggle for Freedom in the Middle East*, New York: Threshold Editions, 2010, adorned with a gushing blurb by Mitt Romney. As he saw things, however, it was a question of a liberal, pro-Western "revolution" along the lines of the "Revolution of the Cedars" in Lebanon in 2005 or the "Green Movement" in Iran in 2009, according to his interpretation of those two events. This is one expression of the vision of the most wild-eyed of the ideologues in the entourage of the George W. Bush administration, such as Michael Ledeen (cited in Chapter 3).

13. See 'Adnan al-Mansar, *Al-Durru wa Ma'danuhu: al-Khilafat bayn al-Hizb al-Dusturi wal-Haraka al-Niqabiyya fi Tunis, 1924–1978. Jadaliyyat al-Tajanus wal-Sira'*, Tunis: Al-Magharibiyya, 2010.

14. On the Gafsa mining basin revolt, see Karine Gantin and Omeyya Seddik, "Revolt in a Tunisian Mining Town," *Le Monde diplomatique*, July 2008. See also Larbi Chouikha and Éric Gobe, "La Tunisie entre la 'révolte du bassin minier de Gafsa' et l'échéance électorale de 2009," *L'Année du Maghreb* 2009, pp. 387–420. A partial version of this article is available online in English: Eric Gobe, "The Gafsa Mining Basin between Riots and a Social Movement: Meaning and Significance of a Protest Movement in Ben Ali's Tunisia," <http://hal .inria.fr/docs/00/55/78/26/PDF/Tunisia_The_Gafsa_mining_basin_between _Riots_and_Social_Movement.pdf>.

15. Hizb al-'Ummal al-Shuyu'i al-Tunisi, "Al-Ihtijajat Taduqq Abwab al-Qasrin," <http://www.albadil.org/spip.php?article1739>.

16. "Tunisie: Un rassemblement de jeune diplômés chômeurs de la ville de Skhira tourne à l'affrontement avec les forces de l'ordre," *Nawaat*, 4 Feb. 2010, <http://nawaat.org/portail/2010/02/04/tunisie-un-rassemblement-de-jeune-di plomes-chomeurs-de-la-ville-de-skhira-tourne-a-laffrontement-avec-les-forces -de-lordre/>.

17. Luiza Toscane, "Victoire de la population à Ben Guerdane," *Nawaat*,

3 Oct. 2010, <http://nawaat.org/portail/2010/10/03/victoire-de-la-population-a-ben-guerdane/>.

18. This brief description of the struggles that took place in Tunisia over the course of the past few years shows, even if we go no further back in time, the weakness of the thesis of "voluntary servitude" or "the force of obedience" that Béatrice Hibou has advanced to explain the stability of Ben Ali's regime. The way the author continues to justify herself even after the uprising indicates how unconvincing her argument is: "In fact, contrary to an analysis widespread among political analysts, in the media, and among former dissidents, political domination did not find its chief incarnation in Ben Ali's absolute power, in the predatory activity of those close to the president, or in the prohibition, enforced by violence and police control, of any sort of political activity. *There were very few dissidents.* Even if repressing or even physically eliminating them had important effects, in that it served as an 'example' and thus spread fear among the population, this potential violence alone does not suffice to explain the *Tunisians' obedience* over a period of decades. Much more profoundly, that obedience was the result of an articulation between, first, latent or insidious violence perpetrated by the police and the control associated with single-party rule and, second, *powerful mechanisms of inclusion.*" ("Tunisie. Économie politique et morale d'un mouvement social," *Politique africaine,* no. 121, March 2011, p. 6—emphasis added). For a good, if indirect refutation of Béatrice Hibou's comments, see the interview that Sadri Khiari granted her in the same issue of *Politique africaine,* "La Révolution tunisienne ne vient pas de nulle part," pp. 23–34. See also Amin Allal and Vincent Geisser, "Tunisie: 'Révolution de jasmin' ou Intifada? *Mouvements,* no. 66, Summer 2011, pp. 62–8.

19. Habib Ayeb, "Social and Political Geography of the Tunisian Revolution: The Alfa Grass Revolution," *Review of African Political Economy,* vol 38, no. 129, Sep. 2011, p. 473.

20. The same dichotomy between the freedoms of capital and labor found another illustration in the eagerness of the occupation authorities in Iraq to liberalize the country's economy without restraint after the 2003 invasion, while maintaining the totalitarian labor code promulgated by Saddam Hussein in 1987.

21. See Hossam el-Hamalawy, "1977: The Lost Revolution," online at <http://www.scribd.com/doc/12893045/1977-Bread-Uprising>.

22. See Marie Duboc, "La contestation sociale en Égypte depuis 2004. Précarisation et mobilisation locale des ouvriers de l'industrie textile," in Sarah Ben Néfissa and Blandine Destremau, eds, *Protestations sociales, révolutions civiles. Transformations du politique dans la Méditerranée arabe, Revue Tiers Monde,* special issue 2011, pp. 95–115. On the Mahalla strikes, see Brecht De Smet, *The Prince and the Pharaoh: The Collaborative Project of Egyptian Workers and Their Intellectuals in the Face of Revolution,* PhD dissertation, Ghent: Ghent University, 2012.

23. See Mustafa Bassiouny and 'Umar Sa'id, *Rayat al-Idrab fi Sama' Misr: 2007 Haraka 'Ummaliya Jadida,* Cairo: Markaz al-Dirasat al-Ishtirakiyya, 2007.

24. See Jamal Muhammad 'Uwayda, *Malhamat I'tisam Muwazzafi al-Dara'ib al-'Iqariyya*, Cairo: Markaz al-Dirasat al-Ishtirakiyya, 2008.

25. These statistics have been gathered by the Cairo Land Center for Human Rights, <http://www.lchr-eg.org/>. On the struggles of this period, see Fatma Ramadan, *Su'ud al-Haraka al-'Ummaliyya wal-Niqabiyya al-Misriyya khilal 'Am 2007*, Cairo: Al-Mirsad al-Niqabi al-'Ummali, Al-Jam'iyya al-Misriyya lil-Nuhud bil-Musharaka al-Mujtama'iyya, n.d., and "Itlala 'ala al-Haraka al-'Ummaliyya fi Misr (2007–2009)," *Al-Hiwar al-Mutammadin*, 25 June 2012, <http://www.ahewar.org/debat/show.art.asp?aid=313257>. Ramadan, one of the best informed observers of working-class struggles in Egypt, is today a member of the executive bureau of the Egyptian Federation of Independent Trade Unions (EFITU). See also Joel Beinin, "A Workers' Social Movement on the Margin of the Global Neoliberal Order, Egypt 2004–2009," in Beinin and Frédéric Vairel, eds, *Social Movements, Mobilization, and Contestation in the Middle East and North Africa*, Stanford, CA: Stanford University Press, 2011, pp. 181–201. See also the analyses written or coauthored by Joel Beinin in 2007–8 for Middle East Research Online, <http://www.merip.org/mero/>. See also Rabab El-Mahdi, "Labour Protests in Egypt: Causes and Meanings," *Review of African Political Economy*, vol 38, no. 129, Sep. 2011, pp. 387–402.

26. See Ekram Ibrahim, "6th of April 2008: A Workers' Strike Which Fired the Egyptian Revolution," *Al-Ahram Online*, 6 April 2012, <http://english.ahram.org.eg/News/38580.aspx>.

27. For a concise overview of the state of the protest movement in the region on the eve of the 2011 uprising, see Marina Ottaway and Amr Hamzawy, "Protest Movements and Political Change in the Arab World," *Policy Outlook*, Washington, DC: Carnegie Endowment for International Peace, 28 Jan. 2011.

28. On Kefaya and the state of the struggles in Egypt two years before the uprising, see Rabab El-Mahdi and Philip Marfleet, eds, *Egypt: Moment of Change*, London: Zed, 2009. See also Maha Abdelrahman, "In Praise of Organisation: Egypt Between Activism and Revolution," *Development and Change*, vol 44, no. 3, May 2013 (forthcoming).

29. See Charlotte Velut and Laurent Bonnefoy, "Tawakkul Karmân: figure de la révolution" in Bonnefoy, Franck Mermier and Marine Poirier, eds, *Yémen. Le tournant révolutionnaire*, Sanaa: Cefas, and Paris: Karthala, 2012, pp. 173–6.

30. Islah Jad, "The NGO-isation of Arab Women's Movements," 2004, <http://www.shebacss.com/docs/sowcere0036-09.pdf>.

31. Doug McAdam, Sidney Tarrow and Charles Tilly, *Dynamics of Contention*, Cambridge, UK: Cambridge University Press, 2001.

32. Ibid., p. 8.

33. Ibid., pp. 331–2.

34. See Jeffrey Ghannam, *Social Media in the Arab World: Leading Up to the Uprisings of 2011*, Washington, DC: Center for International Media Assistance, NED, 3 Feb. 2011.

35. Hamid Dabashi, *The Arab Spring: The End of Postcolonialism*, London: Zed, 2012, p. 239.

36. Tariq Ramadan, *The Arab Awakening: Islam and the New Middle East*,

London: Allen Lane, 2012. Ramadan makes a typically "essentialist" critique of Edward Said, accusing the Palestinian thinker of being "widely accepted" in the West, although he himself does all he can to win acceptance there and has, moreover, achieved "broad" success, even if he remains controversial (as does Said, for that matter).

37. See Eric Toussaint, "The International Context of Global Outrage," CADTM, 30 Dec. 2011, <http://cadtm.org/Breve-retrospective-des-mouvements>.

38. ITU, "Key Global Telecom Indicators for the World Telecommunication Service Sector," <http://www.itu.int/ITU-D/ict/statistics/index.html>.

39. Dubai School of Government, *Arab Social Media Report*, vol 1, no. 1, Jan. 2011.

40. Dubai School of Government, *Arab Social Media Report*, vol 1, no. 2, May 2011.

41. See the reports of the Egyptian government's Markaz al-Ma'lumat wa Da'm Ittikhaz al-Qarar (Information and Decision Support Center, IDSC), esp. *Min al-Internet ila al-Tahrir: 25 Yanayir min Waqi' al-Facebook wal-Twitter, Taqarir Ma'lumatiyya*, vol 5, no. 53, May 2011.

42. Sami Ben Gharbia, "The Internet Freedom Fallacy and the Arab Digital Activism," *Nawaat*, 17 Sep. 2010, <http://nawaat.org/portail/2010/09/17/the-internet-freedom-fallacy-and-the-arab-digital-activism/>. Minor linguistic errors in this article have been silently corrected.

43. Jillian York, "The False Poles of Digital and Traditional Activism," <http://jilliancyork.com/2010/09/27/the-false-poles-of-digital-and-traditional-activism/>. See also IPEMED, *La Confiance dans la société numérique méditerranéenne. Vers un espace .med*, IPEMED Palimpsestes, no. 7, July 2011, which draws the same conclusion in the light of the Arab uprising.

44. Caryle Murphy, "Arab Facebook: The Internet's Role in Politics in the Middle East," *The Majalla*, 13 Nov. 2009, <http://www.majalla.com/eng/2009/11/article5510699>.

45. Ben Gharbia, "The Internet Freedom Fallacy."

46. Mohammed Hachemaoui, "Y a-t-il des tribus dans l'urne? Sociologie d'une énigme électorale (Algérie)," *Cahiers d'études africaines*, vol 52 (1), no. 205, 2012, pp. 103–63. For a comparative study of tribalism's role in Libya and Tunisia, whose societies have undergone modernization to very different degrees, see Muhammad Najib Butalib, *Al-Ab'ad al-Siyasiyya lil-Zahira al-Qabaliyya fi al-Mujtama'at al-'Arabiyya: Muqaraba Susyulujiyya lil-Thawratayn al-Tunisiyya wal-Libiyya*, Doha: al-Markaz al-'Arabi lil-Abhath wa Dirasat al-Siyasat, 2011.

47. For a retired US Army officer's account of the way US occupation forces have used the tribal factor in Iraq in their fight against Al-Qaida, see Lt. Colonel Michael Silverman, *Awakening Victory: How Iraqi Tribes and American Troops Reclaimed Al Anbar and Defeated Al Qaeda in Iraq*, Havertown, PA: Casemate, 2011. The author of another book glorifying this fight has found a very appropriate title for his work, his name for the US troops that have entered the tribal game in Iraq: Bing West, *The Strongest Tribe: War, Politics, and the Endgame in Iraq*, New York: Random House, 2008.

48. Fawwaz Traboulsi, *Al-Dimuqratiyya wal-Thawra*, Beirut: Riad El-Rayyes, 2012, p. 22.

49. Nazih Ayubi, *Overstating the Arab State: Politics and Society in the Middle East*, London: I.B. Tauris, 1995.

50. See Paul Cochrane, "Boon Time for Mercenaries," *Executive*, no. 143, June 2011, <http://www.executive-magazine.com/getarticle.php?article=14309>.

51. Mujib Mashal, "Pakistani Troops Aid Bahrain's Crackdown," *Aljazeera .com*, 30 July 2011, <http://www.aljazeera.com/indepth/features/2011/07/2011 725145048574888.html>.

52. Carmen Becker, "Strategies of Power Consolidation in Syria Under Bashar al-Asad: Modernizing Control over Resources," *Arab Studies Journal*, vol 13/14, no. 2/1, Fall 2005/Spring 2006, p. 87.

53. Barack Obama, "Remarks by the President on Egypt," Washington, DC: White House, 11 Feb. 2011, <http://www.whitehouse.gov/the-press-office/ 2011/02/11/remarks-president-egypt>.

CHAPTER 5

1. Samuel Huntington, *Political Order in Changing Societies*, New Haven, CT: Yale University Press, 1968, ch. 4, pp. 192–263.

2. For accounts of the first weeks of the Tunisian uprising produced as it unfolded, see Nizar Shaqrun, *Riwayat al-Thawra al-Tunisiyya*, Tunis: Dar Mohamed Ali, 2011. See also José Daniel Fierro and Santiago Alba Rico, *Túnez, la Revolución*, Hondarribia: Hiru, 2011.

3. This information is derived from accounts by Ben Ali's wife, Leila Trabelsi, and the head of the presidential guard: Leila Trabelsi, *Ma vérité*, Paris: Editions du Moment, 2012; "La chute du régime Ben Ali racontée par Ali Sariati, le chef de la garde présidentielle," *Le Monde*, 2 April 2011. Another version of events was given to the press on 8 August 2011 by the head of the Anti-Terrorism Brigade, who was obviously intent on magnifying his own role. This account was reported as if it were a scoop by the French website Mediapart; it was taken up by Pierre Puchot, the author of the scoop, in his otherwise well-informed *La Révolution confisquée. Enquête sur la transition démocratique en Tunisie*, Paris: Sindbad/Actes Sud, 2012. This version is unlikely: see "Qui se cache derrière Samir Tarhouni?" *Maghreb Intelligence*, 11 August 2011, <http://www .maghreb-intelligence.com/tunisie/1523-qui-se-cache-derriere-samir-tarhouni .html>.

4. C. Wright Mills, *The Power Elite*, New York: Oxford University Press, 1956.

5. For a critical balance sheet of the first stage of the Tunisian revolution, see Bashir al-Hamdi, *Al-Haq fil-Sulta wal-Thawra wal-Dimuqratiyya. Qira'at fi Masar Thawrat al-Huriyya wal-Karama*, Sidi Bouzid: Donia, 2011, and Farid al-Alibi, *Tunis: al-Intifada wal-Thawra*, Sfax: Nuha, 2011.

6. Hesham Sallam, "Striking Back at Egyptian Workers," *Middle East Report*, vol 41, no. 259, Summer 2011, available online <http://www.merip.org/ mer/mer259/striking-back-egyptian-workers>.

7. 'Adil Zakariyya et al., "Thawrat al-'Ummal: Ihtijajat 'Ummaliyya li Akthar min 300 Alf 'Amil fi 60 Mawqi'an 'Ummaliyyan bi 9 Muhafazat," *Al-Badil*, 9 Feb. 2011.

8. See also "'Asharat al-Idrabat bi Mukhtalaf al-Muhafazat wal-Matalib: Tathbit wa Hawafiz wa Iqalat Mas'ulin," *Al-Masry al-Youm*, 10 Feb. 2011, <http://today.almasryalyoum.com/article2.aspx?ArticleID=287488&IssueID=2042>.

9. "Mawja Jadida min al-Ihtijajat al-'Ummaliyya Tajtah al-Qahira wal-Muhafazat," *Al-Masri al-Youm*, 11 Feb. 2011, <http://today.almasryalyoum.com/article2.aspx?ArticleID=287569&IssueID=2043>.

10. See the 11 Feb. newspaper articles collected at <http://www.id3m.com/D3M/ShowFilesFolders.php?ID=820&Page=336>. See also Fatma Ramadan's contribution (in Arabic) to the website *Al-Hiwar al-Mutammadin*, 12 Aug. 2012, <http://www.ahewar.org/debat/s.asp?aid=319653>, as well as Françoise Clément, Marie Duboc and Omar El Shafei, "Le rôle des mobilisations des travailleurs et du mouvement syndical dans la chute de Moubarak," *Mouvements*, no. 66, Summer 2011, pp. 69–78.

11. The term "military-industrial complex" became famous after Dwight D. Eisenhower used it in his January 1961 farewell address, the last speech of his presidency.

12. See Zeinab Abul-Magd, "The Generals' Secret: Egypt's Ambivalent Market," *Sada*, Washington, DC: Carnegie Endowment for International Peace, 9 Feb. 2012, <http://carnegieendowment.org/sada/index.cfm?fa=show&article=47137&solr_hilite>. See also, by the same author, "The Army and the Economy in Egypt," *Jadaliyya*, 23 Dec. 2011, <http://www.jadaliyya.com/pages/index/3732/the-army-and-the-economy-in-egypt>. On the evolution of the MIC, see LTC Stephen Gotowicki, US Army, "The Military in Egyptian Society" in Phebe Marr, ed, *Egypt at the Crossroads: Domestic Stability and Regional Role*, Washington, DC: National Defense University Press, 1999, pp. 105–25. On its present situation, see Shana Marshall, "Egypt's Other Revolution: Modernizing the Military-Industrial Complex," *Jadaliyya*, 10 Feb. 2012, <www.jadaliyya.com/pages/index/4311/egypts-other-revolution_modernizing-the-military-i>. On the army's role under Mubarak, see Imad Harb, "The Egyptian Military in Politics: Disengagement or Accommodation?" *Middle East Journal*, vol 57, no. 2, Summer 2003, pp. 269–90.

13. Abul-Magd, "The Generals' Secret."

14. *WikiLeaks*, telegram sent from the Cairo embassy on 23 Sep. 2008, <http://wikileaks.org/cable/2008/09/08CAIRO2091.html#>.

15. Gotowicki, "The Military in Egyptian Society," pp. 121–2.

16. On the question of religious sects in Egypt, see Azmi Bishara, *Hal min Mas'ala Qubtiyya fi Misr?* Doha: al-Markaz al-'Arabi lil-Abhath wa Dirasat al-Siyasat, 2012. See also Atef Said, "Al-Mushkila al-Ta'ifiyya fi Misr wal-Badil al-'Ilmani al-Thawri," *Al-Thawra al-Da'ima*, no. 2, Spring 2012, pp. 11–28.

17. For an overview of the first stage of the Yemeni uprising and its various facets, see Laurent Bonnefoy, Franck Mermier and Marine Poirier, eds, *Yémen. Le tournant révolutionnaire*, Sanaa: Cefas, and Paris: Karthala, 2012.

18. Jeremy Sharp, *Yemen: Background and U.S. Relations*, Washington, DC: Congressional Research Service, 8 June 2011, pp. 1–2.

19. Steven Erlanger, "In Yemen, U.S. Faces Leader Who Puts Family First," *New York Times*, 5 Jan. 2010.

20. See "Ali Abdullah Saleh Family in Yemen Govt and Business," *Armies of Liberation*, 8 April 2006, <http://armiesofliberation.com/archives/2006/04/08/ali-abdullah-saleh-family-in-yemen-govt-and-business/>.

21. On Islamic movements in Yemen, see 'Abdul-Malik 'Isa, *Harakat al-Islam al-Siyasi fi al-Yaman*, Beirut: Markaz Dirasat al-Wihda al-'Arabiyya, 2012. On Islah, see also Jillian Schwedler, *Faith in Moderation: Islamist Parties in Jordan and Yemen*, New York: Cambridge University Press, 2006.

22. The way the situation in Yemen has developed confirms Lisa Wedeen's critique of the theory of the "failed state," which ignores the fact that what is designated as an institutional "failure" may be, rather, the result of a power strategy, as was and still is the case in Yemen—*Peripheral Visions: Publics, Power, and Performance in Yemen*, Chicago: Chicago University Press, 2008, esp. chap. 4.

23. "Ahdath al-Thawra fi al-Yaman," *Aljazeera.net*, 13 April 2011, <http://www.aljazeera.net/news/pages/2ff247c6-5abc-4297-a1fd-b1d9f45516a1>.

24. See Jeremy Scahill, "Washington's War in Yemen Backfires" (14 Feb. 2012), *The Nation*, 5 March 2012.

25. According to *Statistical Abstract 2011*, published by the Bahraini Central Informatics Organisation, <http://www.cio.gov.bh>.

26. See International Crisis Group, *Popular Protests in North Africa and the Middle East (III): The Bahrain Revolt*, Middle East/North Africa Report no. 105, 6 April 2011. For a historical overview, see Omar Al Shehabi, "Political Movements in Bahrain: Past, Present, and Future," *Jadaliyya*, 14 Feb. 2012, <http://www.jadaliyya.com/pages/index/4363/political-movements-in-bahrain_past-present-and-fu>.

27. International Crisis Group, *The Bahrain Revolt*, p. 5.

28. See Ali Ahmad al-Diri, "Al-Bahrayn: Dakhil al-Maydan, Kharij al-Ta'ifa," *Bidayat*, no. 1, Winter/Spring 2012, pp. 54–61.

29. See Aryn Baker, "Sunni-Shi'ite Divide Clouds Prospects for Reform in Bahrain," *Time*, 26 Feb. 2011: "Mohammad Bouflasa, a Sunni from a prominent family, stood up on the stage of the first day of the protests to announce, 'I am Sunni, and I am with you.' His disappearance immediately afterwards, say anti-government protesters, is a visible warning from the regime to the pro-reform movement's Sunni sympathizers."

30. Vittorio Longhi and Khalil Bohazza, "Spotlight Interview with Salman Jaffar Al Mahfoodh, Bahrain—GFBTU," ITUC, 1 March 2012, <http://www.ituc-csi.org/spotlight-interview-with-salman,10736.html>.

31. Mujib Mashal, "Pakistani Troops Aid Bahrain's Crackdown," *Aljazeera.com*, 30 July 2011, <http://www.aljazeera.com/indepth/features/2011/07/2011725145048574888.html>.

32. See "Casualties of the 2011–2012 Bahraini Uprising," *Wikipedia*, <http://en.wikipedia.org/wiki/Casualties_of_the_2011%E2%80%932012_Bahraini_uprising>.

33. Brian Murphy, "Saudi Widens Arab Spring Backlash with Bahrain 'Union' Plans," *Associated Press*, 5 March 2012.

34. The Saudi provinces of Al-Ahsa and Qatif as well as the Bahraini archipelago were once part of a big Shiite-populated region known as Bahrain.

35. Leon Trotsky, *Stalin*, trans. Charles Malamuth, London: Hollis and Carter, 1947, p. 421.

36. OPEC, *Annual Statistical Bulletin 2010/2011*, Vienna: OPEC, 2011.

37. UNDP, *Human Development Report 2011*, New York: UNDP, 2011.

38. See Jonathan Bearman, *Qadhafi's Libya*, London: Zed Books, 1986, p. 239.

39. Ali Abdullatif Ahmida talks about the "re-tribalization" and "bedouinization" of the country under Gaddafi in a remarkable essay on the way the dictatorship's social base was constructed: "Libya, Social Origins of Dictatorship, and the Challenge for Democracy," *Journal of the Middle East and Africa*, vol 3, no. 1, 2012, pp. 70–81.

40. Dirk Vandewalle, *A History of Modern Libya*, New York: Cambridge University Press, 2006, p. 149.

41. Ibid., p. 205.

42. See ibid., pp. 150–2, and Hanspeter Mattes, "Challenges to Security Sector Governance in the Middle East: The Libyan Case," working paper, Geneva Centre for the Democratic Control of Armed Forces (DCAF), July 2004.

43. IMF, "IMF Managing Director Dominique Strauss-Kahn's Statement at the Conclusion of His Visit to the Socialist People's Libyan Arab Jamahiriya," 18 Nov. 2008, <http://www.imf.org/external/np/sec/pr/2008/pro8290.htm>.

44. IMF, "The Socialist People's Libyan Arab Jamahiriya—2010 Article IV Consultation, Preliminary Conclusions of the Mission," 28 Oct. 2010, <http://www.imf.org/external/np/ms/2010/102810.htm>. On the IMF's attitude toward the countries of the Arab uprising, see Patrick Bond, "Neoliberal Threats to North Africa," *Review of African Political Economy*, vol 38, no. 129, Sep. 2011, pp. 481–95.

45. Patrick Haimzadeh, *Au Coeur de la Libye de Kadhafi*, Paris: J-C Lattès, 2011, pp. 109–10.

46. See Ashby Monk, "Gaddafi Investment Authority, 2006–2011, RIP," *Oxford SWF Project*, 4 March 2011, <http://oxfordswfproject.com/2011/03/04/gaddafi-investment-authority-2006-2011-rip/>, and Global Witness, "Leaked Gaddafi-Era Documents Expose the Need for Urgent Oil Reforms," 13 April 2012, <http://www.globalwitness.org/library/leaked-documents-expose-need-urgent-oil-reforms-o>.

47. The figure of 30% is an ILO estimate. Although the official Libyan rate (over 20%) was lower, it was nevertheless higher than that of the neighboring states. The new Libyan authorities have raised the figure.

48. afrol News, "Libya Economy Reveals Basis for Protests," 16 Feb. 2011, <http://www.afrol.com/articles/37336>.

49. Ralph Chami et al., *Libya beyond the Revolution: Challenges and Opportunities*, Washington, DC: IMF, 2012.

50. "Sayf al-Islam al-Qadhdhafi Yatawa'ad al-Mutazahirin," *Al-Arabiyya*, 21 Feb. 2011, <http://www.alarabiya.net/articles/2011/02/21/138498.html>.

51. The speech, which lasted about one hour, was transcribed in toto by nationalist Arabs from Jordan, admirers of "the martyr Mouammar Kadhafi": "Nass Kalimat Mu'ammar al-Qadhdhafi Yaum 22 Fibrayir 2011," *Bilad al-'Arab*, 25 Feb. 2012, <http://beladalorb.com/cat22/13198.html>. A rough partial English translation is available at <https://docs.google.com/document/d/1ody5oLJY2QL7k2VuwKonUpSgCUX-_9ATQ-134Xka9fs/edit?hl=en&pli=1>.

52. "Founding Statement of the Interim Transitional National Council," 5 March 2011, <http://www.ntclibya.org/english/founding-statement-of-the -interim-transitional-national-council/>. For the sake of greater precision, the text cited here has been translated from the original Arabic, available at <http://ntclibya.org/arabic/>, *al-Bayanat*.

53. Eberhard Kienle, "Les 'révolutions' arabes," *Critique internationale*, 2012/1, no. 54, p. 106.

54. Youssef Courbage, "La population de la Syrie: des réticences à la transition démographique," in Baudouin Dupret et al., *La Syrie au présent. Reflets d'une société*, Paris: Sindbad/Actes Sud, 2007, p. 189.

55. On the concept of *'asabiyya*, see Chapter 4.

56. Hanna Batatu, *Syria's Peasantry, the Descendants of Its Lesser Rural Notables, and Their Politics*, Princeton, NJ: Princeton University Press, 1999. On the Alawites' ascension in the hierarchy of the Syrian armed forces, see pp. 157–60.

57. Patrick Seale, *Asad: The Struggle for the Middle East*, London: I.B. Tauris, 1990, p. 423. Seale's sanitized biography, based on interviews with Hafez al-Assad, does not so much as mention the six members' religious denomination.

58. Batatu, *Syria's Peasantry*, pp. 232–7.

59. Ibid., p. 226.

60. Ibid., p. 327; see also pp. 217–25.

61. Ibid., p. 227.

62. Reva Bhalla, "Making Sense of the Syrian Crisis," *Stratfor*, 5 May 2011, <http://www.stratfor.com/weekly/20110504-making-sense-syrian-crisis>.

63. Batatu, *Syria's Peasantry*, pp. 206–7.

64. Ibid., p. 237.

65. See Ali El Saleh, "Les 'bourgeoisies' syriennes" in Dupret et al., *La Syrie au présent*, pp. 771–8.

66. See Souhaïl Belhadj and Eberhard Kienle, "Y a-t-il de vraies transformations politiques internes en Syrie?" in ibid., pp. 687–727.

67. Bassam Haddad, "The Syrian Regime's Business Backbone," *Middle East Report*, vol 42, no. 262, Spring 2012, available on line at <http://www.merip. org/mer/mer262/syrian-regimes-business-backbone>. On the business networks forged in Syria and their relation to the government in the framework of what he calls "circumscribed liberalization," see idem, *Business Networks in Syria: The Political Economy of Authoritarian Resilience*, Stanford, CA: Stanford University Press, 2012.

68. See "Rami Makhlouf," *Wikipedia*, <http://en.wikipedia.org/wiki/Rami_Makhlouf>; see also Ignace Leverrier, "Rami Makhlouf, de l'affairisme à

l'illusionnisme," *Un Œil sur la Syrie, Le Monde* Blogs, 28 June 2011, <http://syrie.blog.lemonde.fr/2011/06/28/rami-makhlouf-de-laffairisme-a-lillusionnisme/>.

69. See Mohammed Jamal Barout, *Al-'Aqd al-Akhir fi Tarikh Surya: Jadaliyyat al-Jumud wal-Islah*, Doha: al-Markaz al-'Arabi lil-Abhath wa Dirasat al-Siyasat, 2012.

70. "Alawis had not yet produced a significant stratum of private businessmen and as long as much of the means of production remained state-owned, the state bourgeoisie lacked the secure control deriving from private ownership." Raymond Hinnebusch, *Syria: Revolution from Above*, London: Routledge, 2001, p. 91.

71. See Salwa Ismail, "Changing Social Structures, Shifting Alliances and Authoritarianism in Syria," in Fred Lawson, *Demystifying Syria*, London: Saqi, 2009, pp. 13–28.

72. See Yasir Munif and 'Umar Dahi, "Al-Neoliberaliyya wal-Istibdad fi Suriyya," *Bidayat*, no. 1, Winter/Spring 2012, pp. 72–8.

73. See Batatu, *Syria's Peasantry*.

74. See Samir Aita, "L'économie de la Syrie peut-elle devenir sociale?" in Dupret et al., *La Syrie au présent*, pp. 574–5.

75. See Yasin al-Hajj Salih, "Fi al-Shabbiha wal-Tashbih wa Dawlatahuma," *Kalamon*, no. 5, Winter 2011, available online on *Jadaliyya*, <http://www.jadaliyya.com/pages/index/4468/>. See also "Syria Unrest: Who Are the Shabiha?" *BBC*, 9 May 2012, <http://www.bbc.co.uk/news/world-middle-east-14482968>.

76. Hiba al-Laythi and Khalid Abu-Isma'il, *Al-Faqr fi Suriyya: 1996–2004*, Damascus: UNDP, June 2005.

77. Fayiz Sarah, *Al-Faqr fi Suriyya: Nahwa Tahawwul Jadhri fi Siyasat Mu'alajat al-Faqr*, London: Strategic Research & Communication Centre, 2011.

78. Central Bureau of Statistics (Syria), <http://www.cbssyr.org/>.

79. On Hafez al-Assad's image, see Lisa Wedeen, *Ambiguities of Domination: Politics, Rhetoric, and Symbols in Contemporary Syria*, Chicago: University of Chicago Press, 1999.

80. See Line Khatib, *Islamic Revivalism in Syria: The Rise and Fall of Ba'thist Secularism*, Oxon, UK: Routledge, 2011.

81. "Interview with Syrian President Bashar al-Assad," *Wall Street Journal*, 31 Jan. 2011.

82. The trauma that most closely resembles the Syrians', albeit different in nature and also much more recent, is that of the Algerian civil war triggered by the January 1992 coup d'état; it caused more than 100,000 deaths in the space of a decade. Among all the theories advanced to explain why Algeria had yet to experience an uprising at the time of writing (see, for example, Lahcen Achy, "Why Did Protests in Algeria Fail to Gain Momentum?" *Foreign Policy*, 31 March 2011, <http://mideast.foreignpolicy.com/posts/2011/03/31/why_did_protests_in_algeria_fail_to_gain_momentum>), this is the only plausible one. Similarly, the Saudi regime's use of terror is the main explanation for the fact that the kingdom has not yet exploded.

83. See Rania Abouzeid, "The Syrian Style of Repression: Thugs and Lectures," *Time*, 27 Feb. 2011, <http://www.time.com/time/world/article/0,8599,2055713,00.html>.

84. Muhammad Sayyid Rasas, "Kharita Ijtima'iyya Siyasiyya Iqtisadiyya lil-Ihtijajat fi Suriyya," *Al-Hiwar al-Mutammadin*, 30 July 2011, <http://www.ahewar.org/debat/show.art.asp?aid=269941>.

85. Hassan 'Abbas, *The Dynamics of the Uprising in Syria*, Arab Reform Brief, Mubadarat al-Islah al-'Arabi / Arab Reform Initiative, <www.arab-reform.net>, no. 51, Oct. 2011, p. 9.

86. Youssef Courbage's estimates in "La population de la Syrie," p. 189.

87. Dima Charif, "Gilbert al-Ashqar: Amirka Talhath Wara' Qitar al-Thawrat," *Al-Akhbar*, 22 June 2011, <http://www.al-akhbar.com/node/15106>; English translation in *Al-Akhbar English*, "Gilbert Achcar: The Revolution Has Just Begun," 24 August 2011, <http://english.al-akhbar.com/content/gilbert-achcar-revolution-has-just-begun>, translation modified.

88. I explained all this in my talk before a meeting of the Syrian Opposition (a majority of whom were members of the National Coordinating Committee; Burhan Ghalioun, then president of the SNC, was also present) held in October 2011 in Sweden. An essay based on this talk appeared one month later in Beirut: "Suriyya bayn al-'Askara wal-Tadakhkhul al-'Askari wa Ghiyab al-Istratijiyya," *Al-Akhbar*, 16 Nov. 2011, <http://www.al-akhbar.com/node/25760>; English translation in *Al-Akhbar English*, "Syria: Militarization, Military Intervention and the Absence of Strategy," 18 Nov. 2011, <http://english.al-akhbar.com/content/syria-militarization-military-intervention-and-absence-strategy>.

89. Caroline 'Akum, "Al-'Aqid al-Asa'ad lil-Sharq al-Awsat: Sa Nasta'nif 'Amaliyyatana Dud Quwwat al-Nizam ba'da an Inkashafat Nawayahu," *Al-Sharq al-Awsat*, 5 Nov. 2011.

90. Babeuf, "Manifeste des plébéiens," in *Textes choisis*, Paris: Editions sociales, 1965, p. 218.

91. For a good analysis of the development of the Syrian uprising, see Jean-Pierre Filiu, *Le Nouveau Moyen-Orient. Les peuples à l'heure de la révolution syrienne*, Paris: Fayard, 2013.

92. To date, the fullest study of the organization of the Syrian armed insurrection is Joseph Holliday, *Syria's Maturing Insurgency*, Washington, DC: Institute for the Study of War, 2012.

93. On the role of the "jihadists" in the Syrian insurrection, see Neil Mac-Farquhar and Hwaida Saad, "As Syrian War Drags On, Jihadists Take Bigger Role," *New York Times*, 29 July 2012; Hazim al-Amin, "Idlib: al-Lihya al-Mahalliyya li 'Kata'ib Ahrar al-Sham' Tu'iq Iltihaqaha bi 'al-Jihad al-'Alami,'" *Al-Hayat*, 21 August 2012; and International Crisis Group, *Tentative Jihad: Syria's Fundamentalist Opposition*, Middle East Report no. 131, 12 Oct. 2012.

94. See note 88 above.

95. Razan Zaytunah, "Qa'id Katibat al-Ashtar fil-Rastan: Hakaza Tahawwalna ila al-'Amal al-'Askari," *Al-Hayat*, 27 Jan. 2012.

96. C. J. Chivers, "Many Hands Patch Together Syrian Rebels' Arsenal," *New York Times*, 28 Aug. 2012.

97. Aya Batrawy, "Syria's Wealthy Businesses Feel Civil War Squeeze," *Associated Press*, 18 Oct. 2012.

CHAPTER 6

1. For an interesting analysis of the popularity of conspiracy theories in the Arab region, see Matthew Gray, *Conspiracy Theories in the Arab World: Sources and Politics*, Abingdon, UK: Routledge, 2010.

2. See "WikiLeaks: Clinton I'tamadat Ghasil al-Amwal lil-Munazzamat Misriyya" (with links to the relevant cables), *America in Arabic*, 10 Feb. 2012, <http://americainarabic.org/>.

3. Human Rights Watch, *Delivered into Enemy Hands: US-Led Abuse and Rendition of Opponents to Gaddafi's Libya*, New York: HRW, 2012, p. 1.

4. "Washington Tad'u Salih lil-Istijaba li-Sha'bihi," *Aljazeera.net*, 2 March 2011, <http://www.aljazeera.net/news/pages/be7eb3ac-9881-499f-955a-08b 84518b146>.

5. See Rod Nordland and David Kirkpatrick, "Dossier Details Egypt's Case Against Democracy Groups," *New York Times*, 20 Feb. 2012.

6. "Tunisia: les propos 'effrayants' d'Alliot-Marie suscitent la polémique," *Le Monde*, 13 Jan. 2011, <http://www.lemonde.fr/afrique/article/2011/01/13/ Tunisia-les-propos-effrayants-d-alliot-marie-suscitent-la-polemique_1465278 _3212.html>.

7. "La chute du régime Ben Ali racontée par Ali Sariati, le chef de la garde présidentielle," *Le Monde*, 2 April 2011, and Leila Trabelsi, *Ma vérité*, Paris: Editions du Moment, 2012.

8. MENA, "Tunisian Officer: Washington Tells Dismissed Chief of Staff to 'Take Charge,'" *Egypt Independent*, 16 Jan. 2011, <http://www.egyptindependent .com/news/tunisian-officer-washington-tells-dismissed-chief-staff-take-charge>.

9. Jeremy Sharp, *Egypt: The January 25 Revolution and Implications for U.S. Foreign Policy*, Washington, DC: Congressional Research Service, 11 Feb. 2011, p. 11.

10. "Statement by the Press Secretary on Egypt," The White House, 25 Jan. 2011.

11. "DOD News Briefing with Geoff Morrell from the Pentagon," US Department of Defense, 26 Jan. 2011, <http://www.defense.gov/Transcripts/ Transcript.aspx?TranscriptID=4758>.

12. "Remarks by the President on the Situation in Egypt," Washington, DC: The White House, 28 Jan. 2011, <http://www.whitehouse.gov/the -press-office/2011/01/28/remarks-president-situation-egypt>.

13. "Remarks by the President on a New Beginning, Cairo University, Cairo, Egypt," Washington, DC: The White House, 4 June 2009, <http://www.white house.gov/the-press-office/remarks-president-cairo-university-6-04-09>.

14. On the heavy US defeat in Iraq, see Michael Gordon's investigation report, "Failed Efforts and Challenges of America's Last Months in Iraq," *New York Times*, 22 Sep. 2012.

15. On the Obama administration's weakness vis-à-vis Israel, see Peter Beinart, "Obama Betrayed Ideals on Israel," *Newsweek*, 12 March 2012.

16. See Kareem Fahim, "As Hopes for Reform Fade in Bahrain, Protesters Turn Anger on United States," *New York Times*, 23 June 2012.

17. See, for example, David Kirkpatrick and Steven Lee Myers, "U.S. Hones

Warnings to Egypt as Military Stalls Transition," *New York Times*, 16 Nov. 2011.

18. "Vote for the Brother: A Muslim Brother Is Better than a Mubarak Crony," *The Economist*, 16 June 2012.

19. Matt Bradley and Adam Entous, "U.S. Reaches Out to Islamist Parties," *Wall Street Journal*, 1 July 2011.

20. The US Embassy in Sana'a also stood in direct relation with the Islah Party, as is attested by the diplomatic reports revealed by WikiLeaks.

21. See Helene Cooper and Mark Landler, "U.S. Hopes Assad Can Be Eased Out with Russia's Aid," *New York Times*, 26 May 2012. On the "Yemeni solution" and its limits for Syria, see Fawwaz Traboulsi, "Al-Azma al-Suriyya wa 'al-Hall al-Yamani,'" *Al-Safir*, 13 June 2012.

22. Leon Trotsky, *Between Red & White: A Study of Some Fundamental Questions of Revolution*, Ann Arbor, MI: University of Michigan Library (reprint of the 1922 edition), available online at <http://www.marxists.org/archive/trotsky/1922/red-white/index.htm>.

23. The three following paragraphs are taken from my article, "Libya: A Legitimate and Necessary Debate from an Anti-Imperialist Perspective," *ZNet*, 25 March 2011, <http://www.zcommunications.org/libya-a-legitimate-and-necessary-debate-from-an-anti-imperialist-perspective-by-gilbert-achcar>. The passage has been slightly modified for reasons of style.

24. On the relations between the United States and Gaddafi's regime before the uprising, including US military aid to the regime, see Christopher Blanchard and Jim Zanotti, *Libya: Background and U.S. Relations*, Washington, DC: Congressional Research Service, 18 Feb. 2011.

25. See Human Rights Watch, *Pushed Back, Pushed Around: Italy's Forced Return of Boat Migrants and Asylum Seekers, Libya's Mistreatment of Migrants and Asylum Seekers*, New York: HRW, 2009, and Migreurop, *European Borders: Controls, Detention and Deportations*, 2009/2010 Report, Paris: Migreurop, 2010.

26. See Alessandra Rizzo, "Mediterranean Countries Ask EU to Share Refugees Amid Migrant Waves from North African Unrest," *Associated Press*, 23 Feb. 2011. See also Jean-François Bayart, "Assez de collusions avec le régime de Kadhafi!" *Le Monde*, 13 April 2011.

27. See Richard Krijgsman, "Oil & Gas Companies in Libya—a Who's Who," *Evaluate Energy*, 24 Feb. 2011, <http://www.oil-blog.com/companies/major-ioc/libyan-oil-gas/>, and Energy Information Administration, "Country Analysis Briefs: Libya," June 2012, <www.eia.doe.gov>.

28. Ethan Chorin, *Exit Gaddafi: The Hidden History of the Libyan Revolution*, London: Saqi, 2012, p. 310. The author was a member of the US diplomatic representation in Libya in 2004–6. He has founded an NGO to provide postrevolutionary Libya with medical assistance.

29. Certain people on the left in the West had the ethnocentric indecency to say that it was not certain that a massacre would take place, implying that Benghazi's population should have run the experiment of letting Gaddafi's troops capture the city.

30. The twelve-year embargo inflicted on Iraq between 1991 and 2003 was

well suited to the then depressive oil market. Only in 2000 did the oil price begin moving in the opposite direction, leading the United States to invade the country.

31. Ryan Lizza, "The Consequentialist: How the Arab Spring Remade Obama's Foreign Policy," *The New Yorker*, 2 May 2011. On the other hand, US oil companies, disappointed by the results of their prospecting in Libya in the last few years, were not particularly interested (see Chorin, *Exit Gaddafi*).

32. For the relevant data and a detailed analysis of the NATO intervention, see my "NATO's 'Conspiracy' Against the Libyan Revolution," *Jadaliyya*, 16 August 2011, <http://www.jadaliyya.com/pages/index/2401/natos-conspiracy-against-the-libyan-revolution>.

33. See *Report of the International Commission of Inquiry on Libya*, New York: Human Rights Council, United Nations, 2 March 2012, and Human Rights Watch, *Unacknowledged Deaths: Civilian Casualties in NATO's Air Campaign in Libya*, New York: HRW, 2012.

34. Ian Black, "Post-Gaddafi Libya 'Must Learn from Mistakes Made in Iraq,'" *The Guardian*, 28 June 2011.

35. See my "Self-Deception and Selective Expertise: Bush's Cakewalk into the Iraq Quagmire," *CounterPunch*, 5 May 2004, <http://www.counterpunch.org/2004/05/05/bush-s-cakewalk-into-the-iraq-quagmire/>.

36. The two preceding paragraphs have been taken from my article cited in note 32 above. (The passage has been slightly modified for stylistic reasons.) At the same moment, the International Crisis Group, which functions as a *think tank* for the Western powers, advocated negotiating an agreement with the Gaddafi regime and dispatching an international force to see to it that it was respected: International Crisis Group, *Popular Protest in North Africa and the Middle East (V): Making Sense of Libya*, Middle East / North Africa Report no. 107, 6 June 2011. The main author of this report, Hugh Roberts, director of the ICG's North Africa division between February and July 2011, tried to justify his position in a long essay published in the *London Review of Books* ("Who Said Gaddafi Had to Go?" vol 33, no. 22, 17 Nov. 2011, pp. 8–18). To read this essay today, in light of developments in Libya, is to confirm just how deeply the author grounded his position on mistaken premises. A book by Roberts on Libya is forthcoming. One hopes that he criticizes his past positions in it, the more so as the book will be published by a left-wing publishing firm.

37. Bassem Mroué, "Syria Opposition May Accept Role for Assad's Party," *Associated Press*, 8 Oct. 2012.

38. Ahmad Nur, "Qa'id Thuwwar Halab: Ma'rakatuna Laysat Ma' al-'Alawiyyin," *Aljazeera.net*, 9 Sep. 2012, <http://www.aljazeera.net/news/pages/14df1619-4bd3-424b-a7f4-fa0b4afo6192>.

39. "Libya: Despite Everything, It's Still a Success," *The Economist*, 15 Sep. 2012. The venerable review seems to think that British and European visas are issued in the absence of all xenophobic feelings toward non-Westerners.

40. "Obama: Egypt Is Not US Ally, Nor an Enemy," *BBC*, 3 Sep. 2012, <http://www.bbc.co.uk/news/world-middle-east-19584265>.

41. Karl Marx, "Revolution in China and in Europe," *New York Daily Tri-*

bune, 14 June 1853, <http://www.marxists.org/archive/marx/works/1853/06/14.htm>.

42. See, for example, the reactionary book by John Bradley, *After the Arab Spring: How the Islamists Hijacked the Middle East Revolts*, New York: Palgrave Macmillan, 2012. For Bradley, Jordan's and Morocco's "constitutional monarchies" [*sic*] are the best form of government the Arabs can hope for.

43. I put an article by Hussein Agha and Robert Malley in this category: "This Is Not a Revolution," *New York Review of Books*, vol 59, no. 17, <http://www.nybooks.com/articles/archives/2012/nov/08/not-revolution/>.

44. Karl Marx and Frederick Engels, "Address of the Central Committee to the Communist League," in Marx, *The Revolutions of 1848*, edited and introduced by David Fernbach, London: Verso, 2010, pp. 319–30.

45. Gilbert Achcar, "Eleven Theses on the Current Resurgence of Islamic Fundamentalism," in *Eastern Cauldron: Islam, Afghanistan, Palestine and Iraq in a Marxist Mirror*, New York: Monthly Review Press, and London: Pluto, 2004, pp. 48–59.

46. Robert Fisk, "Exclusive: 'We Believe that the USA Is the Major Player Against Syria and the Rest Are Its Instruments,'" *The Independent*, 28 August 2012.

47. See al-Muldi al-Ahmar, *Al-Intikhabat al-Tunisiyya: Khafaya Fashal al-Qiwa al-Hadathiyya wa Mashakil Najah Hizb al-Nahda al-Islami*, Doha: al-Markaz al-'Arabi lil-Abhath wa Dirasat al-Siyasat, 2011.

48. See Chapter 3.

49. See esp. the article by one of the Brotherhood's ranking leaders, Essam El-Errian, "What the Muslim Brothers Want," *New York Times*, 9 Feb. 2011.

50. Eager to mitigate the impact of the unpopular peace treaty that he concluded with Israel in March 1979 (fewer than six weeks after the Iranian revolution), Sadat had the 1971 constitution amended one year later to include this clause, despite the fact that a large minority of the Egyptian population is Christian.

51. Muhammad Khayr, "'Al-Jazira' wal-Thawra: Fattish 'an 'al-Ikhwan,'" *Al-Akhbar* (Beirut), 21 Dec. 2011. The director of the head office of the Qatari network in Cairo had long been employed in Egypt by a publication of the Muslim Brotherhood before leaving for the Gulf, where he joined the staff of Al Jazeera. He later moved back to Egypt, where he continued to work for the network.

52. See Annie Kriegel, *The French Communists: Profile of a People*, trans. Elaine Halperin, Chicago: University of Chicago Press, 1972. For an application of Kriegel's "counter-society" paradigm to an Arab Islamic party, see Waddah Charara, *Dawlat "Hizbullah": Lubnan Mujtama'an Islamiyyan*, Beirut: Dar al-Nahar, 1996.

53. On the influence of these social services on the rural vote, see Yasmine Moataz Ahmed, "Who Do Egypt's Villagers Vote For? And Why?" *Egypt Independent*, 10 April 2012, <http://www.egyptindependent.com/node/764101>.

54. For a utilization of the concept of anomie, forged by the French sociologist Emile Durkheim, to explain the expansion of Muslim fundamentalism from the last quarter of the twentieth century on, see my *The Clash of Barbarisms:*

The Making of the New World Disorder, 2nd edn, London: Saqi, and Boulder, CO: Paradigm, 2006.

55. Nawal el-Saadawi, "Al-Thawra al-Misriyya al-Thaniya," *Al-Masry al-Youm*, 29 Nov. 2011.

56. The size of the Egyptian electorate is poorly defined. See Hazem Zohny, "40 Million Egyptian Voters? Not Likely," *Ahram Online*, 28 Nov. 2010, <http://english.ahram.org.eg/News/101.aspx>.

57. On the Egyptian Salafists and their conversion to political activism, see Hani Nusayra, *Al-Salafiyya fi Misr: Tahawwulat ma Ba'd al-Thawra*, Cairo: Markaz al-Dirasat al-Siyasiyya wal-Istratijiyya bil-Ahram, 2011; Umayma 'Abdul-Latif, *Al-Salafiyyun fi Misr wal-Siyasa*, Doha: al-Markaz al-'Arabi lil-Abhath wa Dirasat al-Siyasat, 2011; and 'Ammar Ahmad Fayid, *Al-Salafiyyun fi Misr: Min Shar'iyat al-Fatwa ila Shar'iyat al-Intikhab*, Doha: Markaz al-Jazira lil-Dirasat, 2012. See also Ahmad Baha' al-Din Sha'ban, "Maza Yurid al-Wahhabiyyun bi-Misr al-Thawra" in Samir Amin et al., *Al-Dimuqratiyya wal-Thawra fi Misr*, Cairo: al-Dar al-Ishtirakiyya, 2012, pp. 109–27.

58. See Hamdi Qandil, "Balagh ila al-Majlis al'Askari: Natlub al-Tahqiq fi Raf' al-A'lam al-Sa'udiyya," *Al-Masry al-Youm*, 1 Aug. 2011.

59. See my "Orientalism in Reverse: Post-1979 Trends in French Orientalism," *Radical Philosophy*, no. 151, Sep.–Oct. 2008, pp. 20–30. For a hard-hitting critique of culturalist theses about the incompatibility between Islam and secularization, see Aziz Al-Azmeh, *Islams and Modernities*, 3rd edn, London: Verso, 2009.

60. Moussa Grifa, "The Libyan Revolution: Establishing a New Political System and the Transition to Statehood," *Arab Reform Brief*, no. 62, Sep. 2012, Mubadarat al-Islah al-'Arabi / Arab Reform Initiative, <www.arab-reform.net>.

61. "Hushud bi-Jum'at 'al-Dawla al-Madaniyya' bil-Yaman," *Aljazeera .net*, 15 July 2011, <http://www.aljazeera.net/news/pages/d4aa16b3-1e99-4661-a961-1ee891dde30a>.

CONCLUSION

1. See Sebnem Gumuscu and Deniz Sert, "The Power of the Devout Bourgeoisie: The Case of the Justice and Development Party in Turkey," *Middle Eastern Studies*, vol 45, no. 6, Nov. 2009, pp. 953–68.

2. Sebnem Gumuscu, "Economic Liberalization, Devout Bourgeoisie, and Change in Political Islam: Comparing Turkey and Egypt," EUI Working Paper RSCAS 2008/19, Florence: European University Institute, 2008.

3. World Bank, World Databank, <http://databank.worldbank.org/data/Home.aspx>.

4. Ibid.

5. Thirty-nine companies with fewer than 100 employees, thirty-eight with 100 to 500 employees, seventeen with 500 to 1,000 employees, and six with more than 1,000 employees.

6. Klaus Schwab, ed, *The Global Competitiveness Report 2010–2011*, Geneva: World Economic Forum, 2010, available at <http://gcr.weforum.org/gcr2010/>.

7. Klaus Schwab, ed, *The Global Competitiveness Report 2012–2013*, Geneva: World Economic Forum, 2012, p. 11.

8. See the quotations in my article "Al-Intihaziyyun wal-Thawra," *Al-Akhbar* and *Al-Quds al-'Arabi*, 25 Jan. 2012; English translation in *Al-Akhbar English*, "Opportunists and the Revolution," 27 Jan. 2012.

9. Emna El-Hammi, "Tunisie: Voter pour Ennahdha était-ce une arnaque?" *Nawaat*, 8 Dec. 2011, <http://nawaat.org/portail/2011/12/08/tunisie-voter-pour -ennahdha-etait-ce-une-arnaque/>.

10. UTICA, "L'UTICA met en garde contre la situation socio-économique fragile," <http://www.utica.org.tn/website/detail_article2012.php?art_id=1216>.

11. See Oussama Nadjib, "Le patronat tunisien 'libéré' mais en crise se cher-che une nouvelle image," *Maghreb émergent*, 8 Feb. 2011, <http://www.djazair-ess.com/fr/maghrebemergent/2166>.

12. On the debt question in general and Tunisia's and Egypt's debt in par-ticular, see the articles published on the site of the Committee for the Abolition of Third World Debt, <http://cadtm.org>.

13. See Mahmoud Ben Romdhane, "La capacité à emprunter de la Tunisie est loin d'être garantie en 2012," *Maghreb émergent*, 7 Feb. 2012, <http://www .maghrebemergent.info/economie/73-tunisie/8650-mahmoud-ben-romdhane-l -la-capacite-a-emprunter-de-la-tunisie-est-loin-detre-garantie-en-2012-r.html>.

14. Amnesty International, "Tunisian Authorities Must Protect Victims and Their Families in Former Officials' Trial," 12 Feb. 2012, <http://www .amnesty.org/en/library/asset/MDE30/003/2012/en/d651de66-08fb-4c53-880e -d8179476f22a/mde300032012en.html>.

15. Human Rights Watch, "Tunisia: Q&A on the Trial of Ben Ali, Others for Killing Protesters," 11 June 2012, <http://www.hrw.org/news/2012/06/11/ tunisia-qa-trial-ben-ali-others-killing-protesters>.

16. See Iman Muhazzab, "Jadal bi-Sha'n al-Mu'assasa al-'Askariyya fi Tunis," *Aljazeera.net*, 16 Sep. 2012, <http://aljazeera.net/news/pages/49a780 ba-344b-4882-a50a-d6bdce464323>.

17. Céline Lussato, "Tunisie. Messaoudi dénonce 'un nouveau régime dicta-torial,'" *Le Nouvel Observateur*, 30 August 2012, <http://tempsreel.nouvelobs .com/monde/20120830.OBS0825/tunisie-ayoub-messaoudi-denonce-un -regime-dictatorial-theocratique.html>. Under pressure from human rights organizations, the military tribunal had to content itself with condemning Messaoudi to a suspended sentence of four months in prison.

18. See Chapter 5.

19. The expert is Gawdat Bahgat, a professor at the National Defense Uni-versity (NDU) in Washington. Bahgat knows many of the Egyptian officers who have spent time at NDU. He is cited in Craig Whitlock and Greg Jaffe, "Where Egypt Military's Loyalties Lie Remains Unclear," *Washington Post*, 5 Feb. 2011.

20. *WikiLeaks*, cable from the Embassy in Cairo, 23 Sep. 2008, <http:// wikileaks.org/cable/2008/09/08CAIRO2091.html#>.

21. Anes Zaki, "Khabir: al-Taghyir Kana Hatmiyyan bil-Jaysh al-Misri," *Aljazeera.net*, 31 August 2012, <http://www.aljazeera.net/news/pages/73e37525 -42ff-4724-8b7e-7632951dfoc2>. It should also be noted that Morsi named the former commander of the air force chairperson of the board of the Arab Orga-

nization for Industrialization (the Egyptian military industries), and the former commander of the navy head of the Suez Canal Authority. The new defense minister, for his part, sent seventy generals into retirement, several of whom Tantawi had appointed to posts as assistant defense ministers after they had retired.

22. On Khairat al-Shatir and the Brotherhood's capitalists, see Avi Asher-Schapiro, "The GOP Brotherhood of Egypt," *Salon.com*, 26 Jan. 2012, <http://www.salon.com/2012/01/26/the_gop_brotherhood_of_egypt/>.

23. Zeinab Abul-Magd, "Al-Ikhwan al-Ra'smaliyyun," *Al-Tahrir*, 12 Feb. 2012.

24. Sebnem Gumuscu, "Class, Status, and Party: The Changing Face of Political Islam in Turkey and Egypt," *Comparative Political Studies*, vol 43, no. 7, Feb. 2010, pp. 850–1.

25. Ibid, p. 855. For a better account of the differences between Turkish and Arab capitalism, see Alper Dede, "The Arab Uprisings: Debating the 'Turkish Model,' " *Insight Turkey*, vol 13, no. 2, 2011, pp. 23–32.

26. Suzy Hansen, "The Economic Vision of Egypt's Muslim Brotherhood Millionaires," *Bloomberg Businessweek*, 19 April 2012.

27. Nevine Kamel, "One Sure Thing: A Pro-Market Egyptian Constitution," *Ahram Online*, 4 April 2012, <http://english.ahram.org.eg/NewsContent/3/12/38404/Business/Economy/One-sure-thing-A-promarket-Egyptian-constitution-.aspx>.

28. Hansen, "The Economic Vision."

29. See Nadine Marrouchi, "Senior Brotherhood Member Launches Egyptian Business Association," *Egypt Independent*, 26 March 2012, <http://www.egyptindependent.com/node/734126>.

30. Al-Markaz al-Misri lil-Huquq al-Iqtisadiyya wal-Ijtima'iyya, *Al-Huquq al-Iqtisadiyya wal-Ijtima'iyya fil-Shuhur al-Ula lil-Ra'is Mursi: Ma'at Yawm min Siyasat al-Tajahul wal-Tahmish*, Cairo: ECESR, 11 Oct. 2012, p. 6.

31. This information is taken from "Mubarak Era Tycoons Join Egypt President in China," *Al-Ahram Online*, 28 Aug. 2012, <http://english.ahram.org.eg/NewsContent/3/12/51477/Business/Economy/Mubarak-era-tycoons-join-Egypt-President-in-China.aspx>.

32. See Gumuscu, "Economic Liberalization."

33. Staff of the International Monetary Fund, *Economic Transformation in MENA: Delivering on the Promise of Shared Prosperity*, Group of Eight Summit, 27 May 2011, Deauville, France, Washington, DC: IMF, 2011.

34. See Aya Batrawy, "Egypt Vows Structural Reforms, Meets US Executives," *Associated Press*, 9 Sep. 2012.

35. Khaled Hroub, *Fi Madih al-Thawra: al-Nahr dud al-Mustanqa'*, Beirut: Dar al-Saqi, 2012, p. 119.

36. Maxime Rodinson, "On 'Islamic Fundamentalism': An Unpublished Interview with Gilbert Achcar," *Middle East Report*, no. 233, Winter 2004, p. 4.

37. Usama 'Abdul-Salam, "Al-Murshid Yad'u al-Misriyyin lil-Ihtifa' bi-Zikra al-Thawra wa Isti'adat Ruhiha," *Ikhwan Online*, 20 Jan. 2012, <http://www.ikhwanonline.com/new/Article.aspx?ArtID=99730&SecID=230>. On the Muslim Brothers' economic program, see Salah al-'Amrusi, " 'Iqtisad al-Suq

al-Islami': al-Barnamaj al-Iqtisadi wal-Ijtima'i lil-Ikhwan al-Muslimin fi Misr," *Bidayat*, no. 1, Winter/Spring 2012, pp. 79–82.

38. Gilbert Achcar (al-Ashqar), "'17 Disimbir 2010': Bidayat Sayrura Thawriyya Tawilat al-Amad," *Al-Akhbar*, 10 Jan. 2012; English translation: "The Bouazizi Spark: The Beginning of a Long Revolutionary Process," *Al-Akhbar English*, 10 Jan. 2012, <http://english.al-akhbar.com/content/bouazizi-spark-beginning-long-revolutionary-process>. Translation modified.

39. Chemi Shalev, "Full Transcript of Interview with Palestinian Professor Rashid Khalidi," *Haaretz*, 5 Dec. 2011.

40. See 'Adnan al-Mansar, *Al-Durru wa Ma'danuhu: al-Khilafat bayn al-Hizb al-Dusturi wal-Haraka al-Niqabiyya fi Tunis, 1924–1978. Jadaliyyat al-Tajanus wal-Sira'*, Tunis: Al-Magharibiyya, 2010.

41. See Chapter 4.

42. Hamdeen Sabahy, *Naqdur Nabniha min Jadid: al-Barnamaj al-Intikhabi li-Hamdin Sabahi li-Ri'asat Misr*, Cairo: 2012; the sentences cited are on p. 24.

43. See my *The Clash of Barbarisms: The Making of the New World Disorder*, 2nd edn, London: Saqi, and Boulder, CO: Paradigm, 2006.

44. See Olivier Roy, "Révolution post-islamiste," *Le Monde.fr*, 12 Feb. 2011, <http://www.lemonde.fr/idees/article/2011/02/12/revolution-post-islamiste_1478858_3232.html>; see also Asef Bayat, "The Post-Islamist Revolutions," *Foreign Affairs Snapshot*, 26 April 2011, <http://www.foreignaffairs.com/articles/67812/asef-bayat/the-post-islamist-revolutions> and "Arab Revolts: Islamists Aren't Coming!" *Insight Turkey*, vol 13, no. 2, 2011, pp. 9–14.

45. Samir Amin, *The People's Spring: The Future of the Arab Revolution*, Oxford, UK: Pambazuka, 2012, pp. 190–1.

46. In a widely disseminated text that has been partially reproduced in the book cited in the previous note, Samir Amin comments on the "second wave of the awakening of the southern peoples," in which he places the new experiences of the Latin American left as well as the "Springtimes of the Arab Peoples." According to Amin, "These springtimes . . . coincide with the 'autumn of capitalism,' the decline of the capitalism of globalized, financialized, generalized, monopolies. These movements begin, like those of the preceding century, with peoples and states of the system's periphery regaining their independence, retaking the initiative in transforming the world. They are thus above all anti-imperialist movements and so are only potentially anti-capitalist. Should these movements succeed in converging with the other necessary reawakening, that of the workers in the imperialist core, a truly socialist perspective could be opened for the whole human race. But that is in no way a predestined 'historical necessity.' The decline of capitalism might open the way for a long transition toward socialism, but it might equally well put humanity on the road to generalized barbarism." Samir Amin, "2011: An Arab Springtime?" 2 June 2011, available online at <http://monthlyreview.org/commentary/2011-an-arab-springtime#.UIT-EWez7To>; in print in *Monthly Review*, vol 64, no. 5, Oct. 2011.

47. Mona El-Ghobashy, "Politics by Other Means," *Boston Review*, Nov.–Dec. 2011, p. 44. Interesting reflections on the progressive graduation of "street politics," especially the atomized forms of resistance that served as a prelude to

the mass protests, may be found in Asef Bayat, *Life as Politics: How Ordinary People Change the Middle East*, Stanford, CA: Stanford University Press, 2010.

48. Al-Markaz al-Misri lil-Huquq, *Al-Huquq al-Iqtisadiyya wal-Ijtima'iyya fil-Shuhur al-Ula lil-Ra'is Mursi*.

49. Maha Abdelrahman, "A Hierarchy of Struggles? The 'Economic' and the 'Political' in Egypt's Revolution," *Review of African Political Economy*, vol 29, no. 134, Dec. 2012, p. 626.

50. Charles de Gaulle, *Mémoires de guerre*, vol 3, *Le Salut: 1944–1946*, Paris: Plon, 1959, p. 73.

References and Sources

For lack of space, most of the articles from newspapers or press agencies cited in the present book are not included in the following list. Contributions to works by several hands are not cited separately: only the work itself is cited, under the name of the first author mentioned on the cover.

'Abbas, Hassan, *The Dynamics of the Uprising in Syria*, Arab Reform Brief, Mubadarat al-Islah al-'Arabi / Arab Reform Initiative, <www.arab-reform .net>, no. 51, Oct. 2011.

Abdel-Malek, Anouar, *Egypt, Military Society: The Army Regime, the Left, and Social Change under Nasser*, trans. Charles Lam Markmann, New York: Random House, 1968.

Abdelrahman, Maha, "In Praise of Organisation: Egypt Between Activism and Revolution," *Development and Change*, vol 44, no. 3, May 2013 (forthcoming).

———, "A Hierarchy of Struggles? The 'Economic' and the 'Political' in Egypt's Revolution," *Review of African Political Economy*, vol 29, no. 134, Dec. 2012, pp. 614–28.

'Abdul-Fadil, Mahmud, *Ra'smaliyyat al-Mahasib: Dirasa fil-Iqtisad al-Ijtima'i*, Cairo: Dar al-'Ayn, 2011.

'Abdullah, Anwar, *Al-'Ulama' wal-'Arsh: Thuna'iyat al-Sulta fi al-Sa'udiyya*, London: Mu'assasat al-Rafid, 1995.

'Abdul-Latif, Umayma, *Al-Salafiyyun fi Misr wa al-Siyasa*, Doha: al-Markaz al-'Arabi lil-Abhath wa Dirasat al-Siyasat, 2011.

Abouzeid, Rania, "The Syrian Style of Repression: Thugs and Lectures," *Time*, 27 Feb. 2011, <http://www.time.com/time/world/article/0,8599,2055713,00 .html>.

Abul-Magd, Zeinab, "The Army and the Economy in Egypt," *Jadaliyya*, 23 Dec. 2011, <http://www.jadaliyya.com/pages/index/3732/the-army-and-the -economy-in-egypt>.

———, "The Generals' Secret: Egypt's Ambivalent Market," *Sada*, Washington, DC: Carnegie Endowment for International Peace, 9 Feb. 2012, <http://car negieendowment.org/sada/index.cfm?fa=show&article=47137&solr_hilite>.

———, "Al-Ikhwan al-Ra'smaliyyun," *Al-Tahrir*, 12 Feb. 2012.

Aburish, Saïd, *The Rise, Corruption and Coming Fall of the House of Saud*, London: Bloomsbury, 1994.

Achcar, Gilbert, "The Arab World: Absence of Democracy," *Le Monde diplomatique*, June 1997.

———, "The Strategic Triad: USA, Russia, China" and "Rasputin Plays at Chess: How the West Blundered into a New Cold War" in Tariq Ali, ed, *Masters of the Universe? NATO's Balkan Crusade*, London: Verso, 2000, pp. 57–144.

———, *Eastern Cauldron: Islam, Afghanistan, Palestine and Iraq in a Marxist Mirror*, New York: Monthly Review Press, and London: Pluto, 2004.

———, "Fantasy of a Region That Doesn't Exist. Greater Middle East: The US Plan," *Le Monde diplomatique*, April 2004.

———, "Self-Deception and Selective Expertise: Bush's Cakewalk into the Iraq Quagmire," *CounterPunch*, 5 May 2004, <http://www.counterpunch .org/2004/05/05/bush-s-cakewalk-into-the-iraq-quagmire/>.

———, "Arab Spring: Late and Cold," *Le Monde diplomatique*, July 2005.

———, *The Clash of Barbarisms: The Making of the New World Disorder*, 2nd edn, London: Saqi, and Boulder, CO: Paradigm, 2006.

———, "Orientalism in Reverse: Post-1979 Trends in French Orientalism," *Radical Philosophy*, no. 151, Sep.–Oct. 2008, pp. 20–30.

———, "Estabilidad e inestabilidad en Egipto: una mirada de cerca al reciente crecimiento económico" in ICEX, ed, *Claves de la Economía Mundial 2009*, Madrid: Instituto Español de Comercio Exterior, 2009, pp. 455–61; original English text, "Stability and Instability in Egypt: A Closer Look at Recent Egyptian Growth," available at <http://eprints.soas.ac.uk/10365/>.

———, "Al-Yasar al-'Arabi: Hiwar Ajrahu Wa'el 'Abdul-Rahim," *Al-Adab*, no. 4–5, 2010, p. 49.

———, *The Arabs and the Holocaust: The Arab-Israeli War of Narratives*, trans. G. M. Goshgarian, New York: Metropolitan/Picador, 2010; London: Saqi, 2010; 2nd edn, 2011.

———, "Libya: A Legitimate and Necessary Debate from an Anti-Imperialist Perspective," *ZNet*, 25 March 2011, <http://www.zcommunications.org/ libya-a-legitimate-and-necessary-debate-from-an-anti-imperialist-perspec tive-by-gilbert-achcar>.

———, "Gilbert Achcar: The Revolution Has Just Begun," *Al-Akhbar English*, 24 August 2011, <http://english.al-akhbar.com/content/gilbert-achcar-revo lution-has-just-begun>; originally published in Arabic, "Gilbert al-Ashqar: Amirka Talhath Wara' Qitar al-Thawrat" (interview done by Dima Charif), *Al-Akhbar*, 22 June 2011, <http://www.al-akhbar.com/node/15106>.

———, "NATO's 'Conspiracy' Against the Libyan Revolution," *Jadaliyya*, 16 August 2011, <http://www.jadaliyya.com/pages/index/2401/natos-conspir acy-against-the-libyan-revolution>.

———, "Syria: Militarization, Military Intervention and the Absence of Strategy," *Al-Akhbar English*, 18 Nov. 2011, <http://english.al-akhbar.com/con tent/syria-militarization-military-intervention-and-absence-strategy>.

———, "The Bouazizi Spark: The Beginning of a Long Revolutionary Process," *Al-Akhbar English*, 10 Jan. 2012, <http://english.al-akhbar.com/content/ bouazizi-spark-beginning-long-revolutionary-process>.

———, "Opportunists and the Revolution," *Al-Akhbar English*, 27 Jan. 2012, <http://english.al-akhbar.com/node/3724>.

Achy, Lahcen, "Why Did Protests in Algeria Fail to Gain Momentum?" *Foreign Policy*, 31 March 2011, <http://mideast.foreignpolicy.com/posts/2011/03/31/ why_did_protests_in_algeria_fail_to_gain_momentum>.

Adly, Amr, *Mubarak (1990–2011): The State of Corruption*, ARI Thematic Studies, March 2011 [actually March 2012].

afrol News, "Libya Economy Reveals Basis for Protests," 16 Feb. 2011, <http:// www.afrol.com/articles/37336>.

Agha, Hussein and Robert Malley, "This Is Not a Revolution," *New York Review of Books*, vol 59, no. 17, <http://www.nybooks.com/articles/archives/2012/ nov/08/not-revolution/>.

Ahmar (al-), al-Muldi, *Al-Intikhabat al-Tunisiyya: Khafaya Fashal al-Qiwa al-Hadathiyya wa Mashakil Najah Hizb al-Nahda al-Islami*, Doha: al-Markaz al-'Arabi lil-Abhath wa Dirasat al-Siyasat, 2011.

Ahmida, Ali Abdullatif, "Libya, Social Origins of Dictatorship, and the Challenge for Democracy," *Journal of the Middle East and Africa*, vol 3, no. 1, 2012, pp. 70–81.

Alexander, Christopher, *Tunisia: Stability and Reform in the Modern Maghreb*, Oxon, UK: Routledge, 2010.

Alibi (al-), Farid, *Tunis: al-Intifada wal-Thawra*, Sfax: Nuha, 2011.

Allal, Amin and Vincent Geisser, "Tunisie: 'Révolution de jasmin' ou Intifada?" *Mouvements*, no. 66, Summer 2011, pp. 62–8.

Alterman, Jon, *New Media, New Politics? From Satellite Television to the Internet in the Arab World*, Policy Paper no. 48, Washington, DC: The Washington Institute for Near East Policy, 1998.

Althusser, Louis, *For Marx*, trans. Ben Brewster, Harmondsworth, UK: Penguin, 1969.

Amin, Samir et al., *Al-Dimuqratiyya wal-Thawra fi Misr*, Cairo: al-Dar al-Ishtirakiyya, 2012.

———, "2011: An Arab Springtime?" *Monthly Review*, 2 June 2011, <http:// monthlyreview.org/commentary/2011-an-arab-springtime#.UIT-EWez7To>.

———, *The People's Spring: The Future of the Arab Revolution*, Oxford, UK: Pambazuka, 2012.

———, see Riad, Hassan.

'Amrusi (al-), Salah, "'Iqtisad al-Suq al-Islami': al-Barnamaj al-Iqtisadi wal-Ijtima'i lil-Ikhwan al-Muslimin fi Misr," *Bidayat*, no. 1, Winter/Spring 2012, pp. 79–82.

Arab Monetary Fund [Sunduq al-Naqd al-'Arabi], ed, *Tahwilat al-'Amilin fi al-Kharij wal-Tanmiya al-Iqtisadiyya fi al-Duwal al-'Arabiyya*, *Al-Taqrir al-Iqtisadi al-'Arabi al-Muwahhad 2006*, Abu Dhabi: Sunduq al-Naqd al-'Arabi, 2006.

Arab World Initiative, "Research: Broad-based Youth Programs Needed," 15 Jan. 2011, World Bank, <http://arabworld.worldbank.org/content/awi/en/home/featured/youth_programs.html>.

Asher-Schapiro, Avi, "The GOP Brotherhood of Egypt," *Salon.com*, 26 Jan. 2012, <http://www.salon.com/2012/01/26/the_gop_brotherhood_of_egypt/>.

Assad (al-), Bashar, "Interview with Syrian President Bashar al-Assad," *Wall Street Journal*, 31 Jan. 2011.

Awadi (al-), Hesham, *In Pursuit of Legitimacy: The Muslim Brothers and Mubarak, 1982–2000*, London: Tauris Academic Studies, 2004.

Ayeb, Habib, "Social and Political Geography of the Tunisian Revolution: The Alfa Grass Revolution," *Review of African Political Economy*, vol 38, no. 129, Sep. 2011, pp. 467–79.

Ayubi, Nazih, *Bureaucracy & Politics in Contemporary Egypt*, London: Ithaca, 1980.

———, *The State and Public Policies in Egypt Since Sadat*, Reading, UK: Ithaca, 1991.

———, *Overstating the Arab State: Politics and Society in the Middle East*, London: I.B. Tauris, 1995.

Azmeh (Al-), Aziz, *Islams and Modernities*, 3rd edn, London: Verso, 2009.

Babeuf, *Textes choisis*, Paris: Editions sociales, 1965.

Baker, Aryn, "Sunni-Shi'ite Divide Clouds Prospects for Reform in Bahrain," *Time*, 26 Feb. 2011.

Bard, Mitchell, "The 1968 Sale of Phantom Jets to Israel," *Jewish Virtual Library*, <http://www.jewishvirtuallibrary.org/jsource/US-Israel/phantom.html>.

Barout, Mohammed Jamal, "Suriyya 2010: al-Islah aw al-Karitha," *Al-Tajdid al-'Arabi*, 2 June 2005, <http://arabrenewal.info/>.

———, "Tahaddi al-Amn al-Ghaza'i: Ru'yat Mashru' 'Suriyya 2025,'" *Buhuth Iqtisadiyya 'Arabiyya*, no. 43–4, Summer–Autumn 2008, pp. 175–91.

———, *Al-'Aqd al-Akhir fi Tarikh Surya: Jadaliyyat al-Jumud wal-Islah*, Doha: al-Markaz al-'Arabi lil-Abhath wa Dirasat al-Siyasat, 2012.

Bassiouny, Mustafa and 'Umar Sa'id, *Rayat al-Idrab fi Sama' Misr: 2007 Haraka 'Ummaliya Jadida*, Cairo: Markaz al-Dirasat al-Ishtirakiyya, 2007.

Batatu, Hanna, "State and Capitalism in Iraq: A Comment" in *Wealth and Power in the Middle East*, MERIP, no. 142, Sep.–Oct. 1986, pp. 10–12.

———, *Syria's Peasantry, the Descendants of Its Lesser Rural Notables, and Their Politics*, Princeton, NJ: Princeton University Press, 1999.

Battesti, Vincent and François Ireton, eds, *L'Egypte au présent. Inventaire d'une société avant révolution*, Paris: Sindbad/Actes Sud, 2011.

Baumann, Hannes, *Citizen Hariri and Neoliberal Politics in Post-War Lebanon*, PhD dissertation, London: SOAS, University of London, 2012.

Bayat, Asef, *Islam and Democracy: What Is the Real Question?* ISIM paper 8, Amsterdam: Amsterdam University Press, 2007.

———, *Life as Politics: How Ordinary People Change the Middle East*, Stanford, CA: Stanford University Press, 2010.

———, "The Post-Islamist Revolutions," *Foreign Affairs Snapshot*, 26 April

2011, <http://www.foreignaffairs.com/articles/67812/asef-bayat/the-post
-islamist-revolutions>.

———, "Arab Revolts: Islamists Aren't Coming!," *Insight Turkey*, vol 13, no. 2, 2011, pp. 9–14.

BBC, "Syria Unrest: Who Are the Shabiha?," 29 May 2012, <http://www.bbc.co
.uk/news/world-middle-east-14482968>.

Bearman, Jonathan, *Qadhafi's Libya*, London: Zed Books, 1986.

Beblawi, Hazem and Giacomo Luciani, eds, *The Rentier State*, London: Croom Helm, 1987.

Becker, Carmen, "Strategies of Power Consolidation in Syria Under Bashar al-Asad: Modernizing Control Over Resources," *Arab Studies Journal*, vol 13/14, no. 2/1, Autumn 2005/Spring 2006, pp. 65–91.

Beinart, Peter, "Obama Betrayed Ideals on Israel," *Newsweek*, 12 March 2012.

Beinin, Joel and Frédéric Vairel, eds, *Social Movements, Mobilization, and Contestation in the Middle East and North Africa*, Stanford, CA: Stanford University Press, 2011.

Ben Gharbia, Sami, "The Internet Freedom Fallacy and the Arab Digital Activism," *Nawaat*, 17 Sep. 2010, <http://nawaat.org/portail/2010/09/17/the-internet-freedom-fallacy-and-the-arab-digital-activism/>.

Ben Jaballah, Ghazi, "Graduate Unemployment in the Maghreb," *Policy Brief*, Washington, DC: German Marshall Fund, Nov. 2011.

Ben Néfissa, Sarah and Blandine Destremau, eds, *Protestations sociales, révolutions civiles. Transformations du politique dans la Méditerranée arabe*, Revue *Tiers Monde*, special issue 2011.

Ben Romdhane, Mahmoud, *Tunisie: Etat, économie et société. Ressources politiques, légitimation, régulations sociales*, Tunis: Sud Editions, 2011.

Bhalla, Reva, "Making Sense of the Syrian Crisis," *Stratfor*, 5 May 2011, <http://www.stratfor.com/weekly/20110504-making-sense-syrian-crisis>.

Bishara, Azmi, *Hal min Mas'ala Qubtiyya fi Misr?*, Doha: al-Markaz al-'Arabi lil-Abhath wa Dirasat al-Siyasat, 2012.

———, *Fi al-Thawra wa al-Qabiliyya lil-Thawra*, Doha: al-Markaz al-'Arabi lil-Abhath wa Dirasat al-Siyasat, 2012.

Blanchard, Christopher and Jim Zanotti, *Libya: Background and U.S. Relations*, Washington, DC: Congressional Research Service, 18 Feb. 2011.

Blavier, Pierre, "La révolution tunisienne: chômage, expansion scolaire et fracture régionale?" *Actes de la Recherche en Sciences Sociales*, Sep. 2013 (forthcoming).

Bond, Patrick, "Neoliberal Threats to North Africa," *Review of African Political Economy*, vol 38, no. 129, Sep. 2011, pp. 481–95.

Bonnefoy, Laurent, Franck Mermier and Marine Poirier, eds, *Yémen. Le tournant révolutionnaire*, Sanaa: Cefas, and Paris: Karthala, 2012.

Boulila, Ghazi, Chaker Gabsi and Mohamed Haddar, "La pauvreté régionale en Tunisie," study for the international conference convened by the GRI DREEM in Istanbul on 21–23 May 2009, <http://gdri.dreem.free.fr/wp-content/d1-2boulila-chaker-haddar-la-pauvrete-regionale-istalbul-2.pdf>.

Bourdieu, Pierre, *Practical Reason: On the Theory of Action*, Cambridge, UK: Polity, 1998.

———, *Masculine Domination*, trans. Richard Nice, Cambridge, UK: Polity, 2001.

Bradley, John, *After the Arab Spring : How the Islamists Hijacked the Middle East Revolts*, New York: Palgrave Macmillan, 2012.

Brookings Project on U.S. Policy Towards the Islamic World, *An Agenda for Action: The 2002 Doha Conference on U.S. Relations with the Islamic World*, Washington, DC: The Brookings Institution, 2003.

Brown, Anthony Cave, *Oil, God and Gold: The Story of Aramco and the Saudi Kings*, New York: Houghton Mifflin, 1999.

Bush, George W., "Remarks by the President at the 20th Anniversary of the National Endowment for Democracy," Washington, DC: White House, Office of the Press Secretary, 6 Nov. 2003, <http://georgewbush-whitehouse .archives.gov/news/releases/2003/11/20031106-2.html>.

Bush, Ray, *Poverty and Inequality: Persistence and Reproduction in the Global South*, London: Pluto, 2007.

Bush, Ray and Habib Ayeb, eds, *Marginality and Exclusion in Egypt*, London: Zed, 2012.

Butalib, Muhammad Najib, *Al-Ab'ad al-Siyasiyya lil-Zahira al-Qabaliyya fi al-Mujtama'at al-'Arabiyya: Muqaraba Susyulujiyya lil-Thawratayn al-Tunisi-yya wal-Libiyya*, Doha: al-Markaz al-'Arabi lil-Abhath wa Dirasat al-Siyasat, 2011.

Butler, Amy, "Saudi, U.S. Finalize F-15SA Sale," *Aviation Week*, 2 Jan. 2012.

Calvert, John, *Sayyid Qutb and the Origins of Radical Islamism*, New York: Columbia University Press, 2010.

Carré, Olivier, *Mystique et politique: Lecture révolutionnaire du Coran par Sayyid Qutb, Frère musulman radical*, Paris: Presses de la FNSP and Cerf, 1984.

Central Bureau of Statistics (Syria), <http://www.cbssyr.org/>.

Central Informatics Organisation (Bahrain), *Statistical Abstract 2011*, <http://www.cio.gov.bh>.

Central Intelligence Agency, *The Challenge of Ethnic Conflict to National and International Order in the 1990s, Geographic Perspectives: A Conference Report*, Washington, DC: CIA, 1995.

Chami, Ralph et al., *Libya beyond the Revolution: Challenges and Opportunities*, Washington, DC: IMF, 2012.

Chang, Ha-Joon, *Kicking Away the Ladder: Development Strategy in Historical Perspective*, London: Anthem Press, 2003.

Charara, Waddah, *Dawlat "Hizbullah": Lubnan Mujtama'an Islamiyyan*, Beirut: Dar al-Nahar, 1996.

Chaudhry, Kiren Aziz, *The Price of Wealth: Economies and Institutions in the Middle East*, Ithaca, NY: Cornell University Press, 1997.

Chomsky, Noam and Gilbert Achcar, *Perilous Power: The Middle East and U.S. Foreign Policy*, Stephen Shalom, ed, 2nd expanded edn, Boulder, CO: Paradigm Publishers, 2008.

Chorin, Ethan, *Exit Gaddafi: The Hidden History of the Libyan Revolution*, London: Saqi, 2012.

Chouikha, Larbi and Éric Gobe, "La Tunisie entre la 'révolte du bassin minier de Gafsa' et l'échéance électorale de 2009," *L'Année du Maghreb*, 2009, pp. 387–420.

Clément, Françoise, Marie Duboc and Omar El Shafei, "Le rôle des mobilisations des travailleurs et du mouvement syndical dans la chute de Moubarak," *Mouvements*, no. 66, Summer 2011, pp. 69–78.

Cochrane, Paul, "Boon Time for Mercenaries," *Executive*, no. 143, June 2011, <http://www.executive-magazine.com/getarticle.php?article=14309>.

Committee for the Abolition of Third World Debt, <http://cadtm.org>.

Corm, George, *Labor Migration in the Middle East and North Africa: A View from the Region*, Washington, DC: World Bank, ca. 2006.

Courbage, Youssef and Emmanuel Todd, *A Convergence of Civilizations: The Transformation of Muslim Societies Around the World*, trans. George Holoch, New York: Columbia University Press, 2011.

Dabashi, Hamid, *The Arab Spring: The End of Postcolonialism*, London: Zed, 2012.

Darwish, Husam al-Din, *Munaqasha Naqdiyya li-Abhath Muhammad Jamal Barut 'an al-Thawra al-Suriyya*, Doha: al-Markaz al-'Arabi lil-Abhath wa Dirasat al-Siyasat, 2012.

Dede, Alper, "The Arab Uprisings: Debating the 'Turkish Model,'" *Insight Turkey*, vol 13, no. 2, 2011, pp. 23–32.

Defense Industry Daily, "2010–12 Saudi Shopping Spree: F-15s, Helicopters & More," *Defense Industry Daily*, 9 March 2012.

De Smet, Brecht, *The Prince and the Pharaoh: The Collaborative Project of Egyptian Workers and Their Intellectuals in the Face of Revolution*, PhD dissertation, Ghent: Ghent University, 2012.

de Soto, Hernando, "The Free Market Secret of the Arab Revolutions," *Financial Times*, 8 Nov. 2011.

Diouri, Moumen, *A qui appartient le Maroc?* Paris: L'Harmattan, 1992.

Diri (al-), Ali Ahmad, "Al-Bahrayn: Dakhil al-Maydan, Kharij al-Ta'ifa," *Bidayat*, no. 1, Winter/Spring 2012, pp. 54–61.

Disuqi, Abduh Mustafa, "Al-Duktur Sa'id Ramadan, al-Sikritir al-Shakhsi lil-Imam Hasan al-Banna wa Zuj Ibnatihi," *Ikhwan Wiki*, <http://www.ikhwanwiki.com/>.

———, "Al-Tanzim al-'Alami lil-Ikhwan al-Muslimin. Al-Nash'at wal-Tarikh," *Ikhwan Wiki*, <http://www.ikhwanwiki.com/>.

Dreyfuss, Robert, *Devil's Game: How the United States Helped Unleash Fundamentalist Islam*, New York: Henry Holt, 2005.

Dubai Press Club, *Arab Media Outlook 2009–2013*, Dubai: Dubai Press Club, 2010.

Dubai School of Government, *Arab Social Media Report*, vol 1, no. 1, Jan. 2011.

———, *Arab Social Media Report*, vol 1, no. 2, May 2011.

Dupret, Baudouin et al., *La Syrie au présent. Reflets d'une société*, Paris: Sindbad/Actes Sud, 2007.

Eakin, Hugh, "The Strange Power of Qatar," *New York Review of Books*, vol 58, no. 16, 27 Oct. 2011.

Economist (The), "An Old Chinese Myth," *The Economist*, 3 Jan. 2008.

————, "The Upheaval in Egypt: An End or a Beginning?" *The Economist*, 3 Feb. 2011.

————, "Pedalling Prosperity, Special Report: China's Economy," *The Economist*, 26 May 2012.

————, "Vote for the Brother: A Muslim Brother Is Better than a Mubarak Crony," *The Economist*, 16 June 2012.

————, "Libya: Despite Everything, It's Still a Success," *The Economist*, 15 Sep. 2012.

Energy Information Administration (USA), "Country Analysis Briefs: Libya," June 2012, <www.eia.doe.gov>.

Epstein, Gerald, ed, *Capital Flight and Capital Controls in Developing Countries*, Cheltenham, UK: Edward Elgar, 2005.

Erdle, Steffen, *Ben Ali's 'New Tunisia' (1987–2009): A Case Study of Authoritarian Modernization in the Arab World*, Berlin: Klaus Schwarz, 2010.

Erdmann, Gero and Ulf Engel, "Neopatrimonialism Revisited—Beyond a Catch-All Concept," Hamburg: GIGA Working Papers, no. 16, Feb. 2006.

Errian (El-), Essam, "What the Muslim Brothers Want," *The New York Times*, 9 Feb. 2011.

Faruq, 'Abdul-Khaliq, *Iqtisadiyyat al-Fasad fi Misr: Kayfa Jara Ifsad Misr wal-Misriyyin 1974–2010*, Cairo: Maktabat al-Shuruq al-Dawliyya, 2011.

Fayid, 'Ammar Ahmad, *Al-Salafiyyun fi Misr: Min Shar'iyat al-Fatwa ila Shar'iyat al-Intikhab*, Doha: Markaz al-Jazira lil-Dirasat, 2012.

Femia, Francesco and Caitlin Werrell, "Syria: Climate Change, Drought and Social Unrest," The Center for Climate & Security, 29 Feb. 2012, <http://climateand security.org/2012/02/29/syria-climate-change-drought-and-social-unrest/>.

Fierro, José Daniel and Santiago Alba Rico, *Túnez, la Revolución*, Hondarribia: Hiru, 2011.

Filiu, Jean-Pierre, *Le Nouveau Moyen-Orient. Les peuples à l'heure de la révolution syrienne*, Paris: Fayard, 2013.

Freitag, Ulrike, ed, *Saudi-Arabien. Ein Königreich im Wandel?*, Paderborn: Ferdinand Schöningh, 2010.

Fromherz, Allen, *Qatar: A Modern History*, Washington, DC: Georgetown University Press, 2012.

Fukuyama, Francis, "The End of History," *The National Interest*, no. 16, Summer 1989, pp. 3–18.

————, *The End of History and the Last Man*, New York: Avon Books, 1992.

Fuller, Graham, *The Youth Factor: The New Demographics of the Middle East and the Implications for U.S. Policy*, Washington, DC: Brookings Institution, 2003.

Gaddafi, Muammar, "Nass Kalimat Mu'ammar al-Qadhdhafi Yaum 22 Fibrayir 2011," *Bilad al-'Arab*, 25 Feb. 2012, <http://beladalorb.com/cat22/13198. html>.

Gantin, Karine and Omeyya Seddik, "Revolt in a Tunisian Mining Town," *Le Monde diplomatique*, July 2008.

Gatti, Roberta, Diego Angel-Urdinola et al., *Striving for Better Jobs: The Challenge of Informality in the Middle East and North Africa Region*, Washington, DC: World Bank, 2011.

Ghannam, Jeffrey, *Social Media in the Arab World: Leading Up to the Uprisings of 2011*, Washington, DC: Center for International Media Assistance, NED, 3 Feb. 2011.

Ghobashy (El-), Mona, "The Metamorphosis of the Egyptian Muslim Brothers," *International Journal of Middle East Studies*, vol 37, no. 3, August 2005, pp. 373–95.

———, "Politics by Other Means," *Boston Review*, Nov.–Dec. 2011, pp. 39–44.

Global Witness, "Leaked Gaddafi-Era Documents Expose the Need for Urgent Oil Reforms," 13 April 2012, <http://www.globalwitness.org/library/leaked-documents-expose-need-urgent-oil-reforms-0>.

Godelier, Maurice, *Rationality and Irrationality in Economics*, trans. Brian Pearce, New York: Monthly Review Press, 1973.

Gordon, Michael, "Failed Efforts and Challenges of America's Last Months in Iraq," *New York Times*, 22 Sep. 2012.

Graciet, Catherine and Eric Laurent, *Le Roi prédateur*, Paris: Seuil, 2012.

Gräf, Bettina, "IslamOnline.net: Independent, Interactive, Popular," *Arab Media & Society*, no. 4, Winter 2008, <http://www.arabmediasociety.com/?article=576>.

Gräf, Bettina and Jakob Skovgaard-Petersen, eds, *Global Mufti: The Phenomenon of Yusuf al-Qaradawi*, London: Hurst, 2009.

Gray, Matthew, *Conspiracy Theories in the Arab World: Sources and Politics*, Abingdon, UK: Routledge, 2010.

———, *A Theory of "Late Rentierism" in the Arab States of the Gulf*, Qatar: Center for International and Regional Studies—Georgetown University, 2011.

Greenspan, Alan, *The Age of Turbulence: Adventures in a New World*, New York: Penguin Press, 2007.

Grifa, Moussa, "The Libyan Revolution: Establishing a New Political System and the Transition to Statehood," *Arab Reform Brief*, no. 62, Mubadarat al-Islah al-'Arabi / Arab Reform Initiative, <www.arab-reform.net>, Sep. 2012.

Grimmett, Richard, *U.S. Arms Sales: Agreements with and Deliveries to Major Clients, 2003–2010*, Washington, DC: Congressional Research Service, 16 Dec. 2011.

Grimmett, Richard and Paul Kerr, *Conventional Arms Transfers to Developing Nations, 2004–2011*, Washington, DC: Congressional Research Service, 24 August 2012.

Gumuscu, Sebnem, "Economic Liberalization, Devout Bourgeoisie, and Change in Political Islam: Comparing Turkey and Egypt," EUI Working Paper RSCAS 2008/19, Florence: European University Institute, 2008.

———, "Class, Status, and Party: The Changing Face of Political Islam in Turkey and Egypt," *Comparative Political Studies*, vol 43, no. 7, Feb. 2010, pp. 835–61.

Gumuscu, Sebnem and Deniz Sert, "The Power of the Devout Bourgeoisie: The Case of the Justice and Development Party in Turkey," *Middle Eastern Studies*, vol 45, no. 6, Nov. 2009, pp. 953–68.

Hachemaoui, Mohammed, "La rente entrave-t-elle vraiment la démocratie? Réexamen critique des théories de 'l'État rentier' et de la 'malédiction des ressources,'" *Revue française de science politique*, vol 62, no. 2, 2012, pp. 207–30.

———, "Y a-t-il des tribus dans l'urne? Sociologie d'une énigme électorale (Algérie)," *Cahiers d'études africaines*, vol 52 (1), no. 205, 2012, pp. 103–63.

Haddad, Bassam, *Business Networks in Syria: The Political Economy of Authoritarian Resilience*, Stanford, CA: Stanford University Press, 2012.

———, "The Syrian Regime's Business Backbone," *Middle East Report*, vol 42, no. 262, Spring 2012, <http://www.merip.org/mer/mer262/syrian-regimes-business-backbone>.

Haimzadeh, Patrick, *Au Coeur de la Libye de Kadhafi*, Paris: J-C Lattès, 2011.

Hajj Salih (al-), Yasin, "Fi al-Shabbiha wal-Tashbih wa Dawlatahuma," *Kalamon*, no. 5, Winter 2011.

Hakimian, Hassan and Ziba Moshaver, eds, *The State and Global Change: The Political Economy of Transition in the Middle East and North Africa*, Richmond, UK: Curzon, 2001.

Hamalawy (el-), Hossam "1977: The Lost Revolution," <http://www.scribd.com/doc/12893045/1977-Bread-Uprising>.

Hamdi (al-), Bashir, *Al-Haq fil-Sulta wal-Thawra wal-Dimuqratiyya. Qira'at fi Masar Thawrat al-Huriyya wal-Karama*, Sidi Bouzid: Donia, 2011.

Hanieh, Adam, *Capitalism and Class in the Gulf Arab States*, New York: Palgrave Macmillan, 2011.

Hansen, Suzy, "The Economic Vision of Egypt's Muslim Brotherhood Millionaires," *Bloomberg Businessweek*, 19 April 2012.

Harb, Imad, "The Egyptian Military in Politics: Disengagement or Accommodation?" *Middle East Journal*, vol 57, no. 2, Summer 2003, pp. 269–90.

Hasbani, Nadim, "The Geopolitics of Weapons Procurement in the Gulf States," *Defense & Security Analysis*, vol 22, no. 1, March 2006, pp. 73–88.

Headey, Derek and Shenggen Fan, *Reflections on the Global Food Crisis: How Did It Happen? How Has It Hurt? And How Can We Prevent the Next One?* Washington, DC: International Food Policy Research Institute, 2010.

Heinsohn, Gunnar, *Söhne und Weltmacht: Terror im Aufstieg und Fall der Nationen*, Zurich: Orell Füssli Verlag, 2003.

Hendrixson, Anne, "Angry Young Men, Veiled Young Women: Constructing a New Population Threat," *Briefing 34*, Dorset, UK: The Corner House, Dec. 2004.

Hertog, Steffen, *Princes, Brokers, and Bureaucrats: Oil and the State in Saudi Arabia*, Ithaca, NY: Cornell University Press, 2010.

Hibou, Béatrice, *Force of Obedience: The Political Economy of Repression in Tunisia*, Cambridge, UK: Polity, 2011.

———, "Tunisie. Économie politique et morale d'un mouvement social," *Politique africaine*, no. 121, March 2011, pp. 5–22.

Hinnebusch, Raymond, *Syria: Revolution from Above*, London: Routledge, 2001.

Hizb al-'Ummal al-Shuyu'i al-Tunisi, "Al-Ihtijajat Taduqq Abwab al-Qasrin," <http://www.albadil.org/spip.php?article1739>.

Holliday, Joseph, *Syria's Maturing Insurgency*, Washington, DC: Institute for the Study of War, 2012.

Hroub, Khaled, *Fi Madih al-Thawra: al-Nahr dud al-Mustanqa'*, Beirut: Dar al-Saqi, 2012.

Human Rights Watch, *Pushed Back, Pushed Around: Italy's Forced Return of Boat Migrants and Asylum Seekers, Libya's Mistreatment of Migrants and Asylum Seekers*, New York: HRW, 2009.

———, *Delivered into Enemy Hands: US-Led Abuse and Rendition of Opponents to Gaddafi's Libya*, New York: HRW, 2012.

———, *Unacknowledged Deaths: Civilian Casualties in NATO's Air Campaign in Libya*, New York: HRW, 2012.

———, "Tunisia: Q&A on the Trial of Ben Ali, Others for Killing Protesters," 11 June 2012, <http://www.hrw.org/news/2012/06/11/tunisia-qa-trial-ben-ali-others-killing-protesters>.

Huntington, Samuel, *Political Order in Changing Societies*, New Haven, CT: Yale University Press, 1968.

———, *The Third Wave: Democratization in the Late Twentieth Century*, Norman, OK: University of Oklahoma Press, 1991.

———, *The Clash of Civilizations and the Remaking of World Order*, New York: Touchstone, 1997.

Husayn, 'Adil, *Al-Iqtisad al-Misri min al-Istiqlal ila al-Taba'iyya 1974–1979*, 2 vols, Beirut: Dar al-Kalima, 1981.

Ibrahim, Ekram, "6th of April 2008: A Workers' Strike Which Fired the Egyptian Revolution," *Al-Ahram Online*, 6 April 2012, <http://english.ahram.org.eg/News/38580.aspx>.

Institute of International Finance, *Economic Report: Gulf Cooperation Council Countries*, Washington, DC: IIF, 16 Jan. 2008.

———, *GCC Regional Overview*, Washington, DC: IIF, 13 May 2010.

International Commission of Inquiry on Libya, *Report of the International Commission of Inquiry on Libya*, New York: Human Rights Council, United Nations, 2 March 2012.

International Crisis Group, *Popular Protests in North Africa and The Middle East (III): The Bahrain Revolt*, Middle East/North Africa Report no. 105, 6 April 2011.

———, *Popular Protest in North Africa and the Middle East (V): Making Sense of Libya*, Middle East/North Africa Report no. 107, 6 June 2011.

———, *Popular Protests in North Africa and The Middle East (VI): The Syrian People's Slow Motion Revolution*, Middle East/North Africa Report no. 108, 6 July 2011.

———, *Tentative Jihad: Syria's Fundamentalist Opposition*, Middle East Report no. 131, 12 Oct. 2012.

International Labour Office, *Global Employment Trends 2004*, Geneva: ILO, 2004.

———, *World Social Security Report 2010/11: Providing Coverage in Times of Crisis and Beyond*, Geneva: ILO, 2010.

———, *Global Employment Trends 2010*, Geneva: ILO, 2010.

———, *Global Employment Trends for Youth: 2011 Update*, Geneva: ILO, 2011.

———, Department of Statistics, *Statistical Update on Arab States and Territories and North African Countries*, Geneva: ILO, May 2011.

———, *Global Employment Trends 2012*, Geneva: ILO, 2012.

———, *Employment for Stability and Socio-Economic Progress in North Africa: Strategy for North Africa 2011–2015*, Cairo: ILO, 2012.

International Labour Organization, LABORSTA Internet, <http://laborsta.ilo.org/default.html>.

International Monetary Fund, *Regional Economic Outlook: Middle East and Central Asia*, Washington, DC: IMF, 2007.

———, "The Socialist People's Libyan Arab Jamahiriya—2010 Article IV Consultation, Preliminary Conclusions of the Mission," 28 Oct. 2010, <http://www.imf.org/external/np/ms/2010/102810.htm>.

———, *Economic Transformation in MENA: Delivering on the Promise of Shared Prosperity*, Group of Eight Summit, 27 May 2011, Deauville, France, Washington, DC: IMF, 2011.

———, *World Economic Outlook April 2012: Growth Resuming, Dangers Remain*, Washington, DC: IMF, 2012.

International Telecommunication Union, "Key Global Telecom Indicators for the World Telecommunication Service Sector," <http://www.itu.int/ITU-D/ict/statistics/index.html>.

IPEMED, *La Confiance dans la société numérique méditerranéenne. Vers un espace .med*, IPEMED *Palimpsestes*, no. 7, July 2011.

'Isa, 'Abdul-Malik, *Harakat al-Islam al-Siyasi fi al-Yaman*, Beirut: Markaz Dirasat al-Wihda al-'Arabiyya, 2012.

Ismail, Salwa, *Political Life in Cairo's New Quarters: Encountering the Everyday State*, Minneapolis: University of Minnesota Press, 2006.

Jad, Islah, "The NGO-isation of Arab Women's Movements," 2004, <http://www.shebacss.com/docs/sowcere0036-09.pdf>.

Jihaz (Al-) al-Markazi lil-Ta'bi'a al-'Ama wa al-Islah, "Mu'ashshirat al-Faqr Tabqan li Bayanat Bahth al-Dakhl wal-Infaq wal-Istihlak," <http://www.capmas.gov.eg/pdf/studies/pdf/enf1.pdf>.

Johnson, Ian, *A Mosque in Munich: Nazis, the CIA, and the Rise of the Muslim Brotherhood in the West*, New York: Houghton Mifflin Harcourt, 2010.

Kang, David, *Crony Capitalism: Corruption and Development in South Korea and the Philippines*, Cambridge, UK: Cambridge University Press, 2002.

Kapiszewski, Andrzej, "Arab Versus Asian Migrant Workers in the GCC Countries," Beirut: EGM, Population Division, Department of Economic and Social Affairs, United Nations Secretariat, 15–17 May 2006.

Kaplan, David, "Hearts, Minds, and Dollars," *US News & World Report*, 17 April 2005, <http://www.usnews.com/usnews/news/articles/050425/25roots.htm>.

Kar, Dev and Karly Curcio, *Illicit Financial Flows from Developing Countries: 2000–2009*, Washington, DC: Global Financial Integrity, Jan. 2011.

Khafaji (al-), Issam, "State Incubation of Iraqi Capitalism" in *Wealth and Power in the Middle East*, MERIP, no. 142, Sep.–Oct. 1986, pp. 4–9 and 12.

Khalaf, Samir and Roseanne Saad Khalaf, *Arab Youth: Social Mobilisation in Times of Risk*, London: Saqi, 2011.

Khalidi, Rashid, *Sowing Crisis: The Cold War and American Dominance in the Middle East*, Boston, MA: Beacon, 2009.

——, "Full Transcript of Interview with Palestinian Professor Rashid Khalidi" (interview by Chemi Shalev), *Haaretz*, 5 Dec. 2011.

Khan, Mushtaq and Jomo Kwame Sundaram, eds, *Rents, Rent-Seeking and Economic Development: Theory and Evidence in Asia*, Cambridge, UK: Cambridge University Press, 2000.

Khatib, Line, *Islamic Revivalism in Syria: The Rise and Fall of Ba'thist Secularism*, Oxon, UK: Routledge, 2011.

Khiari, Sadri, *Tunisie: le délitement de la cité. Coercition, consentement, résistance*, Paris: Karthala, 2003.

——, "La Révolution tunisienne ne vient pas de nulle part," *Politique africaine*, no. 121, March 2011, pp. 23–34.

Kienle, Eberhard, *A Grand Delusion: Democracy and Economic Reform in Egypt*, London: I.B. Tauris, 2000.

——, "Les 'révolutions' arabes," *Critique internationale*, 2012/1, no. 54, pp. 103–17.

Klasen, Stephan and Francesca Lamanna, "The Impact of Gender Inequality in Education and Employment on Economic Growth in the Middle East and North Africa," Washington, DC: Paper prepared for the World Bank, 2003.

Knowles, Warwick, *Jordan Since 1989: A Study in Political Economy*, London: I.B. Tauris, 2005.

Kraetzschmar, Hendrik Jan, "Electoral Rules, Voter Mobilization and the Islamist Landslide in the Saudi Municipal Elections of 2005," *Contemporary Arab Affairs*, vol 3, no. 4, Oct.–Dec. 2010, pp. 515–33.

Kriegel, Annie, *The French Communists: Profile of a People*, trans. Elaine Halperin, Chicago: University of Chicago Press, 1972.

Krijgsman, Richard, "Oil & Gas Companies in Libya—a Who's Who," *Evaluate Energy*, 24 Feb. 2011, <http://www.oil-blog.com/companies/major-ioc/libyan-oil-gas/>.

Lagarde, Christine, "The Arab Spring, One Year On," IMF, 6 Dec. 2011, <http://www.imf.org/external/np/speeches/2011/120611.htm>.

Lamchichi, Abderrahim, *L'Algérie en crise. Crise économique et changements politiques*, Paris: L'Harmattan, 1991.

Lamloum, Olfa and Bernard Ravanel, eds, *La Tunisie de Ben Ali. La société contre le régime*, Paris: L'Harmattan, 2002.

Lawson, Fred, ed, *Demystifying Syria*, London: Saqi, 2009.

Laythi (al-) Hiba et Khalid Abu-Isma'il, *Al-Faqr fi Suriyya: 1996–2004*, Damascus: UNDP, June 2005.

League of Arab States [Jami'at al-Duwal al-'Arabiyya], Idarat al-Siyasat al-Sukkaniyya wal-Hijra, *Al-Taqrir al-Iqlimi li Hijrat al-'Amal al-'Arabiyya: Hijrat al-Kafa'at al-'Arabiyya, Nazif am Furas 2008*, Cairo: Jami'at al-Duwal al-'Arabiyya, 2009.

Ledeen, Michael, "Creative Destruction: How to Wage a Revolutionary War," *National Review*, 20 Sep. 2001, <http://old.nationalreview.com/contributors/ledeen092001.shtml>.

Lenin, Vladimir, "The Collapse of the Second International," in *Collected Works*, 21, Moscow: Progress Publishers, 1964, pp. 205–59.

Lequiller, François, "Is GDP a Satisfactory Measure of Growth?" *OECD Observer*, no. 246–7, Dec. 2004–Jan. 2005, <http://www.oecdobserver.org/news/fullstory.php/aid/1518/Is_GDP_a_satisfactory_measure_of_growth_.html>.

Leverrier, Ignace, *Un Œil sur la Syrie*, *Le Monde* Blogs, <http://syrie.blog.le monde.fr/>.

Lewis, Bernard, *Islam in History*, Chicago: Open Court, 1993.

Lizza, Ryan, "The Consequentialist: How the Arab Spring Remade Obama's Foreign Policy," *The New Yorker*, 2 May 2011.

Long, David, *The United States and Saudi Arabia: Ambivalent Allies*, Boulder, CO: Westview, 1985.

Longhi, Vittorio and Khalil Bohazza, "Spotlight Interview with Salman Jaffar Al Mahfoodh (Bahrain—GFBTU)," ITUC, 1 March 2012, <http://www.ituc-csi.org/spotlight-interview-with-salman,10736.html>.

Luciani, Giacomo and Steffen Hertog, *Has Arab Business Ever Been, or Will It Be, a Player for Reform? ARI Thematic Study*, Mubadarat al-Islah al-'Arabi / Arab Reform Initiative, Oct. 2010, <www.arab-reform.net>.

Lussato, Céline, "Tunisie. Messaoudi dénonce 'un nouveau régime dictatorial,'" *Le Nouvel Observateur*, 30 August 2012, <http://tempsreel.nouvelobs.com/monde/20120830.OBS0825/tunisie-ayoub-messaoudi-denonce-un-regime-dictatorial-theocratique.html>.

Lynch, Marc, *Voices of the New Arab Public: Iraq, Al-Jazeera, and Middle East Politics Today*, New York: Columbia University Press, 2006.

Ma'had (Al-) al-Watani lil-Ihsa', *Al-Mas'h al-Watani hawl al-Sukkan wal-Tashghil 2010*, Tunis: Wizarat al-Takhtit wal-Ta'awun al-Dawli, June 2011.

Mahdi, Kamil, Anna Würth and Helen Lackner, eds, *Yemen into the Twenty-First Century: Continuity and Change*, Reading, UK: Ithaca, 2007.

Mahdi (El-), Rabab, "Labour Protests in Egypt: Causes and Meanings," *Review of African Political Economy*, vol 38, no. 129, Sep. 2011, pp. 387–402.

Mahdi (El-), Rabab and Philip Marfleet, eds, *Egypt: Moment of Change*, London: Zed, 2009.

Malti, Hocine, *Histoire secrète du pétrole algérien*, Paris: La Découverte, 2010.

Mansar (al-), 'Adnan, *Al-Durru wa Ma'danuhu: al-Khilafat bayn al-Hizb al-Dusturi wal-Haraka al-Niqabiyya fi Tunis, 1924–1978. Jadaliyyat al-Tajanus wal-Sira'*, Tunis: Al-Magharibiyya, 2010.

Markaz al-Ma'lumat wa Da'm Ittikhaz al-Qarar, *Min al-Internet ila al-Tahrir: 25 Yanayir min Waqi' al-Facebook wal-Twitter, Taqarir Ma'lumatiyya*, vol 5, no. 53, May 2011.

Markaz (Al-) al-Misri lil-Huquq al-Iqtisadiyya wal-Ijtima'iyya, *Al-Huquq al-Iqtisadiyya wal-Ijtima'iyya fil-Shuhur al-Ula lil-Ra'is Mursi: Ma'at Yawm min Siyasat al-Tajahul wal-Tahmish*, Cairo: ECESR, 11 Oct. 2012.

Marr, Phebe, ed, *Egypt at the Crossroads: Domestic Stability and Regional Role*, Washington, DC: National Defense University Press, 1999.

Marshall, Shana, "Egypt's Other Revolution: Modernizing the Military-

Industrial Complex," *Jadaliyya*, 10 Feb. 2012, <www.jadaliyya.com/pages/index/4311/egypts-other-revolution_modernizing-the-military-i>.

Marx, Karl, *Wage Labour and Capital*, in *Marx Engels Selected Works (MESW)*, London: Lawrence & Wishart, 1991, pp. 70–90.

——, *The Eighteenth Brumaire of Louis Bonaparte*, *MESW*, pp. 91–171.

——, Preface to *A Contribution to the Critique of Political Economy*, *MESW*, pp. 172–6.

——, *Capital Volume 1*, trans. Ben Fowkes, Harmondsworth: Penguin, 1976.

——, *Grundrisse: Foundations of the Critique of Political Economy*, trans. Martin Nicolaus, London: Penguin, 1993.

Marx, Karl and Frederick Engels, *Manifesto of the Communist Party*, *MESW*, pp. 31–62.

——, "Address of the Central Committee to the Communist League" in Marx, *The Revolutions of 1848*, edited and introduced by David Fernbach, London: Verso, 2010, pp. 319–30.

Mashal, Mujib, "Pakistani Troops Aid Bahrain's Crackdown," *Aljazeera.com*, 30 July 2011, <http://www.aljazeera.com/indepth/features/2011/07/2011725145048574888.html>.

Mattes, Hanspeter, "Challenges to Security Sector Governance in the Middle East: The Libyan Case," working paper, Geneva Centre for the Democratic Control of Armed Forces (DCAF), July 2004.

McAdam, Doug, Sidney Tarrow and Charles Tilly, *Dynamics of Contention*, Cambridge, UK: Cambridge University Press, 2001.

Meijer, Roel, ed, *Global Salafism: Islam's New Religious Movement*, New York: Columbia University Press, 2009.

Ménoret, Pascal, "The Municipal Elections in Saudi Arabia 2005: First Steps on a Democratic Path," *Arab Reform Brief*, Mubadarat al-Islah al-'Arabi / Arab Reform Initiative, <www.arab-reform.net>, n.d.

Migreurop, *European Borders: Controls, Detention and Deportations*, 2009/2010 Report, Paris: Migreurop, 2010.

Milanovic, Branko, *Global Inequality Recalculated: The Effect of New 2005 PPP Estimates on Global Inequality*, Policy Research Working Paper 5061, Washington, DC: World Bank, 2009.

Mills, C. Wright, *The Power Elite*, New York: Oxford University Press, 1956.

Mitchell, Timothy, *Rule of Experts: Egypt, Techno-Politics, Modernity*, Berkeley, CA: University of California Press, 2002.

MNSPR (Poverty Reduction and Economic Management Department), *Arab Republic of Egypt—Reshaping Egypt's Economic Geography: Domestic Integration as a Development Platform*, 2 vols, Washington, DC: World Bank, June 2012.

Moataz Ahmed, Yasmine, "Who Do Egypt's Villagers Vote For? And Why?," *Egypt Independent*, 10 April 2012, <http://www.egyptindependent.com/node/764101>.

Monk, Ashby, "Gaddafi Investment Authority, 2006–2011, RIP," Oxford SWF Project, 4 March 2011, <http://oxfordswfproject.com/2011/03/04/gaddafi-investment-authority-2006-2011-rip/>.

Munif, Yasir and ʿUmar Dahi, "Al-Neoliberaliyya wal-Istibdad fi Suriyya," *Bidayat*, no. 1, Winter/Spring 2012, pp. 72–8.

Murphy, Caryle, "Arab Facebook: The Internet's Role in Politics in the Middle East," *The Majalla*, 13 Nov. 2009, <http://www.majalla.com/eng/2009/11/article5510699>.

Musallam, Adnan, *From Secularism to Jihad: Sayyid Qutb and the Foundations of Radical Islamism*, Westport, CT: Praeger, 2005.

Naba, René, *Les Révolutions arabes*, Paris: Bachari, 2011.

Niblock, Tim with Monica Malik, *The Political Economy of Saudi Arabia*, Oxon, UK: Routledge, 2007.

Nusayra, Hani, *Al-Salafiyya fi Misr: Tahawwulat ma Baʿd al-Thawra*, Cairo: Markaz al-Dirasat al-Siyasiyya wa al-Istratijiyya bil-Ahram, 2011.

Nyrop, Richard et al., *Area Handbook for Egypt*, Washington, DC: The American University, 1976.

Obama, Barack, "Remarks by the President on a New Beginning, Cairo University, Cairo, Egypt," Washington, DC: The White House, 4 June 2009, <http://www.whitehouse.gov/the-press-office/remarks-president-cairo-university-6-04-09>.

———, "Remarks by the President on the Situation in Egypt," Washington, DC: The White House, 28 Jan. 2011, <http://www.whitehouse.gov/the-press-office/2011/01/28/remarks-president-situation-egypt>.

———, "Remarks by the President on Egypt," Washington, DC: The White House, 11 Feb. 2011, <http://www.whitehouse.gov/the-press-office/2011/02/11/remarks-president-egypt>.

———, "Obama: Egypt Is Not US Ally, Nor an Enemy," *BBC*, 3 Sep. 2012, <http://www.bbc.co.uk/news/world-middle-east-19584265>.

OPEC, *Annual Statistical Bulletin 1999*, Vienna: OPEC, 2000.

———, *Annual Statistical Bulletin 2009*, Vienna: OPEC, 2010.

———, *Annual Statistical Bulletin 2010/2011*, Vienna: OPEC, 2011.

Ottaway, Marina and Amr Hamzawy, "Protest Movements and Political Change in the Arab World," *Policy Outlook*, Washington, DC: Carnegie Endowment for International Peace, 28 Jan. 2011.

Owen, Roger, *The Rise and Fall of Arab Presidents for Life*, Cambridge, MA: Harvard University Press, 2012.

Pargeter, Alison, *The Muslim Brotherhood: The Burden of Tradition*, London: Saqi, 2010.

Perlmutter, Amos, "Islam and Democracy Simply Aren't Compatible," *New York Times* and *International Herald Tribune*, 21 Jan. 1992.

Perthes, Volker, *The Political Economy of Syria under Asad*, London: I.B. Tauris, 1995.

Phares, Walid, *The Coming Revolution: Struggle for Freedom in the Middle East*, New York: Threshold Editions, 2010.

Puchot, Pierre, *La Révolution confisquée. Enquête sur la transition démocratique en Tunisie*, Paris: Sindbad/Actes Sud, 2012.

Qaradawi (al-), Yusuf, "Al-Qaradawi Yanfi Talaqqi ʿArd min al-Ikhwan li-Khilafat al-Hudaybi," *Aljazeera.net*, 12 Jan. 2004, <http://www.aljazeera.net/news/pages/558d374a-bc05-4639-b537-85c220dd7e50>.

———, "Al-Isti'fa' min al-'Amal al-Tanzimi fi al-Ikhwan," *Qaradawi.net*, 22 Sep. 2008, <http://qaradawi.net/life/8/940-2011-09-29-12-22-50.html>.

———, "Ma' al-Tanzim al-'Alami lil-Ikhwan," *Qaradawi.net*, 19 Sep. 2011, <http://qaradawi.net/life/8/5194-2011-09-20-12-41-14.html>.

Ramadan, Fatma, *Su'ud al-Haraka al-'Ummaliyya wal-Niqabiyya al-Misriyya khilal 'Am 2007*, Cairo: Al-Mirsad al-Niqabi al-'Ummali, Al-Jam'iyya al-Misriyya lil-Nuhud bil-Musharaka al-Mujtama'iyya, n.d.

———, "Itlala 'ala al-Haraka al-'Ummaliyya fi Misr (2007–2009)," *Al-Hiwar al-Mutammadin*, 25 June 2012, <http://www.ahewar.org/debat/show.art.asp?aid=313257>.

———, "Fi Hiwar Maftuh," *Al-Hiwar al-Mutammadin*, 12 August 2012, <http://www.ahewar.org/debat/s.asp?aid=319653>.

Ramadan, Tariq, *The Arab Awakening: Islam and the New Middle East*, London: Allen Lane, 2012.

Rasheed (Al-), Madawi, *A History of Saudi Arabia*, 2nd edn, Cambridge, UK: Cambridge University Press, 2010.

Riad, Hassan (pseudonym of Samir Amin), *L'Egypte nassérienne*, Paris: Editions de Minuit, 1964.

Rice, Condoleezza, "Interview with The Washington Post Editorial Board," Washington, DC: Department of State, 25 March 2005, <http://2001-2009.state.gov/secretary/rm/2005/43863.htm>.

———, "Remarks at the American University in Cairo," Washington, DC: Department of State, 20 June 2005, <http://2001-2009.state.gov/secretary/rm/2005/48328.htm>.

Roberts, Hugh, "Who Said Gaddafi Had to Go?" *London Review of Books*, vol 33, no. 22, 17 Nov. 2011, p. 8–18.

Rodham Clinton, Hillary, "Secretary of State Hillary Rodham Clinton's Remarks on Receiving the George C. Marshall Foundation Award," George C. Marshall Foundation, 2 June 2011, <http://www.marshallfoundation.org/SecretaryClintonremarksJune22011.htm>.

Rodinson, Maxime, "On 'Islamic Fundamentalism': An Unpublished Interview with Gilbert Achcar," *Middle East Report*, no. 233, Winter 2004, pp. 2–4.

Roy, Olivier, "Révolution post-islamiste," *Le Monde.fr*, 12 Feb. 2011, <http://www.lemonde.fr/idees/article/2011/02/12/revolution-post-islamiste_1478858_3232.html>.

Rubenberg, Cheryl, *Israel and the American National Interest: A Critical Examination*, Chicago: University of Illinois Press, 1986.

Rugh, William, *Arab Mass Media: Newspapers, Radio, and Television in Arab Politics*, Westport, CT: Praeger, 2004.

Saadawi (el-), Nawal, "Al-Thawra al-Misriyya al-Thaniya," *Al-Masry al-Youm*, 29 Nov. 2011.

Saad-Filho, Alfredo and Deborah Johnston, *Neoliberalism: A Critical Reader*, London: Pluto, 2005.

Sabahy, Hamdeen, *Naqdur Nabniha min Jadid : al-Barnamaj al-Intikhabi li-Hamdin Sabahi li-Ri'asat Misr*, Cairo: n.p., 2012.

Sabry, Sarah, *Poverty Lines in Greater Cairo: Underestimating and Misrepre-*

senting Poverty, London: IIED, Human Settlements Programme, Working Paper 21, 2009.

Sadi (Al-), Mahmoud, "Al Jazeera Television: Rhetoric of Deflection," *Arab Media & Society*, no. 15, Spring 2012, <http://www.arabmediasociety.com/?article=786>.

Said, Atef, "Al-Mushkila al-Ta'ifiyya fi Misr wal-Badil al-'Ilmani al-Thawri," *Al-Thawra al-Da'ima*, no. 2, Spring 2012, pp. 11–28.

Sakr, Naomi, *Satellite Realms: Transnational Television, Globalization and the Middle East*, London: I.B. Tauris, 2001.

Salamé, Ghassan, ed, *Democracy without Democrats? The Renewal of Politics in the Muslim World*, London: I.B. Tauris, 1994.

Sallam, Hesham, "Striking Back at Egyptian Workers," *Middle East Report*, vol 41, no. 259, Summer 2011, <http://www.merip.org/mer/mer259/striking-back-egyptian-workers>.

Sarah, Fayiz, *Al-Faqr fi Suriyya: Nahwa Tahawwul Jadhri fi Siyasat Mu'alajat al-Faqr*, London: Strategic Research & Communication Centre, 2011.

Sayed (El-), Mohamed, "Memories of 1977," *Al-Ahram Weekly*, no. 881, 24–30 Jan. 2008, <http://weekly.ahram.org.eg/2008/881/eg5.htm>.

Sayyid Rasas, Muhammad, "Kharita Ijtima'iyya Siyasiyya Iqtisadiyya lil-Ihtijajat fi Suriyya," *Al-Hiwar al-Mutammadin*, 30 July 2011, <http://www.ahewar.org/debat/show.art.asp?aid=269941>.

Scahill, Jeremy, "Washington's War in Yemen Backfires," *The Nation*, 5 March 2012.

Schleifer, Abdallah, "Interview with Sheikh Yusuf al-Qaradawi," *Transnational Broadcasting Studies*, no. 13, Fall 2004, <http://www.tbsjournal.com/Archives/Fall04/interviewyusufqaradawi.htm>.

Schramm, Christophe, *Migration from Egypt, Morocco, and Tunisia: Synthesis of Three Case Studies*, Washington, DC: World Bank, ca. 2006.

Schwab, Klaus, ed, *The Global Competitiveness Report 2010–2011*, Geneva: World Economic Forum, 2010.

———, ed, *The Global Competitiveness Report 2012–2013*, Geneva: World Economic Forum, 2012.

Schwedler, Jillian, *Faith in Moderation: Islamist Parties in Jordan and Yemen*, New York: Cambridge University Press, 2006.

Seale, Patrick, *Asad: The Struggle for the Middle East*, London: I.B. Tauris, 1990.

Security Cooperation Agency, *Historical Facts Book as of September 30, 2010*, Washington, DC: Department of Defense, 2010.

Seurat, Michel, *L'Etat de barbarie*, Paris: Seuil, 1989.

Shaqrun, Nizar, *Riwayat al-Thawra al-Tunisiyya*, Tunis: Dar Mohamed Ali, 2011.

Sharp, Jeremy, *U.S. Democracy Promotion Policy in the Middle East: The Islamist Dilemma*, Washington, DC: Congressional Research Service, 15 June 2006.

———, *Egypt: The January 25 Revolution and Implications for U.S. Foreign Policy*, Washington, DC: Congressional Research Service, 11 Feb. 2011.

——, *Yemen: Background and U.S. Relations*, Washington, DC: Congressional Research Service, 8 June 2011.

Shatir (el-), Khairat, "No Need to Be Afraid of Us," *The Guardian*, 23 Nov. 2005.

Shehabi (Al), Omar, "Political Movements in Bahrain: Past, Present, and Future," *Jadaliyya*, 14 Feb. 2012, <http://www.jadaliyya.com/pages/index/4363/political-movements-in-bahrain_past-present-and-fu>.

Silverman, Lt. Colonel Michael, *Awakening Victory: How Iraqi Tribes and American Troops Reclaimed Al Anbar and Defeated Al Qaeda in Iraq*, Havertown, PA: Casemate, 2011.

SIPRI (Stockholm International Peace Research Institute), SIPRI Database, <http://armstrade.sipri.org/armstrade/html/export_toplist.php>.

Soboul, Albert, *La Révolution française*, Paris: Presses Universitaires de France, 1965.

——, *La Civilisation et la Révolution française*, Paris: Arthaud, 1988.

Taine, Hyppolite-Adolphe, *The Origins of Contemporary France*, vol 2, *The French Revolution*, trans. John Duran, New York: Henry Holt, 1890.

Tammam, Hussam, *Tahawwulat al-Ikhwan al-Muslimin: Tafakkuk al-Idiyulujiya wa Nihayat al-Tanzim*, 2nd edn, Cairo: Madbuli, 2010.

——, "Al-Qaradawi wal-Ikhwan. Qira'at fi Jadaliyyat al-Shaykh wal-Haraka," *Al-Shuruq*, 22–27 August 2011.

Therborn, Göran, "NATO's Demographer," *New Left Review*, II, no. 56, March–April 2009, pp. 136–44.

Toscane, Luiza, "Victoire de la population à Ben Guerdane," *Nawaat*, 3 Oct. 2010, <http://nawaat.org/portail/2010/10/03/victoire-de-la-population-a-ben-guerdane/>.

Toussaint, Eric, "The International Context of Global Outrage," CADTM, 30 Dec. 2011, <http://cadtm.org/Breve-retrospective-des-mouvements>.

Trabelsi, Leila, *Ma vérité*, Paris: Editions du Moment, 2012.

Traboulsi, Fawwaz, *Al-Dimuqratiyya wal-Thawra*, Beirut: Riad El-Rayyes, 2012.

Trofimov, Yaroslav, *The Siege of Mecca: The Forgotten Uprising in Islam's Holiest Shrine and the Birth of al Qaeda*, New York: Doubleday, 2007.

Trotsky, Leon, *Between Red & White: A Study of Some Fundamental Questions of Revolution*, Ann Arbor, MI: University of Michigan Library (reprint of the 1922 edition).

——, *Stalin*, trans. Charles Malamuth, London: Hollis and Carter, 1947.

——, *The Revolution Betrayed: What Is the Soviet Union and Where Is It Going?* trans. Max Eastman, New York: Pathfinder, 1980.

UN, UNdata, <http://data.un.org/>.

UNCTAD, *World Investment Report 2012: Towards a New Generation of Investment Policies*, Geneva: UNCTAD, 2012.

UNDP, *Arab Human Development Report 2009: Challenges to Human Security in the Arab Countries*, New York: UNDP, Regional Bureau for Arab States, 2009.

——, *Human Development Report 2011*, New York: UNDP, 2011.

UNDP, AFESD, *Arab Human Development Report 2003: Building a Knowledge Society*, New York: UNDP, Regional Bureau for Arab States, 2003.

UNDP, AFESD, AGFUND, *Arab Human Development Report 2005: Towards the Rise of Women in the Arab World*, New York: UNDP, Regional Bureau for Arab States, 2006.

UNESCO Institute for Statistics, *Global Education Digest 2011: Comparing Education Statistics Across the World*, Montreal: UNESCO Institute for Statistics, 2011.

UN-Habitat, *The State of Arab Cities 2012: Challenges of Urban Transition*, Nairobi: UN-Habitat, 2012.

UNICEF, *The State of the World's Children 2012: Children in an Urban World*, New York: UNICEF, 2012.

US Census Bureau, International Data Base, <http://www.census.gov/population/international/data/idb/informationGateway.php>.

US Department of State, Foreign Military Financing Account Summary, 23 June 2010, <http://www.state.gov/t/pm/ppa/sat/c14560.htm>.

'Uwayda, Jamal Muhammad, *Malhamat I'tisam Muwazzafi al-Dara'ib al-'Iqariyya*, Cairo: Markaz al-Dirasat al-Ishtirakiyya, 2008.

Vandewalle, Dirk, *Libya since Independence: Oil and State-Building*, Ithaca: Cornell University Press, 1998.

———, *A History of Modern Libya*, New York: Cambridge University Press, 2006.

Wade, Robert, *Governing the Market: Economic Theory and the Role of Government in East Asian Industrialization*, 2nd edn with a new introduction by the author, Princeton, NJ: Princeton University Press, 2004.

Weber, Max, *Economy and Society*, 2 vols, Berkeley: University of California Press, 1978.

———, *The Protestant Ethic and the "Spirit" of Capitalism and Other Writings*, London: Penguin, 2002.

Wedeen, Lisa, *Ambiguities of Domination: Politics, Rhetoric, and Symbols in Contemporary Syria*, Chicago: University of Chicago Press, 1999.

———, *Peripheral Visions: Publics, Power, and Performance in Yemen*, Chicago: Chicago University Press, 2008.

West, Bing, *The Strongest Tribe: War, Politics, and the Endgame in Iraq*, New York: Random House, 2008.

WikiLeaks, <http://www.wikileaks.org/wiki/Main_Page>.

Wikipedia, Arabic, English and French sites, <http://www.wikipedia.org/>.

World Bank, *Gender and Development in the Middle East and North Africa: Women in the Public Sphere*, MENA Development Report, Washington, DC: World Bank, 2004.

———, *Unlocking the Employment Potential in the Middle East and North Africa: Toward a New Social Contract*, MENA Development Report, Washington, DC: World Bank, 2004.

———, *Oil Booms and Revenue Management*, MENA Economic Developments and Prospects 2005, Washington, DC: World Bank, 2005.

———, *World Development Report 2008*, Washington, DC: World Bank, 2007.

———, *MENA Economic Developments and Prospects 2008: Regional Integration for Global Competitiveness*, Washington, DC: World Bank, 2009.

———, *MENA Economic Developments and Prospects 2009: Navigating through the Global Recession*, Washington, DC: World Bank, 2009.

———, *World Development Indicators 2009*, Washington, DC: World Bank, 2009.

———, *Shaping the Future: A Long-Term Perspective of People and Job Mobility for the Middle East and North Africa*, Washington, DC: World Bank, 2009.

———, *World Development Report 2010*, Washington, DC: World Bank, 2009.

———, *World Development Indicators 2010*, Washington, DC: World Bank, 2010.

———, *Economic Integration in the GCC*, Washington, DC: World Bank, 2010.

———, *Global Economic Prospects January 2011: Navigating Strong Currents*, Washington, DC: World Bank, 2011.

———, *MENA Economic Developments and Prospects January 2011: Sustaining the Recovery and Looking Beyond*, Washington, DC: World Bank, 2011.

———, *Migration and Remittances Factbook 2011*, 2nd edn, Washington, DC: World Bank, 2011.

———, *MENA Economic Developments and Prospects September 2011: Investing for Growth and Jobs*, Washington, DC: World Bank, 2011.

———, *World Development Indicators 2012*, Washington, DC: World Bank, 2012.

———, *MENA Region: A Regional Economic Update, April 2012: Enabling Employment Miracles*, Washington, DC: World Bank, 2012.

———, The Changing Wealth of Nations, <http://data.worldbank.org/data-catalog/wealth-of-nations>.

———, World DataBank, <http://databank.worldbank.org/data/home.aspx>.

Yamani, Mai, "The Two Faces of Saudi Arabia," *Survival*, vol 50, no. 1, Feb.–March 2008, pp. 143–56.

Yergin, Daniel, *The Prize: The Epic Quest for Oil, Money and Power*, 3rd edn, London: Simon & Schuster, 2008.

York, Jillian, "The False Poles of Digital and Traditional Activism," 27 Sep. 2010, <http://jilliancyork.com/2010/09/27/the-false-poles-of-digital-and-traditional-activism/>.

Yunis, Sharif, *Sayyid Qutb wal-Usuliyya al-Islamiyya*, Cairo: Dar Tayyiba, 1995.

Zaibi, Fakher, "Evolution du marché de l'emploi en Tunisie," n.d., <http://www.emploi.gov.tn/fileadmin/user_upload/PDF/928081.PDF>.

Zaki, Anis, "Khabir: al-Taghyir Kana Hatmiyyan bil-Jaysh al-Misri," *Al-Jazeera*, 31 August 2012, <http://www.aljazeera.net/news/pages/73e37525-42ff-4724-8b7e-7632951dfoc2>.

Zayani, Mohamed, ed, *The Al Jazeera Phenomenon: Critical Perspectives on New Arab Media*, London: Pluto, 2005.

Zohny, Hazem, "40 Million Egyptian Voters? Not Likely," *Ahram online*, 28 Nov. 2010, <http://english.ahram.org.eg/News/101.aspx>.

Index

Abbas, Mahmoud, 91
Abdel-Jalil, Moustafa, 181
Abdelrahman, Maha, 242
Abdul-Rahman, Hassan, 96
Aboul-Fotouh, Abdel-Moneim, 215–16
Abu Aita, Kamal, 238
Abu Ghazalah, Abdel-Halim, 150
Abul-Magd, Zeinab, 150
Abul-Naga, Fayza, 190–91
adventure capitalism, 65–67
Akef, Mohammed Mahdi, 107
Algeria, 71, 121, 137, 138; Bonapartism,
   69–70; education statistics, 34, 35;
   employment, 66; hunger riots (1988),
   117; *intifah,* 71; Islamic Salvation Front,
   209; neopatrimonialism, 59; population
   growth, 13; rent from natural resources,
   55; social insurance coverage, 23, 25
Alliot-Marie, Michèle, 191
Alterman, Jon, 111–12
Althusser, Louis, 114–15, 116, 260n3
Amazigh, 138
America, Abdel Hakim, 150
American Israel Public Affairs Committee
   (AIPAC), 105
Amin, Samir, 240, 250n42, 279n46
Ammar, Rachid, 145, 224
Anan, Sami, 193, 225–27
anti-imperialism, 197–98, 279n46
Arab-Israeli wars (1967 and 1973), 38, 40,
   47, 70, 71, 84
Arab Spring, 27, 189, 241, 244n7; as result

of US pressure, 91–93. *See also specific
   uprisings under* Bahrain, Egypt, Libya,
   Syria, Tunisia, and Yemen
Arabiya, Al, 259n86
Arafat, Yasser, 91
Asaad, Riyad al-, 184
Ashtar, Hassan al-, 185
Assad, Bashar al-, 45, 73, 175–76, 177, 178,
   189–90
Assad, Hafez al-, 71, 72, 172–75, 176–77,
   179
Assad, Rifaat al-, 179
Ayeb, Habib, 124–25

Babeuf, Gracchus, 184
Bahrain, 80, 122; GDP, 56; General
   Federation of Bahraini Trade Unions
   (GFBTU), 162; population growth,
   13; rent from natural resources, 55;
   sectarian divisions, 160–61, 267n29;
   social insurance coverage, 25; Uprising
   (2011), 161–63, 195; workers'
   movement, 123
Banna, Hassan al-, 97–98, 209
Barout, Mohammed Jamal, 45, 118–19
Batatu, Hanna, 172
Bayat, Asef, 87
Beblawi, Hazem, 55–56
Becker, Carmen, 142–43
Belhaj, Ahlem, 127
Ben Ali, Zine el-Abidine, 59, 72, 145–46,
   191, 192, 251n46, 262n18

Ben Gharbia, Sami, 133, 135
Bendjedid, Chadli, 71
Berlusconi, Silvio, 199
Bizri, Dalal al-, 117–18
bloodless coups d'état, 149
Bonapartism, 68–70, 94, 219–20
Bouazizi, Mohamed, 22, 124–25
Bourdieu, Pierre, 102; *Masculine Domination*, 31, 247n48
bourgeoisie, 57–58, 59, 61, 69, 95, 175, 180–81, 219, 228–29, 251n46
Bourguiba, Habib, 70
breakthrough coups d'état, 144
Bush, George H.W., administration of, 80–81, 83, 86, 194
Bush, George W., administration of, 77, 97, 104, 105, 194, 254n3; and Iraq, 89, 106, 204; and Libya, 199–200; and Muslim Brothers, 106–8; *National Strategy for Combating Terrorism (2003)*, 106; promotion of democracy, 88–93
Bush, Ray, 47

capitalism, 7–9, 10, 36, 50–51, 58–59, 61–67, 71, 72, 228–29, 252n55, 279n46; and Egyptian Muslim Brothers, 98–99, 229–36; genesis of Arab, 67–73; investment problems, 39–41
Castro, Fidel, 197
Central Intelligence Agency (CIA), 28
Chávez, Hugo, 197
Chebbi, Ahmed Najib, 118
Chehab, Fouad, 70
Cheney, Dick, 88
Chile, 73
China, 42, 82, 84, 200, 201, 231–32
Chivers, C. J., 186
Chorin, Ethan, 199
Christian Copts, Egyptian, 154, 275n50
citizen journalism, 133
Clinton, Hillary, 49, 192
colonialism, 67–68, 137
combined development, 136–39, 140, 141, 157
communications technologies, 129–35, 179, 209. *See also* Internet; social media
conservative coups d'état, 145, 153
conspiracy theories, 188–91, 206
coups d'état, 2–3, 72, 144–45, 149, 153
crony capitalism, 58–59, 63–64, 72
culture of emancipation, 131
cyber-activism, 130–35, 168

Dabashi, Hamid, 131
de Soto, Hernando, 22

democracy, 56–58; compatibility with Islam, 87, 90; as parochializer, 86; as partner of neoliberalism, 125; promotion by West of, 85–93, 96–97, 189, 193; and workers' movements, 240–41
democracy paradox, 86
denationalization, 175
derivative rents, 55–56
devout bourgeoisie, 219, 228–29
digital activism, 130–35
Dubai World, 67
Dutch disease, 66

Ebadi, Shirin: *Gender and Development in the Middle East and North Africa*, 31
education: correlation with poverty, 24; employment of graduates, 32–35, 124; investments in, 168
Egypt, 47–48, 58, 71, 111, 122, 238–39; 1952 coup, 2–3; Bonapartism, 69–70; Bread Riots (1977), 74, 125; Coptic Christians, 154, 275n50; education statistics, 35; Egyptian Business Development Association (EBDA), 231; Egyptian Federation of Independent Trade Unions (EFITU), 238; elections (2005), 92–93, 96–97; employment, 66; foreign direct investment, 46; GDP per capita, 11–12, 48, 65, 220; horizontal homogeneity, 140–41; Internet usage in, 132, 133, 134; military, 82, 142, 149–54, 190, 266n1; National Association for Change, 211; population growth, 13; post-Revolution relations with US, 207; Real Estate Tax Authority Union (RETA), 238; rent from natural resources, 55; Revolution (2011), 4, 72, 148–55, 169, 192–94, 195–96, 211–16, 241–42; role of labor, 125–27, 148–49, 238; social insurance coverage, 23, 25; socioeconomic inequalities, 16, 17–19, 20–21; Supreme Council of the Armed Forces (SCAF), 151–52, 153–54, 190, 213, 225; union with Syria, 85. *See also* Muslim Brotherhood, Egyptian; Nasser, Gamal Abdel-
El-Baradei, Mohamed, 211
el-Saadawi, Nawal, 214
Elmessiri, Abdel-Wahab, 117
emigration: remittances, 65, 250n38; as safety valve, 25–26; of tertiary educated, 34–35
Emirate of Qatar. *See* Qatar
employment: and Egyptian Muslim Brotherhood, 98–99; manufacturing vs. construction, 66; in MENA, 23, 24–25,

26; migrant labor, 65; rates, 167–68, 268n47; relationship with investment, 46, 49, 248n18; sectarian differences, 161; by state, 73, 248n18; of women, 29–32, 247n48; of youth, 26–29, 131, 167, 233

Engels, Friedrich, 209; *Communist Manifesto*, 95

Ennahda, 196, 210–11, 213, 220, 221–25

Erbakan, Necmettin, 219

European Union, 106

Ezz, Ahmed, 153

Facebook, 130, 132, 182

First Gulf War, 80–81, 83

food prices, 51–52

force of obedience thesis, 262n18

foreign direct investment (FDI), 46

France, 163–64, 191–92, 201; Revolution (1789–1799), 3–4, 52, 128, 129, 184

freedom of expression, 131

Freud, Sigmund: *Interpretation of Dreams, The*, 114

Fromherz, Allen, 102

Fukuyama, Francis, 86

Fuller, Graham, 27–28, 246n40

G8–Greater Middle East Partnership, 90–91

Gabaly, Sherif El-, 232

Gaddafi, Muammar al-, 73; and Civil War (2011), 169, 170–71, 200, 202; *Green Book*, 164; regime, 72, 164–68, 190, 198–99

Gaddafi, Saif al-Islam, 169–70, 203

Ganzouri, Kamal al-, 154

gender paradox, 31

geographical rents, 55

Ghannouchi, Rached, 98, 210, 225

Ghobashy, Mona El-, 241

Ghonim, Wael, 130

Glorious Thirty Years, 49–50

Gorbachev, Mikhail, 166

Gotowicki, Stephen, 151

governance and development, 62

Great Recession (2007–2009), 41, 51–53

Green Parties, 131

Grifa, Moussa, 216–17

ground rents, 55

Gulf Cooperation Council (GCC), 12, 23, 25, 34, 56; and Bahraini Uprising (2011), 162–63; coups d'état, 145; Egyptian dependency on capital from, 232; employment, 46; and Libyan Civil War (2011), 171; mass clientele, 139–40; migrant labor, 65; neopatrimonial-

ism, 59; stability of monarchies, 65; and Syrian Civil War (2011), 205; US as arms supplier, 82–84; as US creditor, 81–82; World Bank data, 42–44, 248n1; and Yemeni Revolution (2011), 158–59

Gumuscu, Sebnem, 219, 229

Habib, Muhammad, 96

Hachemaoui, Mohammed, 138

Haddad, Bassam, 175–76

Hadi, 'Abd Rabbuh Mansur, 159

Haimzadeh, Patrick, 167

Hajji, Adnane, 123–24

Hamas, 102, 107, 108, 121

Hammi, Emna El-, 221–22

Hanieh, Adam: *Capitalism and Class in the Gulf Arab States*, 252n55

Hariri, Rafic, 91, 177

Hassan, Ammar Ali, 117

Heinsohn, Gunnar, 28

Hertog, Steffen, 45

Hezbollah, 102, 119

Hibou, Béatrice, 262n18

Higazi, Mustafa, 227

Hroub, Khaled, 235

Huntington, Samuel, 85, 86; *Clash of Civilizations, The*, 28, 144

Hussein, Saddam, 60, 71, 72, 73, 86

hydrocarbon exports, 54

Ibn Khaldun, 138

Indyk, Martin, 105

infitah, 38, 71–72, 149, 166, 175, 228; and public investment, 42–43, 45

informal economy, 14, 23–24, 35, 177

inqilab, 2

International Monetary Fund (IMF), 17, 48, 166, 233

Internet, 111, 119, 129, 182; Islamic sites, 107, 132; social media, 130–35, 168, 179, 182, 209; users by country, 131–32, 134

intifada, 2

investment: foreign direct, 46; private, 44–47, 248n1; public, 42–44, 45, 47–48, 50, 248n1; relationship to employment, 46, 49, 248n18

Iran, 82–83, 121–22; and Iraq, 194; Islamic Revolution (1979), 96, 99, 208–9; socioeconomic inequalities, 18; and Syrian Civil War (2011), 186, 205

Iraq, 65, 139; Bonapartism, 70; education statistics, 35; elections (2005), 91; *intifah*, 71; invasion of Kuwait, 81, 99–100; and Iran, 194; neopatrimonialism, 59;

Iraq *(continued)*
　　population growth, 13; rent from
　　natural resources, 55; socioeconomic
　　inequalities, 16, 19; US as arms supplier
　　to, 82; US invasion and occupation of,
　　89, 106, 204; workers' movement, 123
Islah, 196
Islam: compatibility with democracy, 87,
　　90; and Egyptian Constitution, 212,
　　275n50; fundamentalism, 88, 93, 95–96,
　　100, 104, 121–22, 208, 209, 234; Inter-
　　net sites, 107, 132; and new Arabism,
　　111–12; news outlets, 112; Salafist, 104,
　　157, 209, 214–15, 216, 217, 221, 222,
　　230, 240; Shia, 91, 99, 158, 160, 162–
　　63, 178, 209; as solution, 235; Sunni,
　　106, 121, 161, 173–74, 177, 178, 180,
　　181, 185, 187, 209; Wahhabism, 78–79,
　　98, 103, 104, 185, 258n70
Islamic Texas, 78
IslamOnline, 107
Islamophobia, 208
Israel: Arab-Israeli wars (1967 and 1973),
　　38, 40, 47, 70, 71, 84; and Arab Spring,
　　189; and Gaza, 28; and Lebanon, 102;
　　relationship with US, 84–85, 194; and
　　Syrian Civil War (2011-), 205
Italy, 192, 199

Jad, Islah, 128
Japan, 82
Jazeera, Al, 74, 108–13, 210, 212–13,
　　259n86, 259n88, 260n91
Jibril, Mahmoud, 181, 216
Jilani, Hedi, 222
Jordan: crushing of Palestinian resistance,
　　70; education statistics, 33, 35; for-
　　eign direct investment, 46; hunger riots
　　(1989), 74, 117; and Muslim Brothers,
　　122; neopatrimonialism, 59; population
　　growth, 13; social insurance coverage,
　　23; socioeconomic inequalities, 17, 19;
　　and Syrian Civil War (2011), 187

Kadri, Ali, 84
Karman, Tawakkul, 127–28, 156, 157
Kemal, Mustafa, 68–69
Kemalism, 68–69
Khaddam, Abdel-Halim, 173
Khalidi, Rashid, 236–37
Khamis, Mohamed Farid, 232
Khanfar, Wadah, 109, 259n88
Khiari, Sadri, 118
Khomeini, Ayatollah Ruhollah, 209
Kienle, Eberhard, 171

Kilo, Michel, 184
Kramer, Martin, 105
Kurds, 138, 187
Kuwait, 65, 80; employment, 46; GDP,
　　56; invaded by Iraq, 99–100; popula-
　　tion growth, 12–13; rent from natural
　　resources, 55; women in, 92

Lagarde, Christine, 48
Lebanon, 70, 91, 121, 177, 250n38; educa-
　　tion statistics, 33, 35; emigrant remit-
　　tances, 25; foreign direct investment,
　　46; Hezbollah, 102; neopatrimonialism,
　　59; population growth, 13; poverty, 17;
　　social insurance coverage, 23; workers'
　　movement, 123
Ledeen, Michael, 89
Lenin, Vladimir, 116–17, 136
Libya: Bonapartism, 70; Civil War (2011),
　　4, 72, 168–72, 180, 181, 183, 184, 191–
　　92, 197, 200–204, 205–6, 207, 216–17,
　　274n36; General National Congress
　　(GNC), 216, 217; Internet usage in, 134;
　　intifah, 72; National Transitional Coun-
　　cil (NTC), 169, 170; population growth,
　　13; rent from natural resources, 55, 165;
　　republican coup, 72; Republican Guard,
　　174, 175; Revolutionary Guard Corps,
　　166; social insurance coverage, 23. *See
　　also* Gaddafi, Muammar al-
Luciani, Giacomo, 45
Lynch, Marc, 109–10

Makhlouf, Muhammad, 176
Makhlouf, Rami, 176
Maktoum, Sheikh Mohammed bin Rashid
　　Al, 67
Malek, Hassan, 229–30, 232
Malik, Monica, 56–57
Mao Zedong: *Little Red Book,* 164–68
market bourgeoisie, 58, 59, 180–81, 251n46
Marx, Karl, 9, 68, 69, 114, 116–17, 208,
　　209; *Communist Manifesto,* 95; *Con-
　　tribution to the Critique of Politi-
　　cal Economy, A,* 7, 9; *Das Capital,* 55;
　　Grundrisse, 36; *Poverty of Philosophy,
　　The,* 134
mass base, 136, 137–41
Mauritania: neopatrimonialism, 59; popu-
　　lation growth, 13; rent from natural
　　resources, 55; socioeconomic inequali-
　　ties, 16, 17, 19; workers' movement, 123
McAdam, Doug, 129
middle class, 57–58, 95, 130
Middle East and North Africa (MENA)

region: conditions for youth, 28–29; development, 10–12; emigration of tertiary educated, 34–35; employment, 23, 24–25, 26, 29–35, 247n48; factors inhibiting development in, 35–37; foreign direct investment, 46; GDP per capita, 11–12, 13–14, 22, 38, 39–41; gender paradigm in, 31; global recession effects, 51–53; HDI, 14–15; informal economy, 23–24; Internet usage in, 131–32; population, 12–13, 25, 27; poverty rates, 17; private investment rates, 44–47, 248n1; public investment rates, 42–43, 45; relationship with Soviet Union, 77; republican coups, 72; revenue from rents, 54–57; socioeconomic inequalities, 18–22
Middle East Broadcasting Center (MBC), 108, 258n86
migrant labor. See emigration
Mills, C. Wright, 146
mining rents, 55
mismatch thesis, 35
Mitchell, Andrew, 203–4
Morocco, 111, 122; education statistics, 33, 34, 35; employment, 46; hunger riots (1981), 74, 117; neopatrimonialism, 59; population growth, 13; social insurance coverage, 23; socioeconomic inequalities, 16–17, 19; women's movement, 127; workers' movement, 123
Morsi, Mohamed, 231–34; consolidation of power by, 225–27, 278n21; election of, 154, 196, 215, 216; Presidential Program, 235
Mubarak, Hosni, 47, 72, 73, 108, 150, 226, 228; elections (2005), 96; and George W. Bush administration, 92–93, 97; and Obama administration, 192–94; removal from power of, 151–52, 190–91, 211, 212; and Salafists, 214–15
Murphy, Caryle, 135
Muslim Brotherhood, Egyptian, 209, 220, 228–29; founding of, 95–96; and George W. Bush administration, 96–97, 107–8, 259n82; modernists, 99; under Nasser, 97; and neoliberalism, 229–36; and Obama administration, 195–96; and Qatar, 102–4; and Revolution (2011), 153, 154, 211–16; and Saudi Kingdom, 96, 97–98, 99, 103–4
Muslim Brotherhood, Iraqi, 106
Muslim Brotherhood, Libyan, 216
Muslim Brotherhood, Syrian, 106, 173, 179, 182, 185

Muslim Brotherhood, Tunisian, 196, 210–11, 213, 220, 221–25
Muslim Brotherhood, Yemeni, 196; Yemeni Congregation for Reform (Al-Islah), 157
Muslim World League, 98

Naba, René, 113
Nahda, Al-, 218
Nasser, Gamal Abdel-, 47, 48, 149, 150; 1952 coup, 2–3; and Brotherhood, 97; regime of, 69–71
nationalism, 68, 69–70, 79–80, 85, 95, 121, 139
natural gas exports, 54
Nazif, Ahmed, 153
neoliberalism, 43, 53–54, 63, 166, 175, 219–20, 241; of Egyptian Muslim Brothers, 229–36; failures of command economy, 39; and globalized capitalism, 9; as partner of democracy, 125
neopatrimonialism, 58–60, 63, 72–73, 141, 220, 232
nepotism, 58–59, 63–64, 71, 72, 157, 167, 232
New Arab Order, 194
new Arabism, 111–12
Niblock, Tim, 56–57
North Atlantic Treaty Organization (NATO), 218; and Libyan Civil War (2011), 170–71, 189, 201–4, 205–6, 207; and Syrian Civil War (2011), 204–5
North Yemen, 69–70, 71, 72
Nour, Ayman, 92, 97
Numeyri, Gaafar al-, 71–72

Obama, Barack, administration of, 108; and Bahraini Uprising (2011), 195; and Egyptian Revolution (2011), 195–96; and Libyan Civil War (2011), 202; and Muslim Brotherhood, 195–96; and Revolution in Egypt, 192–94; and Syrian Civil War (2011), 196; and Tunisian Revolution (2010–2011), 196; and Yemeni Revolution (2011), 196, 273n20
oil, 160, 165; companies controlling, 81, 199; and democracy, 56–57; enrichment of Muslim Brotherhood, 96; Great Power rivalry, 76–77, 84, 85; as pacifier, 234; prices, 13–14, 38, 40, 64–65, 71, 244n8; and Western intervention in Libya, 201, 274n30
Oman, 12, 55, 80
Organization of Petroleum Exporting Countries (OPEC), 64
Orientalism, 87, 138, 235

Ortega, Daniel, 197
overdetermination, 114–17, 135
Özal, Turgut, 219

Palestine Liberation Organization (PLO), 65
Palestinian Authority, 91, 102, 108
Palestinians: education statistics, 35; emigrant remittances, 25–26; in Gaza, 28; in Jordan, 70; poverty, 16; in Syria, 181
patriarchal culture, 30–31
patrimonialism, 58–60, 63–64, 141–42, 158, 160, 167
Perlmutter, Amos, 87
petroleum. *See* oil
Phares, Walid: *Coming Revolution: Struggle for Freedom in the Middle East, The,* 261n12
Pinochet, Augusto, 73
politically determined capitalism, 62–65
Popular Petition, 210–11
post-Islamism thesis, 240
poverty: correlation with education, 24; correlation with informal economy, 23–24; in Egypt, 16, 17–18; indicators, 15–16
Powell, Colin, 88
production: blockages to, 10, 50–51; in communist mode, 94; contradictions in capitalist mode, 36, 247n62; and overdetermination, 115; privatized, 73; revolution in modes, 8–9
Project for the New American Century, 254n3
proletariat, 95
public space, expansion of, 131
purchasing power parity (PPP), 14–15

Qaida, Al-, 83, 100, 104, 121, 185, 209; in Yemen, 158–59
Qaradawi, Yusuf al-, 103, 104, 107, 112
Qatar, 64, 80, 100–101, 258n70; Egyptian dependency on capital from, 232, 234; and Egyptian Muslim Brothers, 212; GDP per capita, 21; as middleman, 101–3, 104–8; population growth, 12; rent from natural resources, 55; satellite television news network, 108–13, 259n86, 259n88, 260n91; socioeconomic inequalities, 19, 21; and Syrian Civil War (2011), 186–87; and Tunisian Revolution (2010–2011), 210
Qutb, Sayyid, 99, 209

racketeering, 55
Ramadan, Said, 98, 99–100, 257n54
Ramadan, Tariq, 131; *Arab Awakening:*

Islam and the New Middle East, The, 264n36
reactionary coups d'état, 145
reformist coups d'état, 145
regionalism, 138–39, 140, 141
rents, 54–57, 61, 101, 142, 160, 250n38
republican dictatorships, 72–73
resource curse, 60
revolution: coordinated by youth networks, 129–35, 179, 209–10, 211; corrective, 149; definitions of, 2, 10; leaderless, 128; Marxist, 7, 9, 94, 114, 116–17, 120–21; in modes of production, 8–9; and overdetermination, 115–16; palace, 139; pro-Western, 261n12; as process, 4–5; and state apparatus, 141–43; subjective conditions, 117–20; thresholds needed to be crossed, 136. *See also under specific nations*
revolutionary coups d'état, 145
Rice, Condoleezza, 87–88, 92–93, 106, 193
Roberts, Hugh, 274n36
Rodinson, Maxime, 234
Romdhane, Mahmoud Ben, 46
Rousseau, Jean-Jacques: *Confessions,* 22–23; *Declaration of the Rights of Man and the Citizen,* 140
Rubenberg, Cheryl, 84
Rumsfeld, Donald, 88
Russia, 200, 201; Revolutions (1917), 116, 128; and Syrian Civil War (2011), 186, 205. *See also* Soviet Union

Sabahy, Hamdeen, 238–39
Saban, Haim, 105
Sabry, Sarah, 18
Sadat, Anwar al-, 3, 48, 71, 72, 100, 149–51, 228; assassination of, 152; and Muslim Brotherhood, 98
Sadi, Mahmoud Al-, 112–13
Said, Khaled, 130–31
Saleh, Ahmed, 159, 160
Saleh, Ali Abdallah, 71, 72, 73, 155, 156–60, 190
Sarkozy, Nicolas, 191, 201
satellite television, 74, 108–13, 119, 260n96. *See also* Al Jazeera
Saudi Arabian Kingdom, 57, 64, 65, 111, 164, 271n82; and Al Jazeera, 108, 109; and Bahraini Uprising (2011), 162–63; economy, 45; education statistics, 33; and Egyptian Muslim Brotherhood, 96, 97–98, 99–100, 103–4; elections (2005), 91–92; employment, 66; foreign direct investment, 46; government and society,

78–79; nationalism, 79–80; nepotistic capitalism, 71; population growth, 12; relationship with USA, 77–78, 80, 82–83, 87; rent from natural resources, 55; and Syrian Civil War (2011), 186–87; Wahhabism, 78–79; and Yemeni Revolution (2011), 158–59

scale shift, 129

sectarianism, 137–39, 140, 141

self-determination, right to, 197, 198

Shafiq, Ahmed, 153, 216

Shalish, Dhul-Himma, 176

Sharia, 212

Shatir, Khairat al-, 98–99, 107, 228, 229; "No Need to Be Afraid of Us," 107

Shebbi, Abul-Qacem al-, 1

Sieda, Abdulbaset, 204

Sisi, Abdul-Fattah al-, 225

Sistani, Ayatollah Ali al-, 91

Soboul, Albert, 10, 52

social insurance coverage, 23, 25

social media, 130–35, 168, 179, 182, 209

social revolution, 4

socioeconomic inequalities, 16–22

South Africa, 44

Soviet Union, 69, 70, 77, 120–21, 163–64, 197. See also Russia

Spain, 131

speculative trading capitalism, 65–67

Squarcini, Bernard, 191

state bourgeoisie, 58, 180–81

strategic rents, 55

Strauss-Kahn, Dominique, 166

Sudan: Bonapartism, 70; intifah, 71–72; neopatrimonialism, 59; population growth, 13; poverty, 16; rent from natural resources, 55

Suleiman, Omar, 152, 212

symbolic capital, 102–3, 112

symbolic violence, 31, 247n48

Syria, 71, 111, 118–19, 142–43; Bonapartism, 69–70; Civil War (2011), 72, 179–87, 196, 197, 204–6; and conspiracy theory, 190; Corrective Movement (1970), 172–73; education statistics, 33, 35; Free Syrian Army (FSA), 184–85; Internet usage in, 134; investment rates, 45; Islamization of, 178; National Coordinating Committee (NCC), 182–83; population growth, 13; rent from natural resources, 55; sectarianism, 172, 173–74, 177, 181, 185, 270n70; self-employment, 23; social insurance coverage, 23; socioeconomic inequalities, 17, 19; Syrian National Council (SNC), 182, 184, 185, 204; union with Egypt, 85

Tammam, Husam, 104, 107

Tantawi, Hussein, 150–51, 225–27

Tarrow, Sidney, 129

taxation and democracy, 56

Thani, Hamad bin Khalifa, Al, 100–101, 103, 108

thawra, 2

Tilly, Charles, 129

Tlass, Mustafa, 173

Traboulsi, Fawwaz, 139

triangle of power, 146, 147, 149, 150–51

tribalism, 137, 138–39, 140, 141; in Yemen, 156, 157, 158

Trimech, Abdesslem, 124

Trotsky, Leon, 8, 163–64, 197

Tunisia, 1, 70, 111, 118, 121, 262n18; education statistics, 34, 35; employment, 23, 66; foreign direct investment, 46; GDP per capita, 220; horizontal homogeneity, 140–41; hunger riots (1983–1984), 74, 117; Internet usage in, 132, 133, 134; market bourgeoisie, 59, 251n46; neopatrimonialism, 59; population growth, 13; public institutions, 220–21; Revolution (2010–2011), 1–2, 4, 72, 74, 145–48, 152–53, 154–55, 169, 191, 196, 209–10; revolution trigger, 22; social insurance coverage, 23, 25; socioeconomic inequalities, 16, 17, 18, 19; Tunisian General Labor Union (UGTT), 123–25, 145, 146, 147, 210, 237–38; women's movement, 127; workers' movement, 124–25, 126–27

Turkey, 227; employment, 66; Independent Industrialists' and Businessmen's Association (MÜSIAD), 219, 231; Kemalism, 68–69; Kurdish Workers' Party (PKK), 187; Party for Justice and Development (AKP), 99, 105, 218–20, 229, 232; socioeconomic inequalities, 18; and Syrian Civil War (2011), 187, 205

underemployment and unemployment. See employment

Union of Soviet Socialist Republics (USSR). See Russia; Soviet Union

United Arab Emirates (UAE), 64; arms purchases from US, 82; economic crisis (2008–2011), 67; foreign direct investment, 46; population growth, 13, 80; rent from natural resources, 55

United Kingdom, 67–68, 80

United Nations (UN), 201, 202–3; *Arab Human Development Reports,* 17, 20, 50, 74–75; Development Program (UNDP), 14, 17, 54, 74–75; Human Development Index (HDI), 14–15

United States, 67–68; and Arab Spring, 91–93, 189–91; Central Intelligence Agency (CIA), 28; and Egypt post Revolution, 207; and Egyptian military, 142; and Egyptian Muslim Brotherhood, 99–100, 107–8, 259n82; financial aid to MENA, 48; First Gulf War, 80–81, 83; and GCC, 81–84; invasion of Iraq, 81, 106; and Israel, 84–85; and Libya, 207; as power in Arab region, 193–95; and Qatar, 101–2; and Saudi Kingdom, 77–78, 80, 82–83, 87; and Syrian Civil War (2011), 186. *See also administrations of specific presidents*

uprisings, types of, 2

US-Islamic World Forum, 105

Vandewalle, Dirk, 165–66

veto coups d'état, 144

virtual networks, 237. *See also* Internet

voluntary servitude thesis, 262n18

Wahhabism, 78–79, 98, 103, 104, 185, 258n70

War on Terror, 88–89, 104

Weber, Max, 58, 230; *Economy and Society,* 60; *Protestant Ethic and the Spirit of Capitalism, The,* 61

Wedeen, Lisa, 267n22

Westernization as parochializer, 86

Wolfowitz, Paul, 88

women: employment of, 29–32, 49, 247n48; feminist activities, 127–28; in Kuwait, 92; in MENA, 49–50; in Saudi Kingdom, 92

workers' movement, 123–27, 128

World Bank, 15, 17, 20, 35, 41, 45–46, 49, 51, 66; Arab World Initiative, 26; *Migration and Remittances Factbook 2011,* 34–35; World Databank, 44–45; *World Development Reports,* 16

World Economic Forum: *Global Competitiveness Report* (2010), 220

World War I, 80

Yamani, Mai, 79

Yemen, 65; GDP per capita, 21; Internet usage in, 134; population growth, 13; rent from natural resources, 55; Revolution (2011), 155–60, 196, 217, 272n22, 273n20; self-employment, 23; social insurance coverage, 23; socioeconomic inequalities, 16, 17, 19; women's movement, 127–28

Yergin, Daniel, 77

York, Jillian, 134–35

Younes, Abdel-Fattah, 183

Youth Bulge theory, 27–28

youth networks, 129–35

YouTube, 130, 182

Zayani, Mohamed, 109

Zindani, 'Abdul-Majid al-, 217